GRANT SEEKERS GUIDE

HOW TO USE THIS BOOK

STEP ONE

METHOD 1: BY FIELD OF INTEREST

1. Go to the Index of Grantmakers by Field of Interest—page 553.

2. Scan the categories to choose those most appropriate to your mission.

3. Make a list of telephone numbers, email addresses, and web sites.

METHOD 2: BY LOCATION OR REGION

1. Go to the Index of Grantmakers by Geographical Preferences—page 583.

2. Scan the States to choose those most appropriate to your mission.

3. Make a list of telephone numbers, email addresses, and web sites.

METHOD 3: BY FOUNDATION

1. Since the foundations are listed alphabetically, scan the entries looking primarily at the "areas of Interest" and "Application Guidelines" in each foundation entry.

2. Make a list of telephone numbers, email addresses, and web sites prioritizing the entries using your own unique Byzantine methods keeping in mind deadlines and other pertinent facts.

STEP TWO

1. Call the foundations that meet you   whom proposals in your field should be subn...

2. While you have the someone on the phone, confirm the address, and application guidelines, ask for a list of current grantees, and additional material that will round out the information.

3. Make annotations on the pages of the book with the date of your call and the name of the person to whom you spoke. Make any needed changes to the entry, such as a staffing change that has occurred at the foundation.

(*see USER'S GUIDE p. xvii*)

GRANT
SEEKERS
GUIDE

**FOUNDATIONS THAT
SUPPORT SOCIAL &
ECONOMIC JUSTICE**

SIXTH REVISED EDITION

JAMES McGRATH MORRIS AND
LAURA ADLER, EDITORS

MOYER BELL
KINGSTON, RHODE ISLAND &
LANCASTER, UNITED KINGDOM

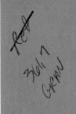

Published by Moyer Bell

Thanks to Elizabeth Austin and Tricia Rubacky.

Sixth Edition

LIBRARY OF CONGRESS CATALOGING-IN-PUBLICATION DATA
Grant seekers guide: funding sourcebook; James McGrath Morris and Laura Adler, editors-Rev. and expanded.

p. cm.
Includes bibliographies and indexes

I. Endowment-United States-Directories.	I. Morris, James McGrath.
HV97.A3G73	2005
361.7'632'02573-dc 1 9	88-12052
ISBN 1-55921-304-3 Pb	CIP

Printed in the United States of America
Printed on acid free paper ∞
Distributed in North America by Acorn Alliance, 549 Old North Road, Kingston, RI 02881, 401-783-5480, www.moyerbellbooks.com and in Europe by Gazelle Book Services Ltd., White Cross Mills, High Town, Lancaster, LA1 4XS England 524-68765, www.gazelle.co.uk

DEDICATION

This book is dedicated to the many people working in the
nonprofit world with a great deal of comittment but without
much recognition. As it is more blessed to give than to
receive, these volunteers give their time and tallent as well as
money.

CONTENTS

Introduction | ix
User's Guide | xvii
Grantmakers | I

CONTENTS

INTRODUCTION TO THE SIXTH EDITION

by James McGrath Morris

To read the *New York Times* in the spring of 2001, one would think that all an organization dedicated to social justice had to do was ask and money would come flowing its way. FOUNDATION GRANTS SURGED LAST YEAR DESPITE SLOWING ECONOMY, read the headline. Reporter Tamar Levin told her readers that "without question, it has been an extraordinary era for philanthropy, with billions of dollars a year in new gifts flowing into existing foundations, some 10,000 new foundations formed, and vast gains in the value of the holding of the largest independent foundations."[1] Foundations doled out $27.6 billion in 2000, more than 18 percent from the previous year.

"Foundations have grown so rapidly since the mid-1990s that not even a volatile stock market and slowing economy could keep them from posting record growth in grant dollars," exulted Sara Engelhardt, president of the Foundation Center.[2]

Unfortunately, if you run the kind of organization for whom the subtitle of this book is an organizing principle, this remarkable growth in philanthropy has not resulted in a commensurate growth of funds for your cause. To be sure, times are better for advocates of social change, but not because of the prodigious growth in the philanthropic community's wealth. Rather if funding for social justice causes has improved it is because of a boot-strap effort by members of the social justice community itself.

The fact that the social justice community continues to be a pariah to organized giving should not, in and of itself, be a surprise. Its goal is radical change. Broadly speaking, as defined by most who use the terms, social change or social justice reflects an approach to creating systemic and fundamental change focused at the root of the social problem, rather than its symptoms, usually by providing those most in need of help with the means, power, or opportunity to solve their own problems; thus the slogan "change, not charity."

---

[1] Tamar Levin, "Foundation Grants Surged Last Year Despite Slowing Economy," *New York Times*, March 27, 2001.
[2] Quoted in Levin, *New York Times*, March 27, 2001.

This approach can be unsettling to those with wealth. Rarely are the privileged comforted by sharing their wealth with people who advocate fundamental social change. As a result only slivers of the philanthropic pie are directed to social justice causes. Chuck Collins, the author of *Robin Hood was Right** and Patricia Maher, executive director of the Haymarket People's Fund, estimated that only two to four percent of the $175 billion distributed by American philanthropy in 1999 went to causes advocating social change. "The lion's share went to churches, the arts, elite private colleges and universities, and hospitals," they wrote. "And even when money was given to support services, such as soup kitchens and homeless shelters, the root causes remained unchanged."[3]

A study by the National Network of Grantmakers (NNG) came to a similar conclusion. In 1998, the NNG calcuated that social and economic justice grant making in the United States accounted for 2.4% of all institutional funding. In dollars and cents, social and economic justice causes attracted only $336 million of the $13.8 billion in domestic grants in 1997.[4]

Too often what money is directed toward dealing with social problems is spent only on relieving solely the symptoms. "This is why charitable efforts often fail to achieve lasting solutions," wrote Collins and Maher. What is needed is to channel money in the direction of movements seeking fundamental social change. "This work requires money. Yet it is exactly these movements that are largely left out of the charitable pie. But it should—and could—be a lot more."[5]

If you have read this far, you are probably nodding your head or maybe letting out a few "Amens." And, if you purchased this book to find the money to support your cause, you are also probably wondering—if not, you ought to be—if, besides this encouraging rhetoric and the endless pages of listings to follow, is there money out there for causes that aspire to bring about social and economic justice? The answer is yes and the amount is growing for several reasons.

---

*Chuck Collins, Pam Rogers, and Joan P. Garner. *Robin Hood was Right: A Guide to Giving Your Money for Social Change*. New York: W.W. Norton, 2001.

[3]Chuck Collins and Patricia Maher, "Charity That Changes Society," *Christian Science Monitor*, April 3, 2000.

[4]They surveyed NNG's membership and combined the findings with those of the Women's Funding Network, controlling for duplication. "Social Change Grantmaking in the U.S. The Mid-1990s," *Research Report—Autumn 1998*, National Network of Grantmakers.

[5]Collins & Maher, *Christian Science Monitor*, April 3, 2000.

First, mainstream foundations underwent prodigious growth in the 1990s thanks to a rising stock market. While it is clear that the vast majority of the money continued to flow to the traditional recipients, seeking a share of these funds should not be entirely discounted simply because your agenda is radical. In 1999, $266 million was distributed to social causes. The Ford Foundation distributed $85 million alone to such causes. The two top recipients were the American Civil Liberties Union, which received thirty grants totaling $10 million and Children's Defense Fund, which received thirty-seven grants of almost $10 million. Sadly, the list of recipients reflects the age-old biases in giving: favoritism toward traditional causes or preference to insider connections still dominate this sector of grant giving.

Second, a new area of funding that may turn out to be more open to social change causes has developed with the growth of minority philanthropy. Economic growth in the 1990s brought more African-Americans and Hispanics into positions of philanthropic leadership. The percent of households in black communities who made charitable donations increased to 53% in 1997 while the number of households in white communities making charitable donations decreased to 69%. Similar trends were also evident in the Hispanic community, which saw its median income grow by 6% in the late 1990s. The increase in minority involvement in philanthropy will alter donation patterns, according to Susan Raymond, Chief Analyst with Changingourworld.com. "In the U.S.," Raymond says, "minority leadership in philanthropy tends to focus resources on deep and historically intractable social problems, seeking to work creatively at the community level.

"While the 'new philanthropy' that generates eight-figure donations to academic centers may grab the headlines," she says, "it is quieter, less flashy minority philanthropy that may be making the most creative investments in street-level solutions to the nation's enduring social and educational inequalities."[6]

Third, alternative sources of funding have also experienced growth in recent years. One such new source is what are called "giving circles." A cross between a book reading club and an investment club, giving circles permit people to pool their money and give collectively to the organizations of their choice. Beth Schultz Klarman, a Boston philanthropist, started such a circle with sixty other women who each pledged to contribute at least $10,000 over a five year period. The circles have not been limited to women. Fifteen African-American men formed the African-American Federation of Greater

---

[6]Susan Raymond, "Minority Philanthropy on the Rise in the U.S.," *http.//www.changingourworld.com.*

Boston, funded with contributions of between $250 and $500 a year from each member.

But more important than these three new trends in funding for social change have been the developments in the foundations who cater to social justice. They have grown greatly in number and strength and for reasons that are very different than those propelling the growth in traditional philanthropy.

Historians will be able to chart the growth of these new organizations through the expansion of the Funding Exchange, a loosely organized alliance of social justice foundations created in 1979. Starting with a handful of organizations, its network now reaches from Oregon to Georgia and New England to Hawaii. Its goal is to have an affiliate in every region of the country. Collectively, the Funding Exchange has had a considerable influence. In recent years the Funding Exchange network grant making has distributed approximately $12 million each year to more than 2,200 organizations.

The Funding Exchange itself maintains several funds whose grants are selected with considerable input from activists. In late 2000, these funds were supporting groups whose agendas included police brutality, workers' rights, lesbian and gay rights, and Hawaiian sovereignty. Most grants were small, in comparison to those distributed by traditional foundations. But the groups who benefit from Funding Exchange grants usually are outside mainstream funding. The California Coalition for Women Prisoners, for example, received a $9,000 grant to support the work of this prisoner-organized and operated group.

Two typical members of the Funding Exchange are Liberty Hill Foundation in California and the McKenzie River Gathering Fund in Oregon. Both have grown considerably in recent years by the convergence of their efforts with an audience more receptive to their message and the development of a new generation of wealth holders more open to alternative forms of philanthropy.

"Social change and economic justice are coming back into vogue," said Tori Osborn, executive director of the Liberty Hill Foundation.[7] The causes of poverty, criminal justice, race, homelessness, low wage, community organizing are beginning to gain support again after a hiatus during the end of the twentieth century, according to Osborn. Additionally gay and lesbian rights issues are finding support beyond their traditional base. "I believe a new social force is stirring—still in its early stages, not yet unified or even clear on its vision. But we see signs every day: The Progressive L.A. Network drew 600 people, many low-income people of color, to a recent conference unveiling an

---

[7]Comments from Tori Osborn come from an interview with the author.

urban policy agenda on transportation, food and nutrition, housing and more, just in time to influence the mayoral race. At Liberty Hill, we see more grassroots activism, new leaders emerging, and more and more momentum."

The foundation that Osborn runs is one of a new breed of philanthropic organizations dedicated to social justice that were created during the past quarter century. Established in 1976 with $69,000 donated by a group of young people inspired by the 1960s movements for social change, the Liberty Hill Foundation supports grassroots organizations in the Los Angeles region. The foundation helps launch and sustain ventures for social change with grants that range from $2,500 to $25,000. Liberty Hill has donated more than $14 million in the past twenty-five years. The foundation now makes about 360 grants a year.

Susan Remmers, Executive Director of the McKenzie River Gathering Foundation, has seen a similar trend in Oregon. The social change message is being increasingly well received, according to Remmers. "There is broader public sentiment among mainstream folks that something is wrong, things could be better, the economy is booming why am I not?" The disparity between perception and reality is making people more open to the idea that problems may have deep seated institutional or system causes. "The mainstream public is beginning to struggle with this concept," she said.[8]

McKenzie River Gathering Foundation has distributed more than $6 million since its founding in 1976 when two activists convened on the banks of the river in the Cascade foothills to decide how to distribute $500,000 in inherited wealth to groups working on social justice causes. Among those receiving grants in 2000 were an AIDS education group working with high-risk populations, an organization seeking to establish a statewide presence to address toxic population, and a Native American tribe trying to preserve its language. In all more than $300,000 went to sixty-one organizations and in the year 2002 the total was expected to rise to $450,000.

Both Liberty Hill and McKenzie River Gathering have experienced substantial growth in their ability to distribute money. But, unlike mainstream funding organizations, this growth has come from their own efforts. McKenzie River Gathering, in particular, has concentrated considerable effort into creating a long-term, diversified development strategy. Its ability to increase the size of its grant making pool by fifty percent is a reflection of the success of that strategy.

The search for money and to broaden its support has not meant a betrayal of

---

[8]Comments from Susan Remmers come from an interview with the author.

its original ideals, said Remmers. In July 2001, the original founders of the McKenzie River Gathering Founcation came together again. While much of the movement fervor present in the 1960s and 1970s that lead to the creation of alternative foundations dissipated in the 1980s and 1990s, the values that grew out of the epoch have not faded. In fact, she said, there was a remarkable continuity of politics and grant making tactics from the founding group to the current staff members. "There has not been a radical shift," said Remmers. "Perhaps the language has changed, but when you get down to it the core values are the same."

A boon to groups working on social change issues is the preference of Funding Exchange members and other alternative foundations to use activists in deciding how to award their grants. The extent of involvement by activists in grant making varies greatly among these foundations. In some they are used as advisors, in others as decision-makers. Since its founding, for instance, the McKenzie River Gathering Foundation has virtually turned over the funding decisions to activists instead of leaving it in the hands of foundation staff. "We are not the norm," admits Remmers.

In the end, it is these few and small foundations that portend the most promising trend for social justice causes. The maturing of the Funding Exchange has increased the power of those who seek long term solutions rather than charity. Tied to this coming of age has also been a reawakening in protest politics. Since the late 1990s, the rise of globalization as an issue has made the climate more favorable for the work of social justice funds, according to Remmers. "There is a resurgence in political analysis, political action, and commitment to take what steps are necessary to advance change," she said.

Coinciding with these trends is the arrival of a new generation of donors. Liberty Hill's Osborn sees evidence of this in her efforts to raise funds. "There is a slow enlightenment process going on," she said. "The sands are shifting in the foundation field." Baby boomers are coming into "philanthropic age." These younger entrepreneurs, high tech folks, are more receptive to donating to social change causes, according to Osborn.

The National Committee for Responsive Philanthropy (NCRP) examined these trends in 2000 and concluded that $10 trillion is being passed from one generation to another in the next decade as the World War II generation dies off. Their study** looked in particular at eight areas of social change philan-

---

**Are We Ready? Social Change Philanthropy and the Coming $10 Trillion Transfer of Wealth*. Washington: National Committee for Responsive Philanthropy, 2000.

thropy and noted some encouraging trends. For example, lesbian, gay, bisexual, and transgender foundations are growing in size and influence. The collective endowments of women's funds are projected to reach $450 million by 2009. "There has been a lot of talk about the coming transfer of wealth, but few people have asked how this windfall will affect our society's most pressing social issues," said John Echohawk, who is both the NCRP chair and executive director of the Native American Rights Funds. "Social change philanthropists are asking those difficult questions and funding the solutions to our most intractable problems."

The focus of attention, in addition to those with inherited wealth, are the new millionaires emerging from the technology sector of the economy. "People treat wealth differently than income," noted James Ferris, a professor in the University of Southern California's School of Policy, Planning and Development. "There's a lot of attention on the new entrepreneurs, are they going to give differently?"[9]

The new philanthropy has certainly spawned a vast number of new foundations. The Foundation Center reports that the number of foundations doubled in the last two decades of the twentieth century. California is home to many of these. "The next ten years will see the West Coast emerging as a real philanthropic power," said Ferris.

But again the promise may be greater than the reality when it comes to social justice causes. Another study by the NCRP looked at seventy-three non-profits in California, home of much of the dot-com wealth. It found that progressive advocacy groups were impoverished in comparison to the conservative public policy organizations. The "new philanthropy" gets much mention in the press. Evidence, however, of it being a supporter of social change is scant. In fact the pattern of giving to well known and "safe" causes, such as disease eradication, than to causes seeking to eradicate social injustice is unlikely to be broken.

In summary, if you are working for a social justice cause this is a better time to be seeking funding. But like the injustices you are fighting, the injustice you face is that greatest share of wealth continues to be beyond your reach.

---

[9]Quoted in Mary McNamara, "The Changing Face of Giving," *Los Angeles Times*, January 9, 2000.

USER'S GUIDE

The pages that follow contain information that has been set neatly into type on crisp white pages. If, after owning the *Grant Seekers Guide* for a few days, the pages remain as they are now, you are not using the work properly. This book's destiny is to be dog-eared, marked up with pen and Highlighter, filled with Post-It notes, and frequently left open on the desk like an overweight ballet dancer unable to rise from doing the splits. Only then will it be working for you.

This is a book to be used, but with caution. Don't depend on it as the ultimate authority. Even as we concluded the fact checking on this edition, changes had occurred in the short time since we first contacted the foundations to update the book. Instead consider the book as a Rolodex of hot leads. When you find a foundation that might support your work, follow the following steps:

★ Call the foundation and obtain the name to whom proposals in your field should be submitted.

★ While you have the someone on the phone, confirm the address, and request application guidelines, list of grantees, and additional material that will round out the information.

★ Annotate the book with the date of your call and the name of the person to whom you spoke. Make any needed changes to the entry, such as a staffing change that has occurred at the foundation.

With all the material in hand, you are ready to proceed to the next step, trying to persuade the foundation to give you money. Again the *Grant Seekers Guide* can help. Look, for example, at the kinds of words that are used to describe the purpose of the foundation to which you are applying. While we wrote the entries, we used words that were often selected by the foundation in answering our queries. For instance, look at the clues provided in the following text:

The Megabucks Foundation provides grants in the areas of education, health, and the environment. The trustees favor projects that offer new approaches over those that are similar to previously funded programs and organizations that have not received prior support.

When shaping and submitting a proposal to such a foundation, one would want to be sure to highlight the innovative aspects of your grant and how you have not received prior support.

Next, you should study the fiscal information provided. If assets are listed, they are at market value as of a fixed date. Comparing the assets of foundation will give you a clear picture of who has the money. The number of grants and the range of sizes, especially the median* grant size, should help you judge the suitability of the sum you are seeking.

Lastly, we have included some foundations that say they do not accept proposals. Consider such a claim as only a means by which overburdened foundations separate the wheat from the chaff. Such foundations, for the most part, fund organizations and projects at the behest of their directors. A smart fundraiser will realize that a subtle campaign to educate these directors of an organization's worthiness may eventually yield results.

In any case, keep in mind the adage of former President Jimmy Carter. You can go fishing and still catch no fish, he used to say. But if you don't go fishing, you will certainly end up without any fish.

---

*Median is, of course, not an average. Rather it indicates that one-half of the grants issued were larger and one-half were smaller.

A TERRITORY RESOURCE

603 Stewart Street, Suite 1007

Seattle, Washington 98101

PHONE: (206) 624-4081

FAX: (206) 382-2640

EMAIL: website@atrfoundation.org

WEB: www.atrfoundation.org

Contact Person

Carol T. Pencke, Executive Director

Purpose

A Territory Resource (ATR) is a public foundation that supports activist, community-based organizations working for social, economic and environmental justice across the Northwest in Washington, Oregon, Idaho, Montana and Wyoming.

Areas of Interest

ATR funds projects solely within the five states of Idaho, Oregon, Washington, Montana, and Wyoming.

ATR restricts its works to organizations that:

- Organize people to work on social justice activities;
- Reach effectively their constituencies and build lasting organizations responsive to those constituencies;
- Attempt activities with a realistic chance of success;
- Develop short- and long-range strategies;
- Represent the diversity of their community or constituency.

Other organizational strengths valued by ATR include direction by skillful volunteer leadership or staff, a self-sustaining financial plan, outreach to new participants, and cooperative working relationships with other organizations open to shared research and development of joint strategies.

Areas of interest for ATR include economic and environmental justice, low-income communities and issues, communities of color and their issues, rural communities and issues, human rights, and coalition building. ATR also provides technical assistance grants for cultural work that promotes progressive social change.

**Financial
Data**

(Year ended 12/31/00)	
Assets:	$ 2,324,722
Total grants paid:	$ 962,035

**Application
Procedures**

A letter describing the program and establishing basic eligibility is required for regular grant applicants. If the project falls within ATR guidelines and priorities, a formal application proposal will be invited. This grant application is due approximately four weeks after the pre-application deadline. The ATR grant review committees and staff evaluate proposals. After an initial screening, site visits will be arranged for a limited number of applicants. Finally, approximately ten weeks after the application deadlines, proposals are considered and approved by the board of directors upon the recommendation of the grant review committees. Applicants will be notified of the board's decision within two weeks of that decision.

Requests for proposals are issued once per year for major grants and cultural grants. ATR offers two, three-year major grants each year. To be eligible, an organization must have received funding from ATR at least once within the last five years, maintain a budget of over $100,000, and undertake what ATR considers a bold new direction. Funding for major grants includes $20,000 in the first and second year, and $10,000 for the third year.

Technical assistance grant proposals are accepted year-round. However, no technical grants are awarded in April. See our website for more information.

**Grant
Limitations**

To be eligible for funding, a project must: work to achieve progressive social change and social justice; address fundamental issues facing the Northwest-Northern Rockies region and its inhabitants; operate in and have a direct bearing on the people of Idaho, Montana, Oregon, Washington, or Wyoming; actively work to make social institutions more just, equitable, and humane; operate in a democratic, nondiscriminatory, humane manner, responsive to the project's constituency; and be a non-profit, tax-exempt 501(c)(3) organization or be sponsored by one.

ATR generally will not fund: projects that can be funded by traditional sources; projects sponsored by a government agency; direct service programs; individuals; publications, conferences, media events, arts/theater productions unless they are an integral part of other ongoing social change activities; or endowments or capital building projects.

Meeting Times

The board of directors meets four times each year, and member meetings are held three times annually. Regular granting meetings occur in May and November. Cultural granting meetings are in February, and technical assistance granting meetings are monthly (except in April, October, and November).

Publications

An annual report is available. See our website for more information.

ABELARD FOUNDATION WEST

%⁄ COMMON COUNSEL FOUNDATION

1221 PRESERVATION PARK WAY, SUITE 101

OAKLAND, CALIFORNIA 94612

PHONE: (510) 834-2995

FAX: 510-834-2998

EMAIL: ccounsel@igc.org

WEB: www.commoncounsel.org

**Contact
Person**

Elizabeth Wilcox, Executive Director

Purpose

The Abelard Foundation supports social change organizations working toward a more democratic, just, and equitable society. Specifically the foundation funds projects that expand and protect civil rights and civil liberties; increase opportunities for the poor, the disenfranchised, and minorities; and expand community involvement in and control over economic and environmental decisions.

**Areas of
Interest**

The foundation provides funds to community-based organizations in the Western United States engaged in organizing, policy development, advocacy, or education on the following issues:

- Environmental justice
- Human rights/civil rights
- Economic justice
- Workers' rights
- Immigrant rights
- Criminal justice
- Native American/sovereignty issues

Most grants are awarded to organizations with a constituent base and interested in strengthening the skills and abilities of their members.

The Abelard staff advises other donors through Common Counsel, a shared grantmaking organization. These donors have interests similar to Abelard's, and also fund more extensively in the areas of environmental justice and youth/leadership development. Common Counsel also provides small technical assistance grants through its Grantee Exchange Fund.

Financial Data

> (Year ended 12/31/00)
> Assets: $ 5,000,000 - $ 6,000,000
> Total grants paid: $ 244,000
> Number of grants paid: 27
> Highest grant: $ 12,000
> Lowest grant: $ 8,000
> Median grant size: $ 10,000

Application Procedures

Organizations working in Hawaii, California, the Pacific Northwest states, the Rocky Mountain states, and the Southwest should follow the application procedures outlined here.

Applicants are encouraged to submit materials for one of two deadlines: January 15 or June 15. Grantseekers should consult the website at www.commoncounsel.org for detailed proposal guidelines.

Interested organizations may contact the foundation submitting a full proposal. Proposals should include the following: a letter summarizing the background and purposes of the organization requesting funds and stating how the funds will be used; a description of the project explaining the problem or issue to be addressed, how the project will address the problem, and why the strategy will be effective; resumes of the people who will do the work; a project schedule; a detailed budget for the project and for the sponsoring organization if the project is part of a larger, ongoing effort; information on fundraising strategies, including the status of current requests and past sources of funding; proof of tax-exempt status; and a list of board members and other references familiar with the organization's work. Abelard accepts the common grant application of National Network of Grantmakers.

Grant Limitations

The foundation does not support: social service programs offering ongoing or direct delivery of services; medical, educational, or cultural institutions; capital expenditures, construction or renovation programs; programs undertaken at government initiative; and scholarship funds or other aids to individuals. Projects whose purpose is primarily to inform in a general way, or to study or research an issue for purpose of public education, and with little or no emphasis on policy change or implementation do not fall within Abelard's funding guidelines. Conferences are supported only when they are closely related to the initiation of new programs or organizations.

Meeting Times

The board of directors meets twice a year, usually in June and November.

Publications

The foundation publishes a brochure describing its work and a list of grantees. The website (www.commoncounsel.org) provides updated guidelines and grants lists.

AETNA FOUNDATION

AETNA INCORPORATED

151 FARMINGTON AVENUE

HARTFORD, CONNECTICUT 06156-3180

PHONE: (860) 273-1932

FAX: (860) 273-4764

EMAIL: aetnafoundation@aetna.com

WEB: www.aetna.com/foundation

Contact Person

Marilda Gandara Alfonso, Vice President and Executive Director

Purpose

The three purposes of Aetna's philanthropic programs are to help preserve a viable society in which to live, work, and do business; to support those programs and organizations that address social problems with innovative solutions; and to provide support in a manner that will stimulate other donors. Its efforts focus primarily on Hartford, Connecticut.

Areas of Interest

For the last several years, the foundation has concentrated its efforts in two areas: immunization and primary health care for children and college programs for minority students.

In the first area, the foundation funds programs to increase the number of children, birth to two years old, who are fully immunized against preventable childhood diseases. As part of the initiative, it also supports education and outreach efforts, and innovative ways to deliver accessible, cost-effective services to children who otherwise would not receive needed health care.

In the second area, the foundation funds programs to increase the successful enrollment and participation of minority students in higher education. Grants target programs that help minority middle students in higher education. In particular, the grants aim to assist minority middle and high school students aspire to and prepare for entry into higher education, and increase their likelihood of success once they enter college.

In addition to the national grants program, the foundation operates an extensive local grants program through selected Aetna field offices. The FOCUS program, administered by field office general managers, makes grants in the interest areas of children's health and minority education.

Of related interest to some nonprofit organizations is Aetna's Corporate Responsibility Investment Committee (CRIC) comprising vice presidents from Bond Investment, Common Stock, Real Estate Investment, Treasurers, Corporate Public Involvement, Law, Employee Benefits, and International divisions. It is entirely separate from the foundation and its purpose is to oversee corporate investments that strengthen community-based enterprises, increase economic development opportunities, leverage Aetna dollars, and provide leadership for new program development.

Financial Data

```
(Year ended    /   /    )
Total Revenue and Support:                    NA
                        Foundation    Corporate
Total Grants Paid              NA              NA
Number of Grants Paid:
Highest Grant
Lowest Grant
Median Grant Size
```

Application Procedures

Grant applications are accepted year round and must be submitted in writing. Grant seekers are encouraged to submit a preliminary inquiry, including the organization's purpose and history; documentation of tax-exempt status; a summary of the program for which funds will be requested; a budget and fundraising strategy; and the amount requested. Staff members will review the inquiry and respond either with an invitation to submit a formal proposal or explanation as to why the project does not meet the foundation's or the company's philanthropic priorities. Exceptions to the program priorities are rare, so the foundation discourages applications that do not fit its priorities.

Organizations seeking a loan from Aetna's Corporate Responsibility Investment Committee should write a letter of no more than three pages addressed to Thomas Q. Callahan. The letter should include the following information: the applicant's name and address; the amount being requested and an explanation of how the money will be used; project name and location; a description of the type of project involved, including those facts that are particularly relevant to CRIC's interests; a description of the applicant's development history, including previous Aetna-supported projects, if applicable; and other sources of support for the project, both private and public. There are no geographic restrictions on this program. CRIC invests on a nationwide basis, and applications are accepted throughout the year.

Grant
Limitations

Grants are restricted to tax-exempt organizations located in the United States and to programs taking place in the United States, with the exception of a small international program started in 1988. About one-third of the grants are concentrated in the Hartford, Connecticut, area. Grants are not made to: individuals; organizations without 501(c)(3) designation or de facto tax-exempt status; capital building, endowment or debt reduction drives; medical research; private secondary and elementary schools; political activities; religious organizations whose programs are restricted to members of a specific denomination; and sporting events, advertising, fund-raising dinners, or similar special events.

Meeting
Times

The board of directors meets quarterly in March, June, September, and December.

Publications

Annual reports are available that include information on the foundation's grant application procedure.

ALASKA CONSERVATION FOUNDATION

441 WEST 5TH AVENUE, SUITE 402

ANCHORAGE, ALASKA 99501-2340

PHONE: (907) 276-1917

FAX: (907) 274-4145

EMAIL: acfinfo@akcf.org

WEB: www.akcf.org

Contact Person

Deborah L. Williams, Executive Director

Purpose

The Alaska Conservation Foundation works to protect the integrity of Alaska's ecosystems and to promote sustainable livelihoods among Alaska's communities and peoples.

Areas of Interest

ACF is a foundation for conservation in the community of Alaska. The foundation's particular interests include: community and grassroots organizing around environmental issues, energy conservation and generation, hazardous waste and toxic substances, clean streams, and wildlands and wildlife protection. It places an emphasis on projects that support organizational growth, membership development, community outreach, and building coalitions to broaden the base of support for protecting the ecosystems that provide for healthy and sustainable communities. Grants are made both for general operating support and for carrying out specifically designated projects.

Financial Data

(Year ended 6/30/99)	
Support and revenue:	$ 3,398,161
Total grants paid:	$ 1,881,203

Application Procedures

The foundation distributes application guidelines upon request. Briefly, a complete application includes information about the organization, structure and legal status of an applicant, and concise information on the organization or proposed project and needs to be served. Lengthy submissions are discouraged. There are two application deadlines. While the dates vary annually, they are generally six weeks in advance of the foundation's February and September grantmaking sessions.

Grant
Limitations

The foundation makes grants only to Alaska-based organizations. No grants are made for endowments, basic research or land acquisition.

Meeting
Times

The board of directors meets three times a year. While the dates are not fixed, meetings usually occur in early February, May, and September.

Publications

The foundation publishes an annual report, quarterly newsletter *Dispatch*, application guidelines and the *Alaska Conservation Directory*.

AMERICAN CONSERVATION ASSOCIATION

PHONE: (212) 649-5600 or (202) 624-9367

1350 New York Avenue, N.W.

Washington, D.C. 20005

Contact Person

Executive Vice President

Purpose

The American Conservation Foundation is a private operating foundation whose purpose is to advance knowledge and understanding of conservation.

Areas of Interest

The foundation awards grants to nonprofit organizations in the United States that help preserve the landscape and natural resources and educate the public in the proper use of these areas. Examples of support are awards in areas such as beautification programs, environmental protection of natural resources, advocacy and regulation, pollution control and animals and wildlife. Operating, continuing, and general support is provided. Support is also provided for special projects, technical assistance, loans, and conferences and seminars.

Financial Data

(Year ended / /)	
Assets:	NA
Total grants paid:	
Total number of grants:	
Highest grant:	
Lowest grant:	
Median grant size:	

Application Procedures

The foundation does not have an application form nor does it publish guidelines for applications. Applicants should submit a letter of inquiry which includes the following: a detailed description of the project and amount of funding requested; a copy of the organization's current year's budget and the project budget; and a list of additional sources of support. One copy of the letter should be submitted, preferably in early spring. The board meets once a year in the fall.

Grant Limitations

Grants are not awarded to individuals, for building funds, endowments, scholarships or fellowships.

Meeting Times

The board meets in the fall, usually in September or October. The executive committee meets as needed.

Publications

None.

AMERICAN FOUNDATION FOR AIDS RESEARCH

120 WALL STREET, 13TH FLOOR

NEW YORK, NEW YORK 10005-3908

PHONE: (212) 806-1696

FAX: (212) 806-1601

EMAIL: grants@amfar.org

WEB: www.amfar.org

Contact Person

Kent Cozad, Grants Administrator

Purpose

The mission of the American Foundation for AIDS Research (AmFAR) is to support the search for a cure, the refinement of prevention techniques, and the improvement of treatment for acquired immunodeficiency syndrome (AIDS) and related disorders. In addition to its grantmaking activities, AmFAR serves as a resource for responsible information on the clinical, psychological, public health and public policy aspects for AIDS.

Areas of Interest

The bulk of AmFAR's grantmating is directed toward basic biomedical research, however AmFAR also awards grants for clinical, behavioral, legal, ethical, and humanistic research and has made a significant commitment of resources to public education and community outreach activities. In addition to traditional written materials, radio, and film aimed at young people and minorities, AmFAR has supported leadership training for corporate executives and educators, efforts to educate employees in the workplace, and community-based networking and organizing.

Financial Data

```
(Year ended   /   /   )
Assets:                              NA
Total grants paid:
Number of grants paid:
Highest grant:
Lowest grant:
Median grant size:
```

**Application
Procedures**

The grant process begins with a formal request-for-proposals (RFP), which is distributed to thousands of researchers worldwide and publicized in HIV/AIDS-related scholarly journals. Investigators are required to submit a letter of intent (LOI), which must be approved prior to submission of a grant application. Applications are solicited from a limited number of researchers each grant cycle, and both LOIs and full proposals are reviewed by AmFAR's Scientific Advisory Committee. The SAC's recommendations are submitted to the Board of Directors for final approval of all grant awards.

**Meeting
Times**

The board of directors of the American Foundation for AIDS Research meets twice a year to award grants.

Publications

AmFAR publishes an annual report, and grant application guidelines are available upon request.

HUGH J. ANDERSEN FOUNDATION

342 5th Avenue, North

BAYPORT, MINNESOTA 55003-1201

PHONE: (651) 439-1557

FAX: (651) 439-9480

EMAIL: bek@srinc.biz

WEB: www.srinc.biz

Contact Person

Brad Kruse, Program Officer

Purpose

The Hugh J. Andersen Foundation, established in 1962, is a private foundation committed to building individual and community capacity. Its resources are focused primarily on the St. Croix Valley, which encompasses Washington County, Minnesota and Pierce, Polk and St. Croix Counties in Wisconsin. A secondary geographic interest is St. Paul, Minnesota.

Areas of Interest

The foundation's areas of interest in order of priority are: organizations that provide human services; organizations that serve children and youth; organizations that provide local educational enrichment opportunities; and organizations engaged in health-related programming.

The foundation is interested in programs that are initiated, supported or require involvement by the constituency for whom benefits are sought. This type of effort develops and builds on individual and community capacities.

Financial Data

(Year ended 2/28/01)	
Assets:	$ 49,467,715
Total grants paid:	$ 2,050,889
Total number of grants:	173
Highest grant:	$ 250,000
Lowest grant:	$ 300
Median grant size:	$ 5,000

**Application
Procedures**

All applicants must complete the foundation's application form which is sent along with the program guidelines. Supporting information includes: a description of organization, its mission, and programming and results; a list of the board of directors and their affiliations, and the qualifications of key management; a copy of the current year's organizational budget and a list of past, current and pending sources of support; a copy of IRS 501(c)(3) tax-exempt determination and a copy of the most recent financial audit. Deadlines for receipt are November 15, March 15, June 15, and September 15.

Letters of inquiry may also be sent and will be reviewed at the next board meeting after receipt. If the board determines that the request falls within its guidelines, a full proposal will be requested from the applicant.

**Grant
Limitations**

Grants are made only to nonprofit public charitable organizations that are tax-exempt under Section 501(c)(3) of the IRS code. It does not make grants or scholarships to individuals, for lobbying activities, fundraising events, travel, private schools, or religious institutions. Major endowment and capital funding is a low priority and the foundation does not fund the entire budget for a project.

**Meeting
Times**

The board of directors meets four times a year.

Publications

The foundation publishes an annual report and application guidelines.

THE APPALACHIAN COMMUNITY FUND

107 West Main

Knoxville, Tennessee 37902

PHONE: (865) 523-5783

FAX: (865) 523-1896

EMAIL:info@appalachiancommunityfund.org

WEB:www.appalachiancommunityfund.org

Contact Person

Gaye Evans, Executive Director

Purpose

The Appalachian Community Fund (AFC) was founded in 1987 to bring new resources and provide grants to groups for community organizing and social change in the central region of Appalachia (eastern Tennessee, eastern Kentucky, southwest Virginia and all of West Virginia). Grants are given to the community-based organizations that address underlying causes of the economic and social distress of the region, and are targeted to organizations and communities with little or no access to other moneys. ACF also seeks to become a sustainable resource to the region through building a long-term resource base and expanding community philanthropy in the region.

The organization does this through:

• Providing resources for community organizing efforts

• Implementing strategies for social change through grantmaking

• Creating a comprehensive development strategy in order to become a sustainable resource in the region

Areas of Interest

ACF's grantmaking program supports organizations where people are organizing themselves to address problems in their own communities and neighborhoods and where organizations develop and grow with democratic structures to be vehicles for change. Issues range from workers' and women's rights to environmental justice, community-based economic development, racism, and youth issues, among others. The focus for our grantmaking is grassroots organizing for social change.

**Financial
Data**

(Year ended 6/30/2000)	
Support and revenue:	$ 337,745
Total grants paid:	$ 245,000
Number of grants paid:	40
Highest grant:	$ 6,200
Lowest grant:	$ 300
Median grant size:	$ 5,000

**Application
Procedures**

Grants made from the General Program have a maximum grant size of $7,500. Last year the average grant was $5,000. We accept proposals for the General Program annually. We also have a Technical Assistance program and a Seize the Moment opportunity program. In the spring we award the Lucille Thornburgh Leadership Development Program grants. For more information on any of these grants programs, please contact the office.

The Board of Directors of the Appalachian Community Fund is made up of activists from the four central Appalachian states. Proposal applications are read by members of the ACF Board, who review and discuss proposals and make decisions on the final grant awards.

**Grant
Limitations**

The Appalachian Community Fund (ACF) funds work that takes place in the central Appalachian region: West Virginia, eastern Kentucky, southwest Virginia, and east Tennessee. We use the Appalachian Regional Commission designation for Appalachian counties in these states. Organizations must have a 501(c)(3) tax exempt status, or 501(c)(3) fiscal sponsor in order to receive ACF funding.

ACF *DOES NOT* FUND:

- Profit-making organizations.
- Electoral lobbying for initiatives or public office.
- Individual efforts.
- Major capital projects.
- Social services unless they demonstrate some analysis and strategies to challenge the systems that lead to oppression.

**Meeting
Times**

Decisions on grant requests are made once a year by the board of directors for the General Program and once a year for the Thornburgh Program. Tech Assistance and Seize the Moment grants may be awarded throughout the year.

Publications

The Appalachian Community Fund publishes an annual report and grant guidelines.

Contact Person

Bernadette Roberts, Program Associate

Purpose

The Arca Foundation supports a wide variety of organizations engaged in exposing the inequities of present day policy, proposing creative alternatives, and mobilizing grassroots support for changing the status quo. Grantmaking is clustered around a specific set of issues, and is limited to activities of national significance and likely to yield tangible public policy results.

Areas of Interest

From time to time the priorities of the foundation change. In general, however, the foundation's areas of interest are:

• United States and Cuba. Projects that seek to rebuild the relationship between the two countries by creating a climate more conducive to dialogue and democratization.

• Campaign finance reform. Projects that try to reformulate the way elections are financed in the United States.

Additionally, the foundation also funds a number of policy-oriented social justice projects that reflect the diverse interests of its board.

Financial Data

(Year ended 12/31/2000)	
Assets:	$72,759,206
Total grants awarded:	$2.8million
Number of grants awarded:	65
Highest grant:	$100,000
Lowest grant:	$500
Median grant size:	$40,000

Application
Procedures

Deadlines for proposals are September 1 for the December board meeting and March 1 for the June board meeting. Organizations wishing to apply for a grant should submit a full proposal which includes a one page cover sheet stating the organization's name and address, contact person, telephone number, annual budget and amount requested; one page summary of the proposal, project and organizational budget, amount requested and amounts and dates of other Arca grants; other project grants received and potential funding sources; a narrative, no more than ten pages long, that contains information on the organization and purpose of the grant. Attachments should include a copy of the IRS determination letter, list of staff with resumes, and list of board of directors and their affiliations.

All proposals are acknowledged in writing within a few weeks of receipt and further information will be requested as needed. Phone calls are discouraged and applicants will be notified in writing shortly after the board's decision.

Grant
Limitations

Only organizations identified as 501(c)(3) and 509(a) tax-exempt charities are eligible for funding. Grantmaking is limited to U.S. based organizations working to affect U.S. policy. The foundation does not fund: organizations that provide direct social services; scholarship funds of scholarly research; capital projects or endowments; individuals or government programs.

Meeting
Times

The board of directors meets in June and December to consider grant proposals.

Publications

The foundation publishes an annual report, which includes application procedures.

THE ARK FOUNDATION

P.O. Box 2244

Orinda, California 94563

PHONE: (925) 253-1260

FAX: (925) 253-9337

EMAIL: llazare@earthlink.net

Contact Person

Linda Lazare, Director

Areas of Interest

The Ark Foundation supports projects in the counties of Alameda and Contra Costa in California, with a specific emphasis on community based projects that promote self esteem and self sufficiency for the individual. A new focus is personal health via vegan diet and exercise.

Financial Data

(Year ended 10/31/00)	
Support and revenue:	$ 55,000
Total grants approved:	$ 46,500
Number of grants approved:	23
Highest grant:	$ 5 ,000
Lowest grant:	$ 500
Median grant size:	$ 1,000

Application Procedures

Organizations interested in applying to the foundation for support should write a preliminary letter (no more than two pages long) describing the organization and the project for which funds are sought. This letter should describe the organization's mission and goals; the objectives of the proposed project, why the organization thinks they can be realistically attained, and the criteria against which the project will be evaluated; the capability of the organization to carry out the proposed project; the relationship of the organization and the project to others working in the same field; the public policy implications or the potential for the project to be used as a model; and a statement describing what, if the project is successful, would be the follow-up.

The letter should also include information on the budget of the proposed project, the amount to be requested from the foundation, and the amount that can be expected from other sources of funding. The enclosures should include the organization's annual report or other program description, the most recent financial statements, and proof of tax-exempt status under Section 501(c)(3) of the Internal Revenue Code.

If the foundation is interested in the proposed project, a more formal proposal may be requested and a site visit or other meeting may be arranged.

Grant Limitations

The foundation provides support only to organizations with tax-exempt status or projects working through a tax-exempt fiscal sponsor. The foundation does not support individuals, endowment campaigns, building funds, or projects that are primarily international.

Meeting Times

The board of directors of the Ark Foundation meets approximately twice a year.

Publications

None.

ASTRAEA NATIONAL LESBIAN ACTION FOUNDATION

PHONE: (212) 529-8021

FAX: (212) 982-3321

EMAIL: info@astraea.org

WEB: www.astraeafoundation.org

116 E. 16TH STREET, 7TH FLOOR

NEW YORK, NEW YORK 10003

Contact Person

Katherine Acey, Executive Director

Purpose

The Astraea National Lesbian Action Foundation provides economic and social support to projects that empower the lives of lesbians. Astraea's primary purpose is to raise and distribute funds to organizations, individuals, and projects that promote a feminist perspective advancing the social, political, economic, educational, and cultural well-being of lesbians and all women and girls. Astraea supports programs and policies that actively work to eliminate those forms of oppression based on race, age, sex, economic exploitation, physical and mental ability, anti-Semitism, and all other factors that affect lesbians and gay men in the United States and internationally.

Areas of Interest

The general grantmaking program funds local, regional, and national organizations that focus on organizing, advocacy, and empowerment services. Projects funded by Astraea are actively working to eliminate all forms of oppression based on sexual orientation, race and ethnicity, age, sex, class, physical and mental ability, and all other factors that affect lesbians in the United States. Cultural and film/video projects are also considered for funding.

Lynn Campbell Memorial Fund supports projects that reflect activism in women's, labor, lesbian and gay social movements, and commitment to social justice.

Margot Karle Scholarship is awarded to a woman student within the City University of New York (CUNY) system who demonstrates a commitment to social activism and financial need.

Lesbian Writers Fund supports the work of lesbian fiction and poetry writers.

**Financial
Data**

> (Year ended   / /   )
> Assets: NA
> Total grants paid:
> Number of grants paid:
> Highest grant:
> Lowest grant:
> Median grant size:

**Application
Procedures**

All applications must be submitted on forms provided by the foundation. Interested organizations should contact the program director by telephone or mail and request an application form. All forms are available online. Completed applications to the foundation must be postmarked by the deadline date of the specific grant program to receive consideration at the next funding cycle.

Deadlines are as follows:

General Grantmaking Program: guidelines posted online

Margot Karle Scholarship: August 15, December 15

Lesbian Writers Fund: March 8

**Grant
Limitations**

The foundation does not fund projects of individuals, except for cultural and media projects that are designed to serve as organizing tools for social change.

**Meeting
Times**

The Community Funding Panel meets twice a year to consider grant request to the general grantmaking program.

Publications

The foundation publishes a brochure outlining its program interests and application procedures and a semi-annual newsletter describing its grantees.

AT&T FOUNDATION

32 Avenue of the Americas

6th Floor

New York, New York 10013

PHONE: (212) 387-4849

FAX: (212) 387-5098

EMAIL: naic@att.com

WEB: www.att.com/foundation

Contact Person

Marilyn Reznick, Executive Director

Purpose

The AT&T Foundation is the company's principal instrument for philanthropy. It provides grants to nonprofit organizations for innovative programs that focus on helping people achieve self-sufficiency and lead productive lives. The foundation maintains four programs: grants, employee volunteerism, donations of products and services, and a range of local initiatives. Most grants are awarded in communities that have a significance AT&T presence.

Areas of Interest

Grants and contributions are made in the areas of education, health and human services, arts and culture, and international projects.

• Arts and Culture. New and innovative artistic projects that foster communications and promote cross-cultural understanding. Priority is given to programs assisting in the creation of new artistic work, bringing the work of women artists of diverse cultures to wider audiences, and supporting initiatives that provide access to all segments of communities.

• Education. Pre-college and higher education programs that improve science and math teaching and learning, and projects that explore the role of technology in education. The objectives of the program are to enhance teaching and research and promote curriculum innovation; improve opportunities for women and minority students and encourage diversification of student and faculty populations; and advance systemic reform, teacher preparation, student achievement and parental involvement at the K-12 level.

• Heath and Human Services. Programs that are national and comprehensive in scope and focus on children and families; accessibility of health and social services to those in need; the advancement of diversity; and the protection of the environment. In the United States grants are made primarily through the United Way, however, the foundation looks for projects that serve as models for other organizations and can be replicated elsewhere.

• International. Organizations based outside the United States performing activities that fall within the focus areas of education, health and human services, and arts and culture. Priority is given to projects that involve innovation/technology.

Financial Data

```
(Year ended   /  /  )
Assets:                          NA
Grants paid:
Number of grants:
Highest grant:
Lowest grant:
Median grant size:
```

Application Procedures

Applicants should review AT&T Foundation's funding guidelines brochure to determine whether a project is appropriate for foundation support. If after reading the guidelines, grant seekers remain unsure, they should request the AT&T Foundation Report by calling 904-636-3898, faxing a request to 904-636-1674, or writing to:

AT&T Foundation Report
Dept. BR.
P.O. Box 45284
Jacksonville, Florida 32232-5284

The foundation accepts proposals throughout the year. Consideration of proposals occurs at the end of January, April, July, and September. There are two ways of applying for grants. If the organization or project is based in the United States and national in scope, the AT&T Foundation headquarters is the appropriate contact point. If the organization and scope is regional or local, the appropriate regional contributions manager listed at the end of this entry should be contacted.

**Grant
Limitations**

The foundation does not award grants to individuals, buy advertisements, or donate equipment. Other excluded organizations and purposes are: organizations not classified as tax-exempt under Section 501(c)(3) of the Internal Revenue Code; organizations whose chief purpose is to influence legislation; political organizations or campaigns; religious organizations which are denominational or sectarian in purpose; operating expenses or capital campaigns; local chapters of national organizations; sports teams or athletic competitions; and banquets or other fundraising events.

It should be noted that within each of the foundation's specific areas of interest there are additional limitations. For more information consult the foundation's application guidelines.

**Meeting
Times**

The board of trustees meets quarterly.

Publications

The foundation publishes a biennial report and list of grants and financial information, and a brochure describing its guidelines and application procedures.

**Regional
Contributions
Coordinators**

As indicated below, local organizations should initiate contact with the foundation by writing to the AT&T Regional Contributions Manager at one of the following addresses:

Organization Location	Foundation Contact
Southern Region	
Alabama, Georgia	1200 Peachtree Street, N.E. Suite 2040 Atlanta, GA 30309
Kentucky, Louisiana, Mississippi, North Carolina, South Carolina, Tennessee, Arkansas, Kansas, Missouri, Oklahoma, Texas, Florida	501 LBJ Freeway, Suite 1007 Dallas, TX 75240 6855 Red Road, 2nd Floor Coral Gables, FL 33143

Eastern Region

Connecticut, Maine, Vermont, Massachusetts, New Hampshire, Rhode Island, Upstate New York	99 Bedford Street Room 402 Boston, MA 02111
Delaware, Pennsylvania	1500 Market Street, 17th Floor Philadelphia, PA 19103
Maryland, Virginia, Washington, D.C., West Virginia	1120 20th Street, N.W. Suite 520-S Washington, DC 20036
New York, New York City	1301 Avenue of the Americas, Room 3018 New York, NY 10019
New Jersey	295 North Maple Ave. Room 2221F2 Basking Ridge, NJ 07920
Illinois, Indiana, Iowa, Minnesota, Nebraska, North Dakota, South Dakota, Wisconsin	227 West Monroe Street 20th Floor Chicago, IL 60606
Michigan, Ohio (except Dayton)	26957 Northwestern Highway Suite 400 Southfield, MI 48034
Dayton, Ohio	1700 S. Patterson Blvd. Area WHQ5E Dayton, OH 45479

Western Region

Northern California, Oregon, Alaska, Hawaii, Nevada, Washington State	795 Folsom Street, Suite 120 San Francisco, CA 94107
Southern California, Arizona, New Mexico	6111 West 6th Street Suite 2200 Los Angeles, CA 90017
Colorado, Idaho, Montana Utah, Wyoming	7979 E. Tufts Ave. Parkway, Suite 1100 Denver, Co 80237

Asia/Pacific

Australia, China, India, Japan, Taiwan	Times Square 28F/Shell Tower 1 Matheson Street Causeway Bay, Hong Kong

Europe/Middle East/Africa

France, Germany, Poland,
The Netherlands,
Russia, Spain, United Kingdom,
North America/Latin American/Caribbean
Canada

Tour Horizon
52 quai de Dion-Bouton
92806 Puteaux Cedex, France

4650 Victoria Park Avenue
Suite 700
Willowdale, Ontario
Canada M2H 3P7

Argentina, Brazil, Colombia
Mexico, Puerto Rico, Venezuela

6855 Red Road, 2nd Floor
Coral Gables, FL 33143

AVON PRODUCTS FOUNDATION

PHONE: (212) 282-5000

FAX: (212) 282-2646

EMAIL: info@avonfoundation.org

WEB: www.avon.com

WORLD HEADQUARTERS

1345 AVENUE OF THE AMERICAS

NEW YORK, NEW YORK 10105-0196

Contact Person

Kathleen Walas, President

Purpose

The Avon Products Foundation is a company-sponsored foundation of Avon Products, Inc., the manufacturer of cosmetics, toiletries, and costume jewelry. The foundation support endeavors that understand and respond to the needs of women and their families, and enable women to reach their full potential.

Areas of Interest

The foundation considers projects which provide assistance for women's programs in four areas: health, education, community and social services, and arts and culture. National programs and New York City projects are administered by the foundation's headquarters in New York. Funding is also available regionally in areas where Avon has regional offices. Contact the regional office for more information in these regions:

Atlanta, Georgia: (770) 271-6100
Morton Grove, Illinois: (847) 966-0200
Newark, Delaware: (302) 453-7700
Pasadena, California: (626) 578-8000
Springdale, Ohio: (513) 551-2000
Suffern, New York: (845) 369-2000

AVON PRODUCTS FOUNDATION

**Financial
Data**

```
(Year ended    /   /   )
Assets:                                    NA
Total grants paid:
Number of grants paid:
Highest grant:
Lowest grant:
Median grant size:
```

**Application
Procedures**

Although the foundation prefers to seek out and request proposals, unsolicited proposals will be accepted and considered. Applicants should contact the appropriate office to determine whether funding should be pursued.

**Grant
Limitations**

Eligibility is limited to national programs and to local and regional programs operating near an Avon location. The foundation does not make grants to individuals for educational or other purposes, political causes or candidates, religious, veteran or fraternal organizations unless the projects benefit the entire community, fundraising events, and courtesy advertising.

**Meeting
Times**

The board of directors meets three times a year.

Publications

The foundation publishes an annual report and application guidelines.

MARY REYNOLDS BABCOCK FOUNDATION

PHONE: (336) 748-9222

FAX: (336) 777-0095

EMAIL: info@mrbf.org

WEB: www.mrbf.org

2920 REYNOLDA ROAD

WINSTON-SALEM, NORTH CAROLINA

27106

Contact Person

Gayle Williams, Executive Director

Purpose

The Mary Reynolds Babcock Foundation's mission is to promote "the well-being and betterment of humankind" by assisting people in the South to build communities that nurture people, spur enterprise, bridge differences, and act with fairness and compassion. In particular, it seeks to be of benefit in areas where poverty prevails or race divides.

Areas of Interest

The foundation places special emphasis on strategies that increase communities' commitment, sense of responsibility, and capacity toward three ends:
- Assuring the well-being of children, youth, and families;
- Bridging the faultlines of race and class;
- Protecting and investing in human and natural resources for the long term.

The foundation is developing guidelines for organizational development, leadership development, and community building program areas.

Financial Data

(Year ended 12/18/00)	
Assets:	$ 118,549,309
Total grants paid:	$ 4,508,986
Number of grants paid:	116
Highest grant:	$ 150,000
Lowest grant:	$ 1,600
Median grant size:	$ 30,000

**Application
Procedures**

Call or write for a copy.

Publications

The foundation publishes an annual report.

BAUMAN FOUNDATION

2040 "S" Street, N.W.

Washington, DC 20009-1110

PHONE: (202) 328-2040

FAX: (202) 328-2003

Contact Persons

Patricia Bauman, Co-Director

John L. Bryant, Jr., Co-Director

Purpose

The Bauman Foundation's goal is to foster activities that encourage systemic social change.

Areas of Interest

The Bauman Foundation's areas of interest focus on programs that revive concepts of the common good through changes in institutions and power relations in economic and political life; stress the connections between human health and the environment (especially the role of toxic chemicals and other environmental factors in chronic diseases) through education and advocacy; implement citizen right-to-know laws and policies; and support widespread public access to information.

Financial Data

(Year ended 6/30/99)	
Assets:	$ 55,980,076
Total Grants Paid:	$ 3,534,954
Total number of grants:	47
Highest grant:	$ 550,000
Lowest grant:	$ 1,000
Median grant size:	

Application Procedures

The Bauman Foundation does not review unsolicited proposals.

**Grant
Limitations**

No grants to individuals. No grants for biomedical and epidemiological research, direct services, organizing (unless part of a broader strategy), or overhead expenses for established institutions. No grants for local or state programs (unless there is a plan for their dissemination and use as models).

**Meeting
Times**

Quarterly.

Publications

None.

THE BELDON FUND

99 Madison Avenue, 8th Floor
New York, NY 10016

PHONE: (212) 616-5600

FAX: (212) 616-5656

EMAIL: info@beldon.org

WEB: www.beldon.org

Contact Person

William J. Roberts, Executive Director

Areas of Interest

The Beldon Fund focuses project and general support grants in three programs: *Human Health and the Environment, Corporate Campaigns*, and *Key States*. These programs are designed to work together to achieve the vision and mission of the Fund. Proposals that work synergistically across programs are encouraged.

The *Human Health and the Environment* program seeks to add new, powerful voices to promote a national consensus on the environment and to activate the public on issues that matter to people in a deeply personal and potent way.

The *Corporate Campaigns* program seeks to answer the constant and growing efforts by many corporations to block the development of a national consensus on the environment and the achievement of real, sustainable progress on the health of our planet.

The *Key States* program focuses on particular states where the power of a growing, energized consensus for environmental protection can be organized and brought to bear on the public policy and policy makers.

Financial Data

(Year ended 12/31/99)	
Assets:	$ 79,301,365
Total grants paid:	$ 2,480,000
Number of grants paid:	15
Highest grant:	$ 800,000
Lowest grant:	$ 25,000

Application Procedures

Organizations seeking grants from the Fund should begin the process by submitting a letter of inquiry in accordance with our Program Guidelines. The Fund grants both general support and project-specific support for one year or for multiple years. We require letters of inquiry from all organizations seeking grants from the Fund, including former grantees and current grantees seeking renewal.

There is no specific limit on the number of requests we will consider from a single organization, nor is there a limit on the number of years we will continuously fund an organization. The amount granted depends on the scope of the project and the size of the applicant's budget. (To learn more about the kinds of grants we provide, please visit our website to review the list of grants that we have awarded in the past.)

The Fund makes grants to public charities classified as tax exempt under section 501(c)(3) of the Internal Revenue Code. If you do not have 501(c)(3) tax-exempt status, please indicate the name of the public charity that serves as your fiscal sponsor.

Grant Limitations

The fund makes grants only to tax-exempt organizations. The fund does not make grants for the following: land acquisition, film and video projects, international programs, litigation, endowment or capital campaigns, grants to individuals, historic preservation, direct social service delivery programs, public or private education, scholarships, or academic research.

Meeting Times

Grant decisions are made throughout the year.

Publications

The fund publishes an annual report.

BEN & JERRY'S FOUNDATION

30 COMMUNITY DRIVE

SO. BURLINGTON, VERMONT 05403

PHONE: (802) 846-1500

WEB: www.benjerry.com/foundation

Contact Person

Rebecca Golden, Director

Purpose

Ben & Jerry's Foundation supports organizations working to change the underlying conditions that create social problems such as racism, sexism, poverty and environmental destruction. The foundation primarily funds small grassroots organizations and is willing to take risks funding new projects and small organizations struggling to survive.

Areas of Interest

The foundation supports projects that, in its words, are:
- Models for social change;
- Infused with a spirit of generosity and hopefulness;
- Directed towards enhancing people's quality of life;
- Examples of creative problem solving.

The foundation will only consider proposals in the focus areas of children and families, disadvantaged groups, and the environment.

Financial Data

(Year ended 12/31/00)	
Assets:	$ 1,369,652
Total grants paid:	$ 622,050
Number of grants paid:	64
Highest grant:	$ 15,000
Lowest grant:	$ 250
Median grant size:	$ 3,000

Application
Procedures

The application process has two stages. The initial application consists of two copies each of a cover page and a one-page letter of interest. This letter should be copied onto the backside of the cover page provided.

Applicants must request a copy of the guidelines and application materials before submitting a proposal. No full proposals will be reviewed without an invitation.

Awards are granted from $500 - $15,000. Each trimester the foundation will fund a small number of grants for $1,000 or less for material items for programs that fit in its three general categories.

Grant
Limitations

The foundation, because of its size, does not offer grants to maintain basic or direct services. In addition, it does not fund state agencies, scholarships to individuals, religious projects, research projects, colleges or universities, or international programs. Donation of funds is limited to organizations with 501(c)(3) status, or who have a sponsoring agency with this status.

Meeting
Times

Initial applications are reviewed on an ongoing basis. The full board meets three times yearly to review full proposals.

Publications

Guidelines, annual report, grants recipient list.

CLAUDE WORTHINGTON BENEDUM FOUNDATION

PHONE: (412) 288-0360

FAX: (412) 288-0366

1400 BENEDUM-TREES BUILDING

223 FOURTH AVENUE

PITTSBURGH, PENNSYLVANIA 15222

WEB: www.fdncenter.org/
grantmaker/benedum

Contact Person

William P. Getty, President

Purpose

The Claude Worthington Benedum Foundation's objective is to provide support for "people helping themselves" in West Virginia. Four current priorities include: improving the quality and cost-effectiveness of education at all levels to enhance economic development; developing more appropriate, better coordinated, higher quality, and cost-effective rural health care services, health promotion projects, and health professions education programs; reshaping the human service delivery system with a focus on the needs of children and families living in poverty and increasing the potential for independent living of the elderly; and helping West Virginians, particularly those living in rural areas, undertake community based development with a focus on local economic development.

A small number of grants are awarded in Pittsburgh, Pennsylvania for support of major university centers which address issues facing West Virginians and for support of major arts organizations.

Areas of Interest

The Benedum Foundation awards grants in five major program areas: education, health, human services, community and economic development, and the arts.

Financial Data

(Year ended 12/31/2000)	
Assets:	$346,406,822
Total grants awarded:	NA

**Application
Procedures**

There are no standard application forms and no deadlines for receipt of proposals. Applicants should contact the foundation for the brochure "Guidelines for Applicants" to determine whether the foundation priorities and resources permit consideration of a request. A description of a complete proposal is included in the brochure. Proposals sent via fax or e-mail will not be accepted.

After receipt of a proposal, the staff determines which projects to recommend for consideration and final action by the board of directors.

Review of grant applications occurs year-round and final approval by the board is in March, June, September, and December.

**Grant
Limitations**

In addition to the geographic restriction identified above, the foundation does not make grants to individuals, for business development by individuals, deficit funding, annual appeals, national health and welfare campaigns, hospital construction, renovation or equipment, medical research, sectarian religious activities, travel, publications, or individual elementary and secondary schools.

**Meeting
Times**

The board of trustees meets four times a year in March, June, September, and December.

Publications

The foundation publishes an annual report and grant guidelines.

THE WILLIAM BINGHAM FOUNDATION

20325 CENTER RIDGE ROAD, #629

ROCKY RIVER, OHIO 44116

PHONE: (440) 331-6350

EMAIL: info@wbinghamfoundation.org

WEB: www.wbinghamfoundation.org

Contact Person

Laura Gilbertson, Director

Areas of Interest

The William Bingham Foundation contributes to a wide variety of organizations in the areas of education, the arts, health, welfare, and environmental issues in the communities in which the foundation's trustees reside. The foundation has given two of its largest grants to environmental programs, one to establish an environmental conflict negotiation fund and another to support research projects and policy development to halt ozone depletion and global climate change resulting from human activities.

Financial Data

(Year ended 12/31/99)	
Assets:	$ 16,162,000
Total grants paid:	$ 1,282,390
Number of grants paid:	32
Highest grant:	$ 100,000
Lowest grant:	$ 5,000

Application Procedures

To initiate a request to the foundation, applicants should submit a letter no longer than two pages outlining the nature of the project, budget requirements, and the amount requested. Telephone inquiries are discouraged. If the project coincides with the foundation's interests, a trustee or the executive director will contact the applicant and request a detailed grant proposal which must be completed at least two months before the semiannual meetings of the trustees. At that time applicants will be asked to provide financial statements and documentation of tax-exempt status. The foundation may request to meet with an applicant in order to evaluate a request. The foundation encourages applicants to seek additional funding from other sources and asks to be informed promptly of other grants received.

Grant Limitations

The foundation prefers to support organizations in the eastern United States and makes awards only to qualified applicants that are tax-exempt under Section 501(c)(3) of the Internal Revenue Code. Grants are not awarded to individuals.

Meeting Times

The board of trustees meets twice a year in the spring and fall, usually in May and October.

Publications

The foundation publishes an annual report.

THE BLUE MOON FUND

(Formerly The W. Alton Jones Foundation)

433 PARK STREET

CHARLOTTESVILLE, VIRGINIA 22902

PHONE: (434) 295-5160

FAX: (434) 295-6894

EMAIL: info@bluemoonfund.org

WEB: www.bluemoonfund.org

Contact Person

Kathy Cornelius, Executive Assistant

Purpose

The goal of the Blue Moon Fund is to protect the earth's life support systems from environmental harm and to eliminate the possibility of nuclear warfare and the massive release of radio active material.

Areas of Interest

The funding work of the foundation is divided into two programs. The first, called the Sustainable Society Program, seeks to promote a sustainable society through five areas:

• Maintaining biodiversity in three watershed areas, the Amazon, Coastal Louisiana, and the Pantanal and Parana-Paraguay River watershed; in three forest ecosystems, the Pacific Northwest (including Southwestern Canada), Irian Jaya, and Siberia; and through international agreements and treaties related to biodiversity and forests.

• Promoting economics for a sustainable planet by creating models which value biodiversity, balance the economy with the environment and assess the full cost of human activity on the planet; promoting the understanding and economic value of biodiversity; balancing economic and environmental needs; promoting sustainable trade policies through international agreements, with an emphasis on the Western Hemisphere; promoting wise policies in the multilateral development banks; and promoting the sustainable use of biological resources.

• Developing new sources of energy usage and addressing the related climate changes by promoting renewable energy in developing countries; developing renewable urban energy policy in Brazil and Russia, Ukraine and the other newly independent states; promoting a hydrogen economy; and supporting multinational climate treaties.

• Eliminating systemic contamination in aquifers; in three areas impacting the health of children—pesticides and endocrine disrupters, air pollution, and lead poisoning; and in Eastern Europe, Russia, and the other newly independent States.

• Environmental law and media, promoting and developing activities that complement the foundation's areas of environmental grantmaking.

The second, known as the Secure Society Program, seeks to build a secure world, free from the nuclear threat through four areas:

• Common Security through global strategy; specific regions—former Soviet Union, the Middle East, including Iran, Northeast Asia (Korea, China, Japan), South Asia (India, Pakistan, China) and Europe (Conference on Security and Cooperation in Europe).

• Eliminating nuclear weapons by stopping development, production and testing; preventing proliferation; preventing use; and dismantling existing weapons.

• Preventing massive release of radioactive material by eliminating plutonium; preventing nuclear accidents; disposing of nuclear waste; and preventing hostile use of radiation.

• Assessing the full costs of being a nuclear state, both economic and societal.

Financial Data

(Year ended 12/31/99)	
Assets:	$426,171,583
Total grants awarded:	$31,035,477
Number of grants awarded:	238
Highest grant:	$440,000
Lowest grant:	$2,000

Application Procedures

Most of the foundation's grantmaking occurs through foundation-initiated programs. Unsolicited inquiries are considered, although proposals not directed toward the foundation's priorities, listed above, are unlikely to be funded. The foundation limits grantmaking in its two program areas to the above.

Before submitting a proposal, a letter of inquiry should be sent to the foundation describing the goals of the project and summarizing, in brief, the means by which these goals will be met and the amount of funding to be requested. The letter should be no more than two pages in length. The foundation responds to all inquiries.

Specifics to be included in the formal proposal will be provided if, in response to a letter of inquiry, a proposal is invited.

Grant Limitations

The foundation is precluded from making grants or loans for non-charitable activities, private individuals or organizations that pass funds on to others, building construction or renovation, scholarships, endowments, or basic research.

Applications to fund conferences, for general support, or for international exchanges are not encouraged.

Meeting Times

The board of trustees meets quaterly to review grant applications.

Publications

The foundation publishes an annual report.

BOETTCHER FOUNDATION

600 17TH STREET, SUITE 2210 SOUTH

DENVER, COLORADO 80202

PHONE: (303) 534-1937

FAX: (303) 534-1934

EMAIL: grants@boettcherfoundation.org

WEB: www.boettcherfoundation.org

Contact Person

Timothy W. Schultz, President and Executive Director

Purpose

The Boettcher Foundation supports projects in Colorado in the areas of education, community and social services, civic and cultural programs, and hospital and health services.

Areas of Interest

The foundation has four grantmaking areas: education, community and social services, civic and cultural programs, and hospital and health services, in order of funding priority. A majority of grants are for capital projects, such as building or equipment needs in the form of challenge grants. A limited number of grants for operating funds are made to organizations familiar to the trustees. The trustees also favor making significant grants for large projects rather than dividing the available funds into small grants to a vast number of recipients.

Financial Data

(Year ended 12/31/00)	
Assets:	$ 224,498,182
Total grants paid:	$ 6,899,328*
Total number of grants:	159
Highest grant:	$ 500,000
Lowest grant:	$ 600
Median grant size:	$ 42,197

*This analysis does not include 161 scholarships totaling $2,521,926.

**Application
Procedures**

> There is no application form for proposals. If the project is within the scope of the foundation's activities and is strictly limited to Colorado, then a brief letter should be submitted before a formal proposal. This letter should concisely state the proposed project as well as its objectives, significance and intended results, the project timetable, and the funding strategy for the project including the total budget for the project. If the staff determines the project to be within its current scope of operations, a detailed and complete application will be requested.
>
> Initial letters are accepted throughout the year. There are no deadlines.

**Grant
Limitations**

> Grantmaking is limited to Colorado. Except for its scholarship and fellowship program, only tax-exempt nonprofit organizations under 501(c)(3) code of the Internal Revenue Service are eligible for funds.

**Meeting
Times**

> The board of trustees meets monthly.

Publications

> The foundation publishes an annual report and grant application guidelines.

BOSTON FOUNDATION

75 ARLINGTON STREET, 10TH FLOOR

BOSTON, MASSACHUSETTS 02116

PHONE: (617) 338-1700

FAX: (617) 338-1606 or 1607

EMAIL: robert.wadsworth@tbf.org

WEB: www.bostonfoundation.org

Contact Persons

Paul S. Grogan, President

Robert R. Wadsworth, Program Director

Purpose

The Boston Foundation is a community foundation to which any donor may make a gift or bequest of any size for the good of the people of greater Boston. Contributions are combined to create a permanent endowment for charitable purposes. The income from this endowment is distributed each year in ways that meet the changing needs of the community.

Areas of Interest

The Boston Foundation reviews funding requests in the spirit of its mission to nurture a sense of community among the people of Greater Boston. In 1992, the Boston Foundation adopted a framework, "Building Family and Community," which is the focus of its current grantmaking from Discretionary Funds. Under this framework, funding priority is given to community-building strategies that help children and their families overcome poverty.

Grants made within this framework include both initiative, targeted specifically to the needs of children, youth, and families, and broader efforts to develop and strengthen Boston's neighborhoods as vibrant livable communities. An emphasis is placed on addressing the causes of poverty and despair, rather than its symptoms or effects.

The foundation typically makes grants for one year at a time.

Financial Data

(Year ended 6/30/00)	
Assets:	$ 702,881,525
Total grants paid:	$ 53,078,132

Application Procedures

Proposals should be submitted approximately twelve weeks before each scheduled meeting of the foundation's board of directors. After submission of a proposal, a conference with the staff is normally necessary before a request can be considered. A longer advance period may be necessary in the case of proposals requiring an unusual amount of preliminary investigation.

Each proposal should include a summarizing cover letter signed by the organization's chief staff officer; a report on the expenditure of any previous grant; a narrative proposal which describes the organization; project and agency budgets; and attachments, including a copy of the organization's most recent Section 501(c)(3) ruling from the IRS, financial statement and audit, a list of board and officers, and an Equity and Diversity Form supplied by the Boston Foundation.

Grant Limitations

Grants are made only to tax-exempt organizations as defined by Section 501(c)(3) of the Internal Revenue Code. The foundation does not consider more than one proposal from the same organization within a twelve-month period. In general grants are not made from discretionary funds for general operating support; medical, scientific, or academic research; scholarships, fellowships, or financial aid; the writing, publication, or distribution of books or articles; conferences or symposia; travel; the production or distribution of films, radio, or television programs; audio and/or video equipment; or capital campaigns.

Furthermore, grants are not generally from discretionary funds to individuals; religious organizations for religious purposes; private or parochial schools; municipalities; organizations outside the Greater Boston area; and national or international organizations.

Meeting Times

The board of directors meets four times a year to consider grant requests, usually in March, June, September, and December.

Publications

The foundation publishes an annual report, a quarterly newsletter, and a brochure that includes application guidelines and procedures.

THE BOSTON GLOBE FOUNDATION

PHONE: (617) 929-2895

FAX: (617) 929-2041

EMAIL: foundation@globe.com

WEB: www.bostonglobe.com/foundation

135 MORRISSEY BOULEVARD

BOSTON, MASSACHUSETTS 02107-2378

Contact Person

William B. Ketter, President

Purpose

The Boston Globe Foundation seeks to assist low income children, teens, and families. The foundation supports projects that will have an effect on children and teens in minority communities and on individuals who have been excluded from equal participation in society. Grants are made to nonprofit agencies in Boston, Cambridge, Somerville, and Chelsea.

Areas of Interest

The foundation focuses its grantmaking in four major program areas: journalism, arts and culture, civic participation and community building. In promoting its goals of "empowerment," the foundation makes it a priority to support community-based agencies. Programs and agencies that provide active self-determined roles for participants, and which use the affected constituents in project design and implementation, receive priority.

The second priority is funding advocacy agencies which influence public policy around needs of low-income populations. In this area, agencies that are not community-based but have a responsive staff and governance and can serve the interest of a given community will be considered for funding.

The foundation also has extensive matching gift programs for cultural organizations and for higher education and it maintains giving programs for scholarships and summer camps.

THE BOSTON GLOBE FOUNDATION

**Financial
Data**

```
(Year ended   /  /   )
Assets:                                NA
Total grants paid:
Number of grants:
Highest grant:
Lowest grant:
Median grant size:
```

**Application
Procedures**

There are no deadlines; requests for grants are accepted throughout the year. It takes approximately three to four months to process a proposal before review by the board. Applicants may apply using the Boston Globe Foundation Proposal Form or by using the Common Proposal Format provided by Associated Grantmakers of Massachusetts with supporting materials. Applicants should contact the foundation office to obtain materials needed for proposals.

The foundation holds bi-weekly informational meetings where staff explain funding priorities and application procedures. Applicants should contact Sylvia Payton at the foundation to obtain information about the meetings.

**Grant
Limitations**

The foundation makes most of its grant awards to organizations in the Greater Boston area. The foundation does not make grants to individuals, nor does it purchase tables or tickets at dinners or other functions, nor does it make contributions in the form of purchasing advertising, and it does not usually make more than one grant per fiscal year to any one organization.

**Meeting
Times**

The board of directors meets three times a year in March, June, and September to consider grant requests.

Publications

The foundation publishes an annual report and grant application forms. Information is available on the foundation's website: www.bostonglobe.com/foundation.

BOSTON WOMEN'S FUND

PHONE: (617) 725-0035

FAX: (617) 725-0277

EMAIL: bwf@bostonwomensfund.org

WEB: www.bostonwomensfund.org

14 Beacon Street, Suite 805

Boston, Massachusetts 02108

Contact Person

Renae Gray, Executive Director

Purpose

The Boston Women's Fund seeks to improve women's lives by supporting grassroots women's groups that are working for social and economic justice in the greater Boston area. Grants of up to $2,500 are awarded to projects that are organized and operated by women and that have limited access to more traditional sources of support. Technical assistance is also provided.

Areas of Interest

The fund focuses on projects that work for social change by organizing women on their own behalf to address economic, sexual, racial, and social inequities. Areas of interest include welfare reform, health care, violence prevention, reproductive freedom, homelessness, workplace equity, and economic development. Special emphasis is given to projects that strive to transcend barriers of race, age, and social class and encourage women of diverse backgrounds to work together; and community organizing projects and direct service projects that empower women who are the most vulnerable and have the least access to resources (e.g., low income women, women of color, single mothers, girls, lesbians, disabled women).

Financial Data

(Year ended / /)	
Assets:	NA
Total grants awarded:	
Number of grants awarded:	
Highest grant:	
Lowest grant:	
Median grant size:	

Application
Procedures

Application deadlines are March 31 and September 30. Interested organizations should telephone the fund for guidelines and application forms. In addition to requiring information about the organization making the request, the purpose of the grant, goals and objectives, and timetables, the proposal should demonstrate: the group is controlled by women; it is committed to working toward a more just, human society free from all forms of inequality; and its policy-making body reflects the population it serves in terms of race, class, age, and sexual orientation. Priority is given to projects with budgets under $150,000.

The application also requires information about income and expenses for the preceding year as well as anticipated income and expenses for the following year. Evidence of tax-exempt status under Section 501(c)(3) must be provided.

Grant
Limitations

The fund makes grants only to organizations in the greater Boston area with proof of tax-exempt status or to projects working with a tax-exempt sponsor. It provides funds to an organization, project, or group only once during any given funding year. It does not support groups with substantial ongoing support or groups linked to large established institutions, alternative businesses (such as food co-ops and work collectives), nonprint media, conferences, cultural projects, and research and special events not integrally linked to organizing. Grants are not made to individuals.

Meeting
Times

The allocations committee meets twice a year, in the spring and fall, to consider grant applications.

Publications

The fund publishes application guidelines and a newsletter.

BOWSHER-BOOHER FOUNDATION

PHONE: (574) 237-3449

WELLS FARGO BANK, INDIANA, N.A.

112 WEST JEFFERSON BOULEVARD

SOUTH BEND, INDIANA 46601

Contact Person

Thomas M. Lower, Senior Vice President

Purpose

The Bowsher-Booher Foundation supports broad charitable, scientific, literacy and educational efforts in St. Joseph County, Indiana, with an emphasis on aiding and empowering the South Bend community's poor, disadvantaged, and distressed.

The foundation supports experimental and innovative approaches to addressing fundamental underlying problems in the South Bend community. It views itself as a catalyst for change, bringing together creative community-minded activists and the range of social, economic, and racial problems threatening the community's well-being.

Areas of Interest

The foundation's areas of interest include children and youth programs, criminal justice programs, healthcare programs, housing, neighborhood renewal, and homeless programs, jobs programs, and family programs in the areas of rights of children, parent support groups, and improving the quality of family relationships. Support is also available for leadership development programs and other programs which are vital to the general health and growth of the South Bend community.

**Financial
Data**

```
(Year ended    /   /   )
Assets:                                    NA
Total grants awarded:
Number of grants awarded:
Highest grant:
Lowest grant:
Median grant size:
```

**Application
Procedures**

Potential applicants should write a brief letter describing their organization, the purpose for which funds are sought, the amount requested, and other sources of funding. In order to receive consideration at subsequent board meetings, letters must be submitted by April 1 or October 1.

**Grant
Limitations**

Grants are made only to support activities of tax-exempt organizations benefiting the residents of South Bend and St. Joseph County, Indiana. The foundation normally does not fund capital construction and endowments. Awards to a single applicant rarely exceed $20,000.

**Meeting
Times**

The board of directors meets twice a year, in May and November, to review grant applications.

Publications

None.

BREAD AND ROSES COMMUNITY FUND

PHONE: (215) 731-1107

FAX: (215) 731-0453

EMAIL: info@breadrosesfund.org

WEB: www.breadrosesfund.org

1500 WALNUT STREET, SUITE 1305

PHILADELPHIA, PENNSYLVANIA 19102

Contact Person

Christie Balka, Executive Director

Purpose

The Bread and Roses Community Fund supports organizations within the five-county greater Philadelphia area and in Camden County, New Jersey, that work for a more equitable distribution of resources, wealth, and power in society.

Areas of Interest

Bread and Roses gives priority to groups that do not have access to traditional funding sources, especially those organizing in poor, working class, or minority communities. Grants are also given to groups that provide support services to organizing efforts. The fund's grantmaking stresses organizations that challenge the root causes of social problems rather than those that treat symptoms.

Areas of interest include: AIDS and health activism, arts and social change, community organizing, economic justice, human rights and civil liberties, lesbian and gay rights, international issues, resources for organizing, women's rights, workers' rights, youth empowerment, environmental activism.

Applications are evaluated using the following criteria: organizations must express a commitment to working toward a society free from all forms of racial, sexual, and economic discrimination and inequality; the activities of the organization must lead to systematic changes that will create a more humane and just society; organizations must challenge existing institutions to become more responsive to the people they serve; organizations must be democratically organized and responsible to the constituencies they serve; and organizations must carry out their work in a non-discriminatory manner.

**Financial
Data**

```
(Year ended    /   /   )
Total grants paid:                    NA
Number of grants paid:
Highest grant: General Fund:
Emergency:
Lowest grant: General Fund:
Emergency:
Median grant size:
```

**Application
Procedures**

Groups interested in applying for a grant from Bread and Roses should telephone the office for application forms. Applicants are required to complete written application forms and submit current literature and background materials. Deadlines are October 1 and March 15.

Once Bread and Roses has ascertained that an application falls within the funding guidelines and is complete, the application is distributed to members of the foundation's eighteen-person community funding board which may choose to interview the group or arrange an on-site visit. Following review and discussion, the funding board recommends approval or rejection and determines the grant size. Rejected groups may submit a written appeal requesting reconsideration. Final approval of funding recommendations is made by the Bread and Roses board of directors.

**Grant
Limitations**

Bread and Roses only funds organizations within the five-county greater Philadelphia area and in Camden County, New Jersey. To be eligible for a grant from Bread and Roses, organizations must have IRS tax exemption or be carrying out tax-exempt work. Groups can apply either for general operating expenses or for specific projects. However, groups with annual budgets over $100,000 cannot submit a general support request; they must apply for a special project grant. Human and social services, such as health clinics and day-care services, and groups linked to larger institutions, generally are not funded. Grants are made only for projects concerning social change activism and organizing, not for direct service projects that provide individual solutions.

**Meeting
Times**

The board of directors meets six times a year. The Community Funding Board meets periodically from October through June to review grant applications.

Publications

The Community Fund publishes reports for donors and a newsletter entitled "Keeping in Touch," and distributes application forms and guidelines upon request.

THE OTTO BREMER FOUNDATION

445 MINNESOTA STREET, SUITE 2250

ST. PAUL, MINNESOTA 55101-2107

PHONE: (651) 227-8036 or
888-291-1123

FAX: (651) 312-3665

EMAIL: obf@bremer.com

WEB: www.ottobremer.org

Contact Person

John Kostishack, Executive Director

Purpose

The Otto Bremer Foundation promotes the social and economic health of the communities served by Bremer-affiliated banks in Minnesota, Montana, North Dakota, and Wisconsin. Its major efforts focus on addressing rural poverty, the changing rural economy, early childhood education, and youth service opportunities. The foundation also makes a small number of regional grants and grants to relieve poverty in the city of St. Paul.

Areas of Interest

The programs of the foundation are organized into five areas of interest:
• Community affairs. Activities that address the needs of the general community and increase citizen participation.
• Education. Internships for minority students at nonprofit organizations with a community service emphasis. Higher education grants are limited to post-secondary educational institutions in Minnesota.
• Health. Efforts to promote individual and community health, environmental quality, and health education.
• Human services. Projects address the needs of children, single parent families, battered women, the elderly, the disabled, and the poor.
• Religious. Programs of religious organizations, especially ecumenical programs, that address critical community needs.

Additionally, the foundation has two areas of project emphasis: projects that promote a better understanding of cultural, racial, religious, or ethnic differences, help identify and confront racism and heal the damage inflicted by racism, and projects that aim at removing barriers that keep rural people in poverty, address the root causes of poverty, and enhance self-sufficiency for low-income people.

The foundation accepts grant applications for projects in program development, operating support, capital (including building and equipment), matching or challenge grants, and internships.

Financial Data

(Year ended 12/31/00)	
Number of grants:	658
Highest grant:	$ 259,235
Lowest grant:	$ 552
Median grant size:	$ 20,445

Application Procedures

Proposals are accepted throughout the year, and there are no deadlines. Applicants should plan to submit proposals for staff review three months prior to the date a funding decision is desired. The foundation encourages initial telephone or written inquiries concerning its interest in a particular project. Applicants are also encouraged to contact the foundation staff for assistance in developing a proposal.

Generally, proposals should include: legal name, address, and brief description of the organization; name and telephone number of the contact person; documentation of the organization's nonprofit and tax-exempt status, including a copy of the ruling from the IRS; evidence that the request is endorsed by the board of directors of the organization with a list of those members; a clear description of the project for which funds are being sought, what it is designed to achieve and how this will be accomplished; the names and qualifications of individuals responsible for implementing the project; a complete project budget, including an indication of the time period in which funds are to be spent; an audited financial statement, if available, for the organization's previous fiscal year, a current operating budget, and a copy of the most recently filed IRS Form 990; an indication of other funding sources to be approached and a description of future funding plans; and a description of the procedures for reporting expenditures and the progress of the project.

Grant Limitations

Grants are only made to organizations whose beneficiaries are residents of Minnesota, North Dakota, Wisconsin, or Montana. Grants are not made to individuals. Grants are restricted to private nonprofit or public tax exempt organizations for purposes defined under section 501 (c)(3) of the Internal Revenue Code. Requests for grants for annual fund drives, benefit events, camps, economic development, or medical research are discouraged. Requests for building endowments other than for the development of community foundations are discouraged. Requests for funds to develop theatrical productions, motion pictures, books, and other artistic or media projects are discouraged. Requests for sporting activities are discouraged. While the Otto Bremer Foundation does fund some post-secondary programs, it does not fund Kindergarten through 12th grade education. The Otto Bremer Foundation does not have a staff discretionary fund.

The Minnesota Common Grant Application is accepted by the Otto Bremer Foundation.

Meeting Times

The board of trustees meets monthly.

Publications

The foundation publishes an annual report.

BRIDGEBUILDERS FOUNDATION

PHONE: (412) 963-0232

FAX: (412) 963-0240

560 EPSILON DRIVE, RIDC PARK

PITTSBURGH, PENNSYLVANIA 15238

Contact Person

Katie Wilson, Executive Director

Purpose

The main objective of the Bridgebuilders Foundation—formerly the Pittsburgh Bridge & Iron Works Charitable Trust—is to provide support for community groups that try to form bridges between various racial, social, and ethnic groups. The foundation is particularly interested in supporting groups that are not able to find funding through conventional channels.

Areas of Interest

Areas of interest include programs that encourage young people to broaden experience and contribute to society, organizations promoting social and economic justice through positive social change and organizations working to promote peace, environmental groups, and programs for youth.

Financial Data

(Year ended 12/31/00)	
Assets:	$ 1,400,000
Total grants approved:	$ 41,000
Number of grants approved:	12
Highest grant:	$ 6,500
Lowest grant:	$ 2,000
Median grant size:	$ 3,000

Application Procedures

All requests should be received by June 1 or November 1 for consideration at the following board meeting. The foundation has no rigid requirements for proposals. The NNG Common Grant Application form is accepted. In general, all funding requests should include:

- a one page summary of the proposal
- a full description of the organization and the proposed project
- a timeline for the project
- a list of other project funding sources
- a detailed budget for the project
- the organization's latest annual report and most recent audited financial statements
- IRS 501(c)(3) tax-exempt status letter
- any other materials (e.g. brochures, press clippings) may be included.

Grant Limitations

The foundation does not make grants to individuals, to United Way campaigns, to traditional health care facilities, or to capital fund drives.

Meeting Times

The board of trustees meets to consider grants twice a year, usually in June and December.

Publications

The foundation publishes an annual report.

THE PATRICK & AIMEE BUTLER FAMILY FOUNDATION

PHONE: (651) 222-2565

FAX: (651) 222-2565 ext. 16

Suite E-1420

EMAIL: kerrieb@butlerfamilyfoundation.org

332 MINNESOTA STREET

WEB: butlerfamilyfoundation.org

ST. PAUL, MINNESOTA 55101-1369

Contact Person

Kerrie Blevins, Foundation Director

Purpose

The Patrick and Aimee Butler Family Foundation provides support for progressive ideas in the areas of arts and culture, environment, social service and social change. Grantmaking is limited to the St. Paul and Minneapolis area.

Areas of Interest

The foundation supports programs in these areas; arts and culture, environment, social service and general philanthropy.

Financial Data

(Year ended 12/31/00)	
Assets:	$ 54,394,211
Total grants paid:	$ 2,878,058
Number of grants paid:	122
Highest grant:	$ 1,249,598
Lowest grant:	$ 3,000
Median grant size:	$ 10,000

Application Procedures

The foundation only accepts applications received on its application form. Requests that do not follow the foundation's procedures are denied. Grants guidelines are distributed in January and the foundation utilizes two grant cycles per year. Please refer to the annual report and guidelines for current year deadlines.

There are two grant cycles per year. Trustees review the proposals in June and October, and notify applicants from whom a full proposal is requested by the end of July and November. Decisions are made at the June and October board meetings and distributions occur within 6 weeks.

Grant Limitations

The foundation's support is primarily limited to the organizations that serve the St. Paul and Minneapolis area. A few grants are made in Greater Minnesota and outside the state. The foundation does not fund grants in the areas of criminal justice, economic development or education, employment and vocational programs, music or dance, videos or films, health, hospitals, loans or grants to individuals, medical research, secondary and elementary education, or projects outside of the United States.

Meeting Times

The board of directors meets twice a year, in the spring and fall, to review proposals.

Publications

The foundation publishes an annual report and guidelines.

THE BYDALE FOUNDATION

PHONE: (914) 428-3232

11 MARTINE AVENUE, SUITE 775

WHITE PLAINS, NEW YORK 10606

Contact Person

Milton D. Solomon, Vice President

Areas of Interest

The Bydale Foundation is a family foundation with diverse grantmaking practices. Its grantmaking is generally restricted to energy and environmental national policy, specifically progressive environmental strategies; domestic economic policy; foreign policy, specifically peace issues, disarmament, and world order; and the arts, primarily traditional programs in New York City, but also some community arts programs.

On occasion, the foundation has supported publications and other media projects related to its priority interests. Seed money and general support are available.

Financial Data

```
(Year ended    /    /    )
Assets:                              NA
Total grants paid:
Number of grants paid:
Highest grant:
Lowest grant:
Median grant size:
```

Application Procedures

The deadline for proposals is November 1. The foundation specifically requests that all inquiries and applications be made in writing. Proposals should be brief and should include a statement of purpose and strategies, staffing capabilities, and detailed budget materials on both the organization and the proposed project. Supporting materials should be included.

Grant
Limitations

The foundation makes grants only to tax-exempt organizations. No grants are made to individuals.

Meeting
Times

The board of directors meets once a year.

Publications

None.

THE MORRIS AND GWENDOLYN CAFRITZ FOUNDATION

PHONE: (202) 223-3100

FAX: (202) 296-7567

EMAIL: info@cafritzfoundation.org

WEB: www.cafritzfoundation.org

1825 K Street, N.W. 14th Floor

Washington, DC 20006

Contact Person

Anne Allen, Executive Director

Purpose

The Morris and Gwendolyn Cafritz Foundation awards grants for direct assistance in the areas of community service, arts and culture, education, and health in the Washington, D.C. metropolitan area.

Areas of Interest

The five general areas of support and organizations supported are: arts and culture, including performing arts groups, media groups, and arts and humanities organizations; education, including schools and their support agencies, colleges and universities, science organizations, and education centers; human services, including agencies, mental health agencies, public health organizations; medicine, including hospitals and medical care facilities; and community improvement and development, including museums, youth development organizations, animal welfare organizations, volunteer bureaus, civil rights groups, and public policy institutes.

Financial Data

(Year ended 4/30/00)	
Assets:	$ 248,202,773
Total grants paid:	$ 13,256,937
Total number of grants:	349
Highest grant:	$ 1,000,000
Lowest grant:	$ 100
Median grant size:	$ 10,000 - $50,000

**Application
Procedures**

Grants are awarded three times a year. Proposals may be submitted at any time and applications received between deadlines will be held until the next deadline date for review. Deadlines for proposals are March 1, July 1, and November 1. The foundation uses the Washington Regional Association of Grantmakers (WRAG) Common Grant Application Format. Applicants should request a copy of this application from the foundation.

**Grant
Limitations**

The foundation does not make grants for capital purposes, endowments, for special events or to individuals. Grants are awarded only to organizations working in the Washington, D.C. metropolitan area. Only tax-exempt non-profit organizations under 501(c)(3) status from the IRS are eligible for funds.

Publications

The foundation publishes an annual report and application guidelines.

CALIFORNIA ADOLESCENT NUTRITION AND FITNESS PROGRAM

PHONE: (510) 644-1533

FAX: (510) 644-1535

EMAIL: info@canfit.org

WEB: www.canfit.org

2140 SHATTUCK AVENUE, SUITE 610

BERKELEY, CALIFORNIA 94704

Contact Person

Arnell J. Hinkle, R.D., M.P.H., Executive Director

Purpose

The California Adolescent Nutrition and Fitness Program (CANFit) seeks to improve the nutritional and health status of California's low-income, African-American, American Indian, Latino, and Asian youth ages ten through fourteen. Its goal is to increase the number of agencies providing nutritional education and physical fitness service to low-income youth.

Areas of Interest

The program provides technical assistance and training to organizations serving their target populations on a wide range of topic areas and issues related to nutrition and fitness. It awards grants to programs which address the multiple influences, such as media, peers, family, or environment, which affect adolescent dietary and exercise behaviors; integrate the cultural, linguistic, social and demographic characteristics of youth; and employ individuals who are credible and respected to deliver the program.

CANFit currently supports two initiatives:

- Community-based. Projects or expansion of existing projects are supported that meet CANFit's mission. Grants up to $10,000 are awarded for planning purposes.

- Policy Development. Social action such as coalition building, technical assistance and advocacy to both legislative and media groups.

**Financial
Data**

(Year ended 12/31/00)	
Total grants paid:	$ 300,000
Total number of grants:	15
Highest grant:	$ 25,000
Lowest grant:	$ 1,000

**Application
Procedures**

Applicants must first submit a letter of intent and cover sheet. Instructions for completing the letter should be requested from CANFit. Applicants whose letter of intent are approved will be invited to submit a full proposal. Applicants should contact CANFit for deadlines.

**Grant
Limitations**

All grants are limited to California.

**Meeting
Times**

The board meets on an "as-needed" basis.

Publications

The program publishes a brochure describing its program and grant guidelines.

CALIFORNIA COMMUNITY FOUNDATION

PHONE: (213) 413-4130

FAX: (213) 622-2979

EMAIL: ccfinfo@ccf-la.org

WEB: www.calfund.org

445 SOUTH FIGUEROA STREET

SUITE 3400

LOS ANGELES, CALIFORNIA 90071

Contact Person

Cindy DiGiamtaomo, Senior Program Assistant

Purpose

The California Community Foundation administers philanthropic gifts and distributes grants to nonprofit agencies in Los Angeles County. Grant requests will only be considered from organizations located in or offering services to the citizens of Los Angeles County.

Areas of Interest

The foundation has established several broad categories in which grants are made. In the past they have included the arts and culture, civic affairs, community development, community education, and health and medicine. The foundation supports technical assistance, program-related investments, seed money, special projects and matching funds.

Financial Data

(Year ended 6/30/00)	
Assets:	$ 547,793,428
Total grants paid:	$ 78,277,334
Number of grants paid:	4952
Highest grant:	$ 16,563,537
Lowest grant:	$ 20
Median grant size:	$ 1,000

Application Procedures

An application form is required and may be obtained by calling the foundation office. Applicants should submit one copy of their proposal with a cover letter typed on the organization's letterhead that is signed by a board officer authorized to sign for the corporation. Attached to the proposal should be one copy of: the list of the organization's governing body, including professional, business, or community affiliations and indicating any paid staff members serving on the board; the complete financial statement for the most recent fiscal year (audited if available) and the organization's most recent IRS Form 990; budgets for the current and immediately preceding year; the current annual report or statement of program activities; and an IRS letter confirming the applicant's tax-exempt status.

Deadlines are September 1 and March 1 for Community Development and Human Services; December 1 and June 1 for most other programs. Art related programs have their own schedules and application forms; applicants should call the foundation office for the most current information.

Grant Limitations

In addition to the geographic limitations above, unless otherwise designated specifically by a donor to the foundation, grants will not be made for: endowments; annual campaigns, dinners, or special events; building campaigns; sectarian purposes; individuals; routine operating support; fellowships, scholarships; loans; special events, conferences, or films.

Meeting Times

Grantmaking decisions are made by the board of governors which meets four times a year.

Publications

The foundation publishes an annual report that encompasses detailed listings of grants and instructions for preparing a proposal. Through its Funding Information Center, the foundation has produced and makes available a comprehensive guide to researching and approaching foundations, *The Funding Information Center Handbook*. The handbook is available free to nonprofit organizations.

THE CARETH FOUNDATION

264 N. Pleasant Street, 2nd Floor

Amherst, Massachusetts 01002

PHONE: (413) 256-0349

FAX: (413) 256-3536

EMAIL: info@proteusfund.org

WEB: www.proteusfund.org

Contact Person

Amy Clough, Grants Manager

Purpose

The purpose of the CarEth Foundation is to promote enduring peace with social, economic, and political justice for all.

Areas of Interest

The foundation supports projects that promote the creation of a global community of peace and justice; promote genuine democracy in the United States, leading to peace and justice; promote just and peaceful conflict resolution.

Financial Data

(Year ended / /)	
Assets:	NA
Total grants paid:	
Number of grants paid:	
Highest grant:	
Lowest grant:	
Median grant size:	

Application Procedures

Applicants should submit a proposal that includes a concise statement of the organization's mission, resources, and approach to the problem being addressed. In any proposal the strategy and rationale for a particular project should be addressed rather than the need for support. The reasons why the applicant's organization is particularly well suited to carry out the proposed project should be articulated. Easily transmitted examples of past work are welcome. The expected results of the project should be described, including outcomes that are less than desirable. Background information—such as project and organization budget, and short biographies of principles—is essential. Applicants are informed of the decisions of the Board of Directors as soon as possible. A brief, written report is expected at the end of the grant year. Grants are generally considered to be one year in duration. The CarEth Foundation accepts the NNG Common Grant Application. The foundation does not accept emailed or faxed proposals.

Grant Limitations

The foundation makes grants only in the area of peace and does not support organizations seeking to influence legislation or partisan elections. Grants are made only to tax-exempt organizations or the projects of tax-exempt organizations, and no grants are made to individuals.

Conferences, speakers' bureaus, and special events are low priorities for support. Furthermore, the foundation does not support projects which will have ended before foundation review of the proposal; coordinating or networking activities; fundraising and capital improvements; human rights projects (unless clearly connected with U.S. foreign or domestic policy); organizations primarily based outside the United States; relief efforts; and proposals from schools, colleges, and universities intended for workshops and courses primarily intended for their own constituencies.

CarEth does not directly fund local, state or regional grassroots organizations whose goal is to educate and mobilize citizens in those locations. Such organizations should seek funding directly from the Peace Development Fund, to whom the CarEth Foundation gives an annual allocation. The CarEth Foundation will directly fund national grassroots organizations, including those with chapters or grassroots strategy.

Meeting Times

The board of directors meets once each spring and fall to consider proposals.

Publications

The foundation distributes a description of its program interests.

CARNEGIE CORPORATION OF NEW YORK

PHONE: (212) 371-3200

FAX: (212) 754-4073

437 MADISON AVENUE

WEB: www.carnegie.org

NEW YORK, NEW YORK 10022

Contact Persons

Vartan Gregorian, President

Daniel Fallon, Program Chair, Education

David C. Speedie, Program Chair, International Peace and Security

Narciso Matos, Program Chair, International Development

Geraldine P. Mannion, Program Chair, Strengthening U.S. Democracy

Purpose

The Carnegie Corporation of New York is a philanthropic foundation created "to promote the advancement and diffusion of knowledge and understanding among the people of the United States." Its charter was later amended to permit the use of funds for the same purposes in certain countries that are or were members of the British overseas Commonwealth. The Corporation seeks to carry out Andrew Carnegie's vision of philanthropy, which he said should aim "to do real and permanent good in this world."

Areas of Interest

Currently, the corporation is concentrating on these programs:

International Peace and Security

The International Peace and Security (IPS) program has three principal areas of focus: Nonproliferation of Weapons of Mass Destruction; Russia and Other Post-Soviet States; and New Dimensions of Security, where the initial focus has been on the clash between the norms of the sanctity of existing international borders and the right to self-determination of an ethnic national group within a state. In the two years of grantmaking in these sub-areas, external events have served to underscore their criticality for global security. The Corporation's Higher Education in the former Soviet Union initiative is also administered under this program rubric.

Education

The twentieth century has passed from the age of the industrial worker to the age of the knowledge worker, in which both general and specialized education have assumed ever greater importance for the personal development of individuals; for the civic, social, and economic strength of the nation; and for the search for solutions to global problems facing humankind. Most educational and political leaders understand that the nation's future depends on the priority given to the development of new knowledge and to investments in human capital formation. For individuals, the benefits of education are increasingly critical, since opportunities to acquire good jobs and a decent standard of living are requiring higher levels of formal education.

International Development

The International Development Program of Carnegie Corporation aims to promote social and economic progress through support of a select number of innovative efforts to close the knowledge gap between African countries and the rest of the world as well as help these countries address the problem internally. The specific themes of the program are:
- Strengthening Selected African Universities
- Enhancing Women's Educational Opportunities at African Universities
- Revitalizing Public Libraries.

Strengthening U.S. Democracy Program

The events surrounding the November 2000 elections dramatically underscored the weak links in the nation's electoral infrastructure system. Today, the world's most technologically advanced nation has a 19th century voting system. In addition, voter participation among the eligible electorate remains abysmally low. Despite a slight increase in the 2000 turnout—about 52 percent of eligible voters participated, up from 48 percent in 1996, the lowest turnout since 1924—large segments of the voting population still stayed home.

Structural problems and barriers are not the only factors limiting full participation in our democracy. Campaign finance abuses, elections dominated by news media "spin" rather than thoughtful debate, and a growing cynicism about the role of government and political leaders at all levels have contributed to an increase in the public's distrust of the electoral process, leaving them with little motivation to participate.

Addressing both the structural and attitudinal barriers to full civic participation in the United States, the Corporation's Strengthening U.S. Democracy Program has as its overarching goal: To increase civic participation in our democracy and to improve the capacity of nonprofit organizations that contribute to a healthy civil society.

Financial Data

(Year ended 9/30/00)	
Assets:	$ 1,900,000,000
Total grants paid:	$ 75,000,000

Application Procedures

The Corporation accepts requests for funding at all times of the year. There are no application deadlines.

Grant decisions are based primarily on the information provided by grantseekers in the Corporation's own detailed proposal formats. Only proposals presented in the Corporation's format will be considered for funding. Grantseekers who would like to approach the foundation with a preliminary request for funding are encouraged to submit a letter of inquiry. If the project described in the letter fits the foundation's guidelines, the sender will be contacted and asked to submit a proposal in the Corporation's format. A request to submit a proposal is not an indication of the Corporation's intention or commitment to award a grant.

Please read the program guidelines and funding restrictions online carefully to determine if your organization and project fit the Corporation's grantmaking strategies. Please call Kathleen Whittemore at (212) 207-6236 for further assistance.

Meeting Times

The board of directors meets in October, December, April, and June.

Publications

The corporation publishes annual and quarterly reports, as well as a brochure.

MARY FLAGLER CARY CHARITABLE TRUST

PHONE: (212) 953-7700

FAX: (212) 953-7720

EMAIL: info@carytrust.org

WEB: www.carytrust.org

122 EAST 42ND STREET, ROOM 3505

NEW YORK, NEW YORK 10168

Contact Person

Edward A. Ames, Trustee

Purpose

The Mary Flagler Cary Charitable Trust supports orchestral music, conservation of natural resources, and urban environmental programs in New York City. The trust makes grants both for general operating support and for specific projects or objectives. The music grants and urban environmental programs are restricted to New York City and conservation grants are limited to the eastern coastal states.

Areas of Interest

In its support of music, the trust's primary interests are the development of young orchestral musicians and the enrichment of musical performance in New York City. Whenever possible, the trust seeks to give help to the disadvantaged, minority group members and women in the pursuit of their music studies and careers. Music grants are made in a number of areas including for institutional support for the advanced training of instrumentalists seeking orchestral careers and for community music schools and other institutions which offer basic music training for young people who would otherwise not have such an opportunity.

In its conservation program, the trust seeks to preserve coastal wetlands and estuaries. Grants are made to protect selected regional ecosystems, including the Nanticoke River Watershed in Delaware and Virginia; the Virginia Coast Reserve in Virginia; the Albermarle and Pamilco Sounds, and the watersheds of four tributary rivers, in North Carolina; the ACE Basin in South Carolina, and the Everglades watershed in Florida.

In its third area of support, urban environment, the trust supports community initiatives and development of local leadership to work on environmental problems within low-income neighborhoods of New York City. Issues of greatest importance to the trust include hazardous waste, lead poisoning, recycling and the need to recapture open space. Programs in the community which provide training and develop local leadership in this area are also given priority.

Financial Data*

(Year ended 6/30/2000)	
Assets:	$135,370,661
Total grants awarded:	$9,292,105
Number of grants awarded:	144
Median grant size:	$20,000

*Grantmaking has been reduced. Please see the website for more information.

Application Procedures

The trust does not use a grant application form. Instead, as a first step, a letter should be sent to the trust containing a concise statement of the program or project, the amount of funding requested and how it fits within the over all budget of the applicant, a brief description of the nature and activities of the applicant, its legal name, and a current list of officers and directors or trustees.

If, after studying a written grant request, the trustees decide that there is a possibility of support, additional information will be requested, including: complete tax information with rulings on tax exemption status under Internal Revenue Code Section 501c)(3); a copy of the applicant's most recent audited financial statement; and an official letter or request on the organization's letterhead, signed by its chief executive officer on behalf of its governing body.

Grant Limitations

The trust does not make grants to private foundations, hospitals, religious organizations, primary or secondary schools, colleges and universities, libraries, or museums. No grants are made for scholarships, fellowships, capital funds, annual campaigns, seed money, emergency funds, deficit financing, or endowment funds, and no loans are made to individuals.

Meeting Times

The trustees meet at least once every month.

Publications

The Mary Flagler Cary Charitable Trust publishes a brochure, program guidelines and general information, and will make a grants list and financial information available on request.

THE ANNIE E. CASEY FOUNDATION

701 St. Paul Street

Baltimore, Maryland 21202

PHONE: (410) 547-6600

FAX: (410) 547-6624

EMAIL: webmail@aecf.org

WEB: www.aecf.org

Contact Person

Office of the President

Purpose

The Annie E. Casey Foundation is a private charitable organization dedicated to improving the lives of disadvantaged children in the United States. It supports projects that foster innovative public policies and human-service reforms which more effectively meet the needs of vulnerable children and their families.

Areas of Interest

The foundation runs a long-term foster care and permanency planning program which helps children who have led troubled lives. Currently, about twenty percent of the foundation's budget supports this program. The balance of its resources goes to five interrelated grant-making areas:

• Increasing awareness of the problems of disadvantaged children and their families, and the need for changes in the public policies and institutions that serve them.

• Strengthening the management capacities necessary for successful reform of child-serving institutions and systems, such as technical assistance, planning, and information systems grants.

• Program demonstration and policy research that enhance programs and practices which are essential to reforming the systems serving children and families. Examples of this would include projects in juvenile justice, childhood immunization, education reform, and housing policies.

• Long-term comprehensive reform initiatives at the state, local, and neighborhood level that demonstrate the potential of educational, service-system, economic, and community-level reform. Projects would include ones that are family focused, flexible and community based in areas such as mental health, rebuilding communities, school reform, and family preservation.

• Evaluating and disseminating information on reforms in service delivery that produce improved outcomes for children. Rigorous evaluations of its major demonstration projects are conducted, and the results provide well-documented examples of what works, what does not, and why.

Financial Data

(Year ended 12/31/00)	
Assets:	$ 3,001,942,131
Total grants paid:	$ 101,012,809
Total number of grants:	1,335
Highest grant:	$ 2,000,000*
Lowest grant:	$ 5,000
Median grant size:	$ 600,000

*This excludes a $29,464,985 grant to Casey Family Services.

Application Procedures

Organizations should first submit a letter of inquiry. This letter should include an outline of the proposal, the goals of the project, the population served, the amount of funds requested, and a brief history of the organization. The foundation will review this letter of inquiry and respond in writing. Letters should be sent to the attention of Planning and Development of The Annie E. Casey Foundation.

Grant Limitations

The foundation does not make grants to individuals, nor does it make capital grants for projects that are not an integral part of a foundation-sponsored initiative.

Meeting Times

The board of trustees meets every other month.

Publications

The foundation publishes an annual report and grant guidelines.

CATHOLIC CAMPAIGN FOR HUMAN DEVELOPMENT

c/o **UNITED STATES CONFERENCE OF CATHOLIC BISHOPS**
3211 4TH STREET, N. E.
WASHINGTON, DC 20017-1194

PHONE: (202) 541-3210

FAX: (202) 541-3329

EMAIL: lmonroe@usccb.org

WEB: www.usccb.org/cchd

Contact Persons

Father Robert Vitillo, Executive Director
Levon Monroe, Grants Administrator

Purpose

The Catholic Campaign for Human Development (CCHD) is an action-oriented education program sponsored by the Catholic Bishops of the United States. It funds projects throughout the country that attack the basic causes of poverty and to empower low income persons.

CCHD specifically encourages applications from poverty organizations working to bring about institutional change. CCHD makes grant awards on a non-denominational basis. However, all activities for which support is sought must conform to the moral teachings of the Catholic Church.

Areas of Interest

Priority is given to projects which are innovative and demonstrate a change from traditional approaches to poverty by attacking the basic causes of poverty and by effecting institutional change; which directly benefit a relatively large number of people; which generate cooperation among and within diverse groups; and which document that as a result of CCHD funding there is the possibility of generating funds from other sources or of becoming self-sufficient. Grant awards range from a minimum of $10,000 to a maximum of $100,000.

CCHD has specific grantmaking criteria. Briefly, all organizations receiving CCHD support must benefit a poverty group where at least fifty percent of those benefitting from the project must be from the low-income community. Members of the poverty group must have the dominant voice in the project; at least fifty percent of those who plan, implement, and make policy, such as the board of directors, should be persons who are involuntarily poor. Projects not meeting this criteria must document why they do not and what steps will be taken for the poverty group to assume leadership and control.

**Financial
Data**

> (Year ended 12/31/98)
> Projected income: $ 13,831,256*
> Total grants paid: $ 10,372,538
> Number of grants paid: 309
>
> *CCHD receives seventy-five percent of the funds collected
> by each diocese on one day specially set aside for a social
> justice collection. This figure is a projection which includes
> CCHD's 1998 share, direct contributions, and investment
> income.

**Application
Procedures**

The deadline for submitting completed application materials to CCHD is
January 31. However, CCHD starts distributing materials in September, and
organizations that want to apply must complete a pre-application. The pre-
application is mandatory and the deadline for submitting it is November 1.

Specific forms are required for both the pre-application and the final
application; these, along with instructions, will be provided upon request.
Interested applicants are urged to contact their local CCHD diocesan office or
the national office staff if they need assistance in completing the process.
Applicants are urged to follow the instructions carefully. Failure to provide
the information requested, in the form requested, will result in a negative
evaluation of the request.

**Grant
Limitations**

CCHD makes grants only to organizations that are tax-exempt under Section
501(c)(3) of the Internal Revenue Code or that are working with a tax-exempt
fiscal agent. The following general classifications do not meet CCHD's funding criteria and guidelines: direct service projects; projects controlled by
government, educational or ecclesiastical bodies; research projects, surveys,
planning and feasibility studies; projects that have been operating for several
years on funds from other funding agencies; projects sponsored by organizations which, at the time of application, receive substantial sums from other
funding sources (unless the applicant documents that the proposed project
cannot be funded by these agencies); and individually owned, for-profit
businesses.

Funding will not be considered for projects which can be funded by the
private or public sector, unless applicants document that they are unable to

obtain funds from these sources. However, proposals which request seed money or matching funds will be considered. No CCHD funds will be granted to organizations that would utilize the money to support other organizations.

Meeting Times

The CCHD advisory committee reviews USCCB proposals in June and non-funded projects are notified. Also in June the committee of bishops reviews the advisory committee recommendations. Funding decisions are announced in July.

Publications

CCHD publishes an annual report, a description of funded projects, application guidelines and instructions (in English and Spanish), and various other educational materials.

THE CHAMPLIN FOUNDATIONS

PHONE: (401) 736-0370

FAX: (401) 736-7248

THE SUMMIT SOUTH

300 CENTERVILLE ROAD, SUITE 300S

WEB: fdncenter.org/grantmaker/champlin

WARWICK, RHODE ISLAND 02886-0226

Contact Person

Keith H. Lang, Executive Director

Purpose

The Champlin Foundations make direct grants for capital needs to organizations which serve the broadest possible segment of the population in Rhode Island.

Areas of Interest

The foundation provides "hands-on" equipment or facilities for those who are served by tax-exempt organizations, such as athletic, educational, or health care institutions. Over the years grants have been made to independent and public schools, colleges and universities; conservation organizations and a zoo; hospital and health care facilities; libraries; youth and fitness agencies; social service agencies; and for historic preservation, the arts, sciences, and humane societies. Additionally, grants have been made for acquisition of land for open space and recreation in Rhode Island.

The foundations stress that their interest is not in administrative buildings or equipment, nor do they provide funding for facilities or equipment for agencies whose prime purpose is counseling, day care, guidance, activities that they consider "program activities."

Financial Data

(Year ended 12/31/00)	
Assets:	$ 490,523,340
Total grants paid:	$ 23,721,810
Total number of grants:	221
Highest grant:	$ 4,000,000
Lowest grant:	$ 429
Median grant size:	$ 25,000 -$65,000

**Application
Procedures**

> Initial contact should be a brief letter of inquiry to the foundation. Letters of inquiry about potential support should be no longer than one page, addressed to the executive director, and should include the following: description of the project and its intended purpose, its cost, and the amount requested from The Champlin Foundations; the status of any fundraising effort, and other sources of funds available. One copy should be submitted with a copy of the organization's 501(c)(3) exemption and 509(a) letter. All letters will be acknowledged and additional information may be requested.
>
> Requests should be submitted between March 1 and June 30 for consideration during the November committee meeting.

**Grant
Limitations**

> Grants are not awarded for program or operating expenses, seed money, feasibility studies, for publications, books, films, etc., to individuals, to organizations outside of Rhode Island; organizations not classified as tax-exempt under Section 501(c)(3) of the Internal Revenue Code, or religious schools. Grants are not awarded on a continuing basis, but applicants may qualify annually.

**Meeting
Times**

> The distribution committee meets annually, in November, to accept or reject grant recommendations. Funds are distributed in December.

Publications

> The foundations publish program policy statements, application guidelines, annual report, and grants list.

BEN B. CHENEY FOUNDATION

PHONE: (253) 572-2442

1201 PACIFIC AVENUE, SUITE 1600

TACOMA, WASHINGTON 98402-4379

EMAIL: info@benbcheneyfoundation.org

WEB: www.benbcheneyfoundation.org

Contact Person

Bradbury F. Cheney, Director

Purpose

The Ben B. Cheney Foundation funds projects that encourage the development of new and innovative approaches to community problems and services or make an investment in equipment or facilities which have long-lasting positive effects on community needs.

Areas of Interest

The foundation provides grants to projects serving communities in Tacoma/Pierce County, Southwest Washington, Southwest Oregon (particularly around the Medford area), and portions of Del Norte, Humboldt, Lassen, Shasta, Siskiyou, and Trinity counties in Northern California.

The foundation will support a wide variety of activities ranging from arts and culture to food banks and senior programs.

Financial Data

(Year ended 12/31/00)	
Assets:	$ 87,911,298
Total grants paid:	$ 3,977,422
Total number of grants:	176
Highest grant:	$ 100,000
Lowest grant:	$ 1,500
Median size:	$ 6,500
(Small grant program for grants under $10,000)	
Median Size	$ 25,000 - $ 30,000
(Grants considered at regular board meetings)	

Application Procedures

Initial requests should be in the form of a preliminary letter (approximately two pages in length) that summarizes the full proposal. The purpose of this letter is to convince the foundation to take the next step in the funding process, which is either a site visit or an office appointment. Typically such a letter shares the history and mission of the organization, the need and opportunity this grant would address, the total cost of the project, a plan for raising other needed funds (both for the specific grant activities and for the long-term sustainability of the project if needed), and the amount you would ask the foundation to grant.

Grant Limitations

Besides its geographic limitations, the foundation generally does not support general operating budgets, projects normally financed by tax funds, religious organizations for sectarian purposes, research, endowments, individuals, production of books, films, or videos, or conferences and seminars. Grants can be made only to private, nonprofit, tax-exempt organizations with 501(c)(3) certification from the IRS.

Meeting Times

The board of trustees meets three times a year to review and approve grant requests.

Publications

The foundation publishes a brochure that includes the application guidelines.

THE CHICAGO COMMUNITY TRUST

111 EAST WACKER DRIVE

SUITE 1400

CHICAGO, ILLINOIS 60601

PHONE: (312) 616-8000

FAX: (312) 616-7955

EMAIL: sandy@cct.org

WEB: www.cct.org

Contact Person

Sandy Cheers, Grants Manager

Purpose

The Chicago Community Trust is a community foundation that provides grants to organizations serving Cook County and the five surrounding counties.

Areas of Interest

The grants are made in the areas of health, basic human needs, arts and humanities, education, and community development. Proposals for operating support, special projects, and capital needs are accepted for consideration if they fall within the areas of interest.

The Trust also maintains special grant programs, including: the Management/ Organizations Development Grant Program; the Joint Trust/Church Program; The Mid-Sized and Small Arts Organizations; and Legal Services Program.

Financial Data

(Year ended 9/30/00)	
Assets:	$ 1,200,000,000
Total grants paid:	$ 35,783,100
Total number of grants:	1,142
Highest grant:	$ 1,000,000
Lowest grant:	$ 100
Median grant size:	$ 10,000 - $50,000

Application Procedures

The Trust staff recommends that prospective grantees contact the Trust prior to submitting a letter of inquiry in order to obtain the most current information about special guidelines or proposals. From time to time, the Trust develops new guidelines for specific programs or areas of interest with procedures which must be met before support will be considered.

Letters of inquiry are accepted throughout the year and decisions are made by the Trust's executive committee three times a year.

Grant Limitations

Except for cases where a donor has designated the beneficiary group or restricted the use of a particular fund, the Trust will generally not make grants for scholarships, individuals, religious purposes, endowments, or operating support of government agencies.

Meeting Times

The Trust's executive committee meets three times a year in January, June, and September to consider grant requests.

Publications

The foundation publishes an annual report, brochure, newsletter, and grant guidelines.

THE CHICAGO FOUNDATION FOR WOMEN

PHONE: (312) 266-1176

FAX: (312) 266-0990

EMAIL: info@cfw.org

230 WEST SUPERIOR STREET, 4TH FLOOR WEB: www.cfw.org

CHICAGO, ILLINOIS 60610-3583

Contact Person

Candace Anderson, Grants Manager

Purpose

The Chicago Foundation for Women funds organizations and projects that address the needs of women of all economic, ethnic, and racial backgrounds. The foundation awards grants to organizations which primarily serve women and girls, with priority given to those which serve low-income and/or minority communities, have trouble accessing other funding sources, and which serve in the Chicago metropolitan area.

Areas of Interest

The foundation accepts proposals focusing on women's issues or concerns in the following categories:

Arts	Leadership Development
Advocacy	Lesbian Women
Day Care Advocacy	Older Women
Domestic Violence	Other Women's Projects
Education	Philanthropy
Employment/Economic	Reproductive Rights
Development	Sexual Assault
Health (Physical & Mental)	Teen Girls
Housing/Homelessness	

The foundation is specifically interested in projects that have a strong advocacy component, that address the root causes of problems, and have an effect on large numbers of women. In the area of advocacy, the Sophia Fund, a special program of the foundation, has an interest in reproductive rights, economic justice, violence against women, public awareness of women's issues, and expanding philanthropy for women. Other projects which the foundation seeks to fund are those which are led by women, create leadership opportunities for women, and facilitate women of diverse backgrounds in working together.

Grants range in size from $500 to $30,000. Grants in the area of social change advocacy and health can be larger. An organization will not be penalized for requesting more.

Financial Data

(Year ended 6/30/00)	
Support and revenue:	$ 6,675,098
Total grants paid:	$ 1,019,800
Number of grants paid:	164
Highest grant:	$ 50,000
Lowest grant:	$ 500

Application Procedures

All applicants must submit a letter of intent and a completed proposal summary form before submitting a full proposal. Full proposals should be submitted only upon request by the foundation and that request will be in writing. This letter of intent should be no more than two pages long and include: a completed proposal summary form (available by calling the foundation office), a summary of the organization's mission, activities, and goals; a summary of the project; dollar amount requested; how many women will benefit from the organization or project and how it will benefit these women; a description of how the organization is involved in systems change advocacy and examples; and a summary of challenges or obstacles to be faced in raising money this year. Three copies of the proposal along with one copy of the IRS 501(c)(3) letter should be submitted.

Letters of intent may be submitted at any time, but they are reviewed only twice—in the spring cycle and fall cycle. For the spring cycle, letters must be received by the first Friday in February; a decision will be rendered by June 30. For the fall cycle, letters must be received by the first Friday in August; a decision will be rendered by December 31.

Grant Limitations

Grants are made only to organizations and projects in the Chicago metropolitan area, and all applicants must have obtained or be eligible for 501(c)(3) status from the IRS, or have the support of a tax-exempt fiscal agent.

The foundation does not support religious organizations for religious purposes, individual efforts, capital drives, endowments, or campaigns to elect candidates to public office.

Projects with budgets over $250,000, except in special circumstances, will not be funded.

Meeting Times

The board of directors meets in the spring and fall to review grant proposals.

Publications

The foundation publishes a brochure, application guidelines, and a newsletter.

CHINOOK FUND

2418 W. 32ND AVENUE

DENVER, COLORADO 80211

PHONE: (303) 455-6905

FAX: (303) 477-1617

EMAIL: office@chinookfund.org

WEB: www.chinookfund.org

Contact Person

Peg Logan, Executive Director
Erica Vigil, Office Manager

Purpose

The Chinook Fund supports efforts in Colorado that challenge and attempt to alter existing economic and social relationships and institutions that are inequitable and undemocratic. This type of change requires an analysis of the root cuaese of social problems and their solutions, followed by action and evaluation of the effectiveness of that action, according to the fund.

Areas of Interest

Chinook funds projects that are working for progressive social change through such means as community organizing, advocacy, and alternative media.

Financial Data

(Year ended 6/30/2001)	
Total grants awarded:	$123,600
Number of grants awarded:	37
Highest grant:	$7,000
Lowest grant:	$500
Median grant size:	$3,000

Applications Procedure

All applicants must complete a five-page application form. Initial contact should be a phone call requesting the application. Proposal deadlines are February 21 for the June meeting and August 21 for the November meeting.

**Grant
Limitations**

The Chinook Fund limits its grantmaking to Colorado. The fund does not support groups whose purpose is to provide direct services; groups with wide access to traditional funding; groups with annual budgets over $250,000; individuals; other foundations or pass-through agencies.

**Meeting
Times**

There are two grantmaking cycles per year. The grantmaking committee meets twice during each cycle.

Publications

The fund publishes the "WINDS OF CHANGE Newsletter."

CIVIL JUSTICE FOUNDATION

1050 31st Street, N.W.
Washington, DC 20007

PHONE: 800-424-2725

FAX: (202) 965-0355

EMAIL: claudia.gordon@atlahq.org

WEB: www.cjfweb.org

Contact Persons

Executive Director

Purpose

The Civil Justice Foundation, established in 1986 by the Association of Trial Lawyers of America, awards grants nationally to progressive grassroots organizations dedicated to injury prevention and advocacy on behalf of injured consumers.

Areas of Interest

The foundation awards grants in the $10,000 range to grassroots advocacy organizations in three areas: groups of injured consumers, injury prevention advocacy work, and research and promotion of public policy on injury control.

Some of the issues that concern this foundation are toxic waste, handgun and domestic violence, access for the physically challenged, lead poisoning, and consumer's health care rights.

Financial Data

(Year ended 7/31/00)	
Assets:	$ 187,929
Total grants paid:	$ 130,000
Total number of grants:	13
Highest grant:	$ 10,000
Lowest grant:	$ 10,000
Median grant size:	$ 10,000

Application Procedures

The Foundation makes grants every July. Letters of proposal for July grants are due in the Foundation office on February 15 of each year. The Foundation reviews the proposals and issues invitations for full grant applications. Please contact the Foundation office for more information on the letter of proposal format.

**Grant
Limitations**

Organizations receiving grants must be classified as tax-exempt under Section 501(c)(3) of the Internal Revenue Code and typically have operating budgets that do not exceed $500,000.

**Meeting
Times**

The board of trustees meets in the winter and in July.

Publications

None.

LIZ CLAIBORNE FOUNDATION

PHONE: (212) 626-5704

FAX: (212) 626-5741

1441 BROADWAY

NEW YORK, NY 10018

Contact Person

Melanie Lyons, Vice President, Philanthropic Programs

Purpose

The Liz Claiborne Foundation provides grants to nonprofit organizations working to advance ways of addressing the problems of children and youth, women, and poverty. Assistance is limited to the New York City area and Hudson County, Los Angeles, CA, West Chester, OH, the North Shore of Massachusetts, Mount Pocono, PA, and New Jersey where the major plant administrative facilities of the corporation are located.

Areas of Interest

The foundation has three areas of interest:

• Empowering girls. Projects that empower girls through leadership, educational development, and positive body images.

• Women. Projects that address long-term solutions to poverty and discrimination; address the causes of violence and abuse against women and their effects; support services for women and families in need; provide services for women with AIDS and their families.

• Entrepreneurial solutions to social problems. Highly innovative projects that alleviate poverty and promote self-sufficiency while encouraging grassroots, community leadership.

Financial Data

> (Year ended / /)
> Assets: NA
> Total grants awarded:
> Number of grants awarded:
> Highest grant:
> Lowest grant:
> Median grant size:

Application Procedures

Proposals submitted to the foundation should contain a statement of the goals, history, and accomplishments of the requesting organization; a statement of purpose of the proposal and project, amount requested and evaluation methods; current organization budget and project budget showing both expenses and income; most recent audited financial statement; list of funding sources, public and private, and amounts contributed, including those pending approval; a list of professional and support staff and their titles; and a copy of the organization's 501 (c)(3) tax-exempt status from the IRS. There are no deadlines for proposals other than being received two months prior to desired review date.

Grant Limitations

Grantmaking is primarily in New York City and Hudson County, Los Angeles, Mount Pocono, PA, West Chester, OH, the North Shore of Massachusetts, and New Jersey. The foundation normally does not fund projects based outside the United States; religious, fraternal, or veterans' organizations; individuals; research; annual or capital campaigns or endowments; benefits/special events; hospital-based programs or single disease organizations; or professional meetings, exhibits, or media projects.

Meeting Times

The board meets monthly to review proposals.

Publications

The foundation publishes application guidelines.

Contact Persons

Michael A. Bailin, President

Susan Notkin, Program Director, Children

Bruce Trachdenberg, Director, Office of Communications

Nancy Roob, Vice President and Director of Institution and Field Building

Purpose

The Edna McConnell Clark Foundation seeks to improve conditions for people who are poor and disadvantaged living in the U.S.

Areas of Interest

Institution and Field Building

During 2000, two areas of the foundation's interest converged as institution and field building, our emerging grantmaking approach, became more focused on the goal of strengthening youth-serving organizations. Distinct activities were carried out in the two areas, yet by the end of the year they had become more unified than separate. As a result, the foundation entered 2001 in a strong position to use the methods of institution and field building to pursue the new, primary objective of helping young people from poor families grow up to be contributing and self-sufficient members of society.

Youth Development

The foundation began 2000 ready to start work on a preliminary strategy in youth development. The strategy, which the foundation's trustees had approved a year earlier, was designed to increase the availability of high-quality activities for young people during their nonschool hours—activities likely to help participants achieve better educational, vocational, and social outcomes.

Program for Children

The Program for Children focuses on keeping children safe and strengthening families. The Community Partnerships for Protecting Children initiative seeks to enhance the capacity of communities to protect children from abuse and neglect by engaging a broad range of stakeholders in assuming responsibility for child safety. Over the past four years, the initiative has assisted four localities—Cedar Rapids, Iowa; Jacksonville, Florida; Louisville, Kentucky; and St. Louis, Missouri—in bringing together diverse partnerships of public and private agencies (including child protective services), neighborhood-based organizations, and parent and resident leaders to establish local systems of community child protection.

New York Neighborhoods

The Program for New York Neighborhoods, which supports continuing and sustainable improvements in living conditions in Central Harlem and South Bronx neighborhoods through the Neighborhood Partners Initiative (NPI), entered its final phase during 2000. Through NPI, the Foundation is working with five lead agencies—Rheedlen Centers for Children and Families and Abyssinian Development Corporation in Central Harlem, and Mid Bronx Senior Citizens Council, Highbridge Community Life Center, and Bronx ACORN in the South Bronx—on improvement projects in their respective communities.

Student Achievement

The Program for Student Achievement currently works with three urban school districts—Corpus Christi, Texas; Long Beach, California; and San Diego, California—to increase the academic achievement of all their middle school students. Since 1995, each district has developed and implemented academic standards for what middle school students should know and be able to do in language arts, math, science, and social studies.

Tropical Disease Research

From 1985 through 1999, the foundation's Program for Tropical Disease Research made substantial investments in projects to control and eliminate trachoma, the world's leading cause of preventable blindness. A bacterial infection of the upper eyelid, trachoma infects approximately 150 million people in Africa, Asia, the Middle East, and some parts of South America and Australia. In 1998, the foundation joined with Pfizer, Inc. to create the International Trachoma Initiative (ITI), which sustains much of the work begun by the foundation.

**Financial
Data**

(Year ended 9/30/00)	
Assets:	$ 712,816,913
Total grants paid:	$ 28,000,539
Highest grant:	$ 4,100,000
Lowest grant:	$ 5,000

**Application
Procedures**

Initially, the foundation wants to view only a brief letter describing the program. If the staff determines that the request falls within the scope of the foundation's priorities, more detailed information and a formal proposal will be requested. Within each application, the staff looks for the strategy, skills, and commitment to accomplish the proposed project as well as the potential of the project to make substantial impact on specific program objectives.

**Grant
Limitations**

The foundation welcomes the opportunity to cooperate with other funders with relevant interests. The foundation will not consider requests for capital purposes, scholarships, endowment or deficit operations, and does not make grants to individuals.

**Meeting
Times**

The board of trustees meets four times per year, in March, June, September, and December.

Publications

The foundation publishes an annual report and a quarterly listing of grants awarded.

ROBERT STERLING CLARK FOUNDATION

PHONE: (212) 288-8900

FAX: (212) 288-1033

EMAIL: rcsf@aol.com

135 EAST 64TH STREET

NEW YORK, NEW YORK 10021-7045

Contact Person

Margaret C. Ayers, Executive Director

Areas of Interest

The Robert Sterling Clark Foundation provides support in three areas: Improving the performance of public institutions in New York City and state, in human services delivery, housing and economic development, environmental management, and budgetary process; strengthening the management of cultural institutions; and ensuring access to family planning services.

In the first area, the foundation funds endeavors designed to monitor human services delivery programs so that funds are not wasted and that recipients of service are well served. It supports programs that ensure the preservation and protection of the environment in accordance with federal and state mandates. It seeks to encourage linkages between the public and private sectors that promote the development of New York's economic base. And, lastly, it promotes improvements in the effectiveness and accountability of city and state agencies.

In its program to strengthen the management of cultural institutions, the foundation's grantmaking takes two forms. It provides grants to cultural institutions and arts service organizations for one-time projects designed to generate new sources of earned or contributed income, reduce operating costs through resource sharing, and improve internal management. Second, the foundation initiates grants to a limited number of small cultural institutions for use in general support. Eligibility is limited to institutions in New York City and the greater metropolitan area.

In its third program priority, the foundation seeks proposals from organizations whose work is aimed at protecting reproductive freedom and insuring access to family planning services. The foundation funds projects at the national level making use of litigation, public policy analysis, public education, and research to achieve these objectives.

**Financial
Data**

(Year ended 10/31/00)	
Assets:	$ 141,216,231
Total grants paid:	$ 5,027,820
Number of grants paid:	129
Highest grant:	$ 150,000
Lowest grant:	$ 1,000
Median grant size:	

**Application
Procedures**

We are interested in learning as much as possible about the applicant. This includes budgets (past, current, projected), audited financial statements, an IRS letter explaining tax status, names and occupations of trustees, and examples of past accomplishments. The individual project proposal should include, in addition to a description of the planned work, a budget, expected outcomes, plans for evaluation, background of those involved and a statement of plans for future support. The main body of the application should not exceed fifteen pages. Also, a one page summary is required.

**Grant
Limitations**

The foundation makes no grants to individuals or for building or endowment funds.

**Meeting
Times**

The board of directors meets quarterly, in January, April, July, and October. The board considers proposals year round.

Publications

The foundation publishes an annual report, and will make available upon request the information sheet "Program Guidelines and Grant Application Procedures."

THE CLEVELAND FOUNDATION

1422 Euclid Avenue, Suite 1400

Cleveland, Ohio 44115-2001

PHONE: (216) 861-3810

FAX: (216) 589-9039

EMAIL: twimberly@clevefdn.org

WEB: www.clevelandfoundation.org

Contact Person

Steven A. Minter, President and Executive Director

Purpose

The Cleveland Foundation, a public charity dedicated to improving the quality of life in Greater Cleveland, is the oldest and second-largest community foundation in the nation. Its establishment in 1914 is cited as one of ten events that most heavily influenced the development of the nonprofit sector in the 20th Century and it continues to be a leader in its field.

The Cleveland Foundation is made up of more than 800 funds created by individuals, families, organizations and corporations. It offers donors of all means the opportunity to have a lasting impact on their community while maximizing income, gift and estate tax benefits.

For more information about the organization, visit www.cleveland foundation.org.

Areas of Interest

Arts and Culture

- Building capacity to manage artistic risk
- Supporting effective arts in education
- Increasing access to and awareness of the arts
- Improving public awareness and support of arts and culture

Civic Affairs

- Improving neighborhood quality of life
- Supporting community development planning
- Promoting workforce development

Economic Development

- Stimulating government-business partnerships
- Strengthening institutions that foster Cleveland's growth
- Supporting programs that assist entrepreneurs

Education

- Assisting with improvement of districts' governance and management
- Strengthening leadership/teaching/parent involvement
- Experimenting with new approaches to public schooling
- Developing systematic research/evaluation/reporting
- Bolstering strategic initiatives of area colleges and universities

Environment

- Supporting parks and open spaces
- Strengthening environmental organizations
- Supporting education, especially for urban youth
- Building citizen awareness and participation

Health

- Supporting health care for indigent and uninsured
- Improving care for people with chronic conditions
- Aiding community transition to managed care/capitation

Social Services

- Strengthening families
- Strengthening agencies that deliver critical services
- Assisting the chronically poor
- Helping agencies respond to public policy changes

Financial Data

(Year ended 12/31/00)	
Assets:	$ 1,600,206,255
Total grants paid:	$ 73,159,657
Number of grants:	1,810
Highest grant:	NA
Lowest grant:	
Median grant size:	

Application Procedures

Your formal application for a grant must include a number of important elements. Because we will need to make copies, please submit your proposal on 8½ × 11-inch paper printed on one side only. Please do not use notebooks or binders, or include any videotape, tape recordings or CDs. Write clearly and simply, using language the lay person can understand. The better organized your proposal, the more persuasive it is likely to be.

Your proposal MUST include the grant request cover sheet and budget form completed in full; otherwise, we cannot begin to assess your request in a timely way. We don't accept proposals by fax or e-mail. In one mailing, we'll need:

• Your full proposal, with the pages numbered (two copies)
• A copy of your organization's tax-exempt letter from the IRS
• Your current annual report or a statement of your agency's most recent activities
• A list of your current board members
• Your current audit or financial statement. If you don't have one, list your provisions for an independent audit or your project's expenses
• Your agency's affirmative action policy or statement of non-discrimination
• Job descriptions and resumes of your project personnel. If you plan to use consultants on the project, include their resumes
• Names of your collaborators on the project, if applicable
• Letters in support of your project or letters from other funding sources who may have expressed interest in supporting the project (optional)

We review proposals on an ongoing basis, so please submit your proposal whenever it is ready. Please see our website for more information.

Grant Limitations

We give most of our grants to nonprofit organizations classified as 501(c)(3). We make some grants to government agencies, but we don't make grants to individuals. We use our funds to support long-term priorities in each grant-making area. We also support good ideas from a wide range of community organizations.

What we support:
• Projects in Greater Cleveland
• Projects that benefit Greater Clevelanders directly
• Programs that meet community needs
• Programs that test new ideas

What we don't support:
• Annual or membership drives
• Most fundraising projects
• Travel (if that's all the project is)
• Police and fire protection
• Government staff positions

- Publications or audiovisual programs unless they're part of a larger project
- Most requests for buildings, land or equipment

We're nonsectarian, so we don't support religious organizations for religious purposes. We do support them for non-religious programs such as hunger centers, job training or child care.

Meeting Times

The distribution committee meets four times a year in March, June, September, and December.

Publications

The foundation publishes an annual report, Guidelines for Grantseekers, and several publications for donors, attorneys and financial planners.

THE COLUMBIA FOUNDATION

1016 LINCOLN BOULEVARD, SUITE 205

SAN FRANCISCO, CALIFORNIA 94129

PHONE: (415) 561-6880

FAX: (415) 561-6883

EMAIL: info@columbia.org

WEB: www.columbia.org

Contact Person

Susan Reed Clark, Executive Director

Purpose

The foundation's broad philanthropic purpose has given it flexibility to respond to changing social conditions. Long-standing interests in world peace, human rights, the environment, cross-cultural and international understanding, the quality of urban life, and the arts have evolved to reflect current conditions and opportunities. The board of directors sets new priorities as conditions change.

Areas of Interest

The program priorities of the foundation are:

Arts and Culture

The goal is to enhance the quality of life through the arts and cultural programs.

Human Rights

The goal is the protection of basic human rights for all: the right to express convictions, to be free from discrimination, and the right of every person to physical and mental integrity. As defined by the Universal Declaration of Human Rights, these rights are not privileges granted by governments, nor can governments abrogate them.

Sustainable Communities and Economies

The goal is to secure quality of life for everyone within the means of nature in a way that is just and equitable to all humanity, other species and to future generations. Columbia Foundation seeks to catalyze significant breakthroughs in the building of sustainable communities and economies, and to bring them to the mainstream of public discourse in civil society and public policy making.

THE COLUMBIA FOUNDATION

Financial Data

(Year ended 5/31/01)	
Assets:	$ 43,600,381
Total grants paid:	$ 3,430,677
Number of grants paid:	86

Application Procedures

Complete proposals that match the foundation's program guidelines should be submitted by the application deadline stated for each respective program area. The foundation will only consider proposals from organizations that qualify as public charities under the laws, rules and regulations of the United States Internal Revenue Service.

The foundation does not accept proposals or letters of inquiry sent by facsimile or the Internet, and strongly discourages them being sent by overnight express services of any kind. Please use the regular postal service. The proposal deadline will be considered met if the postmarked date on your application envelope is on or before the stated program deadline date.

Proposals and letters of inquiry submitted to the foundation should be two-sided and produced on recycled or tree-free paper (see www.conservatree.com for information about paper alternatives). Please staple and number your pages so they are not lost. Do not enclose binders, folders, report covers, or other excess packaging materials. Please do not send videos, CDs, cassettes or other bulky items.

These deadlines are for the submission of full proposals. Letters of inquiry may be submitted at any time, but no later than 30 days prior to the program deadline.

Human Rights: September 1st
Sustainable Communities and Economies: December 15th
Arts and Culture: June 1st (beginning 2002)

The foundation considers proposals in each program area only once a year. The foundation's board of directors makes final grant decisions at a board meeting held approximately three to four months after the program area deadline. Please see our website for complete details on application procedures.

Grant Limitations

Priority is given to the following types of projects: those that promote social change rather than providing an ongoing service; venture funding for new ideas or for efforts to address controversial issues; programs in the early stages of development when the potential is high but funding is scarce; programs that promote the renewal or advancement of community institutions related to the foundation's program priorities; and programs that educate and train community leaders in the principles of sustainable development as the guiding principles for community and economic development. Only tax-exempt 501(c)(3) organizations are considered for funding.

Meeting Times

The board of directors meets four times a year.

Publications

The foundation publishes an annual report and will make available upon request a foundation profile, grants list, and proposal summary sheet.

THE COLUMBUS FOUNDATION

AND AFFILIATED

ORGANIZATIONS

1234 EAST BROAD STREET

COLUMBUS, OHIO 43205

PHONE: (614) 251-4000

FAX: (614) 251-4009

EMAIL: info@columbusfoundation.org

WEB: www.columbusfoundation.org

**Contact
Person**

Lisa Courtice, Vice President for
Community Research and Grants Management
Douglas F. Kridler, President & CEO

Purpose

The Columbus Foundation is committed to improving the quality of community life by assuring that all children enter school prepared to learn; helping adolescents make a positive transition to young adulthood; building the capacity of families to have safe and secure living environments; and making neighborhoods positive environments for living.

**Areas of
Interest**

The foundation accepts proposals in seven broad program areas: advancing philanthropy; arts and humanities; conservation; education; health; social services; and urban affairs. Proposals that relate to one or more of the foundation's strategic grantmaking areas receive higher priority for funding.

**Financial
Data**

(Year ended 12/31/2000)	
Assets:	$677,889,306
Total grants awarded:	$57,605,631
Number of grants awarded:	4,482
Highest grant:	$2,500,000
Lowest grant:	$25
Median grant size:	$15,000

**Application
Procedures**

There is one proposal deadline per year for each of the program areas. Because in several of these program areas grantmaking priorities are related to one or more of the foundations areas of strategic grantmaking, applicants are encouraged to meet or speak with a program officer well in advance of the deadline to discuss how the proposed project relates to the foundation's priorities. The foundation has its own application form and format for the body of the proposal. Applicants should contact the foundation to obtain a copy of its brochure "Information for Grant Applicants" before submitting a proposal. Grant application workshops are regularly scheduled during the year and applicants are encouraged to attend.

Program Area	Deadline Date	Decision Date
Health	April	July
Arts and conservation	November	February
Social services	July	October
Advancing philanthropy and urban affairs	September	December
Education	February	May

Grant Limitations

The foundation makes grants only to tax-exempt public charities under Section 501(c)(3) of the IRS code which have direct relevance to the central Ohio region. Grants are made outside Franklin County when a program is statewide with some benefit in Franklin County or when a project will contribute significantly to the welfare of residents of Franklin County. No grants are made to individuals, for religious purposes, budget deficits, endowments, conferences, scholarly research, or projects that are normally the responsibility of a public agency. Additionally, grants are not made when funds are available elsewhere.

Meeting Times

The governing committee meets in February, April, May, July, September, October, and December.

Publications

The foundation publishes an annual report, a brochure, and grant application guidelines.

COMMUNITY FOUNDATION OF GREATER MEMPHIS

1900 UNION AVENUE

MEMPHIS, TENNESSEE 38104

PHONE: (901) 728-4600

FAX: (901) 722-0010

EMAIL: mwolowicz@cfgm.org

WEB: www.cfgm.org

Contact Person

Andrea L. Reynolds, Vice President, Donor Relations and Program

Areas of Interest

The Community Foundation makes grants from its various funds, including donor-advised, designated, nonprofit designated, field of interest, scholarship, supporting organization and discretionary. Grants primarily support the metropolitan Memphis area, although some are made to organizations outside of the area. The foundation's competitive application process includes Community Building Grants and the Theodora Trezevant Neely Special Endowment Fund.

Financial Data

(Year ended 4/30/00)	
Assets:	$ 190,682,515
Total grants paid:	$ 28,509,823
Number of grants paid:	4,913
Highest grant:	$ 2,000,000
Lowest grant:	$ 100
Median grant:	$ 1,000

Application Procedures

Application procedures exist only for the Community Building Grants, Theodora Trezevant Neely Special Endowment Fund and Scholarship Funds. Other funds typically do not solicit applications or proposals. Only those proposals submitted on the foundation's application forms will be accepted. Please call or email the office for a copy of the applications. Neely is due January 15 each year with awards announced March 31. Community Building

Grants are due October 1 for a December 31 decision; and March 1 for a May 31 decision. Scholarship fund applications are due April 1.

Grant Limitations

Theodora Trezevant Neely Special Endowment Fund supports organizations located in Shelby County. Community Building Grants support organizations in the metropolitan Memphis area. Scholarship funds typically support Shelby County residents, although one fund is nationwide. Only organizations that are tax-exempt under section 501(c)(3) of the Internal Revenue Code are eligible to apply.

Meeting Times

Final decisions on Neely are made March 31. Final decisions on Community Building Grants are made May 31 and December 31. Final decisions for scholarship funds are made June 30.

Publications

The foundation publishes an annual report, newsletters, brochures and information packets on creating donor-advised funds. We also have a website, www.cfgm.org.

Contact Person

Faith Krueger, Chief Administrative Officer

Purpose

The Community Foundation of New Jersey seeks to assist people with social concerns achieve their particular goals in the state, towns, and neighborhoods. Primarily a collection of endowed funds—contributed by many individuals, families, corporations, private foundations, and other charitable organizations—the foundation is directed mainly toward New Jersey and to the issues identified by its donors, community leaders, and experts. Of particular interest to the foundation are the problems of our cities and of needy citizens.

The foundation's efforts focus on:

Grassroots leadership and community development
The AIDS epidemic
Youth education
Family mentoring
Volunteerism
Problems of immigrants and diversity

Other concerns include the arts, day care, health, housing, literacy, urban environment, the elderly, the disabled, and minority small business.

Areas of Interest

The foundation lists the following areas of concern to the residents of New Jersey and to be consistent with its charitable purposes.

• Community Development. Projects that respond to a broad array of community concerns, especially economic development, leadership training, and the empowerment of people so they may successfully address problems and help revitalize their neighborhoods.

• Cultural. To facilitate access for all people to a diverse range of activities, increasing awareness of the needs of new and emerging groups, and supporting well established institutions.

• Education. To prepare students more effectively for employment, encourage teacher initiative, lower student dropout rates, and address illiteracy.

• Environment and Conservation. Projects that preserve the environment, conserve our natural resources, and plan for orderly future development.

• Health. Projects to promote good health, prevent institutionalization, and facilitate access to health care delivery systems to all people.

• Religion. To support the secular role of the church, particularly in inner-city neighborhoods.

• Social Services and Welfare. To identify and respond to changing needs and particular gaps in the social service system and encourage efforts to address significant social problems.

The foundation seeks innovative programs that address important, identified problems. Attention is paid to programs that have specific, quantifiable objectives, leverage additional funding sources, and could be replicated elsewhere in New Jersey to meet similar community problems.

Financial Data

```
(Year ended    /   /   )
Support and revenue:              NA
Total grants paid:
Number of grants paid:
Highest grant:
Lowest grant:
Median grant size:
```

Application Procedures

The foundation holds discretionary, donor-advised and restricted funds. Within these categories are included both program related investment and scholarship funds. Requests for grants are directed to discretionary and program related investment funds held by the foundation.

Discretionary Funds: Applications for discretionary and program related funds must be made to the executive director. A brief, one-page letter describing the program or project should be submitted, including the amount of money requested. If the program falls within guideline priorities and funding capabilities of the foundation, a proposal form will be sent to the applicant. The proposal is then considered by the distribution committee and a recommendation is made to the board of trustees. The following schedule outlines deadlines for each program area:

Program	Deadline for Letter/Application	Notification
AIDS	January 31	March 31
Arts, Education, Environment	March 31	June 30
Health, Social Services	June 30	October 30

Program Related Investment Funds: Grants or loans may be made by several funds held by the Community Foundation. Loans are made generally to women and minorities living in Northwestern Essex County who do not have access to normal financial markets; these loans are for economic development purposes. Loans are also available to nonprofit agencies in Mercer County for capital projects.

**Grant
Limitations**

The foundation makes grants only for charitable or educational activities serving the residents of the state. No grants will be considered for on-going operating budgets nor for the capital needs of agencies. Grants will not be made to individuals nor for sectarian and religious programs from discretionary funds. Funding is for seed projects only; nonstart-up dollars are given only in very special cases. Organizations receiving grants usually must be recognized by the IRS as tax-exempt, nonprofit organizations. Project funding is only for one year; in very special cases, multi-year funding for two to three years may be considered, but projects must be resubmitted each year.

**Meeting
Times**

The board of trustees meets three times a year in March, June, and October.

Publications

The foundation publishes an annual report.

COMPTON FOUNDATION, INC.

PHONE: (650) 328-0101

FAX: (650) 328-0171

535 MIDDLEFIELD ROAD, SUITE 160

MENLO PARK, CALIFORNIA 94025

WEB: www.comptonfoundation.org

Contact Person

Deborah Daughtry, Office and Communications Manager

Purpose

The Compton Foundation's primary concern is the prevention of war, and the amelioration of world conditions that tend to cause conflict. In the eyes of the foundation, primary among these conditions are the increasing pressure and destabilizing effects of excessive population growth, the alarming depletion and unequal distribution of the earth's natural resources, the steady deterioration of the world's environment, and the tenuous status of human rights. The foundation categorizes these global human survival problems into the areas of Peace and World Order, Population, and the Environment.

Areas of Interest

• Peace and World Order. The Compton Foundation supports efforts directed at preventing the proliferation of nuclear and other weapons of destruction; influencing public policy to promote peaceful means of settling international disputes; supporting multi-lateral approaches to international issues; and strengthening existing international institutions.

• Population. Efforts that concern themselves with: the interrelationship between population, peace and environment; the role and status of women in developing countries; U.S. population policy; evaluation of family planning programs in developing countries; problems of illegal immigration from Mexico to the United States; teenage pregnancy prevention; and problems of urban population growth.

• Environment. Projects relating to land, river, and watershed protection and management; adverse environmental consequences of population growth; and energy problems.

COMPTON FOUNDATION, INC.

Financial Data

(Year ended 12/31/99)	
Assets:	$ 118,011,253
Total grants paid:	$ 8,043,315

Application Procedures

Applicants should review the foundation's guidelines before submitting a proposal. Proposals should be approximately three to four pages long and include a description of the organization making the request, the objective of the project, the means by which the project will be accomplished and evaluated, and if applicable, a description of previous work supported by the Compton Foundation.

Items that must come with the proposal include: a list of key people involved; proposed project budget; organization budget; other sources of support; and a copy of the organization's IRS tax-exempt letter.

Deadlines for consideration during the May meeting is March 1 and for the December meeting is October 1. Faxed proposals are not accepted.

Grant Limitations

No grants are made to individuals. Grants are made only to organizations with proof of tax-exempt status from the IRS.

Meeting Times

The board of directors meets in May and December.

Publications

The foundation publishes a biennial report and Policies and Guidelines Brochure.

Contact Person

Susan T. Vandiver, Vice President of Grant Programs

Purpose

The Cowell Foundation invests $9 million annually in community-based non-profit organizations and schools, seeking to improve the quality of life for families in Northern California, low-income and rural communities.

Areas of Interest

We are committed to continuous learning and remain open to experimenting with methods that promise to make a measurable difference in the lives of families and children. Recent work has encouraged and funded comprehensive, integrated leadership and governance structures, supports and services that broadly address neighborhood needs in small rural and urban communities.

Together with grantees, we have learned that the Family Resource Center (FRC) is a very productive model to achieve our vision. FRCs are community hubs where local residents work with public and private partners to develop and sustain comprehensive, integrated, accessible, neighborhood-based services and supports aimed at preventing and solving individual, family and community problems by building on local strengths.

Over the next several years, we will move in new directions while continuing our current program interests. Our plan is to link and integrate funding programs: FRCs, affordable housing, K-12 education and youth development in specific communities. Cowell will actively search out opportunities to invest in comprehensive, FRC-based community building that incorporate youth development, affordable housing and education efforts. Our focus is small, rural and urban, low-income neighborhoods where resources are scarce and local leaders are working jointly with residents across fields and sectors to build enduring community governance structures, services and supports for improved children and family outcomes.

**Financial
Data**

```
(Year ended    /   /   )
Assets:                        NA
Total grants paid:
Total number of grants:
Highest grant:
Lowest grant: less than
Median grant size:
```

**Application
Procedures**

We encourage potential applicants to call before sending a letter or proposal so foundation staff can discuss your project idea with you. Be prepared to explain who will benefit from your project, the results you expect, your budget, and any other sources of support you have in mind. Cowell staff will determine if there is a fit with the foundation's specific grantmaking interests for the year and with the resources we have available.

If staff request a letter of inquiry from you, please cover the following points as briefly as possible:

- What you seek to do and why.
- Who will do the work.
- Specific outcomes expected from the project and when.
- How much the proposed project will cost.
- Amount requested from Cowell.
- Other sources of revenue for the proposed project.
- Information about the sponsoring organization's mission, history, finances, activities, accomplishments and plans for the future.

Please don't send us a formal proposal unless Cowell staff asks for one. If you are asked to submit a proposal, staff will give you a list of what we require.

**Grant
Limitations**

The S. H. Cowell Foundation is a private foundation under California and U.S. law. We accept grant proposals only from tax-exempt, charitable organizations and schools. Cowell generally limits grant making to projects that benefit residents of Northern California. We do not accept proposals that benefit specific individuals or persons with medical or other particular conditions, nor do we consider requests that serve religious purposes or support academic or medical research. Except for school districts seeking to meet education guidelines, Cowell does not fund government agencies for projects that are the normal responsibility of government.

Meeting
Times

The board of trustees meets monthly to consider grant requests.

Publications

The foundation publishes an annual report and grant guidelines.

Contact Person

Susan M. Fish, Grants Administrator

Purpose

The Jessie B. Cox Charitable Trust provides grants to nonprofit organizations in the six New England states in the areas of education, health, the environment and development of philanthropy. The trustees favor projects that offer new approaches over those similar to previously funded programs, and organizations that have not received prior support.

Areas of Interest

The trust provides support for special projects and seed money in these areas:

• Education. Programs that have a significant effect on the availability of academic resources, traditional and innovative; increased access, incentives, and opportunities for education participation by undeserved populations in the area; training opportunities in the visual and performing arts; and skills training for disadvantaged or disabled residents seeking meaningful employment.

• Environment. Programs that protect critical land and wildlife resources; positively effect regional economic development and self-sufficiency; promote energy conservation; increase public awareness of important environmental issues facing the region; and promote cooperation among organizations and communities to solve mutual environmental concerns.

• Health. Research and delivery programs in the prevention and treatment of illness and disability; increase access to health care for the regions' undeserved populations; increase opportunities for careers in the health field; and improve delivery of health services to the poor.

**Financial
Data**

(Year ended 12/30/00)	
Assets:	$ *
Total grants paid:	$ 3,059,230
Number of grants paid:	82
Highest grant:	$ 70,000
Lowest grant:	$ 17,500
Median grant size:	$ 37,000

Not applicable because Cox is a charitable lead annuity trust—$3,059,230 every year in grants.

**Application
Procedures**

The trust requests that applicants first submit a concept paper. The concept paper should include a detailed description of the project, the population served, the problem it addresses, results expected, and evaluation criteria; brief history of the organization and its mission, a preliminary budget, and a copy of IRS determination letter. Following each quarterly meeting the trustees will request full proposals for projects of interest.

Deadlines are January 15 for the March meeting, April 15 for the June meeting, July 15 for the September meeting, and October 15 for the December meeting.

During each quarterly meeting the trustees will request full proposals from projects that fall within their funding priorities.

**Grant
Limitations**

Grants are made only to organizations that are tax-exempt under Section 501(c)(3) of the Internal Revenue Code. The following general classifications are not funded: individuals, capital or building funds, equipment and materials, land acquisition, deficit financing, operating budgets, continuing support, and general endowments. The trust supports programs in the six New England states.

**Meeting
Times**

The trustees meet four times a year in March, June, September, and December.

Publications

The trust publishes an annual report and application guidelines.

THE CROSSROADS FUND

3411 W. Diversey Avenue, Suite 20

Chicago, Illinois 60647-1245

PHONE: (773) 227-7676

FAX: (773) 227-7790

EMAIL: info@crossroadsfund.org

WEB: www.crossroadsfund.org

Contact Persons

Jeanne Kracher, Executive Director

Inhe Choi, Program Director

Purpose

The Crossroads Fund is a public foundation that raises money to provide grants and technical assistance to Chicago-area grassroots organizations working on issues of social and economic justice.

Areas of Interest

Social change is the focus of the fund's grantmaking. It welcomes applications from new organizations and those working on emerging issues. It also seeks groups that represent a diverse population (such as people of color, women, lesbians, gay men, and those with disabilities) and whose diversity is reflected in its leadership.

In order to be considered for a grant, an organization's activities must fall within the scope of the fund's guidelines. Crossroads seeks and supports organizations that are working for a society free of discrimination based on race, sex, age, religion, economic status, sexual orientation, ethnic background, or physical or mental disabilities; struggling for the rights of workers; promoting self-determination in low-income and disenfranchised communities; creating alternative arts and media linked to the struggle for social change; promoting international peace, and organizing locally for a just U.S. foreign policy, or defending political and human rights.

Priority is given to those groups that operate in the Chicago metropolitan area, that are based in minority and other oppressed communities, that operate in a democratic manner and are responsive to the constituencies they serve, that provide direct services only when tied to social change programs or when they are likely to empower the communities served, and that may have difficulty securing funding from larger private and public funding sources.

**Financial
Data**

```
(Year ended   /  /  )
Support and revenue:                    NA
Total grants paid:
Number of grants paid:
Highest grant:
Lowest grant:
Median grant size:
```

**Application
Procedures**

Crossroads has two grant cycles per year. Proposal deadline dates for each year are March 1 and September 1. Interested organizations should telephone or write for complete guidelines and application materials.

All proposals that reach the fund's office or are postmarked by the deadline date will be reviewed. Applications are screened according to whether the group's work falls within the Crossroads' guidelines. Those proposals meeting the guidelines are reviewed by members of the grantmaking committee of the board. An evaluation session is held by the grantmaking committee to select applicants to recommend to the full board for face to face interviews (or site visits). Board members and staff attend interviews, and report back to the full board, where final decisions are made. Grant applicants are notified by mail (and sometimes phone) regarding the status of their application. This process is normally completed within sixteen weeks of the proposal deadline.

Crossroads makes grants for both general operating support and special projects. It will consider applications for up to $7,000. Organizations may receive only one grant a year, and must submit a report on the use of any previous grant received from Crossroads before new proposals will be reviewed.

Crossroads also administers a donor-advised program that offers flexible yet limited grant making in consultation with Crossroads' donors.

**Grant
Limitations**

For regular grant making cycles, Crossroads only supports those organizations with annual budgets of $100,000 or less. Maximum grant amount awarded is $7,000. In addition, Crossroads does not generally support: groups whose sole purpose is to provide direct services, individuals, conferences, research projects, or travel.

Because Crossroads has limited resources and a very specific mission, it is not able to fund every worthwhile project. If there is uncertainty about whether or not a project fits within Crossroads' guidelines, groups should send a brief letter describing its organization, or call the Crossroads staff.

The fund will accept grant applications from organizations regardless of their tax-exempt status so long as their activities clearly fall within tax-exempt guidelines. Fiscal sponsorship for those organizations without tax-exempt status is not required.

The fund is required to make grants only for tax exempt activities. To comply with IRS regulations, the Crossroads Fund cannot: fund organizations involved in electoral campaigns, contribute substantially to support lobbying at the federal, state, or local level; and support private, in contrast to public, interests.

Meeting Times

The board of directors meets bimonthly, and funding decisions are made twice a year.

Publications

The fund publishes an annual report, funding guidelines, application materials, and grants lists.

C.S. FUND

WARSH-MOTT LEGACY

469 BOHEMIAN HIGHWAY

FREESTONE, CALIFORNIA 95472-9579

PHONE: (707) 874-2942

FAX: (707) 874-1734

EMAIL: rosec@csfund.org
kathyk@csfund.org

WEB: www.csfund.org

**Contact
Person**

Roxanne Turnage, Executive Director

Purpose

The goals of the C.S. Fund and the Warsh-Mott Legacy are to support organizations and projects that work to challenge and change individual and institutional habits, behavior, attitudes, and beliefs that endanger humanity. These include the ways in which different people think of their rights of ownership, security, and freedom; the ways in which they form political, religious and social values; the stated and assumed rights and responsibilities among individuals and between citizens and their institutions and the ways they have learned to solve problems. The funds seek to expand the collective thinking beyond habitual limits in order to discover and create imaginative and effective strategies for planetary survival.

**Areas of
Interest**

CS Fund and Warsh-Mott Legacy are currently granting in four categories, each one with a specific emphasis:

Biotechnology

Grantmaking in this area focuses on challenging the genetic engineering of humans. We do not intend to add any new groups to our roster of grantees working on agriculture issues in the U.S. We are directing some resources toward Central and Eastern Europe and the Newly Independent States of the former Soviet Union to encourage activism on the impacts of biotechnology on agriculture in those countries.

Economic Globalization

Our grantmaking in this category balances short term efforts that oppose the NAFTA/WTO/FTAA trade regimes with long term efforts to develop alternative economic models. We are especially concerned about the lack of democracy that permeates the current system.

Food Security

Grantmaking in this category focuses on four elements of food security: seed saving, soil building, protecting pollinators, and preserving traditional knowledge of how food is grown.

Children's Environmental Health

Our central goals in this category are reducing/eliminating pesticide use in schools, and encouraging school lunch programs to serve organic foods. We also support other school-based toxics projects such as those that address facility siting and the use of toxic materials in and around the classroom.

Financial Data

(Year ended 12/31/00)	
Support and revenue:	$ 2,070,214
Total grants paid:	$ 655,000
Number of grants paid:	37
Highest grant:	$ 45,000
Lowest grant:	$ 1,500
Median grant size:	$ 15,000

Application Procedures

Requests for support should be made by letter of inquiry. Hard copy is preferred over fax or e-mail transmission. There are no deadlines for letters of inquiry—they are accepted throughout the year. If your project falls within the foundation's priority areas of interest, a full proposal will be invited.

If a full proposal is requested, it must be received by the first Monday in February for consideration in the spring, or the first Monday in August for consideration in the fall. The foundation provides general support as well as project-specific grants.

Grant Limitations

The funds do not support endowments, capital ventures, emergency requests, or film and video production. Applicant organizations must be classified as a 501(c)(3) by the Internal Revenue Service. Foreign applicants should note that the foundation makes a very limited number of grants abroad.

C.S. FUND

**Meeting
Times**

The Boards of Directors of the CS Fund and the Warsh-Mott Legacy meet twice a year to make funding decisions, usually in April/May and November/December.

Publications

At present, the funds do not publish an annual report. Further information is available on our website at www.csfund.org.

PATRICK AND ANNA M. CUDAHY FUND

PHONE: (414) 271-6020 or (847) 866-0760

FAX: (847) 475-0679

P. O. Box 11978

WEB: www.cudahyfund.org

MILWAUKEE, WISCONSIN 53211-0978

Contact Person

Sister Judith Borchers, Executive Director

Purpose

The Patrick and Anna M. Cudahy Fund is a general purpose, family foundation that directs most of its support to organizations in Wisconsin and Chicago. Occasionally grants are made to national groups, including those that support international (U.S.-based) programs.

Areas of Interest

The fund's interests are broad. A review of its past grants suggests it has four program areas: identification with the dispossessed (including international relief, international self-development projects, advocacy organizations working for systemic change, domestic relief organizations, and domestic self-development projects working for local community change); persistent national issues (including education, arms control, environment, farm policies, race relations, and economics); institutional support (including higher education, youth serving agencies, inner-city education, elderly, medical, disabled, pregnancy prevention, and religion); and arts and culture.

Financial Data

(Year ended / /)	
Assets:	NA
Total grants paid:	
Number of grants paid:	
Highest grant:	
Lowest grant:	
Median grant size:	

Application
Procedures

Deadlines are approximately two months prior to the quarterly board meetings. Call or write the fund for an application form and the deadlines for the coming year.

Proposals should include a brief description of the organization; an outline of the proposed project; a financial summary of both the organization and the project; and a copy of the organization's ruling from the IRS classifying it as tax-exempt under Section 501(c)(3). Completed proposals will be acknowledged by the fund's staff. Where appropriate, site visits and interviews may be conducted. Groups are informed of the decision of the directors within a week of the meeting.

Grant
Limitations

The fund does not make grants to individuals, make loans, or provide support for endowment funds.

Meeting
Times

The board of directors meets quarterly, generally in March, June, September, and December.

Publications

The fund distributes application guidelines and a list of recent grantees.

THE FRANCES L. & EDWIN L. CUMMINGS MEMORIAL FUND

PHONE: (212) 286-1778

FAX: (212) 682-9458

501 FIFTH AVENUE, SUITE 708

NEW YORK, NEW YORK, 10017-6103

Contact Person

Elizabeth Costas, Administrative Director

Purpose

The Cummings Fund purpose is to provide funds for innovative programs that benefit the health and well-being of the citizens in the New York City metropolitan area. This area includes New York City and the urbanized areas of Northeastern New Jersey.

Areas of Interest

The fund seeks to fill existing needs in areas particularly underfunded at present and it encourages smaller and lesser-known community-based organizations to submit grant requests which address the needs of a specific community. It has a particular interest in programs that serve young people. The major field of interests are:

• Social welfare. Projects that address the issues of child abuse, parent education, youth employment and job training, juvenile delinquency, teenage pregnancy, and homelessness.

• Education. Efforts to reform the public education system or programs that serve public school children.

• Health care. Programs that serve the economically and socially disadvantaged populations.

• Medical research. Projects that focus on AIDS and cancer.

Application Procedures

The deadlines for submitting grant requests are April 1 for review in June and October 1 for review in December. Grant requests are accepted from February 1 for the June meeting and from August 1 for the December meeting.

All proposals should be no longer than seven pages and should include an executive summary and a description of the project. This description should include the amount requested and itemized project budget; identification of the population served (including how they will be selected, number involved, and benefits to that population); measurable goals and evaluation methods; indication of the relevance of the program to the organization and its future goals; and plans for future funding.

One original and three copies of the grant proposal should be submitted along with the following supporting information: the organization's operating budget; identification of other potential sources of support; the most recent audited financial statement; and one copy of the IRS tax-exempt letter.

Financial Data

(Year ended 7/31/01)	
Assets:	$ 41,735,542
Total grants paid:	$ 2,365,700
Total number of grants:	56*
Highest grant:	$ 250,000
Lowest grant:	$ 11,200
Median size grant:	$25,000

*Does not include grants $1,000 and under awarded by the Board of Advisors under a program which allows each member to designate up to one thousand dollars to any organization or organizations they choose following each Board meeting.

Grant Limitations

The fund is legally restricted from contributing to the cultural arts. Additionally the fund does not provide grants in the following areas: alcoholism and drug addiction treatment programs, camping programs, capital campaigns, conferences, day care programs, media production, environmental programs, private schools, individuals, research studies or public opinion polls, advocacy groups, scholarships programs, senior citizens' programs, soup kitchens and food banks, well-endowed institutions or organizations which are not tax exempt under 501(c)(3) of the IRS Code. The fund does not usually provide support for general operating expenses, however, occasionally it will agree to review proposals for the development of general endowments (through challenge grants) for organizations addressing the fund's field of interest.

**Meeting
Times**

The board of trustees meets twice a year to consider grant requests.

Publications

The foundation publishes a biennial report including its grant guidelines.

CUMMINS FOUNDATION

PHONE: (812) 377-3114

FAX: (812) 377-7897

500 JACKSON STREET

MAIL CODE 60633, BOX NUMBER 3005   WEB: www.cummins.com

COLUMBUS, INDIANA 47202-3005

Contact Person

Tracy Souza, President

Purpose

The grantmaking activities of the Cummins Foundation represent one portion of the corporate responsibility program of Cummins Company, Inc., the manufacturer of high-speed diesel engines and component parts. The foundation supports local programs in communities in which the company has facilities or subsidiaries.

Areas of Interest

The activities of the Cummins Foundation support three general principles: empowerment, to develop independence and equip people to help themselves and to serve others; inclusiveness, to expand opportunity for those who lack it; and community, to build and sustain quality in common life.

The foundation has four funding priorities:

• Youth and education. Projects that eliminate barriers to the healthy development of young people, encourages organizations serving youth in creative ways, and supports efforts to improve elementary and secondary schools, including key institutions with which Cummins has historic relationships.

• Equity and justice. Efforts to serve those who face discrimination, are dispossessed, or are poorly served by society. It looks for organizations that are responding creatively and vigorously to meet their needs, engaging in constructive public advocacy and working to ensure protection of civil rights for women and racial and ethnic minorities. It also encourages opportunities for leadership development among women and minorities and supports efforts to increase minority economic participation.

• Community development/arts program. Programs that enhance the general environment of Cummins plant communities. In community development, the foundation supports projects that encourage a high quality of life for the entire community. In the arts area, support is aimed primarily at developing opportunities for young or emerging artists in local Cummins communities and encouraging involvement in the arts, especially by youth.

• Public policy program. The program provides a vehicle for the foundation to make general support grants to national organizations working to strengthen the debate on key issues facing society. For the most part, impetus for these grants comes from the board of the foundation and not as a response to unsolicited proposals.

Financial Data

```
(Year ended   /   /   )
Assets:                                   NA
Total grants paid:
Number of grants paid:
Highest grant:
Lowest grant:
Median grant size:
```

Application Procedures

There are no application deadlines. The foundation prefers that initial inquiries be made in writing and that interested applicants prepare a preliminary proposal for the foundation's review. This preliminary application should include a brief description of the problem being addressed, specifically what the program hopes to achieve, and an operating plan and budget, a description of the key leadership, and plans for evaluating the program's effectiveness. If the foundation is interested in considering the proposed program, additional information will be requested.

Applicants should note that Cummins and its subsidiaries have manufacturing plants in Columbus, Seymour, Madison, and Findley, Minnesota; Huntsville, Alabama; Rocky Mount, North Carolina; Charleston, South Carolina; Jamestown, New York; Fostoria, Ohio; Cookeville and Memphis, Tennessee; Lake Mills, Iowa; and Santa Fe Springs, California. Proposals from plant communities outside southern Indiana should be submitted first to the local plant manager.

Grant Limitations

The foundation does not support political causes or candidates, or sectarian religious activities. Grants are not made to individuals.

**Meeting
Times**

The board meets three times a year. The basic framework of the company's annual philanthropy plan and budget are set at the board meeting at the beginning of each year.

Publications

The foundation produces a two-year contribution report every other year.

DADE COMMUNITY FOUNDATION

200 South Biscayne Boulevard

Suite 505

Miami, Florida 33131-2343

PHONE: (305) 371-2711

FAX: (305) 371-5342

EMAIL: cgrant01@bellsouth.net

WEB: www.dadecommunityfoundation.org

**Contact
Person**

    Ruth Shack, President

Purpose

    The Dade Community Foundation seeks to enhance the quality of life for all the residents of Greater Miami. Its resources are committed to resolving Miami's most intractable problems—cultural alienation and lack of community cohesion.

**Areas of
Interest**

    Grants are made in the broad areas of education, health, human services, arts and culture; environment; economic development; and religion. Within these broad categories, the foundation looks for projects that meet the needs of the economically disadvantaged; abused and neglected children; immigrant and refugee populations; those with AIDS; and the homeless.

**Financial
Data**

(Year ended 12/31/01)	
Assets:	$ 70,621,401
Total grants paid:	$ 7,000,000
Total number of grants:	1091
Highest grant:	$25,000
Lowest grant:	$ 1,000
Median grant size:	$3,700

**Application
Procedures**

    The board of governors meets in February to consider requests for discretionary grants. The deadline for receipt of proposals is November 30. There is no formal application form, however the foundation publishes guidelines that describe the specific information required in the proposal. These guidelines and specific information concerning a prospective proposal should be addressed to JoAnne Bander, Vice President, Programs and Projects.

Grant Limitations

The foundation normally does not make grants to individuals, for memberships, for fundraising events or for memorials. Additionally, grants are only made to nonprofit tax-exempt organizations in Dade County as defined in section 501(c)(3) of the IRS Code.

Meeting Times

The board meets annually in February to consider grant requests.

Publications

The foundation publishes an annual report, information for grant seekers, building endowments, giving programs, and occasional papers on foundation topics.

DEER CREEK FOUNDATION

PHONE: (314) 241-3228

720 Olive Street, Suite 1975

St. Louis, Missouri 63101

Contact Person

Mary Stake Hawker, Director

Purpose

The Deer Creek Foundation's purpose is "to advance and preserve governance of society by rule of the majority, with protection of basic rights as provided by the Constitution and the Bill of Rights, and in education in its relation to this concept".

Areas of Interest

The foundation's priority is assisting individuals and groups working on action programs to advance government accountability, civil liberties, and civil rights that promise to have significant regional or national effect. Among its fields of interest are communications and free speech, equal rights, public policy, citizenship, education, film and media, civil and criminal justice, litigation and legal services, minority and ethnic groups and reproductive rights.

Financial Data

(Year ended 12/31/99)	
Assets:	$ 59,000,000
Total grants paid:	$ 2,353,538
Number of grants paid:	66
Highest grant:	$ 175,000
Lowest grant:	$ 1,000

Application Procedures

No specific application form is required. Applicants should submit a proposal stating the objectives of the project, the specific activities planned to achieve those objectives, the qualifications of the organization and individuals concerned, the mechanism for evaluating the results, a project and organizational budget, the latest annual report or audited financial statement (if available), a copy of the applicant's tax-exempt status determination letter from the Internal Revenue Service, a list of the organization's Board of Directors, and a list of current organization and project funders which includes each contribution amount. Ordinarily, preference will be given to applicants which qualify for exemption under Section 501(c)(3) of the Internal Revenue Code, and which are not "private foundations" as defined under Section 509(a). Public instrumentalities performing similar functions are eligible.

Grant Limitations

Grants are made ordinarily to organizations with Section 501(c)(3) tax-exempt status. The foundation does not normally support endowments, construction, equipment purchases, or general operating expenses.

Meeting Times

The board of directors meets in April, September, and December.

Publications

The foundation publishes a brochure containing grant application guidelines and application procedures. A list of past grantees is available upon request.

THE DENVER FOUNDATION

950 SOUTH CHERRY STREET, SUITE 200

DENVER, COLORADO, 80246

PHONE: (303) 300-1790

FAX: (303) 300-6547

EMAIL: jcasey@denverfoundation.org

WEB: www.denverfoundation.org

Contact Person

David Miller, Executive Director

Purpose

The Denver Foundation is a community foundation supporting a wide variety of projects that benefit the residents of Adams, Arapahoe, Boulder, Denver, Douglas, and Jefferson Counties in Colorado. The foundation seeks projects which will enhance the quality of life in these communities in the areas of arts and culture, education, health and human services, and civic concerns.

Areas of Interest

The foundation will consider projects that benefit a broad sector of the community and target those not adequately served by existing resources; pilot or demonstrate new practical approaches to specific community problems; and improve the quality of life through cultural and aesthetic endeavors.

In the area of education, the foundation limits its grantmaking to projects that increase parental and community involvement; address before-school and after-school programming and early childhood education issues; and develop multi-cultural programs which foster mutual respect among differing children and adults.

Application Procedures

Grants are awarded three times a year through a grant application process. All applications that are completed by the deadline will be assigned to a program officer for review. This review often includes a visit to the agency and interview with the organization's representative. Many, but not all, proposals are then presented to an Advisory Committee of the Foundation.

The Denver Foundation has four volunteer advisory committees—Arts and Culture, Civic and Education, Health, and Human Services. Each committee meets regularly with the staff to review proposals and make funding recommendations to the Board of Trustees.

Recommendations of the Advisory Committees are reviewed by the Grant-making Committee and then by the full Board of Trustees. Following the board meeting, agencies are promptly notified of the board's decision and are usually sent a written rationale explaining the board's decision.

Please be certain to obtain a copy of the Grant Guidelines before submitting an application. Contact The Denver Foundation to request a copy in the mail, or visit the web site at www.denverfoundation.org. Each application must be submitted by 5:00 p.m. on the date of the deadline and must include all elements as outlined in the Guidelines to be considered. Decisions are made five months from the date of submission.

For more information, please contact Jim Casey, Grants Manager, The Denver Foundation at 303-300-1790 ext. 131.

Grant Application Deadlines:

October 1
February 1
June 3
October 1

**Financial
Data**

(Year ended 12/31/00)	
Assets:	$ 186,055,446
Total grants paid:	$ 17,000,000
Total number of grants:	700
Highest grant:	
Lowest grant:	
Median grant size:	

**Grant
Limitations**

To qualify for a Denver Foundation Discretionary Grant, an organization must:
• be a 501(c)(3) tax-exempt nonprofit organization in good standing;
• serve residents in Adams, Arapahoe, Boulder, Denver, Douglas or Jefferson County;
• help meet a need not adequately being met by existing community resources.

**Meeting
Times**

The board of trustees meets quarterly.

Publications

The foundation publishes an annual report, information for grant seekers, a newsletter, and a program policy statement.

THE DISCOUNT FOUNDATION

6712 TILDENWOOD LANE

ROCKVILLE, MARYLAND 20852-4320

PHONE: (301) 468-1288

FAX: (301) 468-1289

EMAIL: info@discountfoundation.org

WEB: www.discountfoundation.org

Contact Person

Susan Chinn, Executive Director

Purpose

The Discount Foundation, a small, private grantmaking foundation, focuses on expanding job opportunities, wages, and benefits for poor and working people, including participants in state and local workfare programs.

The foundation supports community education, community organizing, and citizen participation in efforts to improve the economic and social well-being of the poor and their families.

The foundation has a strong commitment to developing leaders and building citizen organizations in poor, urban communities of color.

Areas of Interest

Discount awards grants in three areas:

- Increasing job opportunities, wages, benefits, and job security for the poor

  Discount supports projects to improve wages and benefits for poor and working people. Examples include campaigns for: a living wage, a higher minimum wage, protecting temporary workers, publicly funded living-wage work, and corporate and public accountability that ties tax subsidies to wage and benefit standards.

- Moving from welfare to work with dignity

  Discount supports organizing projects to link welfare/workfare participants with local institutions—for example, community organizations, labor unions, churches, and congregations—to demand meaningful employment training and support and permanent living-wage jobs that don't displace other low-wage workers.

- Supporting the right to join a union

  Discount assists projects that defend the rights of workers to join a union and bargain collectively.

**Financial
Data**

(Year ended 9/30/99)	
Assets:	$ 8,811,925
Total grants paid:	$ 440,500
Number of grants paid:	25
Highest grant:	$ 25,000
Lowest grant:	$ 5,000
Median grant size:	$ 14,000

**Application
Procedures**

Discount has a two-step process

1. Information Letter.

Submit a one-page informational letter by October 15th. Please do not send a proposal. In the letter briefly describe:
• Your organization
• Its goals and objectives
• The specific project for which you seek support
' After reviewing these letters, the foundation will ask a limited number of organizations to submit a proposal. No proposal will be accepted without prior review and authorization.

2. Proposal Package.

If you are asked to submit a proposal on behalf of your organization, you must complete and return a cover sheet supplied by Discount, grant proposal, IRS letter, and budget information by January 11th.

**Grant
Limitations**

Grants are only made to publicly supported charitable organizations whose Section 501(c)(3) status is confirmed by a current IRS determination or ruling letter. Discount supports activities in Connecticut, Delaware, Illinois, Indiana, Maryland, Massachusetts, Michigan, New Jersey, New York, Ohio, Pennsylvania, Rhode Island, Washington, D.C., and Wisconsin. In a few cases, the foundation may request proposals from outside these states. The foundation does not support capital campaigns and capital projects, endowments, government agencies, schools, religious programs, publications, research projects, tours and trips, or services to individuals.

Meeting Times

The board of directors meets once a year, in the spring.

Publications

Application guidelines are distributed upon request.

GERALDINE R. DODGE FOUNDATION, INC.

PHONE: (973) 540-8442

FAX: (973) 540-1211

EMAIL: info@grdodge.org

WEB: www.grdodge.org

163 MADISON AVENUE

P. O. BOX 1239

MORRISTOWN, NEW JERSEY 07962-1239

Contact Person

David Grant, Executive Director

Purpose

The Geraldine R. Dodge Foundation concentrates its grantmaking activities in New Jersey, with a specific interest in the local Morristown/Madison area. The areas of emphasis include education, the arts, welfare of animals, and public issues. The foundation's public interest program supports projects working in fields such as teen pregnancy and sexuality, the environment, reduction of hazardous waste, energy, and public policy.

Areas of Interest

Our giving in **Education** focuses on elevating the profession of teaching and fostering the continuous improvement of public education at the primary and secondary levels. We seek to support innovative educational thinking, which will ultimately have practical application in New Jersey. Areas of interest include: the early training and ongoing professional development of teachers; the role of the principal and superintendent as educational leaders; systemic change in schools; access to educational excellence for underserved populations; and the creation of model curricula, instruction, and assessments.

Our giving in the **Arts** is focused on New Jersey's cultural institutions and those national organizations which serve New Jersey artists or advance the arts in New Jersey. Priorities include supporting artistic excellence, with emphasis on the development of new and vital works; fostering the improvement of instruction in artistic disciplines; and helping to stabilize arts organizations integral to the lives of their communities.

Our giving in **Morris County** assists organizations which have a major impact on: strengthening families and communities; protecting the environment; improving the quality of K-12 education; fostering excellence in the arts; encouraging partnerships among the county's not-for-profit and for-profit organizations; and stimulating leadership among people of all ages.

Additionally, the foundation is in the first stages of developing an early childhood initiative in Morris County.

Our giving in the **Welfare of Animals** is national in scope and focuses on major undertakings that encourage the humane treatment of both companion and wild animals. The New Jersey Animal Assistance Program is our signature effort aiming to diminish the numbers of unwanted pets and to improve the conditions under which surrendered animals are kept.

Our environmental giving in **Critical Issues** currently has a focus on New Jersey land-use issues through: the preservation of vital open space (the Highlands region, Pine Barrens, and Delaware Bayshore area); encouraging municipalities to implement land-use plans that are in concert with the New Jersey State Plan; and making NJ cities more livable through creation of open spaces, greenways, and development of brownfields. Other areas of Critical Issues giving center on conservation of natural resources in NJ and the northeast, population and reproductive issues, and informing the public about environmental issues.

**Financial
Data**

(Year ended 12/31/00)	
Assets:	$ 328,490,000
Total grants paid:	$ 24,623,000
Number of grants paid:	383
Highest grant:	$ 375,000
Lowest grant:	$ 10,000

**Application
Procedures**

Applicants are advised to submit a one-page letter of inquiry to determine if a project falls within our guidelines. If a project has been funded in the past, a letter of inquiry is not necessary. Letters of inquiry may be submitted throughout the year, but must be received at least two weeks prior to the corresponding proposal submission deadline. Letters may be e-mailed to info@grdodge.org (without attachments) or sent standard mail. Applicants will be notified whether or not to submit a full proposal. The organization must either have 501(c)(3) status under the Internal Revenue code, or be a public entity. A team of program staff will review proposals received and determine which organizations fall within our current grantmaking strategy. A limited number of applicants will be visited by foundation staff to discuss proposals further. As funding decisions are made, applicants will be notified in writing.

Proposals should be submitted to the foundation's executive director and postmarked no later than the following deadlines to allow time for staff review: March 1 for the Arts; June 1 for Welfare of Animals, Morris County and Critical Issues; and November 1 for Education.

Grant Limitations

For effective focus of the foundation's energies, it is necessary to exclude from consideration such major fields as high education, health, and religion. Similarly, support for capital programs, equipment purchases, indirect costs, endowment funds, and deficit reduction are outside the guidelines.

Except through foundation-based initiatives, we do not support scholarship funds nor make direct awards to individuals. Also, we do not consider grants to conduit organizations. Because both federal law and the foundation's charter prohibit funding of any efforts to influence legislation, proposals should not request funding for lobbying efforts.

Meeting Times

The board of trustees meets quarterly.

Publications

The foundation distributes an annual report that includes a description of its grants and application guidelines.

THE DOUTY FOUNDATION

PHONE: (610) 828-8145

FAX: (610) 834-8175

P.O. Box 540

PLYMOUTH MEETING, PENNSYLVANIA 19462

Contact Person

Judith L. Bardes, Executive Director

Purpose

The Alfred and Mary Douty Foundation is a private grantmaking organization which supports projects that provide educational opportunities for disadvantaged people and social services. Grantmaking is concentrated in the Greater Philadelphia area with preference given to projects benefiting Montgomery and Philadelphia counties.

Areas of Interest

Projects which are educational or have the potential for positive social change and benefit disadvantaged people are the major focus of the foundation. General operation support is sometimes provided to small organizations. Most grants do not exceed $5,000 and are made for a one-year period.

Financial Data

(Year ended 12/31/00)	
Assets:	$ 7,742,068
Total grants paid:	$ 292,450
Number of grants paid:	
Highest grant:	$10,000
Lowest grant:	$ 750
Median grant size:	$3,000

Application Procedures

Deadlines for proposals are February 15, April 15, and October 15. Applicants must include seven copies of the foundation's proposal cover sheet which can be obtained by calling the foundation. One copy of the proposal should be sent along with the cover sheet and should include: name and purpose of the applicant organization; purpose of the grant; special nature of the project; leadership involved in the project; amount of funds requested and needed including other funds available; financial reports; leadership of the organization, including board of directors; and one copy of tax-exempt letter from the IRS.

Grant
Limitations

The foundation's support is primarily limited to the organizations that serve the greater Philadelphia area. Grants are not made for religious or political purposes; to organizations which discriminate on the basis or race, ethnic origin, sexual or religious preference, age or gender; or to organizations which are not tax-exempt under 501(c) (3). Organizations with annual budgets greater than $2 million are discouraged from applying for grants.

Meeting
Times

The board of directors meets three times a year to review grant requests.

Publications

The foundation publishes an annual report and grant guidelines.

THE EDUCATIONAL FOUNDATION OF AMERICA

PHONE: (203) 226-6498

FAX: (203) 227-0424

EMAIL: efa@efaw.org

WEB: www.efaw.org

35 CHURCH LANE

WESTPORT, CT 06880-3589

Contact Person

Diane M. Allison, Executive Director

Purpose

The Educational Foundation of America provides grants for work dealing with energy, environment, reproductive rights and population issues, Native Americans, the arts, education, medicine, and peace. The foundation prefers to fund smaller organizations, pilot projects, and projects designed to have long term effects, either environmentally or in a particular policy area.

Areas of Interest

The foundation is concerned with three main issues: protecting and conserving the environment; human overpopulation; and furthering of Native American education and preserving of indigenous cultures. The foundation also funds projects in the arts, specifically projects addressing the decline of theater audiences; education, specifically innovative programs for at-risk youth and substance abuse; and smaller projects in medicine and peace/conflict resolution.

Financial Data

(Year ended 12/31/00)	
Assets:	$ 206,311,046
Total grants paid:	$ 13,780,196
Total number of grants:	256
Highest grant:	$ 150,000
Lowest grant:	$ 15,000

THE EDUCATIONAL FOUNDATION OF AMERICA

Application Procedures

Before submitting a full proposal, applicants are required to submit a letter of inquiry. Full details are available on the foundation's web site. This letter should be no longer than two pages and signed by an officer of the organization. The letter should describe the organization's mission, location, region of focus, past and current projects, names and descriptions of founders and affiliation with other organizations. It should briefly and concisely state the proposed project as well as its objectives, significance and intended results, the project timetable, and the funding strategy for the project including the total budget for the project and the organization. This letter should be accompanied by a copy of the applicant's proof of tax-exempt status under the Internal Revenue Code. The foundation's staff will review the letter of inquiry and notify the organization whether or not to submit a full proposal. Inquiries and proposals are accepted throughout the year. There are no deadlines.

Grant Limitations

The foundation normally does not make grants for endowment or endowed faculty chairs, building programs, religious purposes, grants to individuals, annual fund-raising campaigns, indirect overhead or general support. Projects that focus on the United States are preferred. Only tax-exempt nonprofit organizations under 501(c)(3) status from the IRS are eligible for funds.

Meeting Times

The board of trustees meets once each quarter to consider grant requests.

Publications

The foundation maintains a web site at www.efaw.org.

THE O.P. AND W.E. EDWARDS FOUNDATION

PHONE: (406) 446-1077

FAX: (406) 446-1363

EMAIL: joeder@mac.com

WEB: www.fdncenter.org/grantmaker

/edwards

P.O. Box 2445

RED LODGE, MONTANA 59068

Contact Person

Jo Ann Eder, President

Purpose

The O.P. and W.E. Edwards Foundation is a small, unstaffed foundation with a particular interest in young people. Although most of its grants were specified in the donor's bequest, there is a discretionary grantmaking fund. With this fund, the foundation supports groups with strong neighborhood ties that are able to intervene effectively at those critical times in a youth's life when he or she most needs help and support.

Interests also include preventive programs to help socially and economically deprived children get the start they need to take advantage of later opportunities. It tends to favor organizations which take a comprehensive approach to these problems either within their own programs or as integral parts of a network of services in their communities. There are no geographic restrictions.

Areas of Interest

In the area of direct services to at-risk youth, the foundation looks for small programs that can work with young people in as most complete manner as feasible. Organizations should have strong leadership with a recognized presence in the community and be able to follow through effectively on their contacts with their target population. This population should include, but need not be limited to, economically and socially disadvantaged youth. The foundation is also interested in supporting projects in special issue areas such as truancy, juvenile delinquency and juvenile justice, teenage parenting, youth employability, chemical dependency, and the responsiveness of institutions.

In the prevention area, the foundation supports small organizations targeting economically disadvantaged children (and perhaps their families) at risk of becoming dependent on social services later in their lives. This can include: work with young children in day care or after school programs; family issues such as parenting skills, child abuse and neglect, and domestic violence; and youth empowerment in general through implementation of prevention curricula in schools, focused educational outreach and follow-up activities, and training of service providers in prevention.

Most of the foundation's efforts are for economic development in poor neighborhoods in support of its programmatic focus on economically disadvantaged people. Recently grants have generally been grouped in the following categories: start-up funds for new, untested programs where a successful demonstration is likely to attract other longer term support; grants for new projects of established organizations which are either likely to be institutionalized or have only a limited duration; interim general support for organizations which, although undergoing a transition, seem likely to stabilize in the near future; and long term annual support of certain organizations when needed.

Financial Data

(Year ended 8/31/00)	
Assets:	$ 5,500,000
Total grants paid:	$ 1,238,700
Number of grants paid:	51
Highest grant:	$ 75,000
Lowest grant:	$ 1,000
Median grant size:	$ 20,000

Application Procedures

The foundation does not accept unsolicited requests for funding. Grants are made in response to proposals the board of trustees solicits from organizations about which one or more trustees are closely acquainted.

Meeting Times

The board of trustees meets as needed to make grant decisions.

Publications

The fund distributes a description of its program interests and grantmaking policies on request.

EL POMAR FOUNDATION

10 Lake Circle

Colorado Springs, Colorado 80906

PHONE: (719) 633-7733

FAX: (719) 577-5702

EMAIL: grants@elpomar.org

WEB: www.elpomar.org

**Contact
Person**

Matt Carpenter, Program Officer

Purpose

The El Pomar Foundation supports community projects that it believes make a difference in the lives of the people of Colorado.

**Areas of
Interest**

The foundation awards grants in arts and humanities, civic and community, education, health, and human services. Additionally, it runs several grant initiatives which reward individuals who are committed to serving their communities and increase students' awareness of community issues and provide them with funds to address these issues in their own ways.

**Financial
Data**

(Year ended 12/31/99)	
Assets:	$ 452,314,792
Total grants paid:	$ 14,299,734*
Total number of grants:	367
Highest grant:	$ 2,000,000
Lowest grant:	$ 1,000

*This amount and the following analysis does not include grant program initiatives and program related investments.

**Application
Procedures**

The foundation does not have an application form. Proposals may be submitted at any time. Applicants should submit one copy of a proposal which includes name and address of organization; brief history, mission, and principal programs and accomplishments of organization; a concise statement of purpose or request for the project, expected contributions to population served, and criteria for evaluation; organizational budget and budget of project; and identification of other requests for aid over the last three years. Supporting documentation should include a copy of the organization's tax exempt status under IRS Sections 501(c)(3) and 509(a); audited financial statement for the last three years including the latest IRS Form 990; relationship and capacity of person signing application; a list of members of the governing body; and a statement that the grant's purpose has been approved by the applicant's governing body. Applications should be addressed to the Board of Trustees. Applicants also should furnish up to three pictures (photographs, architectural renderings, images from an existing publication, etc.) that portray the specific project or general operations of the organization. Pictures will be used in the presentation to the Board of Trustees. Applicants should not incur any costs related to this request. El Pomar Foundation will retain the photographs unless otherwise requested by the organization.

Grant Limitations

Grantmaking is limited to tax-exempt, charitable Colorado organizations and activities that take place in Colorado. Grants are not awarded to tax-supported institutions or public schools; organizations which distribute money to recipients of its own selection; organizations which do not have fiscal responsibility for the project; religious organizations for religious purposes; individuals or institutions for conferences, travel, or meetings; to cover deficits, debt elimination, or endowments; media projects; or to influence legislation or support candidates for political office.

Meeting Times

The board meets seven to nine times a year.

Publications

The foundation publishes an annual report and grant guidelines.

EMSA FUND, INC.
PHONE: 303-443-2723

827 Oakdale Road

Atlanta, Georgia 30307

(404) 373-1222

3761 Moffit Court

Boulder, Colorado 80304

Contact Persons

Alice Franklin, President (Georgia)

Andy Franklin, Chairman (Colorado)

Areas of Interest

The EMSA Fund, Inc. is a small, unstaffed family foundation. Its grant-making is focused on progressive grassroots organizations that promote self-determination in low income and traditionally disenfranchised communities, protect the environment, create alternative visual and performing arts, and address responsible foreign policy and peace.

It prefers advocacy organizations rather than direct service providers and rarely funds activities with broad public appeal and support. Most of its grants are directed toward local organizations in Georgia and Colorado, although awards are occasionally made to national organizations headquartered in these two states.

Financial Data

```
(Year ended    /   /   )
 Assets:                              NA
 Total grants paid:
 Number of grants paid:
 Highest grant:
 Lowest grant:
 Median grant size:
```

Application Procedures

The fund does not use application forms and has no deadlines. All inquiries should be in writing. As an initial contact, the fund prefers to receive a brief, two-page letter detailing the proposed project and information about the organization, the need to be met, past accomplishments (and disappointments), and expected results. Budget information, including the specific amount requested from the fund, should be provided, as well as proof of tax-exempt status (or proof of the tax-exempt status of a solid fiscal sponsor). Supporting materials such as brochures or newspaper clippings may be submitted. If additional information is needed, the fund will contact the applicant.

Grant Limitations

The fund does not make grants to individuals, for disease research, or to organizations with broad public appeal.

Meeting Times

Decisions on grant requests are made quarterly or more frequently.

Publications

None.

THE ENGELBERG FOUNDATION

PHONE: (212) 877-4050 ext. 233

FAX: (212) 787-7108

30 WEST 68TH STREET

NEW YORK, NEW YORK 10023

Contact Person

Rabbi Balfour Brickner, Executive Director

Purpose

The Engelberg Foundation is a private foundation that advances health care, education, and social services in the metropolitian New York City area. The foundation provides seed money for innovative pilot programs which have the potential for development to a point where other public or private institutions may provide more support to expand the programs. Additionally, the foundation supports projects which will help participants develop programs and strategies designed to benefit their own lives or communities.

Areas of Interest

In the health care area, the foundation support projects that improve primary health care and preventive medical and dental services for the working poor in urban neighborhoods; provide improved health education, counseling, and family planning services for adolescents; and foster scientific and social research in areas related to improved health care. In the educational area, the foundation supports programs designed to enrich the education, social development, and self-confidence of underprivileged children and encourage the pursuit of careers in health care services.

The foundation does not make grants of less than $25,000 per year unless a grant is to support an existing program which is considered to have exceptional merit. There is no upper limit on the amount or length of a grant, although all grants will be time limited and renewals or extensions will be based solely on the success of a program in meeting its objectives.

**Financial
Data**

```
(Year ended    /   /   )
Assets: in excess of                    NA
Total grants paid:
Total number of grants:
Highest grant:
Lowest grant:
Median grant size:
```

**Application
Procedures**

There are no formal application forms. Requests for grants should be made in writing to the executive director. Telephone solicitations and inquiries are discouraged. Written requests should contain a complete description of the organization requesting the funds, the program for which the funds are sought, an overall budget for the program, the sources from which such funding has or will be obtained, the identity and backgrounds of the key personnel responsible for the program, and any other information which will assist the foundation in evaluating the request.

**Grant
Limitations**

The foundation makes grants only to qualified charitable organizations under IRS Code 501(c)(3).

**Meeting
Times**

The executive director is the only employee. He and the Engelberg family make all funding decisions for the foundation.

Publications

The foundation publishes an information brochure.

FANNIE MAE FOUNDATION

PHONE: (202) 274-8057

4000 WISCONSIN AVENUE, N.W.

NORTH TOWER, SUITE ONE

WEB: www.fanniemaefoundation.org

WASHINGTON, DC 20016

Contact Person

Grants Management Department

Purpose

The Fannie Mae Foundation creates affordable homeownership and housing opportunities through innovative partnerships and initiatives that build healthy, vibrant communities across the United States. The Foundation is specially committed to improving the quality of life for the people of its hometown, Washington, D.C., and to enhancing the livability of the city's neighborhoods.

Areas of Interest

The foundation has three areas of interest. They are:

Increasing the Affordable Housing Supply

Eligible organizations are those working city-, county- , region-, or nationwide to increase the supply of affordable housing by undertaking one or more of the following activities:

• Producing high-quality, affordable homeownership and rental units at scale for low- and moderate-income individuals and families through new construction or rehabilitation in ways that build individual wealth and create stronger, more vibrant communities.
• Preserving, at scale, affordable rental units that are at risk of conversion to market rate housing specifically, preserving such housing for low- and moderate-income individuals and families in ways that build individual wealth and create stronger, more vibrant communities.
• Providing low- and moderate-income individuals and families with owner-occupied rehabilitation services and other related products and services that help to preserve the housing stock, sustain homeownership, build individual wealth, and create stronger, more vibrant communities.

• Financing the production or preservation of such affordable housing in ways that build individual and community wealth and create stronger, more vibrant communities.

• Promoting the increased production and/or preservation of affordable housing through the development and implementation of system reforms or exploration of catalytic opportunities, for example through building the capacity of nonprofit developers, intermediaries and networks; sharing best practices and lessons learned; supporting innovative solutions to such critical challenges that can create development opportunities.

• Building support for, and/or reducing barriers or disincentives to increasing the supply of affordable housing.

• Engaging in efforts that may potentially be replicated or increase efficiencies in the affordable housing field.

Increase Sustainable Homeownership, Build Indiviual/Community Wealth
Eligible organizations are those with proven experience providing comprehensive pre- and post-purchase homeownership counseling and education resulting in sustainable homeownership that builds individual and community wealth. Competitive applicants will have the following characteristics:

• Offer or provide access to comprehensive, quality, affordable, connected homeownership services, including financial and home-buyer counseling; flexible, affordable loan products; real estate, insurance, legal, and home rehabilitation services; housing supply in areas with the potential for price appreciation; competitive refinance products; and post-purchase counseling.

• Work city- , county- , or region-wide or as part of a collaborative.

• Are certified by HUD or have some other industry-acknowledged stamp of approval including affiliation with a nationally recognized network.

• Demonstrate demand for their services and outreach plans to attract participants with the potential to achieve wealth-building homeownership.

• Serve a reasonable number of people, given the size of the market in which they work and the needs of its residents.

• Have a proven track record in increasing the number of low- to moderate-income homeowners in their market and tracking their success over time.

• Connect their programs and services with broader regional efforts to increase individual and community wealth.

Create Healthy and Vibrant Neighborhoods in Washington, D.C.
Housing

Eligible organizations are those working to create healthy, vibrant neighborhoods in the District of Columbia by preserving rental and homeownership units (multi- and single-family) that are at risk of conversion to market-rate housing. The Foundation will give priority to organizations engaged in preserving housing that is affordable for Washington, D.C., residents earning up to 60 percent of the area median income. The Foundation also will review requests to support the preservation or production of housing for residents earning up to 80 percent of the area median income.

The Foundation accepts applications from organizations that meet both the general selection criteria above and one or more of the following specific criteria:

• A proven track record in increasing the supply of affordable housing through the preservation of rental or homeownership units.
• A proven track record in civic engagement efforts that support the preservation of affordable rental or homeownership units (priority will be given to civic engagement efforts focused on developing grassroots leadership).
• A proven track record in housing counseling efforts that educate residents in financial management/literacy and/or give pre- and post-purchase counseling.

Education
Eligible organizations are those working in the District of Columbia to:

• Improve adult literacy in Washington, D.C.
• Improve education by providing teacher professional development, curriculum content aligned with District of Columbia Public School curriculum standards, or principal training in instructional leadership.

Financial Data

Please see our Annual Report, which can be found on our web site at www.fanniemaefoundation.org.

Application Procedures

The Foundation awards most of its grants by soliciting proposals from organizations with the demonstrated ability to create strong partnerships with the Foundation. We also set aside a limited amount of grant funding to be awarded through a competitive process. Information on our competitive grant application process can be found on our web site at www.fanniemaefoundation.org.

SAMUEL S. FELS FUND

1616 WALNUT STREET, SUITE 800

PHILADELPHIA, PENNSYLVANIA 19103

PHONE: (215) 731-9455

FAX: (215) 731-9457

WEB: www.samfels.org

Contact Person

Helen Cunningham, Executive Director

Purpose

The Samuel S. Fels Fund is a Philadelphia foundation with interests in human services, education, and the arts. Within these broad categories, the fund seeks to support projects that help to demonstrate and evaluate ways to prevent, lessen, or resolve contemporary social problems, or that seek to provide permanent improvement in the provision of services.

Areas of Interest

The fund's priorities are organizations and projects located within the city of Philadelphia and directed toward making permanent improvements in community services, specifically in the areas of education, the arts, and community programs. The fund prefers to make grants on a modest scale that will have maximum impact upon institutions and service patterns in Philadelphia. The fund seeks programs that monitor public responsibilities, strengthen neighborhood life, and improve public education. The fund also promotes increased stability for arts organizations.

Financial Data

(Year ended 12/31/00)	
Assets:	$ 55,617,574
Total grants paid:	$ 2,239,673
Number of grants paid:	180
Highest grant:	$ 200,000
Lowest grant:	$ 1,000
Median grant size:	$ 9,000

Application
Procedures

Grant proposals are considered throughout the year, except for arts applications, which are reviewed only twice annually, in January and May. In general, the fund accepts only one proposal from an organization per year. The fund provides applicants with a proposal outline on request. Preliminary inquiries concerning possible applications may be made by telephone. The fund specifically discourages preliminary letters or abbreviated proposals, since only full proposals are accepted for board consideration.

The full proposal should include a cover sheet (also provided by the fund). The body of the proposal should include, in no more than five pages, the following information: a summary of the proposal; background on the organization, including its history and the history of the problem to be addressed, its purpose and goals, a summary of activities and accomplishments (with highlights of the past year including people involved and specific events), the constituency or membership, and a description of interaction with other organizations; the funding request and plans for the coming year, including a description of the organization (or project) program objectives and events and activities planned, number of people involved, number of staff involved, and a timetable; and a description of how the program will be evaluated.

Attachments should include resumes of top staff; a board of directors list including addresses and occupation (indicating any minority, low-income, consumer and/or neighborhood representatives); an annual operating budget for the organization and a project budget (if appropriate); a list of funding sources including past major contributors and amounts, recent applications with results, and anticipated future funding sources; a recent financial statement (audited if available); an annual report (if available); relevant newspaper or magazine articles about the organization's program; and a copy of the most recent IRS letter certifying the applicant's tax-exempt status (and a copy of the IRS letter formally approving a change of name, if appropriate).

Notification of approval or decline of a grant is usually provided within two weeks after a decision by the board of directors. Progress reports from approved grantees stating what has been accomplished and providing appropriate financial reports are required by the fund at least annually.

Grant
Limitations

Only organizations located in the city of Philadelphia, PA are eligible. The fund generally excludes from its grantmaking program contributions to building and development funds, scholarships, fellowships, and grants-in-aid to individuals for travel. Ordinarily the fund also avoids making grants for continuing major programs of large institutions and contributions to endowment funds and to national organizations.

**Meeting
Times**

The board of directors meets eight times a year to consider grant applications.

Publications

The fund publishes an annual report.

FIELD FOUNDATION OF ILLINOIS

PHONE: (312) 831-0910

FAX: (312) 831-0961

200 S. Wacker Drive, Suite 3860

WEB: www.fieldfoundation.org

Chicago, Illinois 60606

Contact Person

Aurie Pennick, Executive Director

Purpose

The Field Foundation of Illinois makes an effort to play a constructive and responsible role in supporting young, struggling, grassroots, community-based programs and older, established institutions in the greater Chicago area.

Areas of Interest

The foundation considers only applications in the fields of health, community welfare, education, culture, conservation, and urban and community affairs from institutions and agencies primarily serving the people of the Chicago metropolitan area.

Preference is given to innovative approaches to solving specific problems. In addition, the board looks at the need for the project, the applicant's ability to meet this need effectively, and the use of volunteers when applicable. Operating support is provided up to three years.

The two newest grantmaking programs are the primary and secondary school education program and the environment program. The first provides grants, up to $20,000, to individual schools to improve curriculum, teaching quality, parental involvement. The second supports innovative initiatives in environmental protection and conservation at the neighborhood level in Chicago metropolitan communities.

Application Procedures

The foundation has no application forms but requires brief, concise proposals for funding. A proposal should describe in detail the amount of support requested, length of funding, anticipated outcomes, implementation plans, personnel and their qualifications, evaluation plans, and total project cost and other funding sources once grant period is over. Supporting documentation should include brief history of organization, budget for current financial year and most recent audited financial statement, list of board of directors and their affiliations, and a copy of the IRS 501(c)(3) tax-exempt letter. There are no deadlines for submission, but the board meets three times a year to review proposals.

Financial Data

(Year ended 4/30/00)	
Assets:	$ 51,317,536
Total grants paid:	$ 1,947,428
Number of grants paid:	117
Highest grant:	$ 100,000
Lowest grant:	$ 5,000
Median grant size:	$ 24,000

Grant Limitations

The foundation supports only projects primarily serving the people of the Chicago metropolitan area. Operating support of a program will normally be of a short duration, generally one to three years. Requests for continuing operating support will not be considered.

No grants for regular operating support are made to member agencies of the United Way of Metropolitan Chicago, or to member agencies of other community chests in the metropolitan area. The foundation does not support: scholarships, fellowships, or other requests from individuals; medical research or national health agency appeals; organizations or committees whose efforts are aimed at influencing legislation; private schools; conferences, seminars, or meetings; the costs of printed materials; organizations working to achieve religious purposes; general operating budgets of neighborhood health centers or clinics, day care centers for children, or small cultural groups.

Meeting Times

The board of directors meets three times a year.

Publications

The foundation publishes an annual report.

THE FORD FOUNDATION

320 East 43rd Street

New York, New York 10017

PHONE: (212) 573-5000

FAX: (212) 351-3677

EMAIL:office-secretary@fordfound.org

WEB:www.fordfound.org

Contact Person

Barron M. Tenny, Secretary

Purpose

The Ford Foundation is a worldwide foundation supporting innovative people and institutions who have fresh ideas about ways to improve human welfare. Its goals are to:

Strengthen democratic values,
Reduce poverty and injustice,
Promote international cooperation, and
Advance human achievement

Areas of Interest

Asset Building and Community Development

The Asset Building and Community Development program helps strengthen and increase the effectiveness of people and organizations working to find solutions to problems of poverty and injustice. Sixty-five staff members focus grant resources on six fields in three program units in New York and abroad.

We support people who leverage human, social, financial and environmental assets to promote social change. Grants support vibrant and robust social movements, institutions and partnerships that analyze contemporary social and economic needs and devise responses to them.

Human Development and Reproductive Health

The Human Development and Reproductive Health unit coordinates efforts to build human assets while strengthening the relationships and social networks that people need to improve their lives. We work in two fields to accomplish these goals:

• With children, youth and families we support organizations and promote policies that help families mobilize human and social assets to overcome poverty and discrimination.

• In sexuality and reproductive health we focus on the social, cultural and economic factors that affect sexuality and reproductive health. Emphasis is given to nongovernmental organizations, researchers and government agencies acting on the expanded understanding of sexuality and reproductive health reached at major United Nations conferences in the last decade. A primary concern is empowering women to participate in improving reproductive health and related policies.

Economic Development

The Economic Development unit seeks to make durable economic improvements in the lives of the disadvantaged. The unit coordinates efforts in two fields:

• In development finance and economic security we support organizations that help businesses create employment opportunities and help low-income people acquire, develop and maintain savings, investments, businesses, homes, land and other assets.

• In work-force development we support organizations that help improve the ways low-income people develop marketable job skills and acquire and retain reliable employment that provides livable wages.

Community and Resource Development

The Community and Resource Development unit coordinates work in two fields that aim to create conditions for the development of sustainable and equitable communities.

• In environment and development we help people and groups acquire, protect and improve land, water, forests, wildlife and other natural assets in ways that help reduce poverty and injustice.

• In community development we seek to improve the quality of life and opportunities for positive change in urban and rural communities. Our goal is to develop community-based institutions that mobilize and leverage philanthropic capital, investment capital, social capital and natural resources in a responsible and fair manner.

In all these units, grant making is also helping to establish and fortify organizations and institutions that support asset building through research, training, policy analysis and advocacy.

Grant making aims to help low-income people and communities build the financial, human, social and natural resource assets they need to overcome poverty and injustice. By supporting and building strong fields, we will be able to continue devising strategies appropriate to new situations.

Peace and Social Justice Program

The Human Rights and International Cooperation unit coordinates efforts in two fields:

- In human rights we promote access to justice and the protection of civil, political, economic, social and cultural rights.
- In international cooperation we encourage cooperation between nations toward a more peaceful and equitable international order based on pluralism and tolerance.

The unit supports organizations working on international human rights as well as the rights of women, members of minority groups and refugees. New initiatives are exploring diverse approaches to achieving reconciliation and justice at the end of a period of massive crimes against human rights. Grant making focuses on the International Criminal Court as well as discrete efforts in countries as diverse as Nigeria, Argentina, Indonesia, Russia and South Africa. Grants for international cooperation focus on foreign policy, resolving conflicts, encouraging peacemaking and curbing nuclear proliferation. New work is fostering greater recognition of developing-country economic issues in the regulation of global markets and the decision making of multilateral institutions like the International Monetary Fund and the World Trade Organization.

The second unit, Governance and Civil Society, also works in two fields:

- In governance we foster effective, transparent, accountable and responsible governmental institutions guided by the rule of law and dedicated to reducing inequality.
- In civil society our goal is to strengthen the civic and political participation of people and groups in charting the future of their societies.

The unit supports efforts to improve government performance, build public awareness of budget and tax issues and confront the challenges posed by government decentralization. To address concerns about electoral reform, campaign finance, voting and women in politics, a new grant-making emphasis will focus on political equality in the United States.

Through work on civil society, grants will seek to increase participation in public affairs beyond voting while strengthening civil society organizations and the practice of philanthropy needed to guarantee their long-term sustainability. Another new grant-making portfolio focuses on global civil society and on the role of transnational citizens' coalitions in addressing the world's pressing social problems.

The Peace and Social Justice program is committed to documenting our work and sharing the knowledge gained among staff members, grantees and others. One example of this commitment is the Budget and Fiscal Analysis

Network (BFAN), which facilitates learning, capacity building and the sharing of experience across 20 countries on how citizens can promote transparency, accountability and participation in government budgeting. In a similar vein, the foundation recently established the Network on Economic, Social and Cultural Rights to help advocates, government officials and NGO's develop ways to enforce these new categories of rights.

Education, Media, Arts and Culture Program

The Education, Media, Arts and Culture program focuses on strengthening the roles leaders in these sectors play in broadening knowledge, opportunity, creativity and freedom of expression. Nearly 30 staff members pursue these goals in two program units in our New York headquarters and in our overseas offices.

Education, Knowledge and Religion (EKR)

The Education, Knowledge and Religion (EKR) unit seeks to enhance educational opportunity, especially for low-income and chronically disadvantaged groups, and to address the challenges of diversity using interdisciplinary and collaborative approaches. The unit works in three fields to pursue these goals:
• In education reform we seek to enhance the capacity of schools and higher education institutions to broaden access while pursuing higher levels of student achievement, especially for historically underserved groups. In this way, we help reduce poverty and inequality by promoting better educational practices for all students.
• In higher education and scholarship our goal is to expand knowledge and deepen scholarship, curriculum and public understanding of pluralism and identity. We support social science training as a means of educating a new generation of leaders and scholars who can be more effective in their civic roles, helping to chart the future of their societies.
• In religion, society and culture we are pursuing a deeper understanding of religion as a powerful force in contemporary life and a resource for strengthening the cultural values and social practices that support democracy, human achievement, justice, equity and cooperation.

Media, Arts and Culture (MAC)

The Media, Arts and Culture (MAC) unit seeks to strengthen the arts and media as important contributors to the communities and societies in which they function. The unit works in two fields to accomplish these goals:
• In media our work aims to promote free and responsible news media and to develop infrastructures that serve the civic needs of society and its diverse

constituencies. In addition, we support the development of media policy and high-quality productions that enrich public dialogue on such issues as building democratic values and pluralism.

• In arts and culture our goal is to strengthen opportunities for artistic creativity and cultural expression that will generate the hope, understanding, courage and confidence necessary to help citizens fulfill their potential.

Program-Related Investments (PRI's)

Each year the foundation invests a portion of its endowment in projects that advance philanthropic purposes in various areas of the foundation's interest. The Trustees have earmarked up to $180 million of the corpus for these investments. The investments are in the form of debt or equity financing or loan guarantees. As of September 30, 2000, $136.7 million in investments and $115,000 in guarantees were outstanding and $25.7 million in funding commitments were in process. During the fiscal year, new PRI loan commitments of $16.5 million were made, and $14.3 million were disbursed. Principal repayments of $11.4 million and investment income of $1.3 million were received.

Financial Data

(Year ended 9/30/00)	
Assets:	$ 14,659,683,000
Total grants paid:	$ 653,205,000
Number of grants paid:	2,639
Median grant size:	$ 120,000

Application Procedures

Before a detailed, formal application is made, applicants are urged to consult the foundation's most recent annual report and statement of current interests. A brief letter of inquiry is advisable in order to determine whether the foundation's interests and funds permit consideration of a proposal. If a proposal is submitted, it should be noted that there are no application forms. Proposals should set forth: objectives; the proposed program for pursuing objectives; qualifications of persons engaged in the work; a detailed budget; present means of support and status of applications to other funding sources; and tax-exempt status of the applicant.

Applications are considered throughout the year. Normally, applicants may expect to receive an initial indication of whether the proposed request falls within the foundation's interests and budgetary limitations within one month after submitting an inquiry. Domestic applications should be sent to the Secretary, Ford Foundation, at the address in New York City. Applicants in foreign areas where the foundation has an office should direct proposals to the nearest foundation office.

Grant Limitations

Most of the foundation's grant funds are given to organizations. While the foundation also makes grants to individuals, such grants are: few in number relative to the demand; limited to research, training, and other activities related to the foundation's program interests; and subject to IRS limitations and requirements. The foundation does not award undergraduate scholarships, nor are grants awarded for purely local or personal needs. Most support for graduate fellowships is funneled through grants to universities and other organizations, which are responsible for the selection of recipients.

Grants are not made for medical projects (except as they affect population problems), programs for which substantial government support is readily available, religious activities are such, routine operating costs of institutions, or, except in rare cases, for the construction or maintenance of buildings.

Meeting Times

The board of trustees meets three times a year.

Publications

Of particular relevance to potential grantees are the following Ford Foundation publications: the annual report, which contains a complete review of grants and financing, and the booklet titled "Current Interests," which includes grant application procedures. A list of publications and films may be obtained from the Ford Foundation, Office of Reports. The Ford Foundation "Report" contains articles about the Foundation's grantmaking activities, and is published four times a year.

FOUNDATION FOR THE CAROLINAS

PHONE: (704) 973-4500

FAX: (704) 973-4599

EMAIL: djonas@fftc.org

217 SOUTH TRYON STREET

WEB: www.fftc.org

CHARLOTTE, NORTH CAROLINA 28202

Contact Person

Donald K. Jonas, Ph.D., Senior Vice President, Community Philanthropy

Areas of Interest

The Foundation for the Carolinas is a community foundation serving North and South Carolina, with a particular long-standing interest in the Charlotte-Mecklenburg area.

In distributing its unrestricted grant funds, the foundation gives priority to seed grants to organizations in the Charlotte, North Carolina area initiating promising new projects, to innovative and efficient approaches for meeting community needs and opportunities, to challenge gifts that require other donors to make matching gifts, to organizations working cooperatively with other programs in their community, and to applicants that demonstrate a plan for funding and likely support from other sources. Most grants are $5,000 and less.

Financial Data

(Year ended 12/31/94–99)	
Assets:	$ 245,000,000
Total grants paid:	$ 30,000,000

Application Procedures

The deadlines for submitting complete, formal proposals to the foundation are February 1, May 1, June 1, and October 1. Application forms are available on request.

Applicants should provide one copy of their proposal and one copy of their most recent audit to the foundation by the required deadline. Attachments to the application form should include: a cover letter (not more than two pages)

addressing concisely the objectives and background of the project, a demonstrated need for the project, specific plans and timetables, current and long-term funding plans of the organization, and the qualifications of the applicant organization and the personnel who will be responsible for the project. Applicants should also provide an overall budget for the organization as well as a budget for the specific project (showing income and expenditures), a list of members of the applicant organization's governing body, and a copy of the applicant's official notice of tax-exempt status from the Internal Revenue Service.

Grant Limitations

The foundation limits its discretionary funding to organizations in the Charlotte, North Carolina area recognized by the IRS as tax-exempt under Section 501(c)(3) of the Internal Revenue Code and serving the communities from which the foundation derives its support. Generally, the foundation does not support capital campaigns, general operating budgets of existing organizations, publication of books, conferences, production of videos, purchase of computers or vehicles.

Meeting Times

The distribution committee meets in February, June, and October to review grant proposals.

Publications

The foundation publishes an annual report.

FOUNDATION FOR THE MID SOUTH

PHONE: (601) 355-8167

FAX: (601) 355-6499

1230 RAYMOND ROAD, BOX 700

WEB: www.fndmidsouth.org

JACKSON, MISSISSIPPI 39204

Contact Persons

George Penick, President

Beverly Divers-White, Vice President

Steven Cooper, Project Director, Philanthropy and the Black Church

Barbara Hunter-Cox, Project Director, Mid South Middle Start

Lynn McGee, Program Manager for Workforce Alliance

Purpose

The Foundation For the Mid South is a non-profit organization that serves the delta regions of Arkansas, Louisiana and Mississippi. The foundation makes grants and initiates programs in the areas of economic development, education, and families and children. It works in partnership with community-based organizations across the region, transcending political, racial and economic barriers to build the communities, resources and leadership in the region.

Areas of Interest

The foundation awards grants to organizations that address issues in economic development, education, families and children, leadership development, and the Black church.

Financial Data

(Year ended 12/31/00)	
Assets:	$ 17,580,927
Total grants paid:	$ 565,194
Total number of grants:	53
Highest grant:	$ 10,000
Lowest grant:	$ 1,500
Median grant size:	$ 5,000

**Application
Procedures**

Applicants should first contact the foundation for current grant guidelines in their area of interest.

**Grant
Limitations**

Grant limitations vary according to program area and type of grant awarded.

**Meeting
Times**

The board of trustees meets three times a year in winter, summer and fall.

Publications

The foundation publishes an annual report, grant guidelines, a quarterly newsletter, a membership brochure, and "MapFacts."

THE FREDDIE MAC FOUNDATION

PHONE: (703) 918-8888

FAX: (703) 918-8895

Mailstop 259

EMAIL: see website

8200 Jones Branch Drive

WEB: www.freddiemacfoundation.org

McLean, Virginia 22102

Contact Person

Tia Waller-Pryde, Grants Manager

Purpose

The Freddie Mac Foundation supports programs that strengthen the health, education, and welfare of children and youth and provide family support services. Funds are provided to a variety of nonprofit organizations serving children and their families which are located in metropolitan Washington, D.C. as well as statewide initiatives in Maryland and Virginia. Some funding is available for national projects.

Areas of Interest

Comprehensive programs that focus on prevention and young children, ages birth to five, will be given first priority. The three areas that are given priority for funding are:

• Education. Projects that strive to prepare children for the future. Areas included are innovative early childhood education and child development programs; school age programs focusing on critically needed skills; programs that encourage parental involvement; and innovative vocational education programs.

• Strengthening families. Projects that focus on the prevention of child abuse and neglect.

• Systems reform. Programs that advocate for coordinated, prevention-focused, child- and family-friendly projects. Included in this area are advocacy organizations (both local and national), demonstration projects, and replication of proven programs that stimulate system reform and public-private partnership and foundation-driven efforts to affect systems and policies.

Financial Data

```
(Year ended    /  /   )
Assets:                              NA
Total grants paid:
Total number of grants:
Highest grant:
Lowest grant:
Median grant size:
```

Application Procedures

Applicants should request guidelines from the foundation. Prior to submitting a proposal, applicants should also telephone the foundation to ensure the acceptability of the proposal. The Washington Regional Association of Grantmakers Common Application Form is the preferred format for proposals. There are two deadlines for submission of proposals: April 2 with notification by July 23, and September 4 with notification by December 3.

Grant Limitations

The foundation awards grants only to nonprofit tax-exempt charitable organizations under IRS code 501(c)(3); and to organizations that do not discriminate in the hiring of staff on the basis or race, religion, sex, national origin, or disabilities. Additionally it does not provide funds for individuals, training or promotion of religious doctrine, or for incurring a debt liability. The maximum grant award is $50,000.

Meeting Times

The board of trustees meets quarterly to consider grant requests.

Publications

The foundation publishes an annual report and an informational packet.

FUND FOR THE CITY OF NEW YORK

121 AVENUE OF THE AMERICAS

SIXTH FLOOR

NEW YORK, NEW YORK 10013

PHONE: (212) 925-6675

FAX: (212) 925-5675

EMAIL: smccrea@fcny.org

WEB: www.fcny.org

Contact Person

Mary McCormick, President

Purpose

The Fund for the City of New York is an independent private operating foundation and public charity established by the Ford Foundation in 1968. The fund's mandate is to be responsive to the problems of New York City and to opportunities to improve the performance of its government and the quality of life of its citizens.

Areas of Interest

The fund seeks to improve the functioning of New York City government agencies and nonprofit organizations by introducing innovative programs, technologies, and methodologies and concentrates its programs in the areas of children and youth, community development, the urban environment, and AIDS. It operates a broad array of programs and acts as management consultant, computer and information technologist, banker, grant maker, neutral convener and broker, and incubator of new programs.

The fund's main areas of current work are listed below followed by a pair of examples in each case:

• Technology and Information: vehicle routing for New York City school buses and case tracking for New York State Division of Human Rights.

• Government Management: large-scale planning for TB control and HHC managed care and international exchanges between New York City/Chicago/Los Angeles and Japan.

• Youth Development: Youth Development Institute to recast youth policies and networks for youth development strengthening youth programs.

• Organizational Assistance: bridge financing for nonprofits through the Cash Flow Loan Program and administrative help for new enterprises through the Incubator Program.

**Financial
Data**

> (Year ended   /   /   )
> Support and revenue: NA
> Total grants paid:
> Number of grants paid:
> Highest grant:
> Lowest grant:
> Median grant size:

**Application
Procedures**

Organizations interested in grants, cash flow loans, or information on the Nonprofit Computer Exchange and other programs should call the fund for application procedures and/or information.

Grantseekers are asked to submit a proposal or a brief letter describing their project. If the proposed project fits the fund's guidelines, staff will contact the applicant and request further information.

Eligible applicants for cash flow loans of up to $50,000 (made against delayed payments on government contracts or, occasionally, foundation or corporate grants) will be asked to submit a letter containing a brief program description; details on the contract, its purpose, amount, status within the bureaucracy; the reasons why the loan is required, how much is needed, and exactly how the funds will be used; a definite repayment schedule based on when money is expected from the funding source; and the name and phone number of an official who can verify the information provided. The applicant must also submit copies of the contract, a copy of the IRS ruling under section 501(c)(3); most recent financial report and a list of board members.

**Grant
Limitations**

Grants are restricted to projects with an intended bearing on New York City and are limited to qualifying charitable organizations. The fund does make grants to individuals, nor does it support endowment or capital campaigns. The fund does not provide support to academic programs.

**Meeting
Times**

The board meets three times a year.

Publications

The fund publishes a periodic annual report and makes available information about its programs upon request.

FUND FOR SOUTHERN COMMUNITIES

315 WEST PONCE DE LEON, SUITE 1061

DECATUR, GEORGIA 30030

PHONE: (404) 371-8404

FAX: (404) 371-8496

EMAIL: grants@fundforsouth.org

WEB: www.fundforsouth.org

Contact Persons

Alice Eason Jenkins, Executive Director

Purpose

The Fund for Southern Communities is a community-based public foundation supporting social change in the South. Through its fundraising and grantmaking programs, The fund seeks to be an effective link between individuals desiring to fund progressive endeavors and a broad range of community organizations which need their support.

Areas of Interest

The fund invites applications from organizations: working against discrimination based on race, sex, age, religion, economic status, sexual preference, ethnic background, or physical and mental disabilities; struggling for the rights of workers; promoting self-determination in low income and disenfranchised communities; protecting the environment and developing appropriate technologies; creating alternative arts and media; promoting peace and responsible U.S. foreign policy; and working for an equitable distribution of economic and political power.

A variety of issues are supported, including but not limited to: community organizing, women's rights, civil rights, anti-racist organizing, workers' rights, lesbian and gay rights, environmental justice, community economic development, alternative culture and media, militarism and peace, civil liberties, and Native American rights.

FUND FOR SOUTHERN COMMUNITIES

**Financial
Data**

(Year ended 6/30/01)	
Support and revenue:	$ 600,000
Total grants paid:	$ 355,000
Number of grants paid:	100
Highest grant:	$ 10,000
Lowest grant:	$ 1,000
Median grant size:	$ 3,000

**Application
Procedures**

The fund accepts applications throughout the year, and makes grants twice a year, in the spring and fall. To obtain an application, telephone or write to the fund. Staff is available to answer questions about eligibility before an application is completed. Complete instructions come with the application package.

After an initial review of the applications, the board selects the strongest proposals and requests interviews. At this time applicants no longer under consideration are notified. Following a second evaluation by the board, final decisions are made. The whole process takes about three months.

**Grant
Limitations**

Although requests must be submitted from projects/programs operating in North Carolina, South Carolina, or Georgia, a project may operate in one or more of these states. The fund awards seed grants to new projects, general support and project grants to small organizations. Direct service applicants are discouraged from applying, unless the services are tied to social change programs or are likely to empower the community to be served.

**Meeting
Times**

The board of directors meets twice a year to make grant awards.

Publications

The fund publishes an annual report, grants listings, a fall and spring newsletter, brochures, and application form.

THE FUNDING EXCHANGE/ NATIONAL GRANTS PROGRAMS

666 BROADWAY, SUITE 500

NEW YORK, NEW YORK 10012

PHONE: (212) 529-5300

FAX: (212) 982-9272

EMAIL: info@fex.org

WEB: www.fex.org

Contact Persons

Charlene Allen, Director of Grantmaking

Purpose

The Funding Exchange is a national network of alternative foundations committed to funding progressive grassroots organizing. Member funds, based in different cities or regions of the country, are autonomous, with their own leadership boards and grantmaking guidelines, and should be approached directly. A current list of the Funding Exchange member funds is available from the national office in New York.

The Funding Exchange national grantmaking program includes:

• The Paul Robeson Fund for Independent Media, which support film, video and radio production on social and political issues;

• The OUT Fund for Lesbian and Gay Liberation, which support radical organizing against heterosexism and homophobia;

• The Saguaro Fund, which support community organizing, primarily in communities of color in the United States and Puerto Rico;

• The Ignacio Martin-Baró Fund, which support grassroots projects which foster psychological well-being, social consciousness and active resistance in communities affected by violence, particularly in Central America, southern Africa and the Philippines, and

• The Donor-Advised Program, which funds a broad range of community-based organizations challenging social and economic injustice, and working to change the circumstances and the social and institutional systems that lead to oppression.

Areas of Interest

In general, the Funding Exchange gives high priority to organizations that are working with historically powerless constituencies for a more equitable distribution of wealth and power in society, organizing in communities and work places around basic economic and social issues, working actively against oppression based on class, gender, race, sexual orientation, age and physical or mental disabilities, operating in a democratic manner and involving the constituencies they serve, both in their leadership and their membership, and limited in their access to traditional sources of funding.

Nearly all national grantmaking program funds go to U.S. based projects, but some overseas projects do receive funding, primarily in Central America, the Caribbean (particularly Puerto Rico, Cuba, and Haiti), the Philippines, southern Africa, South America and the Middle East. Priorities for international funding include groups that are building political and economic self-determination, and encourage North/South and South/South dialogue. The Martin-Baró Fund, which makes most of its grants to groups outside the U.S. has a special application format. This is increasingly true for overseas funding. Grantseekers should obtain the guidelines booklet for more details regarding international funding priorities and procedures before submitting any material for review.

Financial Data

```
(Year ended    /   /   )
Assets:                            NA
Total grants paid:
Total number of grants:
Highest grant:
Lowest grant:
Median grant size:
```

Application Procedures

Contact the national office for the guidelines booklet, which details the application procedures and lists the relevant deadlines. In most cases, grant seekers should send a letter of inquiry by a specified date. Grantseekers who are asked to submit a full proposal will receive an application package.

In most cases, grant seekers will be applying to national grants program, not to specific funds or the donor-advised program; the grants department staff will route applications to the appropriate fund. There are different application procedures for the Robeson Fund, the Martin-Baró Fund, and some international grants. Grantseekers should begin by obtaining the current guidelines booklet.

**Grant
Limitations**

The Funding Exchange national grants program does not fund capital campaigns, endowments or deficit financing, organizations with relatively large budgets (generally over $1 million) and access to traditional or mainstream funding sources, such as the federal government or the United Way, individuals, research projects or fellowships, publications or cultural endeavors which do not demonstrate a capacity to organize the recipients of those services around specific issues; and other foundations.

**Meeting
Times**

Meeting times vary but most grant decisions are made in the spring and fall. Check the guidelines brochure for details.

Publications

The fund publishes a grant lists and guidelines brochure.

GENERAL MILLS FOUNDATION*

ONE GENERAL MILLS BOULEVARD

GOLDEN VALLEY, MN 55426

PHONE: (763) 764-2211

FAX: (763) 764-4114

WEB: www.generalmills.com/foundation

Contact Person

Chris Shea, President

Purpose

The General Mills Foundation serves as a channel through which General Mills, Inc. makes philanthropic contributions. The foundation seeks to balance its support between established organizations and small, developing programs that promise to make important contributions in the future.

Areas of Interest

The foundation makes grants in the three general areas of education, health and social action, and arts and culture. In education, General Mills supports programs that emphasize student achievement and opportunity, literacy and efforts to improve the quality of educational services. In health and social actions, the foundation funds projects that provide high-quality services to children and youth, such as parent education and strengthening the family. The foundation's support of arts and culture provides grants for programs that enhance and sustain excellence in performing and visual arts.

The foundation supports organizations who: offer direct services to the public; provide services for families, young children and school-age youth; engage involvement by General Mills employees; and have concentrations of General Mill's employees in their communities.

Application Procedures

The foundation strongly requests that all initial inquiries be made by mail, not by telephone or personal visit. The foundation does not require application forms. A brief letter with supporting documentation is an acceptable application. There are no application deadlines; proposals are accepted at any time.

* The General Mills Foundation has now merged with the Pillsbury Company Foundation.

The letter should include: a description of the purpose for which the grant is sought; specific details on how this purpose will be achieved by the grant; description of the constituency that will benefit from the project; evidence that the persons proposing the project are able to carry it to completion; a planned method of evaluation; a specific budget for the project, as well as the operating budget for the organization's current fiscal year, showing anticipated sources of revenue, as well as expenses; a brief description of the organization requesting support, with a list of officers and board members; an audited financial statement and the most recent IRS Form 990 (including Schedule A); a major donor list for the most recent and the current fiscal years listing the amount of support from each and sources of assured or anticipated support for the proposed project; and proof of Section 501(c)(3) tax-exempt status.

It is the practice of the foundation to seek additional relevant information on pending proposals from agencies and donars in the coummunity that are likely to be well-informed concerning a particular program or organization.

Financial Data

```
(Year ended   /  /  )
Assets:                        NA
Total grants paid:
Number of grants paid:
Highest grant:
Lowest grant:
Median grant size:
```

Grant Limitations

The foundation will not make grants to individuals; religious organizations for religious purposes; political campaigns; organizations without their own Sections 401(c)(3) and 509(a) rulings from the IRS; organizations designed primarily for lobbying; support travel by groups or individuals; national or local campaigns to eliminate or control specific diseases; basic or applied research, including but not limited to science, medicine, engineering, or energy; and recreation.

In general the foundation does not favor grants to: subsidize publications, whether in print, on film, or for television; support conferences, seminars, workships, or symposia; endowment campaigns or to capital funds for educational institutions; and fund-raising campaigns.

**Meeting
Times**

The board of trustees meets periodically throughout the year.

Publications

The foundation publishes a brochure containing application guidelines.

GENERAL SERVICE FOUNDATION

557 North Mill Street, Suite 201

Aspen, Colorado 81611

PHONE: (970) 920-6834

FAX: (970) 920-4578

EMAIL: info@generalservice.org

WEB: www.generalservice.org

Contact Persons

Robert W. Musser, President

Lani Shaw and Robert Musser, Resources

Lani Shaw, Julie Richardson and Robin Halby, Reproductive Health
and Rights

Julie Richardson and Mary Estrin, International Peace

Purpose

The General Service Foundation supports programs that address three basic long-term national and international issues of international peace, reproductive health and rights, and natural resources. In general the foundation prefers to support experimental, demonstration, research projects, and programs.

Areas of Interest

Within each area of activity, the foundation has established broad guidelines. For example, in the international peace program, the foundation is particularly interested in research and education on U.S. international relations that will contribute to international peace; international working groups concerned with increasing understanding and cooperation; and research and education on the relationships between economic and political development and international peace. It **will not** support work addressing the military aspects of this issue.

The foundation is also concerned with the related issues of rapid population growth and unintended pregnancies, and the availability of quality reproductive health care and access to that care. It funds research for policy analysis, litigation, public education, and advocacy. Grants are awarded for projects in the United States and Latin America that address the needs of low-income women, minority women, and adolescents.

In its support of issues concerning the use of natural resources, the foundation prefers programs that improve the use, management, and quantity of water in the United States (particularly west of the Mississippi River). The goal of the foundation's Resources program is to preserve and protect aquatic and riparian ecosystems in rivers and their tributaries in the primary geographic areas of Washington, Oregon, Idaho, Montana, Wyoming, Colorado, New Mexico, Utah and Arizona.

Financial Data

(Year ended 12/31/00)

Assets:	$ 75,643,248
Total grants paid:	$ 4,450,869*
Number of grants paid:	129
Highest grant:	$ 90,000 (2-year grant)
Lowest grant:	$ 4,900
Median grant size:	unknown

*This excludes 16 discretionary grants made to arts organizations totaling $80,000. The foundation does not fund the arts through unsolicited project proposals. Rather grants are made from a small discretionary fund and are distributed only at the personal request of a director.

Application Procedures

There are two deadlines for letters of inquiry, February 1 and September 1. The board meets twice a year in the spring and fall to review requested proposals.

Letters of inquiry describing the project should be sent to the foundation before a formal proposal is submitted. If the project fits within the foundations's guidelines, and funding is available, an application will be sent to be completed and returned with a formal proposal.

The following information will be required for the proposal: name and address of the tax-exempt organization which will be responsible for the grant with proof that the applicant is currently tax-exempt and not a private foundation; brief statements of the purpose for which funds are sought, evidence supporting the need for the project, the project objectives, the amount requested, the person responsible for administration, qualifications of the organization and individuals responsible for carrying out the project and what will be accomplished; a one- or two-page summary of the proposed project or program, focusing on the solution to the problem; a budget for the project or program; a statement regarding other funding obtained or requested and the plan for long-term funding; and a copy of the applicant organization's last annual report (if available), or information including the organization's programs, its annual budget and financial statements, and a list of directors and officers.

**Grant
Limitations**

The foundation does not make contributions to operating budgets, nor to annual campaigns of established organizations. The foundation does not ordinarily contribute to capital (physical plant, equipment, endowment), to individuals, or to relief programs.

**Meeting
Times**

The board of directors meets twice a year, in the spring and fall.

Publications

The foundation does not publish an annual report. Please check www.general service.org for more past grantee information.

THE WALLACE ALEXANDER GERBODE FOUNDATION

111 Pine Street, Suite 1515

San Francisco, California 94111

PHONE: (415) 391-0911

FAX: (415) 391-4587

EMAIL: info@gerbode.org

WEB: www.fdncenter.org/grantmaker /gerbode

Contact Person

Thomas C. Layton, President

Purpose

The Wallace Alexander Gerbode Foundation supports programs and projects with potential to produce noticeable effect in areas from arts to citizen participation in the San Francisco Bay Area and Hawaii.

Areas of Interest

The foundation's interests lie generally under the following categories:

Arts and culture
Environment
Population
Reproductive rights
Citizen participation/building communities/inclusiveness
Strength of the philanthropic process and the nonprofit sector
Media projects (very specifically focused on issues being addressed currently by the foundation's grantees)

Application Procedures

There is no standard format for application to the foundation and proposals are accepted throughout the year. The foundation prefers that initial contact be made in a letter of inquiry, including a short description of the project, the proposed budget, confirmation of appropriate IRS tax-exempt status, and board list.

**Financial
Data**

(Year ended 12/31/99)	
Assets:	$ 84,921,250
Total grants paid:	$ 2,965,604
Number of grants paid:	127
Highest grant:	$ 100,000
Lowest grant:	$ 1,000

**Grant
Limitations**

The foundation generally does not support: direct services, deficit budgets, general operating funds, building and equipment funds, endowments, general fundraising campaigns, religious purposes, private schools, publications, scholarships, and grants to individuals.

**Meeting
Times**

The board of directors meets four times a year.

Publications

The foundation publishes an annual report. A statement of program policy and grant application guidelines is available upon request.

THE BENJAMIN S. GERSON FAMILY FOUNDATION

PHONE: (216) 621-2901

FAX: (216) 621-8198

℅ **FOUNDATION MANAGEMENT SERVICES**

1422 EUCLID AVENUE, SUITE 627

CLEVELAND, OHIO 44115

Contact Persons

Thomas Gerson, Chairperson

Kim Cowan, Consultant/Foundation Management

Purpose

The Benjamin S. Gerson Family Foundation was established in 1973 to support organizations working to effect progressive social change, remedy inequities, increase access of opportunity, and promote self-help, as well as those organizations working for preservation of existing freedoms and values. Except for national advocacy organizations, the majority of grants support programs in greater Cleveland, Ohio.

Areas of Interest

Grants are made in a number of areas, including programs for women, civil rights and civil liberties, and local community organizations. Grants for operational programs are almost always confined to the greater Cleveland area. However, grants may be made to national organizations working on issues of concern to the foundation.

Grants generally range between $1,000 and $15,000. Preference is given to organizations which can benefit from small grants and may not have ready access to other resources. Support for programs or projects are made to community or grassroots organizations, to innovative or experimental groups, or by well-established organizations provided they serve populations in which the foundation is primarily interested.

Financial Data

(Year ended 12/31/00)	
Assets:	$ 3,781,785
Total grants paid:	$ 200,550
Number of grants paid:	25
Highest grant:	$ 15,000
Lowest grant:	$ 400
Median grant size:	$ 5,000

Application Procedures

The deadline for submitting applications is September 15. Organizations wishing to apply should submit two complete copies of a brief proposal and two copies of the following information: the objectives of the program, how the funds will be used, the expected outcomes, and the anticipated length of the project. The formal proposal should include a short history of the organization and its current activities; a statement of the need or problem to be addressed (with reference to specific objectives, plans for implementation, and staff qualifications) and the project's budget, other sources of funding, and plans for future funding if the project is to be ongoing. Copies of the organization's proof of tax-exempt status, current budget, annual report, and audited financial statements should also be provided. The contact person's name, title, and telephone number should also be clearly identified.

For requests of $1,000 or less, the only financial information required is a copy of the organization's most recent financial statement.

Grant Limitations

The foundation does not provide support for individuals, religious purposes, or to meet budget deficits, nor do they fund media projects, conferences, publications or pure research. Requests for capital campaigns, endowments, conferences, and research are funded only infrequently.

Meeting Times

The board of directors meets once a year, in December, to consider grant requests.

Publications

The foundation distributes guidelines upon request.

THE GLOBAL FUND FOR WOMEN

1375 SUTTER STREET, SUITE 400
SAN FRANCISCO, CA 94109

PHONE: (415) 202-7640

FAX: (415) 202-8604

EMAIL: gfw@globalfundforwomen.org

WEB: www.globalfundforwomen.org

Contact Person

Kavita N. Ramdas, President and CEO

Purpose

The Global Fund for Women is a nonprofit grantmaking foundation that seeds, strengthens and links women's rights organizations in every part of the world. Our grants help expand the choices available to women and ensure that women's voices are heard at the local, national and international levels. We are the only U.S.-based foundation that exclusively funds women's groups overseas.

Areas of Interest

The Global Fund provides grants to women's rights groups based outside the United States. These associations of women work on a broad range of human rights issues that include: economic opportunity, increasing girls' access to education, stopping violence against women, improving health and reproductive rights, increasing women's access to technology, strengthening women's political participation, challenging traditional customs that are harmful to women, promoting the rights of women with disabilities, ensuring lesbian rights, and supporting local women's philanthropy.

Financial Data

(Year ended 6/30/00)	
Assets:	$ 5,200,000
Total grants paid:	$ 3,400,000
Total number of grants:	363
Highest grant:	$ 15,000
Lowest grant:	$ 500
Median grant size:	$ 7,500

Application Procedures

The Global Fund accepts grant requests in any language or format. Letters of inquiry or grant applications may be handwritten or typed, and may be sent to our office in San Francisco by post or fax or by email to proposals@global fundforwomen.org. More details about our criteria and an application format are available on-line at www.globalfundforwomen.org.

A diverse and professional program staff review grant applications. Our review process is informed by the local knowledge and expertise of our 120-member Advisory Council. All final decisions are made by the Global Fund's Board of Directors, a 12-member body that reflects the international diversity of our network. Due to the high number of proposals we receive, it takes 4-6 months to review a request. We accept applications throughout the year and award grants every 2-3 months.

Grant Limitations

The fund supports groups that demonstrate a clear commitment to women's equality and female human rights; are governed and directed primarily by women; have defined plans to strengthen the work of the group over time; and may be unlikely to obtain funding from other sources. Grants are not given to individuals and are made to women's groups outside the United States.

Meeting Times

The Board of Directors makes grant decisions 5-6 times a year, and meets formally at least twice a year.

Publications

The Global Fund publishes an annual report, brochures, and a newsletter. We have also published *Linking Women Globally*, a multi-lingual directory of past grantees. More information is available on our website.

RICHARD AND RHODA GOLDMAN FUND

PHONE: (415) 788-1090

FAX: (415) 788-7890

ONE LOMBARD STREET, SUITE 303

WEB: www.goldmanfund.org

SAN FRANCISCO, CALIFORNIA 94111

Contact Person

Letter of Inquiry

Purpose

The Richard and Rhoda Goldman Fund supports programs that will enhance the quality of life of residents of the San Francisco Bay Area.

Areas of Interest

The fund directs the majority of its grants toward organizations and projects addressing problems related to the elderly, the environment, population, children and youth, violence prevention.

Financial Data

(Year ended 12/31/00)	
Endowment:	$ 429,418,960
Total grants paid:	$ 32,540,477
Number of grants paid:	877
Highest grant:	$ 1,500,000
Lowest grant:	$ 5,000*
Median grant size:	$ 7,500

*The Fund does not accept applications for grants of $5,000 or less. Grants of this amount are made only at the discretion of the board.

Application Procedures

Grantseekers should write a letter of inquiry, no longer than two pages, that contains a one-paragraph summary describing the project, total project budget, amount requested, and short descriptive project title. Additionally, the letter should identify the primary contact, including title, address, and telephone number. The body of the letter should include a description of the project, (necessity, objectives, significance and plans for implementation), itemized project budget, amount requested, other sources of funding, the organization's total annual budget, and a copy of the IRS tax-exempt letter.

If the fund is interested in potentially supporting a project, an invitation to submit a full proposal with be sent to the applicant. Letters of inquiry are accepted at any time. There are no deadlines for submission of proposals.

Grant Limitations

The fund does not support deficit budgets, endowments, general fundraising campaigns, conferences, grants or scholarships to individuals, or basic research. It will only consider applications from organizations certified by the IRS as public charities.

Meeting Times

The board of directors meets quarterly to make grant decisions.

Publications

The fund publishes an annual report.

MORRIS GOLDSEKER FOUNDATION OF MARYLAND

PHONE: (410) 837-5100

FAX: (410) 837-7927

EMAIL: tdebord@goldsekerfoundation.org

WEB: www.goldsekerfoundation.org

1040 PARK AVENUE, SUITE 310

BALTIMORE, MARYLAND 21201

Contact Person

Timothy D. Armbruster, President

Purpose

The purpose of the Morris Goldseker Foundation of Maryland is to improve broadly the quality of life in metropolitan Baltimore, especially for the disadvantaged. Of particular interest to the foundation are programs that increase access and opportunity, promote independence and personal achievement, strengthen institutions and systems of delivery, attract other resources, improve efficiency of operations, address long-term solutions to community problems, strengthen neighborhoods, and the private, nonprofit sector.

Areas of Interest

The foundation has identified five program interests: community affairs, education, health, human services, and neighborhood development. It has elected, however, not to set specific priorities within these areas, preferring to remain flexible.

Applicants are encouraged to demonstrate how ongoing programs, once initiated, will be sustained, as usually the foundation does not award grants for longer than one year and does not consider itself a long-term source of funds. Priority is given to projects not normally financed with public funds.

Financial Data

(Two years ended / /)	
Assets:	NA
Total grants awarded:	
Number of grants:	
Highest grant:	
Lowest grant:	
Median grant size:	

Application Procedures

To apply for support a brief preliminary letter describing the project should be submitted to the foundation. The letter should include background information about the applicant, a statement of need and objectives, methods for accomplishing objectives, a proposed program budget, and the amount sought from the foundation. Evidence of Section 501(c)(3) and 509(a) tax-exempt status should also be provided. The foundation staff will review the materials and promptly notify applicants if a more fully developed proposal is appropriate. If so, a proposal development form and appropriate guidelines will be supplied, and the staff will answer questions and provide such other assistance as may be necessary.

Preliminary letters and grant proposals are welcomed throughout the year. There are, however, specific deadlines for submitting fully developed proposals. These deadlines are: December 1, April 1, and August 1. Applicants are advised to submit preliminary letters as early as possible before the deadlines, because the proposal development process may be time-consuming.

Grant Limitations

The foundation does not consider advocacy and/or political action groups as prime interests for grantmaking. It does not have a program in cultural affairs, and does not award grants in support of endowments, individuals, building campaigns, deficit financing, annual giving, publications, and religious purposes. Usually the foundation does not award grants in support of operating budgets, and grants are not typically made to organizations formed for the purpose of raising or allocating funds. Grant activities are restricted to the Baltimore metropolitan area, and principally Baltimore City.

Meeting Times

The selection committee and trustees consider grant requests three times annually, in March, June, and October.

Publications

The foundation publishes an annual report and a brochure outlining program guidelines.

PHILIP L. GRAHAM FUND

PHONE: (202) 334-6640

FAX: (202) 334-4498

EMAIL: plgfund@washpost.com

1150 15TH STREET, N.W.

WASHINGTON, D.C. 20071

Contact Person

Candice Bryant, President

Purpose

The Philip L. Graham Fund awards grants for charitable, scientific, literary and educational concerns including raising the standards of excellence in professional journalism and helping to enhance and improve the quality of life in communities in the Washington, D.C. metropolitan area.

Areas of Interest

The fund conducts its grantmaking activity in two broadly defined categories, journalism and community assistance. Journalism grants are directed to academic programs at the post-graduate level; minority journalist training and scholarship; legal and First Amendment concerns; and programs whose goal is to improve the practice of professional journalism.

Community assistance grants are made in the areas of arts and humanities, civic and community projects, education, and human services to support special needs or projects of organizations formed in and operating for the benefit of the Washington, D.C. metropolitian area. Of particular interest are programs that address a specific need, promote self-sufficiency or produce a lasting benefit. Among the issues supported by the fund in recent years were hunger, homelessness, infant care, battered women, and educational reform programs. Grants from the fund went to support such programs and activities as direct services, building funds and capital campaigns.

PHILIP L. GRAHAM FUND

**Financial
Data**

```
(Year ended    /   /   )
Assets:                                    NA
Total grants paid:
Number of grants:
Highest grant paid:
Lowest grant paid:
Median grant size:
```

**Application
Procedures**

Deadlines for receipt of proposals are March 1, June 1, and September 1. The
fund has no application forms. The preferred format is a brief letter containing
the following information: a general statement describing the organization, its
purposes and its goals; a description of the project for which funding is sought
and its anticipated benefits; a project budget; the specific amount requested
from the fund and a list of other funding sources from which the organization
is seeking assistance, if any; a copy of the organization's most recent financial
statement; a copy of the IRS determination of tax-exempt status; and if the
program is expected to be a continuing one, information on how it will be
funded in the future.

**Grant
Limitations**

The fund makes grants only to organizations that are tax-exempt public
charities as defined in Section 501(c)(3) of the Internal Revenue Code. The
fund makes grants primarily in the Washington, D.C. metropolitan area. No
grants are made to individuals, or for research, conferences, workshops,
seminars, or travel expense; production of films or publications; tickets for
benefits or support for fundraisers; courtesy advertising; annual campaigns; or
sectarian religious purposes. Grants usually are not made for general support
or for national purposes or concerns.

**Meeting
Times**

The board of trustees meets four times a year.

Publications

The fund publishes an annual summary of grants and application guidelines.

THE GREATER CINCINNATI FOUNDATION

PHONE: (513) 241-2880

FAX: (513) 852-6886

EMAIL: see website

WEB: www.greatercincinnatifdn.org

200 West Fourth Street

Cincinnati, Ohio 45202

Contact Person

Ellen Gilligan, Vice President of Grants and Programs

Purpose

The Greater Cincinnati Foundation is a community foundation whose mission is to improve the quality of life for the people of Hamilton County and contiguous counties in Ohio, Kentucky, and Indiana. The foundation supports projects that are likely to address diversity and positive change; help nonprofit organizations manage themselves and their finances more effectively; focus on prevention; encourage cooperation and eliminate duplication of service; and stimulate others to participate in problem-solving.

Areas of Interest

Grants from the unrestricted and field of interest funds are made within six general funding categories: arts and culture; community progress; education; environment; health; and human services.

The foundation is willing to consider any proposal that could have a major effect on the community, especially if no other funding is available from other sources.

Application Procedures

The foundation encourages applicants to call and consult with program staff before starting to write a proposal. Inquiries are accepted throughout the year.

Grant Limitations

The foundation normally does not make grants to individuals, for operating expenses of existing organizations, religious organizations for religious purposes, endowments, scholarships, annual fundraising drives, travel grants, schools, hospitals, nursing homes and retirement centers, and community services which are primarily supported by tax dollars.

Only nonprofit charitable organizations designated 501(c)(3) by the IRS operating in the Greater Cincinnati area are eligible for grants.

Financial Data

(Year ended 12/31/00)	
Assets:	$ 402,370,503
Total grants approved:	$ 3,691,872*
Total number of grants:	244
Highest grant:	$ 250,000
Lowest grant:	$ 5,000
Median grant size:	$ 115,000**

*This analysis is for unrestricted and field of interest funds.

**Does not include mini-grant program, and special initiatives.

Meeting Times

The board meets quarterly, in March, June, September, and December, to consider funding requests.

Publications

The foundation publishes an annual report and grant guidelines.

THE GREATER KANSAS CITY COMMUNITY FOUNDATION

PHONE: (816) 842-0944

FAX: (816) 842-8079

WEB: www.gkccf.org

1055 BROADWAY, SUITE 130

KANSAS CITY, MISSOURI 64105

Contact Person

Janice C. Kreamer, President and CEO

Purpose

Community foundations can be a valuable ally to nonprofits and a partner in meeting the needs of the community. There are nearly 600 community foundations nationwide, which manage more than $30 billion in assets. However, community foundations vary in their focus from region to region, making it difficult for nonprofits to effectively engage foundation resources.

Many community foundations have adopted the donor-focused model, which engages donors by connecting them to the rewards and satisfaction of giving. Community foundations have adopted this model to help donors achieve their charitable dreams by making giving easy, flexible, and effective. For example, the Greater Kansas City Community Foundation determined that it is in the business of "connecting donors to what they care about and to the needs of the community."

Areas of Interest

The Greater Kansas City Community Foundation takes the time to develop personal relationships with donors, understanding their interests and motivations to develop a sense of what charitable inclinations are present and waiting to be tapped. To make the most effective use of charitable dollars entering the community, the Community Foundation offers donors access to research about nonprofits and charitable planning services which then enables donors to be more intentional in their giving. The Community Foundation also measures the success of charitable giving by evaluating and reporting the effectiveness and outcome of each donor's gift.

The Community Foundation's credibility and expertise positions it as not only an outstanding tool for donors but also as a community leader. The Community Foundation has led coalitions of partners to tackle homelessness, drug and alcohol abuse, children's advocacy and youth development. In each of these cases, the Community Foundation marshaled not only financial resources, but leadership and advocacy resources as well.

By knowing donor's charitable intentions and the community's needs, community foundations can connect donors to nonprofits that will realize the donor's charitable dreams thereby engaging the donor in a longer-term relationship between the nonprofit community and the donor.

**Financial
Data**

(Year ended 12/31/00)	
Assets:	$ 719,476,000
Total grants paid:	$ 90,145,000
Total number of grants:	7,240
Highest grant:	$ 8,501,911
Median grant size:	$ 11,818

**Application
Procedures**

Please visit our website for more information.

**Grant
Limitations**

Please visit our website for more information.

THE GEORGE GUND FOUNDATION

1845 GUILDHALL BUILDING

45 PROSPECT AVENUE WEST

CLEVELAND, OHIO 44115

PHONE: (216) 241-3114

FAX: (216) 241-6560

EMAIL: info@gundfdn.org

WEB: www.gundfdn.org

Contact Person

David Abbott, Executive Director

Purpose

The programs of the George Gund Foundation are directed toward enhancing the ability of individuals to understand the social, cultural, economic, and physical environments in which they live and increasing their proficiency to cope with changes that are constantly taking place.

Preference is given to pilot projects, innovative programs, and studies that hold the promise of significant benefits with broad applicability. Most of the foundation's grants are awarded to organizations in northern Ohio. Grantees are encouraged, however, to disseminate their work broadly, since problems in this region are often relevant to other parts of the country and the world.

Areas of Interest

The foundation has established six program areas:

Arts

The foundation encourages a lively, diverse arts community in Greater Cleveland by funding projects that emphasize artistic quality, innovative programming and organizational development and stability. Increased collaboration among organizations and greater cultural diversity in programming, audiences and organizations are priorities. The foundation has an interest in arts education, with emphasis on curriculum-related partnerships between arts organizations and the Cleveland Public Schools.

Civic Affairs

The foundation is concerned with improving the ability of government and citizens to address important public policy issues and problems. Priorities within this program area are encouraging education and research designed to make government organizations and functions more effective, increasing and improving the quality of citizen participation in public affairs and enhancing the ability of all citizens to live together harmoniously and with respect for each other's rights. Projects that address these issues in Greater Cleveland are given the highest priority.

Economic Development and Revitalization

Grantmaking is directed primarily toward Cleveland, although projects in Greater Cleveland and programs of state-wide significance in Ohio are considered. A high priority is given to programs that create jobs and livable neighborhoods for inner-city residents. Projects concerned with neighborhood physical revitalization generally are not considered directly by the foundation but are referred to Neighborhood Progress, Inc., a local intermediary supported by the foundation. Proposals that improve urban planning capabilities, promote quality urban design and encourage the creation and enhancement of amenities in Greater Cleveland are seriously considered.

Education

Higher education support is directed to both public and private colleges and universities in Northeast Ohio and includes an interest in improving minorities' access to and retention in these institutions, strengthening faculty development and academic programs and providing seed money for new programs. Grants are often targeted toward projects responsive to the foundation's other program objectives. Grantmaking in the area of primary and secondary education is focused primarily within Cuyahoga County, with emphasis on improving educational programs for low-income and minority youth, especially in the Cleveland Public Schools. The emphasis is on projects dealing with public school improvement, community and parental involvement, policy development, staff development and program evaluation. In addition, limited support is provided to national organizations that address school improvement policy issues. Early childhood grantmaking focuses on programs that strengthen the child care system in Greater Cleveland as well as projects that provide early intervention for disadvantaged preschoolers.

Environment

Primary grantmaking emphasis in the Cleveland bioregion is on the protection of ecosystems and natural features. Efforts to develop a broader ecological perspective for the region and encourage citizen awareness and advocacy are encouraged. Grantmaking in Ohio is focused on state-wide issues and state-wide organizations promoting improved public policy or providing coordination and support for local environmental groups. Local projects outside Greater Cleveland will not be considered. Grant making in the Great Lakes basin emphasizes region-wide protection of biological resources and strengthening the infrastructure of the environmental community. The foundation has a special interest in programs that develop leadership and management capacity in nonprofit environmental organizations. Priority in this area is given to programs that train and link networks of organizations.

Human Services

The foundation places high priority on programs within Cuyahoga County that enhance child welfare and protection and increase the stability of families. It is concerned with ameliorating the effects of poverty and social disorganization in the Cleveland area, including programs that address welfare-to-work transition, interpersonal violence and basic human needs. The foundation is interested in increasing the capacity of local social service agencies to better meet the needs of the disadvantaged and in improving social welfare policy at the local, state and federal levels. Local funding efforts in the health field are primarily oriented toward community health, with priority given to programs affecting children. Grantmaking also supports local AIDS prevention, education and direct services and projects related to the development of national AIDS policy. The foundation is committed to the principle of reproductive choice and supports key national planning and reproductive rights organizations.

Financial Data

```
(Year ended    /   /   )
Assets:                              NA
Total grants awarded:
Total number of grants:
Highest grant:
Lowest grant:
Median grant size:
```

Application Procedures

Proposals submission deadlines are January 15, April 15, August 15, and October 15. Each proposal should include a one-page summary describing the project and the amount of funds being requested. The proposal should also include: organizational background, project description, time-line, key personnel, methods of evaluation, project budget, organizational budget, and such supporting documents as board list, brochures, and IRS letter.

Proposals are considered by the foundation's trustees in March, June, September, and December. Deadlines for submitting proposals for consideration at the next regularly scheduled meeting of the trustees are December 30, March 30, June 30, and September 30. Faxed proposals not accepted.

All proposals are screened and evaluated by the staff before presentation at trustee meetings. Organizations submitting proposals outside of the foundation's interests and priorities will be notified promptly.

Grant Limitations

The foundation does not make direct awards to individuals nor does it administer programs that it supports. Grants are limited to purposes and activities in the United States, and the great majority of grants are limited to Cuyahoga County and Northeast Ohio. With the exception of the foundation's special initiative program on retinal degenerative disease research, the foundation does not make grants in the health or medical fields. Grants for general operating support will be considered only if the need is for a limited duration and will substantially strengthen the work and improve the future position of the organization. Rarely does the foundation consider building or endowment grants.

All grantees must have satisfied IRS requirements as nonprofit, tax-exempt agencies having public charity status, or be approved as qualified government-related agencies or religious institutions.

Meeting Times

The board of trustees meets quarterly in March, June, September, and December.

Publications

The foundation publishes an annual report.

EVELYN AND WALTER HAAS, JR. FUND

PHONE: (415) 856-1400

FAX: (415) 856-1500

1 MARKET STREET, SUITE 400

WEB: www.haasjr.org

SAN FRANCISCO, CALIFORNIA 94105

Contact Person

Clayton Juan, Grants Administrator

Purpose

The Evelyn and Walter Haas, Jr. Fund was organized to support cultural, educational, and human welfare projects that enrich the lives of residents of the San Francisco Bay Area by promoting various strategies that will lead to increased self-sufficiency.

Areas of Interest

The fund's program areas promote strengthening children, youth, families, and the elderly, strengthening neighborhoods and communities, and enhancing nonprofit leadership and governance.

Financial Data

(Year ended 12/31/00)	
Assets:	
Total grants paid:	$ 21,340,210
Number of grants paid:	359
Highest grant:	$ 1,700,000
Lowest grant:	$ 100
Median grant size:	$ 55,000

Application Procedures

Before a formal application to the fund is made, applicants should submit a brief one- or two-page letter outlining the purpose of and need for the project, background of the sponsoring organization, project budget, the amount requested, and potential and actual sources of funding.

If the fund requests a formal proposal, the proposal should include: a full description of the objectives, scope, and anticipated outcome of the project; the plan for continuing the project after completion of the fund support; a budget for the project, a current financial report and a statement of actual income (including sources) and disbursements for the last fiscal year; the names and qualifications of key personnel; a list of the members of the organization's governing body; and an IRS letter of determination indicating that the applicant is a public charity.

The fund will acknowledge all requests upon receipt and applicants will be notified of the final disposition of their request within 90 days.

Grant Limitations

The fund does not normally provide support to individuals. While the trustees occasionally initiate grants to organizations outside the Bay Area, financial support is generally restricted to programs in San Francisco and Alameda Counties. The foundation does not make grants to other private foundations, general fundraising campaigns, or for deficit budgets, religious purposes, conferences, publications, or research projects.

Meeting Times

The board of trustees meets periodically, at least three times per year.

Publications

The fund publishes an annual report.

HARDER FOUNDATION

401 BROADWAY

TACOMA, WASHINGTON 98402

PHONE: (253) 593-2121

FAX: (253) 593-2122

EMAIL: harder1@wamail.net

Contact Persons

Del Langbauer, President (Washington)

Purpose

The Harder Foundation makes grants solely for work on environmental issues. The foundation subscribes to the view that where many individuals each use common resources in such a way as to maximize their own gain at little personal short term cost, it exhausts the resource and brings serious hardship to all who are dependent upon it. When restoration of the resource is possible, it is often at great cost and it must be borne by all citizens.

Areas of Interest

Particular interests include preservation of wilderness areas and ecosystem protection; preservation of biological species in their natural habitat; preservation of clean air, clear water, and clean soil, and removal of chemical and other man-made pollutants; conservation of natural resources; and controlling population growth. Generally, the foundation seeks to support activities that will provide the greatest possible improvement in environmental quality for the least possible cost. It also wants some reasonable assurance that measurable environmental benefits will occur during the time frame of the grant.

The foundation makes grants to state or local groups for environmental projects of statewide or regional significance. Each year the foundation also makes a portion of its grants budget available for general support, particularly for small organizations that need basic operating expenses. Often such general support grants are made to organizations which have recently completed successful project grants with the foundation. Occasionally, they are made to new organizations recently formed to resolve an especially important environmental problem. In the latter case, the background and qualifications of officers and staff are especially important. In addition, since 1985 a limited number of foundation-initiated endowment grants have been made to provide endowment funds for organizations with records of unusually successful environmental programs.

Financial Data

(Year ended 12/31/00)	
Assets:	$ 31,386,000
Total grants paid:	$ 1,370,000
Number of grants paid:	56
Highest grant:	$ 100,000
Lowest grant:	$ 1,500
Median grant size:	$ 15,000

Application Procedures

Applicants should write the main office of the foundation and request a current copy of the guidelines for grant proposals. The deadline for grant applications is, generally, August 15 of each year.

Grant Limitations

The foundation makes grants only to tax-exempt organizations. Support is not available for environmental education, capital construction projects, individuals, and organizations sponsored by friends or acquaintances of foundation trustees. Research proposals will be considered only when they are in direct support of a developed plan for specific action to alleviate a pressing environmental problem. The foundation will not support projects normally funded by public tax funds.

Grants will be made only in the following states: Washington, Oregon, Idaho, Montana, Wyoming, Colorado, Utah, Nevada, Alaska, and Florida.

Meeting Times

The board of trustees meets once a year, in February.

Publications

The foundation publishes an annual report and distributes a program policy statement and application guidelines.

THE HAWAII COMMUNITY FOUNDATION

PHONE: (808)537-6333

FAX: (808)521-6286

EMAIL: information@hcf-hawaii.org

WEB: www.hawaiicommunityfoudation.org

1164 BISHOP STREET

SUITE 800

HONOLULU, HAWAII 96813

Contact Person

Kalei Kaha'ulelio, Program Officer

Purpose

Hawaii Community Foundation helps people make a difference by inspiring the spirit of giving and by investing in people and solutions to benefit every island community.

Areas of Interest

The foundation funds works in:

Aging

Supports programs that help the aging population stay healthy and contribute fully to their communities.

Culture

Support is provided to build strong cultural organizations and encourage diversity. Eligible organizations include those that promote and preserve the traditions and integrity of dance, art, music, literature, language and theater.

Education

Business Education

Assists in increasing the knowledge and skills neccessary in the business sector. Programs include those that focus on improving general business skills, learning about finance and banking or developing small business plans.

Family Literacy

Promotes parent and child interaction around literacy in Hawaii.

Literacy

Focuses on improving literacy skills in Hawaii.

Service Learning

Promotes participation in civic life by private school students and teachers through collaborative service learning projects. Preference is given to those private schools that collaborate with public schools in their community.

Geographic Areas

Ewa Beach

Supports activities and programs to improve the quality of life of Ewa Beach residents including children, youth and the elderly.

Kauai

Supports organizations and projects on the island, including culture, education, environment, health and human services. Preference is given to projects that build organizational capacity.

Lānai

Supports projects to benefit the island community. Grantmaking focus is on recreational, educational and cultural activities with special emphasis on seniors and youth.

West Hawaii

Supports programs that improve the quality of life for residents of West Hawaii (North Kohala through Hawaiian Ocean View Estates). Preference is given to projects that include people working together in the community.

Health

Supports programs that encourage individuals, agencies and communities to play a proactive role in choices affecting health.

Human Services

Children and Youth

Supports programs that help children, ages 6-20, develop critical thinking skills, learn about their own culture and that of others, or settle disputes and differences peacefully.

Residential Treatment

Supports programs that provide on-site treatment in a residential setting. Treatment should address residents' physical/mental health problems, provide preventative treatment, or enhance the quality of their lives. Preference is given to facilities that are small, community-based, home-like settings.

Medical Research

Supports studies in health services, clinical research and basic medical research. Preference is given to projects that assist the work of young investigators. Disease-specific areas include cancer, heart disease, lung disease, Alzheimer's disease or juvenile diabetes.

Natural Resouorces Conservation

Promotes the conservation and restoration of Hawaii's native terrestrial and marine ecosystems.

Neighborhood/Community Development

Supports projects on several islands initiated by community groups that want to improve the quality of life in their neighborhoods. Funding and technical assistance is provided to groups to help strengthen organizational and leadership skills. Grantseekers do not need to be a 501(c)(3) organization. Government agencies, large nonprofit organizations and groups not controlled by neighbors are not eligible.

Persons-in-Need

Provides assistance to eligible Hawaii residents in financial need. Current funds focus on children and the elderly. Grants are awarded to qualified individuals through community-based agencies.

Scholarships

Assists Hawaii residents in college or university studies. Funds provide grants to students who meet specific eligibility requirements determined by each fund's donors.

Women

Supports programs that promote and provide opportunities for girls and women to reach their full potential.

Youth Volunteerism

Na 'Ōpio o Ke Ala Hōkū supports activities that promote the development of youth through volunteerism.

Financial Data

```
(Year ended 12/31/99)
Assets:                        $ 233,342,853*
Total grants paid:             $ 9,742,041
Number of grants paid:             1,639
Highest grant:                 $ 50,000
Lowest grant:                  $ 20
Median grant size:             $ 10,000

*Combined market value of all funds.
```

Application Procedures

Before writing a proposal the foundation recommends that grantseekers telephone to learn about the submission process. The foundation publishes an information book, "Grantseekers Guide," which outlines in detail the information which must be included in proposals. Deadlines vary for each program.

Grant Limitations

The foundation will only consider programs and projects carried out by Hawaii organizations. The organizations must be tax-exempt public charities as defined in Section 501(c)(3) of the Internal Revenue Code. Additionally the foundation does not fund endowments, loans, emergency support, large major capital projects, on-going support, deficit funding, tuition aid programs, and individuals (with the exception of scholarship programs).

Publications

The foundation publishes an annual report and an information booklet on application procedures.

HAYMARKET PEOPLE'S FUND

42 SEAVERNS AVENUE

BOSTON, MASSACHUSETTS 02130

PHONE: (617) 522-7676

FAX: (617) 522-9580

EMAIL: haymarket@igc.org

WEB: www.haymarket.org

Contact Persons

Patricia Maher, Executive Director

Tommie Hollis-Younger, Grants Coordinator

Purpose

Haymarket People's Fund is an activist-controlled foundation committed to radical social change. Founded in 1974, Haymarket envisions a democratic system based on collective ownership and control of our society's resources and an equitable distribution of wealth and power within and beyond our national borders, the end of all economic, political, and social exploitation of one human being by another, respect for and protection of the environment, an affirmation of cultural diversity, respect for the dignity and inherent value of all individuals, freedom from all forms of discrimination and oppression including those based on class, race, ethnicity, sex sexual orientation, age, and disability, and a dedication to equality, solidarity, internationalism, and peace.

Areas of Interest

To be considered for funding, an organization must conduct its work within New England, and engage in grassroots organizing for progressive institutional change.

In addition, the organization must demonstrate a clear strategy aimed at an equitable redistribution of wealth and power; a strong indigenous leadership, representative of and accountable to the organization's membership; an on-going effort to develop new leadership; a commitment to building the organization and involving previously unorganized people; the organizational capacity to successfully raise funds, manage funds, and carry out plans; and an organizing campaign or project with specific goals.

Financial
Data

(Year ended 6/30/01)	
Total grants paid:	$ 960,841
Number of grants paid:	249
Highest grant:	$ 10,000
Lowest grant:	$ 750
Median grant size:	$ 5,000

Application
Procedures

Applicants must submit a completed application, available from the fund. Most grants are under $10,000. Emergency grants are available for up to $750 outside of the special grant cycle, and a decision is reached usually within two to three weeks.

Grant
Limitations

Haymarket continues to emphasize funding of small grassroots organizations, but will consider organizations with budgets greater than $100,000, if their work is consistent with the fund's philosophy.

Haymarket does not fund individuals, government agencies, organizations not engaged in grassroots organizing or outside of New England, or alternative businesses.

Meeting
Times

All applications that reach the fund's offices by the deadline date will be reviewed and acknowledged by mail.

After all applications are received, each grant application is reviewed by members of the Haymarket Regional Funding Board in the appropriate region (Maine, New Hampshire, Rhode Island, Connecticut, Massachusetts, and Vermont). An interview is then set up with the applicants who have submitted the strongest applications. The Regional Funding Board will decide the final grant recipients. Grant applicants are notified by mail or phone about the decision.

This process normally is completed within six to eight weeks of the proposal deadline.

Publications

The fund publishes an annual report and a biannual newsletter. Complete information on application procedures and guidelines as well as an audited financial statement are available upon request. The application and guidelines are also available on Haymarket's website: www.haymarket.org.

THE EDWARD W. HAZEN FOUNDATION

309 Fɪꜰᴛʜ Aᴠᴇɴᴜᴇ, Rᴏᴏᴍ 200-3

Nᴇᴡ Yᴏʀᴋ, Nᴇᴡ Yᴏʀᴋ 10016

PHONE: (212) 889-3034

FAX: (212) 889-3039

EMAIL: hazen@hazenfoundation.org

WEB: www.hazenfoundation.org

Contact Person

President

Purpose and Areas of Interest

The foundation supports school reform and youth development. In the area of school reform, it is primarily interested in parent organizing and training initiatives. Similarly in the area of youth development, it favors proposals that focus on youth organizing around social issues or issues of concern to youth.

The foundation seeks to further its programs objectives by supporting the efforts of community-based, and other nonprofit agencies, that view people from diverse backgrounds as partners. The foundation favors proposals from organizations which demonstrate a commitment to diversifying their boards and staff. The foundation will work primarily with organizations in the following cities and regions: Baltimore, District of Columbia, Philadelphia, New York City, Miami, the Mississippi Delta, Chicago, Texas (city to be determined), and Los Angeles.

Financial Data

(Year ended 12/31/00)	
Assets:	N/A
Total grants paid:	$ 1,843,540
Number of grants paid:	99
Highest grant:	$ 100,000
Lowest grant:	$ 1,000

Application Procedures

Applicants should first submit a letter of inquiry of no more than two pages highlighting the goals, objectives, approach, target population, duration, and total cost of the project for which funding is sought. Additional materials, such as video, audio cassettes, books, and articles should not be sent unless they are specifically requested by the foundation staff.

After an initial review, if, in the opinion of staff, the project outline addresses the foundation's mission and program interests, a grant application will be sent. Grant applications should be returned no later than January 15th for spring board meetings, and July 15th for fall board meetings.

Grant Limitations

Approximately $2,000,000 will be awarded annually. Grants are made only to federally tax-exempt non-profit organizations. The foundation does not make grants to individuals, schools or school districts. Similarly, the foundation does not fund social-service programs, scholarships or fellowships; nor provide funds toward ongoing operational expenses, deficit funding, building construction or maintenance.

Meeting Times

The board of trustees meets twice a year, in the spring and fall.

Publications

The foundation has current editions of the annual report available. It also publishes "Guidelines for Grantseekers."

HEADWATERS FUND

122 West Franklin Avenue, Suite 518

Minneapolis, Minnesota 55404

PHONE: (612) 879-0602

FAX: (612) 879-0613 *2

EMAIL: info@headwatersfoundation.org

WEB: www.headwatersfoundation.org

Contact Person

Monica Bryand, Program Officer

Purpose

The Headwaters Fund is a social justice foundation that provides grants and technical support to small social change groups and organizations that address the root causes of injustice in Minnesota and Wisconsin. The fund supports progressive social change nationally and internationally.

Areas of Interest

The fund makes grants to organizations with constituent leadership, representing low-income, minority, and other local disenfranchised communities. The organizations can be geography-, issue-, or constituency-based groups who support the elimination of social, economic, and racial injustice in our society. The fund makes four types of grants each with its own funding limits.

• Empowerment. Grants up to $5,000 are targeted to organizations working on organizational identity, constituency building, education, self-definition, community leadership development, and self-determination.

• Strategic. Grants up to $10,000 are available to groups with strong organizational capacity for work which will have a strategic impact on systems change and where Headwaters' support will make a critical difference. Two-year funding is available.

• Exceptional. Grants up to $15,000 to previous grantees who have shown both exceptional success and critical need. Separate guidelines and procedures apply to these grants. Awards in this area are rare. Two-year funding is available.

• Special Opportunity. Grants up to $1,000 are available on an ongoing basis to help groups meet needs that arise outside of the normal Headwaters grant cycles. These grants are intended to help groups respond to unexpected needs, situations, and opportunities not included in their regular budget process.

Headwaters is committed to the growth of vital grassroots groups. In addition to its grantmaking program it has expanded its support of community with a capacity building initiative that provides technical assistance grants, hosts workshops and training sessions, convenes grassroots organizations, and offers information and referral.

Financial Data

(Year ended 6/30/00)	
Total grants paid:	$ 330,000
Highest grant:	$ 30,000
Lowest grant:	$ 500
Median grant size:	$ 10,000

Application Procedures

Funds are dispersed through two funds. Fund of the Sacred Circle provides grants to American Indian-led organizations in Minnesota and/or Wisconsin. Deadline is July 1. Social Change Fund provides grants to an array of constituent-led groups in Minnesota only. Deadline is February 1. Interested groups are encouraged to call and request a grant information and application booklet. The fund holds an open information meeting approximately one month before deadline. If projects are new to grantmaking or if the organization members were not able to attend the open meeting, they can request a meeting with any grants staff to review the criteria of their individual project.

Proposals are read by staff to determine whether they fit the grant proposal general guidelines; then the proposals are sent to the grants committee. This committee comprises community activists who guide the remainder of the process and decide who receives a site visit, and determines the slate of recommendations for funding that is sent to the board (which also contains community activists) for approval.

If the proposal is a repeat request for funds from Headwaters, the application should be clear about the continued necessity and the role the fund can play, or be clear about the new project or proposal for which funds are being requested. Reports from previous grant(s) must be on file. Attach any supporting documents, letters, or publications to the proposal but make certain that all important information (listed in the guidelines) is contained in the basic seven-page proposal. Five copies of the basic proposal should be sent along with a copy of the supplied cover sheet.

Grant Limitations

Projects must have budgets under $250,000 and must involve social change and not social service.

**Meeting
Times**

Each funding cycle takes about four months to complete. The grants committee meets about six weeks after the deadline to review proposals to decide on a list for site visits. Site visits are attended by two committee members and one staff member. Following the site visits the grants committee meets on recommendations for funding. The board of directors meets the last Monday on alternate months.

Publications

The fund publishes an annual report, quarterly newsletters, a grant information and application booklet, and the "Grassroots Fundraising Video Series."

THE HEWLETT FOUNDATION

2121 SAND HILL ROAD

MENLO PARK, CALIFORNIA 94025

PHONE: (650) 234-4500

FAX: (650) 234-4501

EMAIL: hjackson@hewlett.org

WEB: www.hewlett.org

Contact Person

Paul Brest, President

Purpose

The Hewlett Foundation is a private foundation with broad charitable interests. Its purpose is to support projects in the religious, scientific, literacy, and educational areas nationwide. The foundation reserves a portion of its funds for projects in the San Francisco Bay Area.

Areas of Interest

The foundation's resources are concentrated on the performing arts; education; population issues; environmental issues; conflict resolution and family and community development. The foundation will consider general, program, or project support grants, and opportunities to fund programs with other grantmakers.

• Performing Arts. Classical music ensembles, professional theater and opera companies, and ballet and modern dance organizations for artistic, managerial, and institutional development. The foundation also makes some grants to groups providing services to Bay Area nonprofit film and video organizations.

• Education. Projects that improve elementary, secondary, or higher education. Grants in the elementary and secondary area are generally limited to California public schools, especially those in the San Francisco Bay area.

• Population. Training of population experts, policy-related research, and family planning and other fertility-reducing programs.

• Environment. Decision-making on environmental issues, encouraging more intelligent and rewarding uses of the natural environment for education, conservation, and development. In 1994 a new program was adopted: Grants will be awarded to organizations working on issues that affect the fragile ecosystems lying west of the 100th meridian, the traditional line separating the arid West from the temperate Eastern North America.

• Conflict Resolution. Alternatives to litigation and legislation and the process by which disputes are resolved. Grants, whose overall purpose is to support the development of the field as a whole, are made in five specific categories: theory development, support for mediators and other practitioners of third-party intervention techniques, institutional support for organizations that train or educate potential users about conflict resolution, policy reform, and international conflict resolution development.

• Family and Community Development. Organizations in the San Francisco Bay Area in the categories of children's policy, community development, family support, homelessness, affordable housing, minority leadership development, and youth community service.

Financial Data

(Year ended   /   /   ) Assets: NA Total grants paid: Number of grants paid: Highest grant: Lowest grant: Median grant size:

Application Procedures

Initial contact with the foundation should be made by a brief letter of inquiry. The letter should contain a statement of the applicant's need for funds and enough factual information to enable staff to determine whether the application falls within the foundation's program or perhaps warrants consideration as a special project.

All inquiries are reviewed by the president and by a relevant program officer. The program officer will either, in consultation with the president, decline requests that seem unlikely to result in a project the foundation can support; request further information, if needed, for a decision; or present the request to the rest of the staff for discussion. Applicants who receive a favorable response to their initial inquiry will be invited to submit a formal proposal.

Deadlines for proposals vary by program area and applicants should call the foundation for these deadlines.

Grant Limitations

Normally the foundation will not make grants or loans to individuals; grants for basic research; capital construction fund contributions; grants in the medical or health-related fields; general fundraising drives; or grants intended directly or indirectly either to support candidates for political office or to influence legislation.

In addition, there are limitations within each program area. In the performing arts, the foundation does not consider requests in: the visual or literary arts; the humanities; elementary and secondary school programs; college or university proposals; community art classes; ethnic arts including crafts, folk arts, popular music, and ethnic dance; recreational, therapeutic, and social service arts programs; individuals; one-time events such as seminars, conferences, festivals, or cultural foreign exchange programs; or touring costs. In education, the foundation does not support proposals to fund student aid; construction; equipment purchases including computers; education research; basic scientific research; health research; or health education programs. In the area of population, the foundation will not consider support for biomedical research on reproduction; nor will it fund population education programs directed toward the general public. The Hewlett Foundation is wholly independent of the Hewlett-Packard Company Foundation.

Meeting Times

The board of directors meets quarterly to consider grant applications.

Publications

The foundation publishes a brochure which contains specific guidelines for applicants.

THE HUNT ALTERNATIVES FUND

625 MOUNT AUBURN STREET

CAMBRIDGE, MA 02138

PHONE: (617) 868-3918

FAX: (617) 995-1982

EMAIL: information@
huntalternatives.org

WEB: huntalternativesfund.org

Contact Person

Sarah Gauger, Executive Director

Purpose

The Hunt Alternatives Fund awards grants to organizations that seek innovative solutions to poverty, discrimination, and other forms of social disenfranchisement. Grants are provided to enable organizations to broaden their knowledge, experience, funding, and community support. In 1993, the Hunt Alternatives Fund split into two organizations. The Hunt Alternatives Fund is now based in Cambridge. The Sister Fund, in New York, now awards grants in the New York metropolitan area. (See Sister Fund entry on page 419.)

Areas of Interest

The fund has three program areas:
• ARTWorks for Kids. ARTWorks seeks to strengthen arts programs targeting disadvantaged and disengaged children. These organizations strive to help children use art in order to reach their full potential. Based in the greater Boston Metropolitan area, the fund helps art organizations advocate for sustained support, whether these organizations work in the classroom, after-school programs, or in the larger community.
• Civic Engagement. This program area is an extension of the community-based work in which the foundation engaged in its former Denver base. The fund seeks to promote civic engagement in the U.S. by collaborating with institutional partners to identify and train leaders in initiatives to create a more engaged and just society. The fund will make a few unsolicited grants to partners doing work in this field.
• Women Waging Peace. This program advocates for the full participation of women in local and global peace processes. Women Waging Peace is a coalition of over 200 members and focuses on collaborating on workable solutions to long-standing conflicts.

The fund fosters the long-term viability of nonprofit organizations by helping them identify new or increased sources of assistance and develop strategies for self-sufficiency. Program, project support, staff support, start-up funds, matching and challenge grants, technical assistance, leadership development, and general operating support is provided. Grants range in size from $3,000 to $30,000, with an average grant between $15,000 to $20,000.

Application Procedures

Deadlines vary from year to year and can change without notice. Applicants should call for current information, and submit a request well in advance of the need for funding. The fund accepts the Common Grant Application format, which can be obtained from the fund as well. The fund requires a completed proposal with all supporting documentation attached before it will consider an applicant.

Grant Limitations

The fund only supports public charities recognized by the IRS. It does not support government agencies, capital campaigns, building improvement or endowments, individuals, individual schools or scholarships, medicine/health, art/culture, education or religion, except when the primary focus of the project addresses issues in the purpose statement, or historical efforts, recreation, research, and environmental issues.

Meeting Times

The board of directors meets twice yearly to make funding decisions.

Publications

The fund publishes a twice-yearly report, "Alternatives", that describes grants awarded during the year and news of the fund. It also publishes application guidelines.

THE HYAMS FOUNDATION

175 FEDERAL STREET, 14TH FLOOR

BOSTON, MASSACHUSETTS 02110

PHONE: (617) 426-5600

FAX: (617) 426-5696

EMAIL: info@hyamsfoundation.org

WEB: www.hyamsfoundation.org

Contact Persons

Elizabeth B. Smith, Executive Director

Susan R. Perry, Administrative Manager

Purpose

The mission of the Hyams Foundation is to increase economic and social justice and power within low-income communities. The foundation believes that investing in strategies that enable low-income people to increase their economic security, build wealth and become active participants in their communities will have the greatest social return in these times. The foundation will carry out its mission by: supporting civic participation by low-income communities; promoting economic development that benefits low-income neighborhoods and their residents; and developing the talents and skills of low-income communities in Boston and Chelsea and funds organizations outside of these geographic areas only through special funding initiatives.

Areas of Interest

The foundation makes grants in three program areas:

• Civic Participation, which includes Community Organizing, Leadership Development, Voter and Citizen Participation and Public Policy Advocacy.

• Community Economic Development, which includes Workforce Development, Building Individual and Neighborhood Assets and Job Creation.

• Youth Development, which includes Academic Enrichment, Leadership Development and Activism, Skill and Talent Development and Summer Programs.

THE HYAMS FOUNDATION

**Financial
Data**

(Year ended 12/31/99)	
Assets:	$ 131,800,980
Total grants paid:	$ 4,408,669
Number of grants paid:	210
Median grant size:	$ 23,000

**Application
Procedures**

A single application should be made to the Hyams Foundation, rather than individual or duplicate applications to the separate funds.* A revised grant form is available on our website. Deadlines are as follows: November 1 for the February meeting; March 1 for the June meeting; July 1 for the October meeting.

The main body of the proposal should not exceed ten pages. Attachments should include copies of IRS determination letters establishing that the organization is a tax-exempt public charity and proof of incorporation in Massachusetts (with first-time proposals).

Applicants should not request an appointment before submitting a written proposal. When the staff determines that a proposal meets the eligibility requirements and is complete, a meeting with the applicant organization's director will be requested. The review process takes from two to six months.

Grant recipients are expected to submit a financial statement (audited, if possible) as well as a full report on the program funded. The report should include a statement of the progress made on the program, goals as set forth in the original proposal, the number of persons actually served by the program, income and expenses for the project, specifically, and the organization as a whole, the number of staff employed, and program achievements, as well as problems encountered.

**Grant
Limitations**

Applicants must be Massachusetts charitable corporations and tax-exempt public charities as defined in Section 501(c)(3) of the Internal Revenue Code. Grants are made only to organizations located in and serving the cities of Boston and Chelsea, Massachusetts.

---

*General inquiries should be directed to the administrative assistant to the directors rather than to the executive director.

The trustees will not consider applications from educational institutions for standard educational or capital programs. Consideration will be given only to experimental programs of educational institutions designed to meet the social welfare needs of the community. In addition, no grants are made for educational curriculum development, conferences, film production, or scholarships; to any municipal, state, or federal agency; to national or regional organizations; to religious organizations for religious purposes; to hospital capital campaigns; or to one organization for the programs of another which is not tax-exempt.

Meeting Times

The board of trustees meets approximately six times a year, from September through June.

Publications

The Hyams Foundation publishes an annual report that includes detailed information on guidelines and application procedures, financial information, and a full list of grants.

Contact Person

Jim Canales, President

Purpose

The James Irvine Foundation is dedicated to enhancing the social, economic, and physical quality of life in California, and to enriching the intellectual and cultural environment.

Specifically, the foundation seeks to enhance equal opportunity; to improve the economic and social well-being of the disadvantaged and their communities; to foster communication, understanding, and cooperation among diverse groups; to promote civic participation, social responsibility, public understanding of issues, and sound public policy development; and to enrich the quality and diversity of educational, cultural, health, and human services programs statewide.

Areas of Interest

Grants are made for higher education, the arts, health care and AIDS, community services and youth programs both to well-established institutions and to less mature organizations which exhibit the capacity to realize their potential. Of particular interest are projects that encourage and sustain leadership, seek solutions to new as well as long-standing problems, and strive to leverage results. The foundation supports demonstration projects and collaborative projects, as well as programs with a statewide focus or the potential for significant regional impact.

The foundation will consider requests for institutional and program development, policy studies and capital projects; it specifies, in the latter case, that it expects applicants to attract most of the funds from other sources and to demonstrate the financial capacity to support continuing operational costs without further recourse to the foundation.

**Financial
Data**

> The following analysis is based on grants paid
> in 2000:
> Assets: $ 1,509,641,005
> Total grants paid: $ 37,165,963

**Application
Procedures**

Prospective applicants should submit a preliminary letter of inquiry briefly outlining the project or need for which support is sought. The letter and enclosures should provide general information about the applicant organization, including a financial statement identifying all income sources; project scope, budget, and timetable; and plans for funding the activity. Copies of federal and state tax exemption letters and evidence that the applicant is a public charity should accompany the letter.

Letters of inquiry are accepted year round. Applications for the community economic development, health, higher education, and special projects programs should be submitted to the San Francisco office. Applications for the arts, civic culture, and children, youth, and family programs should be submitted to the Los Angeles office.

Foundation staff will suggest a meeting with applicants whose preliminary requests appear to be in keeping with the foundation's current interests and funding guidelines. Additional information and a site visit may be scheduled. Projects selected at this stage will then go on to one of the foundation's two distribution committees for further consideration and possible recommendation to the board.

The board takes formal action on grant requests several times a year.

**Grant
Limitations**

By trust provisions, grants are limited to charitable uses in the state of California and for the benefit of charities which do not receive a substantial part of their support from taxation nor exist primarily to benefit tax-supported entities. Grants are generally not made to sectarian or religious organizations or private pre-collegiate schools for activities primarily benefitting their own members; for basic research; for films or publishing activities; or for festivals or conferences.

**Meeting
Times**

> The distribution committees of the foundation meet twice a year, generally in May and November, to consider applications. These meetings are followed by a meeting of the board of directors at which final action is taken.

Publications

> The foundation publishes an annual report which includes a full list and description of grants and information for potential applicants.

ITTLESON FOUNDATION

15 EAST 67 STREET

NEW YORK, NEW YORK 10021

PHONE: (212) 794-2008

FAX: (212) 794-0351

WEB: www.ittlesonfoundation.org

Contact Person

Anthony C. Wood, Executive Director

Purpose

The Ittleson Foundation provides seed money for the start-up of innovative programs that improve the social welfare of citizens of the United States. Priority is given to pilot projects, test and demonstration projects, and applied research projects of national scope and which result in a product or outcome of some consequence in the real world.

Areas of Interest

Current areas of interest are mental health, the environment, criminal justice, and AIDS. Mental health has been the primary focus since its inception and the foundation looks for innovative projects that address underserved populations such as the elderly, poor, and people of color. Violence prevention and support and care for people with AIDS are also priorities. Pilot environmental projects that test new approaches to solving environmental problems, bring about changes through policy research, or add to the working knowledge through applied research are funded. The foundation also seeks projects which educate young people in the environmental field.

Financial Data

(Year ended 12/31/01)	
Assets:	$ 26,478,115
Total grants paid:	$ 1,125,000
Number of grants paid:	30
Highest grant:	$ 250,000
Lowest grant:	$ 5,000
Median grant size:	$ 25,000

Application
Procedures

The foundation has no application forms or deadlines. Applicants should write a brief letter to the executive director describing the work for which the funds are being sought along with a budget. If the activity falls within the current scope of the foundation's interests, applicants will be asked to supply additional information as it may be required.

The board meets twice a year. Initial letters of inquiry received before April 1 will be reviewed during the spring meeting and letters received before September 1 will be reviewed during the fall meeting.

Grant
Limitations

The foundation does not usually contribute to the humanities or cultural projects, to general education, or to social agencies offering direct services to individuals. Furthermore, the foundation does not offer fellowships or scholarships of any kind, travel grants, or grants-in-aid to individuals.

Meeting
Times

The board meets twice a year, in the fall and spring.

Publications

The foundation's annual report is available on its website.

JEWISH FUND FOR JUSTICE

260 FIFTH AVENUE, SUITE 701

NEW YORK, NEW YORK 10001

PHONE: (212) 213-2113

FAX: (212) 213-2233

EMAIL: jfjustice@jfjustice.org

WEB: www.jfjustice.org

Contact Person

Lee Winkleman, Director of Grantmaking

Purpose

The Jewish Fund for Justice assists grassroots organizations working directly with low-income people to combat poverty in their own communities. The fund adds a Jewish presence to inter-denominational efforts grappling with the causes of poverty and links Jewish social action with community action through technical assistance, public education, and outreach.

Areas of Interest

The fund makes grants on a nondenominational basis to projects concerned with women in poverty, neighborhood revitalization, at-risk youth, jobs and economic development, multi-issue faith-based organizing, and new Americans.

Financial Data

(Year ended 6/30/00)	
Assets:	$ 2,275,271
Total grants paid:	$ 1,235,000
Number of grants paid:	85
Highest grant:	$ 25,000
Lowest grant:	$ 500
Median grant size:	$ 12,500

Application Procedures

The fund requires that an applicant start the process by calling the program officer to discuss the proposal. If the proposal falls within the fund's interest area, guidelines and an application form will be sent. Application deadlines for the fund's two grant cycles are December 15 and June 1.

Grant Limitations

The fund only supports organizations that are tax-exempt or working with a tax-exempt fiscal agent. In addition, the fund does not support research, social service programs that do not have an advocacy or organizing component, capital expenditures, and media and publication projects.

Publications

The fund publishes an annual report. See our website for grant guidelines.

THE JEWISH HEALTHCARE FOUNDATION OF PITTSBURGH

PHONE: (412) 594-2550

FAX: (412) 232-6240

EMAIL: info@jhf.org

WEB: www.jhf.org

CENTER CITY TOWER, SUITE 2330

650 SMITHFIELD STREET

PITTSBURGH, PENNSYLVANIA 15222

Contact Person

Nancy Zionts

Purpose

To support and foster the healthcare services, healthcare education and to respond to the health-related needs of the elderly, underprivileged, indigent and underserved populations in western Pennsylvania. The foundation will assist in the treatment and care of those who are elderly, sick, infirm, or in any way afflicted with physical or mental disease, in both the Jewish and general communities.

Areas of Interest

The foundation has three areas of interest:

• **Advancing Health: Biomedical, Technological and Informatics Discovery**—the existing technology could reduce medical error and variation, consumer confusion, overcapacity, and the resulting high costs and inferior outcomes. In communities with strong medical research and technology innovators, the quality of care improves. Best practices become available and diffused more quickly. The foundation seeks to fund start-ups, recruiting entrepreneurial individuals and firms to develop industry clusters and specialty centers, and to establish global networks, which will speed up discovery so that people will live longer, healthier and more productive lives.

• **Financing Health: Strengthening Health Systems and Expanding Insurance Coverage**—the foundation supports issues of enrollment, entitlement, coverage and benefits and how they affect access, quality, disease management, prevention and early detection by seeding new financing and delivery models and rallying community leadership to identify, support and reward the highest quality, error-free care.

• **Integrating Health: Physical, Behavioral, Environmental**—the foundation supports the integration of physical, behavioral and environmental health which would improve the health status of all Americans. Integrating services for the frail and vulnerable, across the continuum of acute, rehabilitation, end-of-life, home-based and residential health care into systems that are population specific, extending beyond traditional medical providers to civic organizations, insurers, employers and consumers. The foundation will accomplish this by creating financing and incentives for treatment and services based on the latest research discoveries and best practices, producing better outcomes.

Financial Data

(Year ended 12/31/00)	
Assets:	$ 133,500,000
Total grants paid:	$ 6,165,478
Total number of grants:	120

Application Procedures

Four copies of a preliminary letter of intent should be submitted first. This letter of intent should not exceed six pages and should include the program description, program objectives, proposed intervention, timetable, anticipated outcome, innovative aspects, community education and research and/or evaluation components, likelihood of success, partnerships, and long-term plans. Applicants should also submit supporting materials identifying name and address of the contact person, institutional and personnel qualifications, budget, list of the board of directors, letter of 501(c)(3) status, and most recent financial statements.

There are no deadlines for submissions of letters of intent.

Grant Limitations

Projects must be health related and address the foundation priorities. Applications must be IRS tax-exempt charities. The foundation normally does not make grants to organizations outside western Pennsylvania, for general operations, endowment programs, capital needs, operating deficits or retirement of debt, political campaigns, scholarships, fellowships, individual research grants, or individual travel.

Meeting Times

The board meets on a regular basis.

Publications

The foundation publishes an annual report, grant guidelines, and a program policy statement.

THE ROBERT WOOD JOHNSON FOUNDATION

PHONE: (609) 452-8701

FAX: (609) 627-7582

EMAIL: see website

WEB: www.rwjf.org

P. O. Box 2316

Princeton, New Jersey 08543-2316

Contact Person

Richard J. Toth, Director, Office of Proposal Management

Purpose

The Robert Wood Johnson Foundation is interested in improving health and health care in the United States. Its resources are concentrated on improving access to personal health care, improving the way services are organized and provided to people with chronic health conditions, and reducing the harm caused by substance abuse. The foundation also seeks projects which help address the problem of escalating health care expenditures.

Areas of Interest

The foundation defines its role as one that assists development and testing of new and previously untried approaches to health care problems; demonstrations to assess objectively the operational effectiveness and value of selected new health care arrangements and approaches that have proven effective in more limited settings; and projects designed to promote the broader diffusion of programs that have been objectively shown to improve health status or to make health care more affordable.

RWJF's grantmaking under our Health priority addresses five interest areas—several of which relate to our long-standing goal of reducing the personal, social, and economic harm caused by substance abuse—tobacco, alcohol, and illicit drugs.

- **Tobacco**

Decreasing the number of Americans who use tobacco.

- **Alcohol and Illegal Drugs**

Reducing the negative health and social consequences of alcohol and illegal drug abuse.

- **Health and Behavior**

Increasing physical activity among Americans and promoting health behavior change as part of routine medical care.

- **Community Health**

Understanding how social isolation contributes to poor health and strengthening social support and connectedness.

- **Population-Based Health Sciences**

Promoting leadership and tool developments for population-wide approaches to health improvement.

Grantmaking under our Health Care priority is centered around the six interest areas below. Most relate to our goals of assuring access to basic health care at reasonable cost and improving care and support for people with chronic health conditions.

- **Insurance Coverage**

Increasing the number of Americans with health insurance.

- **Priority Populations**

Improving access to health care for underserved population groups.

- **Information/Tracking**

Improving public and private policymaking by making available timely, accurate, and relevant information about the health system.

- **Clinical Care Management**

Helping reduce the gap between what is known about the best ways to care for people with chronic disease and what is actually practiced.

- **Supportive Services**

Preparing for increased future demand for long-term support and services.

- **End-of-Life Care**

Increasing the number of Americans who receive high-quality palliative care at the end of life.

Application Procedures

Grant applications are accepted throughout the year, and there are no formal application forms. Before submitting a full proposal, applicants should prepare a letter of intent. This letter should briefly and concisely state the proposed project as well as its objectives and significance; the qualifications of the organization and the individuals involved; the mechanisms for evaluating results; the project timetable; evaluation methods; and a budget. The letter should be accompanied by a copy of the applicant's proof of tax-exempt status under the Internal Revenue Code. Proposal letters should be addressed to the proposal manager. If the foundation requests a full proposal, full instructions will be sent regarding what information is needed and by what date. It usually takes from six months to one year after an initial proposal letter is received for a grant award to be made.

Financial Data

(Year ended 12/31/00)	
Assets:	$ 8,793,792,000
Total grants paid:	$ 399,486,662
Number grants paid:	821
Highest grant:	$ 24,844,280
Lowest grant:	$ 1,293
Median grant size:	$ 198,246

Grant Limitations

Ordinarily preference will be given to organizations that have qualified for exemption under Section 501(c)(3) of the Internal Revenue Code and that are not private foundations as defined in Section 509(a). Public instrumentalities and government agencies are eligible for support.

The foundation's guidelines normally preclude support for ongoing general operating expenses; endowment, construction or equipment; basic biomedical research; international activities or programs and institutions outside the United States; and direct support to individuals.

Meeting Times

The board of trustees meets quarterly.

Publications

The foundation publishes an annual report and application guidelines.

JOVID FOUNDATION

5335 WISCONSIN, AVENUE, N.W.

SUITE 440

WASHINGTON, DC 20015-2003

PHONE: (202) 686-2616

FAX: (202) 686-2621

EMAIL: jovidfoundation@yahoo.com

WEB: www.fdncenter.org/grantmaker/jovid

Contact Person

Bob Wittig, Executive Director

Purpose

The Jovid Foundation assists nonprofit organizations in the District of Columbia whose work is aimed at helping people in or at risk of long-term poverty to become self-sufficient. Because the foundation is small and seeks to make a real difference to the projects it funds, it is particularly interested in neighborhood-based efforts.

Areas of Interest

The foundation's grantmaking focuses in the area of employment and training and evaluation of these programs.

Financial Data

(Year ended 12/31/2000)	
Assets:	$8,171,677
Total grants awarded:	$775,940
Number of grants awarded:	49
Highest grant:	$200,000
Lowest grant:	$1,000
Median grant size:	$10,000

Application Procedures

Organizations seeking support should first send a brief one- or two-page letter to the foundation, outlining the project and projected cost. The letter should concisely describe the organization, the specific program for which funds are sought, the community to be served, the total budget for the program and the amount sought. If the project falls within the foundation guidelines the board will invite a formal proposal. Unsolicited proposals will not be accepted or considered for review. The foundation urges prospective applicants to allow enough time for review of an initial letter to meet the grant proposal deadlines if a proposal is solicited.

Grantseekers should contact the foundation for deadlines in the current grantmaking schedule.

Grant Limitations

Grants are awarded in Washington, DC. Only one grant per year is awarded to any one organization.

Meeting Times

The board of trustees meets four times a year in March, June, September, and December.

Publications

The foundation publishes an annual report and grant guidelines.

THE JOYCE FOUNDATION

70 WEST MADISON STREET, SUITE 2750

CHICAGO, ILLINOIS 60602

PHONE: (312) 782-2464

FAX: (312) 782-4160

EMAIL: info@joycefdn.org

WEB: www.joycefdn.org

Contact Persons

Education: Warren Chapman, Fausto Ramos Gómez, and Peter Mich
Employment: Kara Kellaher Mikulich, Unmi Song, and Jennifer Phillips
Environment: Margaret O'Dell and James Seidita
Gun Violence: Roseanna Ander
Money and Politics: Lawrence Hansen
Culture: Ellen Alberding
Associate Program Officer: Shelley Davis

Areas of Interest

The Joyce Foundation supports efforts to protect the natural environment of the Great Lakes, to reduce poverty and violence in the region, and to ensure that its people have access to good schools, decent jobs, and a diverse and thriving culture. We are especially interested in improving public policies, because public systems such as education and welfare directly affect the lives of so many people, and because public policies help shape private sector decisions about jobs, the environment, and the health of our communities. To ensure that public policies truly reflect public rather than private interests, we support efforts to reform the system of financing election campaigns.

Priority is given to applications that are designed to improve public policies; help minorities and the disadvantaged; recognize the interrelationships that exist among program areas; and, stress regional and interstate cooperation.

Support is also provided through the special opportunities fund and the president's discretionary fund.

The issues of interest to the foundation are:

Education

The Joyce Foundation supports efforts to reform public schools in Chicago, Cleveland, and Milwaukee to ensure that all children, regardless of race, gender or economic circumstances, get an education that prepares them for lives as thoughtful and productive citizens. Recognizing that each city's schools are unique, the foundation looks for proposals that support reform in each district and reinforce basic reform concepts, including equitable allocation of resources. Proposals must address one or more of the following program interests:

• investing in teaching: supporting innovative strategies to develop and attract diverse, highly qualified teachers for hard-to-staff subject areas, schools, and districts;

• strengthening community engagement and leadership: identifying, informing and supporting leaders at the school and community level and enabling them to participate meaningfully in school decision-making;

• advancing technology-supported reform: fostering broad application of successful, technology-based innovation to promote district-wide improvements in the reform of teaching and learning;

• promoting minority achievement: using proven strategies for helping minority students achieve at high levels.

Employment

To reduce poverty in the Midwest the Joyce Foundation focuses on issues confronting low-income workers, the problems they face getting and keeping jobs and the barriers to moving up the job ladder. Addressing such issues can help improve the working lives and economic conditions of tens of thousands of Midwest families.

The goal of the Joyce Foundation's Employment Program is to support efforts to develop public policies that improve the education, skills, learning opportunities, and advancement potential of low-wage workers, including current and former welfare recipients. It supports initiatives that promise to:

• improve state job-training and welfare-to-work policies to provide high-quality workforce preparation for low-income people;

• help translate lessons about successful workforce preparation strategies into policy;

• make sure that welfare policies incorporate effective education and training strategies that can move people not just off the welfare rolls but toward economic self-sufficiency;

• explore development of publicly-funded jobs programs for people who lack skills and work experience to break into the private job market;

• assess the impact of state and federal welfare policies on the economic prospects of poor people to help guide the policymaking process.

Environment

Protecting the natural environment of the Great Lakes region has been a long-time commitment of the Joyce Foundation. The foundation supports the development, testing, and implementation of policy-based, prevention-oriented, scientifically sound solutions to the environmental challenges facing the region. It supports work that promises to:

• protect and improve Great Lakes water quality, especially by finding and implementing solutions to environmental problems;

• maintain and strengthen the network of environmental groups working to improve the Great Lakes ecosystem;

• reduce the production, use, and discharge of toxic substances in agricultural and industrial processes;

• use the opportunity of the restructuring of the electric utility industry to promote more efficient use of energy and increased reliance of cleaner energy sources;

• ensure that government decision-making on transportation and land use, especially at the state level, takes environmental considerations into account.

Gun Violence

Gun violence takes the lives of more than 30,000 Americans each year and injures thousands more. The Joyce Foundation seeks to reduce that toll by addressing gun violence as a public health problem, with strategies that emphasize prevention. The foundation will consider proposals aimed at:

• strengthening public policies that deal with gun violence as a public health issue;

• supporting policy-relevant research by scholars and institutions that collect and analyze gun violence data from a public health perspective and examine prevention strategies;

• supporting efforts that lead to the treatment and regulation of guns as a consumer product, with appropriate design and safety standards;

• supporting effective Midwest-based coalitions and national coalitions with a strong Midwest presence that address gun violence as a public health issue and promote policies that reflect that view;

• encouraging and strengthening the activity of medical professionals in addressing gun violence as a public health issue;

• communicating public-health policy and research to Midwest and national policymakers.

Money and Politics

To prevent political corruption, ensure all citizens equal access to their elected representatives, and restore fairness and competition to elections, Americans must address the problem of money in politics.

The goal of the Joyce Foundation's Money and Politics Program is to improve the system of financing state and federal election campaigns. Achieving that goal will likely require broad, sustained efforts including data collection and analysis, policy development and advocacy, public education, grassroots organizing, coalition-building, communications, and litigation. The foundation supports exemplary projects that:

• promote federal and state-level (Midwest) campaign finance reforms;

• seek a better balance between the constitutionally protected rights of citizens to raise, give and spend campaign funds and the public's interest in preserving the integrity of the political process;

• improve financial disclosure of campaign finance records, increase public access to them, and strengthen enforcement of campaign finance laws.

Culture

The Joyce Foundation supports the efforts of Chicago-area cultural institutions to serve and represent the city's diverse populations. The foundation is interested in projects that address current urban issues, enhance cross-cultural understanding, and bring diverse audiences together to share common cultural experiences. We look for efforts that:

• stress the involvement of communities that are often overlooked;

• lead minority audiences to identify mainstream institutions as inviting both their attendance and their collaboration in planning relevant programming;

• help create a stable group of minority-based arts organizations; and

• encourage more of Chicago's people to see the arts as integral to their lives.

Financial Data

(Year ended 12/31/00)	
Assets:	$ 861,793,069
Total Grants Paid:	$ 39,596,622
Total Number of Grants:	254
Highest Grant:	$ 405,000
Lowest Grant:	$ 22,000
Median Grant:	$ 267,894

Application Procedures

The foundation accepts grant inquiries throughout the year. Applicants should submit a brief description of their project in writing before sending a full proposal. Applicants are encouraged to make an initial contact with the foundation well before the proposal deadline, so that a program officer can evaluate the request and discuss whether it sould be developed into a formal grant proposal. Past experience indicates that this preliminary review process is far more likely to yield successful proposals.

If the initial review indicates that funding is possible, a full proposal is requested. To be considered for funding, an organization should submit a written proposal and the application cover sheet, a copy of which is included in both the foundation's "Program and Grant Appplications Guidelines" and "Annual Report" publications.

The following information should be included: description of the organization, including a summary of its background, purpose, objectives, and experience in the area for which funds are sought; information on the project, including organizational and project background, explanation and documentation of need, plans for implementation, means of assessing results, and plans for dissemination of project findings; itemized project budget with narrative and proposed funding sources, amount of funds requested from Joyce, their proposed use, and time period; names and qualifications of people involved in the project; organizational expenses and income for previous, current, and coming fiscal year; list of board members, their titles, outside affiliations, and telephone numbers; a copy of IRS tax-exempt letter under Sections 509(a) and 501(c)(3); audited financial statement (if available) or Form 990 for the most recently completed fiscal year.

If the review of the proposal is positive, it is discussed at a joint meeting of the staff and the directors.

Grant Limitations

Our program areas are Education, Employment, Environment, Gun Violence, Money and Politics, and Culture. We focus our grantmaking on initiatives that promise to have an impact on the Great Lakes region, specifically the states of Illinois, Indiana, Iowa, Michigan, Minnesota, Ohio and Wisconsin. A limited number of environment grants are made to organizations in Canada. Education grantmaking focuses on public schools in Chicago, Cleveland and Milwaukee. Culture grants are restricted to the Chicago metropolitan area. We do not generally support capital proposals, endowment campaigns, religious activities, direct service programs, or scholarships.

**Meeting
Times**

The board of directors meets three times a year, in March, July, and December to consider grant requests.

Publications

The foundation publishes an annual report, "Program and Grant Application Guidelines," and a newsletter, "Work In Progress," which contain information on grantmaking activities.

W. K. KELLOGG FOUNDATION

ONE MICHIGAN AVENUE EAST

BATTLE CREEK, MICHIGAN 49017-4058

PHONE: (269) 968-1611

FAX: (269) 968-0413

EMAIL: see website

WEB: www.wkkf.org

Contact Person

Debbie Rey, Manager of Grant Proposals

Purpose

The W. K. Kellogg Foundation was established in 1930 "to help people help themselves through the practical application of knowledge and resources to improve their quality of life and that of future generations." Its programming activities center around the common vision of a world in which each person has a sense of worth; accepts responsibility for self, family, community, and societal well-being; and has the capacity to be productive, and to help create nurturing families, responsive institutions, and healthy communities.

Areas of Interest

To achieve the greatest impact, the foundation targets its grants toward specific areas. These include: health; food systems and rural development; youth and education; and philanthropy and volunteerism. Within these areas, attention is given to the cross-cutting themes of leadership; information and communication technology; capitalizing on diversity; and social and economic community development programming. Grants are concentrated in the United States, Latin America and the Caribbean, and the southern African countries of Botswana, Lesotho, Mozambique, South Africa, Swaziland, and Zimbabwe.

U.S. Programming Areas

Health

Improve the health of people in communities through increased access to integrated, comprehensive health care systems that are organized around public health, prevention, and primary health care, and that are guided, managed, and staffed by a broad range of appropriately prepared personnel.

Philanthropy and Volunteerism

To increase the ranks of new givers and to nurture emerging forms of philanthropy.

Food Systems and Rural Development

To help meet the needs for a safe and nutritious diet while ensuring that food production systems are environmentally sensitive, economically viable, sustainable over the long term, and socially responsible, and to fund collaborative, comprehensive approaches to rural development that emphasize community problem solving, leadership development, delivery of human services, and training of local government officials.

Youth and Education

Support healthy infant, child, and youth development by mobilizing, strengthening, and aligning systems that affect children's learning.

Greater Battle Creek

To engage with the community as a partner in helping people achieve their full educational and economic potential in order to create a more just, healthy, and sustainable community.

Application Procedures

Although there is no application form, proposals must conform to specified program priorities. Initial contact should be a proposal letter that contains a statement of problem, results expected, timetable, detailed description of project and amount of funding requested, and qualifications of key personnel. Additional supporting documentation should include a copy of current year organizational budget, additional sources (and amount) of support, copy of IRS tax-exempt status, list of board of directors and other key people and their affiliations, and plans for cooperation with other organizations.

If after an evaluation, the proposal is within the foundation's guidelines and current interest areas, the organization may be asked to develop a more detailed proposal possibly including a conference and Kellogg staff investigation.

Financial Data

```
(Year ended 8/31/00)
Assets:                     $ 4,853,383,875
Total grants paid:          $ 186,605,961
Total number of grants:             1,148
Highest grant:              $ 6,773,734
Lowest grant:                     $ 300
Median grant:               $ 225,000
```

Grant Limitations

Grantmaking is primarily in the United States, Latin America and the Caribbean, and southern Africa. Support is also provided to international fellowship programs in other countries.

The foundation does not award grants to individuals (except through fellowship programs), for religious purposes, building or endowment funds, research, development campaigns, films, equipment, publications, conferences, operating budgets, annual campaigns, emergency funds, deficit financing, or renovation projects. Organizations not classified as tax-exempt under Section 501(c)(3) of the Internal Revenue Code are also not funded.

Meeting Times

The board of trustees meets monthly.

Publications

The foundation publishes an annual report, brochure, newsletter, and application guidelines.

THE HENRY P. KENDALL FOUNDATION

176 FEDERAL STREET

BOSTON, MASSACHUSETTS 02110

PHONE: (617) 951-2525

FAX: (617) 443-1977

EMAIL: maries@kendall.org

WEB: www.kendall.org

Contact Person

Theodore M. Smith, Executive Director

Purpose

The Henry P. Kendall Foundation, established in 1957, focuses almost entirely on the environment and securing its physical, biological and aesthetic wealth for future generations.

Areas of Interest

The foundation's geographic priorities for grants are New England and the Maritime Provinces of Eastern Canada and the Pacific Northwest, including Western Canada and Alaska—the "shoulders" of North America. Marine, coastal, mountain, forest, and fresh water systems lie at the heart of the program which seeks to protect and restore ecosystem integrity, emphasizing the stewardship of nature's extraordinary diversity.

Current program themes are:
- Gulf of Maine Ecosystem—creating a community-based research and management paradigm to secure the long-term health of the gulf's ecosystem.
- The Northeastern Landscape—building a science-based approach to landscape conservation in the forests stretching from the Adirondack Mountains to coastal New Brunswick.
- Northeast Climate Change Initiative—developing a civil society approach to climate change by demonstrating that reducing greenhouse gas emissions in this region is technically feasible, economically beneficial, socially marketable and politically palatable, primarily through *Clean Air-Cool Planet*.
- North Country Institutional Capacity-Building—adding strength to leading Canadian and Alaskan conservation organizations.
- Yellowstone to Yukon—building a science-based approach to landscape conservation in the Rocky Mountains of Canada and the U.S.
- Watershed Innovations in North America—spurring national advances in watershed management through developing distinguished leadership, sound

science, reliable financing, and community support for watershed-based stewardship.

- Public Lands Management—stimulating improvements in the performance of public land management agencies in protecting ecological integrity.
- Special Project Initiatives—supporting innovative efforts to promote stewardship, such as grassroots environmental advocacy in New England, urban greenspace initiatives in Boston, advances in conservation biology, and high-leverage opportunities in environmental education.

Financial Data

(Year ended 12/31/00)	
Assets:	$ 92,170,575
Total grants paid:	$ 3,492,293
Number of grants paid:	80
Highest grant:	$ 717,355
Lowest grant:	$ 3,000
Median grant size:	$ 5,000 - $99,000

Application Procedures

If you decide that your interests fall within the Kendall Foundation program, please write a letter of no more than two pages which:

- Describes, in the first paragraph, the purpose for which you seek funding and the amount of money you are requesting;
- Outlines the background or the context of the issue to be addressed, the strategy being employed, the timetable, and the budget;
- Describes your organization, its mission, and its annual budget;
- Lists other sources of financing you already have or intend to seek.

You should attach a copy of your organization's IRS determination letter, a list of board members, and a curriculum vitae of the chief executive. Applications from or in conjunction with an organization acting as fiscal sponsor for a project should include, in addition to the sponsor's IRS determination letter, a letter from the fiscal sponsor confirming that its board has adopted the project and that it maintains active oversight of the project. Additional printed material—e.g., annual report or newsletter—may be attached as background pieces. (Note: the foundation often asks for further documentation, but only after its preliminary review indicates that the information would be helpful in the review process.)

The Kendall Foundation prefers letters which are concise, well-organized, jargon-free, and printed on high post-consumer-content recycled paper. Proposals sent by email are not accepted. Audio and video tapes will not be considered in the proposal review process.

Requests normally are reviewed in three cycles: Decisions on requests postmarked by February 1 are made in March; those postmarked by May 1 are made in June; and those postmarked by October 1 in November. Requests are usually acknowledged within two to three weeks of their receipt.

Grant Limitations

The Kendall Foundation normally makes grants only to those non-profit organizations which are classified as public charities under Section 501(c)(3) of the U.S. Internal Revenue Code or are Canadian organizations deemed equivalent by the foundation.

The foundation provides funding for general operating needs—normally where the money can be used for strategic purposes—and for specific programs and initiatives. Activities funded include advocacy, public education, policy research and analysis, on-the-ground resource management experiments, and institutional development.

The foundation normally does not make grants for endowments or capital fund campaigns, land acquisition, television and film projects, fellowships, basic scientific research, building construction or maintenance, equipment, debt reduction, or conferences or conference participation unrelated to current foundation institutional grants. Nor does the foundation normally fund waste clean-ups, toxics or air/water pollution prevention or pollution monitoring initiatives, individual land trusts, or species-specific preservation efforts.

Grants are normally made for one or two years and typically range from $5,000 to $50,000 with the average being closer to the lower end. The annual grant budget is approximately $3 million.

Meeting Times

The board of directors meets as required.

Publications

The foundation publishes an annual report and maintains a web site.

JOHN S. AND JAMES L. KNIGHT FOUNDATION

WACHOVIA FINANCIAL CENTER

200 SOUTH BISCAYNE BOULEVARD, SUITE 3300

MIAMI, FLORIDA 33131

PHONE: (305) 908-2600

FAX: (305) 908-2698

EMAIL: web@knightfdn.org

WEB: www.knightfdn.org

Contact Person

Grants Administrator

Purpose

The John S. and James L. Knight Foundation promotes excellence in journalism worldwide and invests in the vitality of twenty-six U.S. communities.

Areas of Interest

The foundation has three major grant programs:

Journalism Program

The Journalism Program is international in scope. Grants are made to U.S.-based organizations and institutions that offer special promise of advancing the quality and effectiveness of a free press and understand its role in a thriving democratic society. The foundation gives particular emphasis to the education of current and future journalists, the defense of a free press at home and worldwide. We also encourage approaches to quality journalism across all forms of media. Interested organizations should submit a letter of inquiry to the Foundation.

Knight Community Partners Program

The Knight Community Partners Program aims to improve the quality of life in twenty-six U.S. communities where the Knight brothers owned newspapers. It honors the values they brought to their business and their philanthropy. At its heart, the program seeks to improve the lives of individuals.

In the Knight Community Partners Program, the approaches we use will be as varied and complex as the places themselves. But in each Knight town and city, we want people to come together and define their priorities. In addition to grantmaking, we'll convene, serve as facilitators, help evaluate and disseminate what we learn together. Our ultimate objective is to collaborate with organizations and individuals to work toward a limited number of clearly defined goals.

Out notion of quality of life includes numerous components, and we are open to local ideas that may not fit within our preferences. In general, we believe the Knight community partnerships should foster a strong public education system, a housing and community development network that is available to everyone who needs it, ample assistance for children and families, citizen engagement in civic and democratic life, a vital and multifaceted cultural life, and positive human relations across lines of race, ethnicity and class. Underlying everything is an economy that offers employment opportunities to all who seek work.

As we see it, Knight's Community Partners Program can best succeed by developing long-term strategies focused on a few critical priorities. In particular, we believe Knight communities share opportunities and obligations in the following six priority areas:

• Education: To help all residents gain the knowledge and skills necessary to reach economic self-sufficiency, remain active learners, be good parents and effective citizens in a democracy. To provide an environment in which talented individuals refine and develop their abilities.

• Well-being of children and families: To provide all children and youth with opportunities for positive growth and development and to give all parents resources they need to strengthen their families.

• Housing and community development: To provide all residents with access to affordable and decent housing in safe, drug-free neighborhoods. To provide a continuum that includes everything from services for the homeless to affordable opportunities for home ownership.

• Economic development: To help all adults gain access to jobs. To build alliances among government, business and nonprofit sectors to create economic opportunities for residents.

• Civic engagement/positive human relations: To encourage and enable all residents to participate effectively in the democratic process, form ties to local institutions and strengthen relationships with one another.

• Vitality of cultural life: To provide all residents access to a wide variety of artistic and cultural pursuits. To nourish creativity in children, youth and adults.

National Venture Fund:

The National Venture Fund supports innovative opportunities and initiatives at the national level that relate directly or indirectly to Knight's work in its twenty-six communities. The Venture Fund welcomes proposals from U.S.-

based organizations committed to high standards of planning, evaluation and communication.

Those interested should submit a letter of inquiry to the Foundation.

Geographic Areas

California:	Long Beach	Cities of Long Beach and Signal Hill
	San Jose	Santa Clara, southern Alameda and southern San Mateo counties
Colorado:	Boulder	Boulder County
Florida:	Boca Raton	Palm Beach County
	Bradenton	Manatee County
	Miami	Miami-Dade and Broward counties
	Tallahassee	Leon County
Georgia:	Columbus	Muscogee County, Ga.; Phenix City, Ala.
	Macon	Bibb County
	Milledgeville	Baldwin County
Indiana:	Fort Wayne	Allen County
	Gary	Lake County
Kansas:	Wichita	Sedgwick County
Kentucky:	Lexington	Fayette, Bourbon, Clark, Jessamine, Madison, Montgomery, Scott and Woodford counties
Michigan:	Detroit	Wayne, Macomb, Oakland and Washtenaw counties
Minnesota:	Duluth	St. Louis County, Minn.; City of Superior, Wis.
	St. Paul	Ramsey County
Mississippi:	Biloxi	Harrison County
North Carolina:	Charlotte	Mecklenburg, Cabarrus, Union counties, N.C.; York County, S.C.
North Dakota:	Grand Forks	Grand Forks County, N.D.; Polk County, Minn.
Ohio:	Akron	Summit County
Pennsylvania:	Philadelphia	Philadelphia, Bucks, Chester, Delaware and Montgomery counties, Pa; City of Camden, N.J.
South Carolina:	Columbia	Richland County
	Myrtle Beach	Horry County
South Dakota:	Aberdeen	Brown County

Financial Data

(Year ended 12/31/00)	
Assets:	$ 2,199,000,000
Total grants paid:	$ 70,000,000
Number of grants:	356
Highest grant:	$ 9,000,000
Lowest grant:	$ 5,000
Median grant size:	$ 100,000

Application Procedures

Applicants are asked to submit a one or two page letter of inquiry before submitting proposals. Faxed or electronic submissions will not be accepted.

Grant Limitations

Requests for support of fundraising events; requests to cover operating deficits; charities operated by service clubs; activities that are normally the responsibility of government (The foundation will, in selective cases, join with units of government in supporting special projects); medical research; organizations or projects whose mission is to prevent, eradicate and/or alleviate the effects of a specific disease; requests from hospitals (unless they are for community-wide capital campaigns with a stated goal and beginning and ending dates or for specific projects that meet foundation goals), activities to propagate a religious faith or restricted to one religion or denomination; support of political candidates; memorials; international programs and organizations, except U.S.-based organizations supporting a free press arouond the world; a second request for a capital campaign for which the foundation previously approved a grant; conferences; group travel; honoraria for distinguished guests—except in initiatives of the foundation in all three cases; a second proposal from any institution or organization that has applied for support in the last twelve months, whether the result of the previous application was positive or negative.

Meeting Times

The board of trustees meets quarterly, in March, June, September, and December.

Publications

The foundation publishes an annual report and makes a current list of eligible cities available on request. In addition it publishes a quarterly newsletter (April, July, October, January), and Knight Commission report "A Call to Action: Reconnecting College Sports and Higher Education." (2001)

THE KRESGE FOUNDATION

P. O. Box 3151

3215 West Big Beaver Road

Troy, Michigan 48007-3151

PHONE: (248) 643-9630

FAX: (248) 643-0588

EMAIL: webmaster@kresge.org

WEB: www.kresge.org

Contact Person

John E. Marshall, III, President and CEO

Purpose

The Kresge Foundation, an independent private foundation, seeks to provide challenge grants for capital projects, especially for construction and renovation of buildings, and for the purchase of major equipment and real estate.

Areas of Interest

Grants are made to organizations operating in the fields of higher education, health and long-term care, human services, science and the environment, art and the humanities, and public affairs. Higher education and hospital organizations must have full accreditation. There is no predetermined grant budget by type of project or by field, nor are there geographical restrictions.

Eligible projects include construction of facilities, renovation of facilities, purchase of major equipment or an integrated system at a cost of at least $300,000, and purchase of real estate. The foundation does not grant initial funds or total project costs.

Financial Data

(Year ended / /)	
Asssets:	NA
Total grants paid:	
Number of grants paid:	
Highest grant:	
Lowest grant:	
Median grant size:	

Application Procedures

There are no application deadlines; proposals are accepted throughout the year. However organizations can make only one application in any one year.

The foundation's application guidelines list important considerations concerning an organization's application for funding, including their fund raising plans and project timetables. Applicants should obtain a copy of the guidelines and review them carefully before submitting a proposal. The foundation's application forms and an outline of information required in proposals are available from the foundation. Applications are acknowledged when received, and a specific timetable for review is provided at that time. Grant decisions are usually reached within five months of application receipt. Written and telephone inquiries are encouraged prior to the submission of a full proposal.

Typical grantees will have raised some funds before applying to the foundation and will have outlined a fundraising strategy, incorporating the use of a Kresge challenge grant, for securing the balance of funds needed to complete the project. Any long-term financing (five years or more), regulatory approval (e.g., certificates of need, zoning) or purchase agreements (real estate) required for completion of the project must be formally committed or imminent (within one to two months of submission) prior to applying.

Grant Limitations

Requests specifically toward debt retirement, furnishings, church building projects, or projects which are complete at the time of application are not eligible for foundation support. The foundation does not make grants to individuals.

Meeting Times

The board of trustees meets regularly. Grant decisions are announced in March, May, June, September, November, and December.

Publications

The foundation publishes an annual report and distributes a brochure describing its policies and application procedures.

LEVI STRAUSS FOUNDATION

LEVI'S PLAZA

1155 BATTERY STREET

SAN FRANCISCO, CALIFORNIA 94111

PHONE: (415) 501-6579

FAX: (415) 501-6575

WEB: www.levistrauss.com

Contact Person

Theresa Fay-Bustillos, Executive Director

Purpose

The Levi Strauss Foundation provides grants to nonprofit organizations in nearly 40 countries arouond the world with an emphasis on where LS & Co. has a presence. Some grants are made to national and regional organizations.

Areas of Interest

Community partnership programs address the needs of disadvantaged and underserved people through three series of grants:

• Community-based economic empowerment. Programs that enable low-income people to help themselves through: job creation and community-based economic development; job training, placement and access; leadership development aimed at strengthening the economic development capacity of community organizations and their leaders; and micro-enterprise development.

• AIDS prevention. Projects that provide education and HIV prevention services for poor and underserved people. The foundation is specifically interested in programs that: provide risk reduction education for those with high-risk behaviors; and provide services targeted to populations severely affected by AIDS.

• Social justice. Projects that address racial prejudice and improve race relations. In 1991, the Levi Strauss Foundation launched Project Change that supports coalitions of local residents that reflect the diversity of the community. The coalitions examine the state of race relations in their communities, devise strategies to combat racism, and recommend local projects that influence individual attitudes and behaviors and tackle institutional racism. A small number of grants to programs outside Project Change communities are made to programs that seek to remove racial and other discriminatory barriers, ease tensions between groups, promote diversity in community leadership, and prevent violent acts of racial and cultural prejudice.

The second manner by which the foundation seeks to work in its areas of interest is through its community involvement teams that support and encourage volunteerism and community service by Levi Strauss & Co. employees. Team members volunteer their time and raise funds for community projects of their choice. The foundation supports these activities by making grants to programs that the teams select.

Financial Data

(Year ended 12/31/00)	
Assets:	$ 114,618,305
Total grants paid:	$ 12,543,436
Number of grants paid:	770
Highest grant:	$ 950,000
Lowest grant:	$ 5,000

Application Procedures

The major giving program is the community partnership grants program.

Initial applications should be made by sending a two- to three-page letter that includes a brief statement of the organization's history and goals; purpose of the project and grant request; how the program fits the foundation's guidelines; target population to be served; and amount requested, project budget, and other sources of funds anticipated or committed. If the foundation determines that the project falls within the guidelines, a full proposal will be requested and an application outline provided. The application and review process usually takes thirty days, and all applicants are notified of the disposition of their requests.

Grant Limitations

The foundation will not provide support to organizations which in their constitution or practice discriminate against a person or group on the basis of age, political affiliation, race, national origin, ethnicity, gender, disability, sexual orientation, or religious belief.

Any organization receiving funding must be a public charity with tax-exempt status under Section 501(c)(3) of the Internal Revenue Code or a public entity and have a board or advisory group that is reflective of the population or community being served. With the exception of an employee dependent scholarship program, the foundation does not make grants to individuals.

**Meeting
Times**

The board of directors meets three times a year, in April, July, and December.

Publications

The foundation does not publish an annual report. The guidelines and a list of approved grants are at www.levistrauss.com/responsibility/foundation.

THE MAX AND ANNA LEVINSON FOUNDATION

PHONE: (505) 995-8802

FAX: (505) 995-8982

EMAIL: info@levinsonfoundation.org

WEB: www.levinsonfoundation.org

P. O. Box 6309

Santa Fe, New Mexico 87502-6309

Contact Person

Charlotte Talberth, Executive Director

Purpose

The Levinson Foundation is a small, private foundation concerned with the development of a more humane and rewarding society in which people have a greater ability and opportunity to determine directions for the future. Specifically it seeks projects and organizations working on environmental, social, and Jewish issues in a manner that combines dedication and genuine concern with rigorous analysis and strategic plans, and administrative and technical competence. The foundation accepts proposals from any and all locations but prefers projects with broad implications for society. Proposals for seed funding, start-up, and small organizations are especially encouraged.

Areas of Interest

The foundation funds organizations and projects of national and international benefit in the fields of environmental, social, and Jewish issues.

• Environment. Projects that include preservation of ecosystems and biological diversity; alternative energy and energy efficiency; toxics; alternative agriculture; environmental restoration, natural resource conservation, and sustainable communities.

• Social. Projects that include urban and rural community economic development; multiculturalism; human rights, youth leadership and empowerment; conflict resolution and aid to survivors of violence, and health care.

• Jewish/Israel. Projects that include Jewish culture and spirituality; history and education; Eastern and world Jewry; the Israeli peace movement, and social and environmental issues in Israel.

Whatever the specific area of interest, the foundation encourages projects which are concerned with promoting community, social justice, a healthy environment, and a sustainable economy, either by developing alternatives to the status quo or by responsibly modifying existing systems, institutions, conditions, and attitudes which block promising innovation.

THE MAX AND ANNA LEVINSON FOUNDATION

**Financial
Data**

```
(Year ended    /    /    )
Assets:                                    NA
Total grants paid:
Number of grants:
Highest grant:
Lowest grant:
Median grant size:
```

**Application
Procedures**

Initial approach may be by letter of inquiry rather than by full proposal. There is no required format for applications. Proposals should be brief, two to six pages, and should address the following questions: What is the "problem" or "opportunity" seeking to be addressed, including the scope, significance, and impact? Relevant to the above, what specific change is the applicant seeking to bring about? What are the activities to be carried out for which funding is sought? Why does the applicant believe the efforts described above, if successful, will achieve the changes outlined in the answer to the second question? What criteria will be used to evaluate the extent to which the project's goals have been achieved?

The foundation also requires budget information, relevant information about organization and key individuals and federal tax status (including a copy of the 501(c)(3) letter for the organization or its fiscal sponsor).

**Grant
Limitations**

Grants are awarded once a year and are mostly in the $10,000 to $20,000 range. The foundation does not consider grants for capital programs or traditional charitable programs. It cannot provide on-going support for the basic programs of any single organization. It is rarely able to fund organizations with budgets in excess of $500,000 per year. Materials sent via fax will not be accepted. The deadline to submit proposals is April 1 with grants awarded in June.

**Meeting
Times**

The board of directors meets every eight months.

Publications

The foundation does not publish an annual report. However, proposal guidelines, grants lists, and application forms are available on request.

LIBERTY HILL FOUNDATION

2121 CLOVERFIELD BOULEVARD, SUITE 113

SANTA MONICA, CALIFORNIA 90404

PHONE: (310) 453-3611

FAX: (310) 453-7806

EMAIL: info@libertyhill.org

WEB: www.libertyhill.org

Contact Person

Torie Osborn, Executive Director

Purpose

The Liberty Hill Foundation is a unique partnership of donors and community activists working to build a new Los Angeles based on a vision of social and racial equality, environmental sustainability and economic justice, and a shared sense of social responsibility. "Change, Not Charity" is our driving philosophy. We believe that those people most affected by social and economic inequality possess the knowledge and ideas to fix problems and improve communities—what they need are the resources to make their dreams a reality.

Areas of Interest

Liberty Hill's grantmaking programs support grassroots organizations in L.A. County that empower people and challenge the policies, institutions and attitudes fostering inequality. We give away more than $2 million each year, mostly through small grants—$500 to $25,000—that launch and sustain emerging ventures for social change. Liberty Hill's grantmaking is directed by seasoned community leaders who represent a broad array of experiences, backgrounds and expertise, guaranteeing the flexibility and integrity of our grantmaking.

We also provide training and technical assistance to community groups, convene activists and donors around critical issues facing our region, and work to strengthen the progressive voice in philanthropy.

Our unique contribution to Southern California philanthropy lies in finding the new ideas, new voices and new leaders in L.A. and giving them the resources they need to succeed. A grant from Liberty Hill to a promising and innovative grassroots group often provides a seal of credibility that opens the door to other funding sources, ensuring the viability of effective community-based organizations.

A public foundation, we raise our grantmaking and operational budget each year from individuals, foundations and socially responsible businesses. Our unique base of donors has allowed us to tap into resources that could not otherwise be accessed by grassroots organizations.

Liberty Hill helps bring democracy alive by serving as a bridge between two seemingly opposite worlds: one of wealth and privilege, the other of poverty and powerlessness. The bonds of commonality created at Liberty Hill hold the promise of a more just, safe and peaceful world where all are treated with dignity and respect.

Financial Data

(Year ended 6/30/00)	
Assets:	
Support and revenue:	$ 4,566,266
Total grants awarded:	$ 680,750

Application Procedures

Liberty Hill Foundation welcomes proposals from groups operating anywhere in Los Angeles County. Our funding is targeted to grassroots, community organizing projects that are working to bring about systemic social change. We give priority to groups that do not have access to traditional funding sources (government, foundations, private funders, etc.). Groups can apply for general support or project-specific funding. Guidelines and applications for each fund are available upon request.

Seed Fund

This fund provides grants to emerging and developing community-based organizations that work for social, racial, and economic justice. It helps groups establish themselves to become effective organizers through constituency building, leadership, and outreach.

Grant range: $1,000 - $15,000
Deadline: September 1
Contact: Margarita Ramirez

Fund for a New Los Angeles

This fund provides grants to groups that are actively organizing for racial equality and economic justice. Grants are targeted to organizations that have a proven track record, mature leadership, and solid constituency. The goal of the fund is to help these organizations build strong institutions.

Grant range: $20,000 - $35,000
Deadline: April 1
Contact: Margarita Ramirez

Environmental Justice Fund

This fund makes grants to grassroots organizations that are working to decrease exposure to toxic substances in neighborhoods and workplaces, particularly in communities of color and low-income areas. Groups engaged in community organizing, applied research, policy advocacy, litigation, or popular education are eligible.

Grant range: $5,000 - $35,000
Deadline: November 1
Contact: Lina Paredes

Lesbian and Gay Community Fund

This fund provides critical support to new or ongoing projects addressing the issues of marginalized lesbian, gay, bisexual, and transgendered (LGBT) communities. Grants are targeted to groups actively working for institutional, policy, or public opinion changes that improve LGBT life and wellbeing, promote positive identities, and build alliances between LGBT and straight communities.

Grant range: $1,000 - $15,000
Deadline: February 1
Contact: Lina Paredes

Social Entrepreneurial Fund

This funding initiative is designed to increase the wealth of poor communities through micro-enterprises, community and worker-owned businesses. Applicants must demonstrate a viable business plan that leads to social benefits such as job training or sustainable employment for disadvantaged individuals (such as homeless, high-risk youth, or immigrants) or the provision of a much-needed service (such as child care).

Grant range: $10,000 - $25,000
Deadline: June 1
Contact: Michele Prichard

Special Opportunity Fund

These grants fulfill a variety of organizational needs, particularly in the areas of capacity building, technical assistance, and training. Some examples are strategic planning, organizer training, leadership development, technical assistance, and special and timely education and outreach campaigns. Applicants must first meet Liberty Hill's general funding criteria.

Grant range: Up to $2,500
Funds available year-round
Contact: Margarita Ramirez

Publications

Publications include: annual report, quarterly newsletter (Connexus), brochures (general, Donor-Advised services, LA Lesbian and Gay Community Fund), Hearts & Minds Newsletter, grant applications.

AGNES M. LINDSAY TRUST

660 CHESTNUT STREET

MANCHESTER, NEW HAMPSHIRE 03104

PHONE: 1-866-669-1366 or (603) 669-1366

FAX: (603) 665-8114

EMAIL: admin@lindsaytrust.org

WEB: www.lindsaytrust.org

Contact Person

Susan Bouchard, Administrative Director

Purpose and Areas of Interest

The Agnes M. Lindsay Trust provides capital grants (capital campaigns, renovations, computer equipment, furniture, etc.) to projects in the areas of child welfare, the education of poor students from rural areas, and to agencies and institutions working in the health, welfare, and handicapped areas. The trust's grantmaking is limited to New Hampshire, Massachusetts, Maine, and Vermont.

Financial Data

(Year ended 12/31/00)	
Assets:	$ 38,543,176
Total grants paid:	$ 2,024,411
Total number of grants:	273
Highest grant:	$ 40,000
Lowest grant:	$ 1,000
Median grant size:	$1,000 - $15,000

Application Procedures

The trust accepts proposals throughout the year. Proposals should contain a brochure of the program's purpose; recent financial report and statement of income and expenses for the last two years; copy of current budget; list of capital items with costs, if involved; a copy of tax-exempt 501(c)(3) status from the IRS; and a Proposal Summary Form. Visit our website at www.lindsay trust.org to obtain this form.

**Grant
Limitations**

The trust prefers grants for capital requirements and will consider start-up funds for new projects if project has a good chance of success, and rarely gives grants for operating funds. Additionally, grants are not given to public entities, sectarian organizations, or to individuals and/or students requesting grants for scholarship aid for their own personal use. Only organizations with an IRS determination letter, 501(c)(3), and located in the states of New Hampshire, Massachusetts, Maine, and Vermont are eligible.

**Meeting
Times**

The board of trustees meets monthly to consider grant requests.

Publications

Visit our website at www.lindsaytrust.org.

LYNDHURST FOUNDATION

517 EAST FIFTH STREET

CHATTANOOGA, TN 37403-1826

PHONE: (423) 756-0767

FAX: (423) 756-0770

EMAIL: jmurrah@lyndhurstfoundation.org

WEB: www.lyndhurstfoundation.org

Contact Person

Jack Murrah, President

Purpose and Areas of Interest

Lyndhurst grants are distributed primarily at the initiative of the foundation. From January 2000 through December 2004, the foundation will focus its grantmaking on the activities listed below. Telephone inquiries are welcome.

In Chattanooga

- continued development of the Tennessee Riverpark and urban greenways network
- revitalization of inner-city neighborhoods, with an emphasis on safety and crime prevention, family support and early childhood development, education and youth development, physical infrastructure, and economic development
- strengthening of the city's arts and cultural life through support of the growth of the annual campaign of Allied Arts and the endowment of the Hunter Museum of American Art
- protection and enhancement of the community's natural environment
- the improvement of the community's elementary and secondary public schools through standards-based reform initiatives
- the continued development of improved housing opportunities for people of modest means
- urban design, planning, transportation, and resource conservation projects that bolster commercial, recreational, and residential development within Chattanooga's urban core

Elsewhere

- protection and enhancement of the natural environment of the Southeast, with a focus on the Southern Appalachian mountains in the five-state area of Tennessee, Georgia, South Carolina, North Carolina, and Alabama

- charter school initiatives in Tennessee and activities associated with the national Rural School and Community Trust project
- activities of particular interest to individual trustees of the foundation

Financial Data

(Year ended 12/31/00)	
Assets:	$ 159,124,201
Total grants paid:	$ 10,822,959
Number of grants paid:	48
Highest grant:	$ 5,220,000
Lowest grant:	$ 2,500
Median grant size:	$ 50,000

Application Procedures

Grants are currently distributed primarily at the foundation's initiative. In most categories, uninvited requests are not approved.

In those instances where an organization has been invited to submit a proposal, applicants are encouraged to send a brief letter—three pages or less—that states clearly and specifically what is being asked of the foundation and what is the objective of the project. In addition, the following information (where applicable) should be attached.

- A description of the sponsoring organization
- A list of the board of directors and staff
- A copy of the organization's annual budget (both income and expenditures)
- An estimated project budget with line items
- A copy of the organization's tax-exempt ruling from the Internal Revenue Service

Grant requests are reviewed at quarterly board meetings, usually in January, April, June and October. Please contact the foundation for deadlines.

For further information please write or call Catherine Cox at:

Lyndhurst Foundation
517 East Fifth Street
Chattanooga, Tennessee 37403-1826
Voice (423) 756-0767
Fax (423) 756-0770
Website www.lyndhurstfoundation.org

**Grant
Limitations**

The foundation's grantmaking activities are concentrated in the Southeast, with a special focus on Chattanooga. Grants to individuals are made only at the initiative of the foundation.

**Meeting
Times**

The board of directors meets four times a year.

Publications

The foundation publishes an annual report.

THE JOHN D. AND CATHERINE T. MACARTHUR FOUNDATION

140 SOUTH DEARBORN STREET

CHICAGO, ILLINOIS 60603

PHONE: (312) 726-8000

FAX: (312) 920-6258

EMAIL: 4answers@macfound.org

WEBSITE: www.macfound.org

Contact Persons

Richard Kaplan, Office of Grants Management

Purpose

The John D. and Catherine T. MacArthur Foundation is a private, independent grantmaking institution dedicated to helping groups and individuals foster lasting improvement in the human condition. The foundation seeks the development of healthy individuals and effective communities; peace within and among nations; responsible choices about human reproduction; and a global ecosystem capable of supporting healthy human societies. The foundation pursues this mission by supporting research, policy development, dissemination, education and training, and practice.

The foundation makes grants through two major integrated programs—one on human and community development, the other on global security and sustainability—and two special programs. The Program on Human and Community Development supports national research and policy work and—in Chicago and Palm Beach County, Florida—direct local efforts. The Program on Global Security and Sustainability focuses on arms reduction and security policy, ecosystems conservation and policy, population, and on cross-cutting themes.

The foundation's two other programs are the General Program, which undertakes special initiatives and supports projects that promote excellence and diversity in the media, and the MacArthur Fellows Program, which awards fellowships to exceptionally creative individuals, regardless of field of endeavor.

Areas of Interest

• The **Program on Human and Community Development** supports the development of healthy individuals and effective communities. Healthy individuals are those who enjoy physical and mental health, realize their creative and productive potential, and add value to their communities. By effective communities the foundation means more than congenial places to live. Effective communities consist of webs of relationships among people and institutions that support individual growth and participation in civic life. The depth, quality, and content of such relationships help determine how well communities enhance individual development.

• The object of the **Program on Global Security and Sustainability** is to promote peace within and among countries, healthy ecosystems worldwide, and responsible reproductive choices. The foundation encourages work that recognizes the interactions among peace, sustainable development, reproductive health, and the protection of human rights.

• The **General Program** makes a limited number of grants each year in support of projects that advance the broad purposes of the Foundation but do not fall within the areas addressed by its topical programs (Program on Human and Community Development and Program on Global Security and Sustainability). The program makes grants in a small number of areas of special interest, which change from time to time; in support of public-interest media projects; and for other relevant purposes.

• The **MacArthur Fellows Program** provides unrestricted fellowships to exceptionally talented and promising individuals who have shown evidence of originality, dedication to creative pursuits, and capacity for self-direction. The foundation awards Fellows an income over five years so that they may have the time and the freedom to fulfill their potential by devoting themselves to their own endeavors at their own pace. The foundation hopes that this freedom from financial constraints will lead to discoveries or other significant contributions to society that otherwise might not be made.

Financial Data

(Year ended 12/31/99)	
Assets:	$ 4,720,044,000
Total grants paid:	$ 206,706,210

Application Procedures

The MacArthur Foundation's grantmaking decisions usually result from an interactive process between the organization seeking a grant and the foundation staff. Except for grants under special competitions (see below), there are no fixed deadlines. The foundation reviews proposals and makes grants throughout the year. The first step in the process is to send a letter of inquiry directed to the Office of Grants Management. We suggest a short letter, typically two to three pages, accompanied by a one-page summary containing the following standard information about your organization.

One-page summary

- Name of your organization (and acronym if commonly used)
- Name of parent organization, if any
- Name of chief executive officer or person holding similar position
- Organization's address (and courier address if different)
- Organization's phone number, fax number, and e-mail address, if any
- Name and title of the principal contact person if different from the above
- Address (and courier address if different)
- Phone number, fax number, and e-mail address, if any, of principal contact
- Web address, if any

Letter of inquiry

There is no set format, but letters of inquiry generally include the following:
- Name or topic of the proposed project or work to be done
- A brief statement (two or three sentences) of the purpose and nature of the project
- The significance of the issue addressed by the project and how it relates to the foundation's interests and program goals
- How the project will address the issue
- How the issue relates to your organization, and why your organization is qualified to undertake the project
- Country or geographic region where the work will take place
- Time period for which funding is requested
- Information about those who will be helped by and interested in the project and how you will communicate with them
- Amount of funding requested from MacArthur and total project cost (estimates are acceptable)

You are welcome to enclose attachments that you feel would help the foundation understand your project.

Grant Limitations

The foundation does not support political activities or attempts to influence action and specific legislation. We do not provide scholarships or tuition assistance for undergraduate, graduate, or postgraduate studies; nor do we support annual fundraising drives, institutional benefits, honorary functions, or similar projects.

**Meeting
times**

The board of directors meets regularly.

Publications

The foundation publishes an annual report and individual program descriptions, as well as a general programs and policies brochure.

A.L. MAILMAN FAMILY FOUNDATION

707 WESTCHESTER AVENUE

WHITE PLAINS, NEW YORK 10604

PHONE: (914) 683-8089

FAX: (914) 686-5519

EMAIL: almf@mailman.org

WEB: www.mailman.org

Contact Person

Luba H. Lynch, Executive Director

Purpose

The A.L. Mailman Family Foundation seeks to help strengthen families in their ability to support their children. It focuses its support on early care and education, family support and early intervention, giving special priority to projects designed to make systemic changes.

Areas of Interest

The foundation awards grants in three major areas:

• Early care and education. Policy relevant research, systemic change, and material development and dissemination. Policy research which provides insight into improving child care standards and quality care is a priority along with projects which promote the restructuring of social systems to be family-focused and family-supportive. Most of the foundation's grants are made in this program area.

• Family support. Projects that strive to strengthen families and enhance parents' ability to nurture their children.

• Moral education and social responsibility. Projects that support educational approaches which promote social justice and the development of moral responsibility in children and youth.

**Financial
Data**

(Year ended 12/31/00)	
Assets:	$ 30,412,921
Total grants paid:	$ 1,696,172
Number of grants paid:	22
Highest grant:	$ 50,000
Lowest grant:	$ 5,000
Median grant size:	$ 30,000

**Application
Procedures**

The deadlines for submitting proposals are January 15 and June 15. The first step in initiating a proposal is a letter of inquiry briefly describing the proposed project, the amount requested, the budget and other funding sources, and attaching a copy of the applicant's proof of tax-exempt status from the IRS. If the foundation is interested, applicants will be invited to submit a full proposal.

A full grant application should include a two-page summary of the proposal; a description of the problem or issue that the proposed project will address; a statement on how the project relates to the foundation's interests; a review of similar efforts in the field and a rationale for the specific approach of the project; a fully developed project description and plans for implementation; staff qualifications and biographies; an assessment of the project's future implications and special contributions to the field; a plan for monitoring and evaluation; dissemination or replication plans; a detailed budget listing committed funds and potential funders with whom proposals are pending; and a projection of future funding needs with proposed strategies to meet those budgetary needs without the foundation's continued support. Attached to the application should be: a list of the members of the applicant's governing body and/or advisory committee members; and a letter from the governing body of the organization approving the project.

**Grant
Limitations**

The foundation does not provide support for individuals, ongoing direct services, general operating expenses, capital expenditures, and endowment campaigns.

**Meeting
Times**

The board of directors meets twice a year to review grant proposals.

Publications

The foundation publishes an annual report.

MARIANIST SHARING FUND

PHONE: (314) 533-1207

FAX: (314) 533-0778

4425 West Pine Boulevard

Saint Louis, Missouri 63108

WEB: www.marianist.org

Contact Person

Darla Benton, Program Officer

Purpose

The Marianist Sharing fund was established in 1975 by the New York Province of the Marianist Brothers and Priests (Society of Mary) to finance projects of social change that improve lives and build community. It provides grants to projects to bring about institutional change by addressing the basic social, economic, and political causes of poverty. Additionally, the fund supports projects which develop local leadership through community organizations and which encourage community participation.

Areas of Interest

Two areas of interest are:

• Matching grants for projects that promote justice in social structures and institutions and focus on direct community organizing within the East Coast states and Puerto Rico.

• Alternative investments that allow nonprofit, social change groups to use the money for capital investment in their work.

Financial Data

(Year ended 6/30/00)	
Assets:	Not endowed
Total grants paid:	$ 113,500
Total number of grants:	18
Highest grant:	$ 10,000
Lowest grant:	$ 4,000
Median grant:	$ 6,300

Application
Procedures

The fund allocates money each year by the Marianists from their unrestricted income. Grant applications are due September 1. Potential applicants should call the fund to request information and a grant application form.

Grant
Limitations

The fund does not provide for direct services, such as day care centers, recreation programs, community centers, scholarships, etc.; for projects controlled by the government; for research projects; for individuals or for-profit businesses; or for partisan political activities.

Meeting
Times

The Marianists meet once a year, usually in October, to make grant decisions.

Publications

The fund publishes an annual report and grant guidelines.

MARIN COMMUNITY FOUNDATION

5 HAMILTON LANDING, SUITE 200

NOVATO, CALIFORNIA 94949

PHONE: (415) 464-2500

FAX: (415) 464-2555

EMAIL: info@marincf.org

WEB: www.marincf.org

Contact Person

Thomas Peters, President

Purpose

The purpose of the Marin Community Foundation is to improve the quality of life for residents of Marin County through grantmaking, loan programs, and community programs of technical assistance and service.

Areas of Interest

The foundation and its affiliated trusts provide grants in three issue areas: community action and education, health and welfare, and arts and humanities. The foundation's priorities are homelessness and poverty, affordable housing, arts in education, strengthening major arts organizations, early childhood education, drug and alcohol abuse, school reform, at-risk youth, and advocacy for children.

• Human Needs. Projects that promote the health and well-being of the community and improve the lives of those who face disabling physical, mental and social problems. Areas of interest are access to services, independent living, coordindated service delivery and community education.

• Education and Training. Projects that contribute to developing and maintaining quality education and training opportunities for all. Areas of interest are: school restructuring and redesign, school drop out prevention, literacy and basic skills, and lifelong learning.

• Community Development. Projects that enhace the economic and social viability of low- and moderate-income communities and their residents. Areas of interest are economic development, affordable housing, leadership and technical development, and civic responsibility and advocacy.

• Religion. Projects in the community's religious and spiritual life. Areas of interest are faith and spiritual development, interfaith, interdenominational and cross-cultural cooperation, and leadership development.

• Environment. Projects that support the conservation of natural environment in the community. Areas of interest are environmental quality, land conservation, and environmental education.

• Arts. Projects that encourage the development of a rich cultural environment through the arts. Areas of interest are arts in the community, arts in the schools, and community involvement.

Financial Data

(Year ended 6/30/00)	
Assets:	$ 1,200,000,000
Total grants paid:	$ 51,600,000

Application Procedures

Before applying for a grant, applicants should contact a program officer to determine if a proposed project is consistent with the foundation's goals. If a project falls into this category, the applicant will be asked to submit a brief proposal letter. Proposal letters for all programs except the community development program are accepted on a continuing basis throughout the year. The community development program applications need to be submitted by February 15, June 15, and October 15.

Contents for proposal letters and supporting documentation are included in the foundation's publication, "Programs, Guidelines, and Application."

Grant Limitations

The foundation normally does not make grants to individuals, for basic research, for the start-up of new nonprofit organizations which duplicate existing services, or for for-profit purposes. Additionally, each program area has specific limitations and are described in the publication listed above, "Programs, Guidelines, and Application."

Meeting Times

The board of trustees meets bi-monthly to consider grant requests.

Publications

The foundation publishes an annual report and grant guidelines.

THE JOHN AND MARY R. MARKLE FOUNDATION

PHONE: (212) 489-6655

FAX: (212) 765-9690

EMAIL: info@markle.org

WEB: www.markle.org

10 ROCKEFELLER PLAZA, 16TH FLOOR

NEW YORK, NEW YORK 10020-1903

Contact Persons

Zoë Baird, President

Karen Byers, Managing Director and Chief Financial Officer

Purpose

Emerging communications media and information technology create unprecedented opportunity to improve people's lives. The Markle Foundation works to realize this potential and promotes the development of communications industries that address public needs.

Markle pursues its goals through a range of activities, including analysis, research, public information and the development of innovative media products and services. We create and operate many of our own projects—using not only grants but also investments and strategic alliances with non-profits and businesses.

Areas of Interest

Some of the most promising areas for Markle to meet public needs are in the following programs: Policy for a Networked Society, Interactive Media for Children, and Information Technolgies for Better Health. To capture opportunities in our rapidly changing world that fall outside these priorities, Markle also maintains an Opportunity Fund.

Policy for a Networked Society

This program aims to enhance the public voice on communications policy matters.

As emerging communications technologies cause unprecedented change in our lives, core aspects of our social, political, economic and legal systems are in flux as a result of ever-expanding computing power, convergence, and the rise of a networked world. Decision-making control is shifting in ways that are both hopeful and troubling. Individuals and communities are more empowered than ever before to look after their own interests. Yet as government retrenches and the policies that impact our lives are increasingly shaped in the private sector, it is unclear where and how the public interest will be represented as the next generation of communications policies evolve.

The Policy for a Networked Society program addresses these questions and works to enhance the public voice in the consideration and resolution of domestic and international policies that are surfacing in this new communications environment.

The program is creating a body of research and a global policy network of leaders from the academy, industry, nonprofit community and government to develop principles of regulation on critical policy issues and to represent the public interest as policies are developed and debated. The protection of democratic values, individual liberties, universal access and consumer interests are priorities of the program's activities.

Interactive Media for Children

This program works to gain in-depth knowledge about nature of interactive media, and promotes the use of that knowledge in the creation of beneficial children's products.

It's no secret that today's children are growing up in a media-saturated environment. Televison still dominates their waking hours, but hand-held video games, computer games and programs, and even interactive stuffed animals, are competing heavily for our children's time. Many are on the Internet before they enter school. And parents face tough new challenges. What products and experiences are appropriate for kids? Which ones will help them build positive skills? Which ones should be avoided, in what way, and at what ages?

Markle's Interactive Media for Children program is leading a comprehensive research effort into the cognitive, emotional, physical and developmental needs of children and the potential of interactive technologies to meet them. We are also working with key content producers and companies to integrate this knowledge into innovative games, toys and programs.

In addition, the program studies parents' evolving needs and concerns relative to the new media environment, and aims to create tools that they can use to make informed, responsible decisions for their children.

Information Technologies for Better Health

The overarching goal of the Markle health program is to accelerate the rate at which information technology enables consumers and the health system that supports them to improve health and health care.

One of the primary reasons Americans go online is to find health information. The expanding role of information technology offers unprecedented access to health care information and, increasingly, services. This evolution is gradually enabling individuals to assume a more central position in managing their health and health care. For the health consumer, the Internet, personal medical records, and other health management tools present important opportunities to actively maintain personal wellness, manage chronic illness, and make informed decisions about health care services. For the health care industry, information systems that can assist health care providers in reducing medical errors, enable research on treatment outcomes, and make vital information available at the point of care provide many opportunities for improvement.

Despite the potential for these significant gains, numerous barriers and significant challenges limit the realization of technology's full potential in the health arena. For the health consumer, concerns most often cited include privacy and security of health data, and the quality of online health information. For the health care industry, the complexity of medical data, the failure to adopt information standards, the fragmentation of the health system, privacy and security concerns, and the capital requirements necessary to upgrade or replace existing systems hinder the development and widespread use of information systems.

The Markle health program hopes to encourage the realization of information technology's potential to improve health and health care through four primary strategies: influencing policy, supporting research, incubating solutions, and engaging the public.

The Opportunity Fund

Information and communication technology creates an enormous opportunity for global participation in the networked economy and society. Not only do new technologies offer the potential for equity and improvement in the most critical areas of life, they can also dramatically affect the ability of individuals to be connected, empowered, and active in the world around them.

As a society, we are in the middle of an information revolution, and models and expectations have not yet been set for what can be accomplished. Experimentation and risk-taking are a critical element of Markle's strategy to create public interest applications in this new environment. Unlike Markle's other main programs that have beginning-to-end strategies for investing in a single area, the Opportunity Fund is designed to encompass a wide range of possible applications, and to seed innovative and transformative areas of development. Often, Opportunity Fund projects have the potential to serve as models that can be leveraged into greater activity and resources. For this reason, the program components are flexible and should be expected to grow and shift as the environment and opportunities for important public interest work evolve.

While all of Markle's work is characterized by an ability to act quickly and take risks, the Opportunity Fund ensures that intellectual and financial resources are available for such projects.

We do not accept unsolicited proposals for projects from this fund.

Financial Data

> (Year ended 12/31/00)
> Assets: $ 200,000,000

Application Procedures

The foundation does not have a formal application procedure for submitting a proposal, instead it requests a letter of inquiry preceding a full proposal. This letter should include a brief outline of the project, its purpose, expected outcomes, plan of action and principal staff, and the amount requested.

Grant Limitations

The foundation rarely awards funds for production of films, radio, or television programs. Support is not provided for endowments, building or for individual scholarships.

Meeting Times

The board of directors meets three times a year in November, March, and June.

Publications

The foundation publishes an annual report.

MCKENZIE RIVER GATHERING FOUNDATION

2705 EAST BURNSIDE, SUITE 210

PORTLAND, OREGON 97214

PHONE: (800) 489-6743

FAX: (503) 232-1731

EMAIL: info@mrgfoundation.org

WEB: www.mrgfoundation.org

Contact Person

Anita Rodgers, Grants Director

Purpose

The McKenzie River Gathering Foundation is an activist-controlled fundraising foundation supporting progressive groups based in Oregon.

Areas of Interest

Generally the foundation's grants may be grouped in the following manner: human rights, economic justice, environmental protection, peace, and international solidarity. Specific issues have included anti-bigotry, racial justice, domestic violence, homeless rights, labor organizing, HIV/AIDS, reproductive rights, lesbian and gay liberation, ancient forest protection, sustainable economic justice, watershed protection, air quality, progressive media, anti-militarism, and international self-determination. MRG emphasizes funding of projects with a commitment to diversity in their outreach and group composition, with a clearly-developed organizing focus, with less access to traditional funding sources.

Financial Data

(Year ended 6/30/00)	
Assets:	$ 3,631,528
Total grants paid:	$ 931,158
Number of grants paid:	69

Application Procedures

The foundation has two funding cycles per year, one each in the spring and fall. Applicants are encouraged to contact the foundation's Eugene office to discuss the proposed project, obtain application forms (which are required), and ascertain application deadlines. The process itself includes an oral presentation in an open meeting conducted by the grantmaking committee, where applicants are asked to make a presentation to the group on their project and to respond to questions from committee members and other applicants.

Grant Limitations

All groups must be based in Oregon. The foundation does not generally fund medical facilities, schools, or social services unless these projects are promoting social change beyond their basic function. MRG does not support proposals submitted by individuals. Groups with budgets over $200,000 are seldom funded and most grantees have a budget of less than $100,000. The great majority of grants are in the $4,000 to $6,000 range. MRG's maximum grant amount of $10,000 is the upper limit for the wide range of grant sizes awarded. Very few groups will be funded at the upper end of the grant range.

Meeting Times

The board of directors meets twice a year, no later than December 31 and June 30.

Publications

The foundation publishes an annual report and newsletter. Application forms and guidelines are available upon request.

THE MCKNIGHT FOUNDATION

600 TCF TOWER

121 SOUTH 8TH STREET

MINNEAPOLIS, MINNESOTA 55402

PHONE: (612) 333-4220

FAX: (612) 332-3833

EMAIL: info@mcknight.org

WEB: www.mcknight.org

Contact Person

Rip Rapson, President

Purpose

The McKnight Foundation funds projects that serve the poor and disadvantaged. Specifically, it seeks to respond to the needs of individuals in ways that will lead to their full potential as human beings. Through its grantmaking, the foundation supports community resources aimed at addressing those needs. In so doing, the foundation also strives to enhance the ability and willingness of public and private institutions to respond efficiently and humanely to the changing needs of groups and individuals. It supports organizations that demonstrate effective leadership and administration and that appear likely to benefit their area of concern and their community.

Grantmaking activity is concentrated in Minnesota and proposals from organizations outside Minnesota ordinarily will not be considered. However, the directors occasionally may take the initiative to identify projects outside the state for support.

Areas of Interest

The foundation's primary concern is meeting the needs of people who are poor or disadvantaged. It is especially interested in helping to sustain and strengthen organizations and institutions serving a demonstrated community need. Support may take many forms, including support for ongoing programs or operations, for the development or implementation of special projects, for capital needs or for other purposes. Bridge grants to newer organizations are also funded. Priorities include human services, health, and education. Of lesser importance are such programs as those focusing on chemical dependency, the needs of the elderly and long-term care; the needs of people with disabilities; and leadership development. International giving is a small part of the foundation's work. Grantseekers should contact the foundation for information on current priorities.

- Human Services. Projects that address early childhood development (child care); address the needs of youth-at-risk and troubled families; provide help for hard-to-employ people; preserve housing for low-income families; strengthen neighborhood-based human services and opportunities; and change institutions to improve their ability to help poor or disadvantaged people to achieve more satisfying and productive lives.
- Health. Projects advancing public understanding and prevention of AIDS.
- Education. Projects that improve chances for success for young people and adults not served by traditional schools and projects that result in substantial change within the current educational system. The foundation looks for projects with promise for systemwide reforms.

Financial Data

```
(Year ended   /  /   )
Assets:                              NA
Total grants paid:
Number of grants paid:
Highest grant:
Lowest grant:
Media grant size:
```

Application Procedures

The foundation requires that organizations considering submitting a proposal write a brief letter describing the organization and summarizing the proposed project and amount of support to be requested.

Deadlines for the receipt of letters of inquiry are March 1, June 1, September 1, and December 1. Based on a preliminary review, the staff will advise the applicant whether a complete proposal should be submitted and by what date. Letters are accepted at any time and telephone discussions with program staff are encouraged.

Grant Limitations

The foundation will not approve grants to religious organizations for religious purposes, however they may apply for support for activities that benefit the larger community. Grants are not made directly to individuals except to recipients of the McKnight Awards in Human Service. Eligible applicants must be classified by the IRS as tax-exempt public charities, and must maintain adequate accounting procedures.

**Meeting
Times**

The board of directors meets quarterly, in March, June, September, and December.

Publications

The McKnight Foundation publishes an annual report which includes a list of grants and a description of programs and priorities, a quarterly grants list, and policies and procedures for grantmaking.

JOYCE MERTZ-GILMORE FOUNDATION

218 EAST 18TH STREET

NEW YORK, NEW YORK 10003-3694

PHONE: (212) 475-1137

FAX: (212) 777-5226

EMAIL: info@mertzgilmore.org

WEB: www.mertzgilmore.org

Contact Person

Jay Beckner, Executive Director

Purpose

The Joyce Mertz-Gilmore Foundation is a private foundation that maintains environment, human rights, world security, and New York City grantmaking programs. While the foundation prefers to make general support grants to organizations whose work closely parallels the interests described below, it also supports specific programs or projects when appropriate.

Areas of Interest

- Human Rights. The foundation provides support in the following areas:
  - Protection and support of human rights worldwide. Organizations that monitor and investigate human rights abuses, advocate non-politicized application of international human rights law, encourage the free flow of information within and between countries, or work to build the capacity of non-governmental human rights groups in developing countries, Central Europe, and the former Soviet republics.
  - Protection and support of refugee rights worldwide. Organizations that work on policy issues, advocacy and information dissemination related to refugees, and a limited number of leadership development efforts within refugee communities. The foundation has a particular interest in community development approaches which draw upon the resources and knowledge of refugees themselves, and empower refugees to advance their own needs and rights.
  - Protection and extension of rights in the United States. National or regional efforts to protect and extend the rights of lesbians and gay men and immigrants and refugees, particularly if their legal status is in question. The foundation provides support to groups which undertake advocacy and policy work, citizen awareness activities or litigation to establish clear precedents for protecting the civil rights of these groups.

- Democratic development. Efforts to promote building of the capacity and infrastructure of the voluntary sectors in Central Europe and the former Soviet republics.
- The Environment. Organizations working to promote increased energy efficiency now and a renewable energy future. Grantmaking focuses on efforts to influence and change national energy policy and promote efficiency and renewables through state and local utility regulation.

The foundation also is interested in concrete initiatives linking an efficient and renewable future to the economic and social development of local communities and in efforts to increase public awareness and citizen action. Projects that target low-income and underserved populations in the United States or in developing countries, and that have potential for broader application or replication will receive priority consideration.

The foundation also supports a limited number of other environmental efforts, particularly those focused on issues affecting the metropolitan region of New York City and New York State.

- World Security. Projects that promote a non-military dependent sustainable future with innovative national and regional policy research and analysis related to economic restructuring, conversion, and the limitation and control of arms transfers around the world, and the development of broad-based local coalitions established to explore and undertake new approaches to the economic revitalization of communities that have been or will be hardest hit by decreasing military spending.

The foundation also supports a limited number of projects that explore new thinking about regional or global institutions and structures that can promote and increase world security. Of particular interest are: projects exploring an expanded, more effective role for the United Nations; new configurations of political or economic institutions in post-Cold War Europe; new structures and institutions to establish, regulate or monitor agreements affecting the "global commons" or to establish regional consortia, networks, or policy groups to work on common defense, environment, or human rights concerns.

- New York City's human & built environment. Projects that focus on HIV/AIDS, community development and stabilization advocacy, organizational development and technical assistance.
- Arts in New York City. The foundation makes modest grants for institutional support of the performing arts.

**Financial
Data**

(Year ended 12/31/99)	
Assets:	$ 124,351,430
Total grants paid:	$ 9,574,068
Number of grants paid:	
Highest grant:	
Lowest grant:	
Median grant size:	Not available

**Application
Procedures**

If your organization's mission falls within the foundation's program interests, please submit an inquiry letter of no more than two pages describing that mission and the purpose of the request. Do not send full proposals, video or audio cassettes, press clippings, books, or other materials unless they are requested.

**Grant
Limitations**

Foundation grants are made only to nonprofit, charitable organizations with proof of tax-exempt status. The foundation does not provide funds for endowments, building construction or maintenance, primary operational support, political purposes such as lobbying or propaganda, programs consisting solely or primarily of conferences, sectarian religious concerns, individual scholarships, fellowships, loans or travel, film or television production, publications, or annual fund appeals. It does not make grants to other private foundations. Within the New York City programs funds are not provided for direct social services.

**Meeting
Times**

The board of directors meets semi-annually in the spring and fall to consider grant applications.

Publications

The foundation distributes a grants list, an application form, a brochure, and other information describing its programs and priorities.

EUGENE AND AGNES E. MEYER FOUNDATION

1400 16TH ST. N.W., SUITE 360

WASHINGTON, DC 20036

PHONE: (202) 483-8294

FAX: (202) 328-6850

EMAIL: smunoz@meyerfdn.org

WEB: www.meyerfoundation.org

Contact Person

Steven Munoz

Purpose

The Meyer Foundation works to develop Greater Washington as a community by supporting capable, community-based nonprofit organizations that foster the well-being of all people in the region. We are especially concerned about low-income people and creating healthy neighborhoods. We value and seek to promote the region's diversity.

We accomplish our work by:

• Identifying visionary and talented nonprofit leaders.

• Making early and strategic investments in nonprofit organizations.

• Strengthening the organizational capacity of nonprofits in the region.

• Promoting a strong and influential nonprofit sector.

• Building partnerships to foster the sector's work.

• Serving as a resource to other donors who want to make effective charitable investments in the region.

Areas of Interest

The foundation makes grants for a wide variety of projects, principally grouped into the following categories: community service, education, health and mental health, law and justice, arts and humanities, and neighborhood development and housing.

EUGENE AND AGNES E. MEYER FOUNDATION

Financial Data

(Year ended 12/31/00)	
Assets:	$ 133,407,533
Total grants paid:	$ 5,543,004
Number of grants paid:	234
Highest grant:	$ 500,000
Lowest grant:	$ 1,000
Median grant size:	$ 20,000

Application Procedures

The Meyer Foundation uses a two-step application process:

• Step One—Eligible candidates interested in requesting a grant from the Meyer Foundation are required to first submit a letter of inquiry (LOI). Please visit the foundation's Web site at www.meyerfoundation.org or call for complete application guidelines, forms and submission instructions.

• Step Two—The letter of inquiry will be reviewed by the foundation. Applicants will be notified about the foundation's interest within two months following the submission deadline. If selected for further consideration, a program officer will follow-up to discuss the request. At that time, a full proposal may be invited and the program officer and applicant will agree upon its submission date. A request for submission of a full proposal in no way guarantees eventual funding of the request. Uninvited proposals will not be accepted.

For the proposal itself, applicants are requested to use the Washington Regional Association of Grantmakers Common Grant Application format. It is helpful to refer to the foundation's annual report. All applications are subject to staff review, possibly including an interview and site visit. Notification of the board's decision is made in writing by the end of the month in which the board meets.

Grant Limitations

The foundation does not contribute to programs that are national or international in scope. It distributes its funds to tax-exempt organizations and makes no grants to individuals. As a general rule, the foundation does not support projects that are sectarian in character nor does it support capital campaigns or endowment drives.

To be eligible for consideration, applicants must be:

• A nonprofit agency with tax-exempt status under section 501(c)(3) of the Internal Revenue Code and organized and operated for charitable purposes.

- Located within and primarily serving the Washington, DC region which is defined as: District of Columbia; Montgomery, Prince George's, Calvert, Charles, and St. Mary's counties in Maryland; Arlington, Fairfax, Loudoun, Prince William, and Stafford counties in Northern Virginia; and the cities of Alexandria, Falls Church, Manassas and Manassas Park in Virginia.

**Meeting
Times**

The board of directors meets five times per year. Three of these meetings are reserved for review of proposals.

Publications

The foundation publishes an annual report.

MEYER MEMORIAL TRUST

425 N.W. TENTH AVENUE, SUITE 400

PORTLAND, OREGON 97209

PHONE: (503) 228-5512

FAX: (503) 228-5840

EMAIL: mmt@mmt.org

WEB: www.mmt.org

Contact Person

Charles S. Rooks, Executive Director

Purpose

The Meyer Memorial Trust, one of the largest foundations in the Pacific Northwest, supports projects working with children at risk, assisting teachers, and other social welfare issues.

Areas of Interest

The trust operates three grantmaking programs. Each program has its own geographic limitations and guidelines:

• General Purpose Grants Program—Grants under this program support projects related to arts and humanities, education, health, community development, social welfare, and a variety of other activities. Such grants are limited to Oregon and Clark County, Washington. There are no limitations on the size or duration of the grants that may be requested under this program. In reviewing requests, the trust looks for proposals that have the promise of broad-scale or long-term impact on significant issues.

• Small Grants Program—Small grants range up to $12,000. A request for $12,000 or less that is ineligible for the Small Grants program may be submitted under the trust's General Purpose program. This program is limited to organizations in Oregon and Clark County, Washington. The Small Grants program allows the trust to assist a large number of worthy organizations with a wide variety of small projects that are limited in scope but nevertheless signifcant for the applicant organization. It is unlikely that many of these grants will go to large organizations.

• Support for Teacher Initiative—In 1994 the trust launched a program to give special emphasis to individual teachers' ideas for improving the way learning takes place in their particular classrooms. The common denominator for funding projects is their promise for stimulating and facilitating more effective learning by some or all students in the classroom. The program provides two types of support: 1) grants to individual teachers of up to $1,500 and 2) grants to teams of teachers working jointly on projects within the same school or different schools of up to $5,000. In each category, the amount of the grant can be larger, up to $2,000 for individuals, and up to $7,000 for teams, if the project involves a collaborative effort with businesses or community groups that supply a matching contribution through cash of in-kind donations.

Financial Data

(Year ended 3/31/01)	
Assets:	$ 495,800,000
Total grants paid:	$ 23,607,542
Total number of grants:	292
Highest grant:	$ 1,500,000
Lowest grant:	$ 667

Application Procedures

Each of the three programs has its own application deadlines. The support of teacher initiatives program deadline is February 1. The general purpose grants program accepts proposals any time. Formal proposals are required in order for the trust to determine if a project is within its grantmaking interests. The small grants program has three application deadlines, January 15, April 15, and October 15. A proposal should not be submitted more than one month before a deadline. Each of these programs also has its own guidelines and applicants may request these from the trust.

The trust urges all applicants to read its grant application guidelines and determine that the organization and type of project envisioned are eligible for consideration. Applicants must submit all the following information before a proposal will be considered: a completed grant application cover sheet (included in the guidelines); a description of the organization and the project; a detailed budget; statement of financial condition; copies of tax-exempt status; and a list of names and primary affiliations or the organization's board of directors.

Grant Limitations

The trust awards grants to qualified tax-exempt organizations in Oregon and Clark County, Washington. Applicants normally have tax exemptions under section 501(c)(3) of the IRS Code. Additionally, the trust normally does not make direct grants, scholarships, or loans to individuals; endowments; general fund drives or annual appeals; debt retirement or operational deficits; religious organizations for sectarian projects; indirect or overhead costs except as related to grant project; or for influencing elections or legislation.

Meeting Times

The board of trustees meets regularly to consider grant requests.

Publications

The trust publishes an annual report and grant guidelines.

THE MILKEN FAMILY FOUNDATION

1250 FOURTH STREET

SANTA MONICA, CALIFORNIA 90401-1353

PHONE: (310) 570-4800

FAX: (310) 570-4801

EMAIL: comm-gov@mff.org

WEB: www.mff.org

**Contact
Person**

Dr. Julius Lesner, Executive Director

Purpose

The Milken Family Foundation seeks to assist people to make life better for themselves and for those around them. The foundation concentrates its funding in areas where there is the greatest potential for effective positive change and it seeks out partnerships with those who are working to solve society's problems. Programs designed to answer basic human needs, that are innovative, and that can be easily replicated across the country are given preference.

**Areas of
Interest**

The foundation's areas of interest are education, community services, health care and medical research, and human welfare. The foundation also supports a limited number of other programs which do not fall into these major funding areas.

• Education. Projects that support pre-school through 12th grade education, curriculum improvement, parental involvement, civic education, drug abuse education and special education. Additional funding is made to higher education, libraries and educational facilities.

• Community Services. Projects that connect the needs and resources of educational institutions and the communities in which they are located. Major support is provided for community development programs, cultural centers and activities and community centers.

• Health Care. Research projects that support the effective delivery of physical and mental health care to all who need it; support the development of facilities; and support medical research with emphasis on cancer and epilepsy.

• Human Welfare. Projects that support child welfare programs, community welfare programs, homelessness, hunger programs, and the physically handicapped.

Other programs fall into the categories of conservation and animal welfare, legal assistance, international programs, social action and religious programs.

**Financial
Data**

```
(Year ended   /  /  )
Assets:                              NA
Total grants paid:
Total number of grants:
Highest grant:
Lowest grant:3,000
Median grant size:
```

**Application
Procedures**

Organizations seeking support should first send a brief written statement, not more than three pages long, which should contain a description of project goals, procedures and personnel; brief background of organization including number of years in operation, other areas of activity, applicant's qualifications for support, and previous and current sources of funding; amount of request, project total, detailed budget, and plans for obtaining total funding; and a copy of the IRS 501(c)(3) exemption letter. Supporting printed material may be attached.

**Grant
Limitations**

Organizations seeking funding must be tax-exempt as identified under IRS Code 501(c)(3).

**Meeting
Times**

The board meets on an as-needed basis.

Publications

The foundation publishes a mission statement and grant guidelines.

THE MINNEAPOLIS FOUNDATION

PHONE: (612) 672-3878

FAX: (612) 672-3846

800 IDS CENTER

EMAIL: email@mplsfoundation.org

80 SOUTH EIGHTH STREET

WEB: www.MinneapolisFoundation.org

MINNEAPOLIS, MINNESOTA 55402

Contact Person

Emmett D. Carson, President and CEO

Purpose

The Minneapolis Foundation is a community foundation established to facilitate philanthropy and improve the quality of life in the region. The foundation administers a broad range of restricted and unrestricted funds and makes grants for a variety of purposes and projects.

Areas of Interest

Competitive grants (those made through an application process open to the public) are awarded in the following areas: Children, Youth and Families; Community Capacity Building; Economically Healthy Neighborhoods; Low Income Senior Citizens; People with Disabilities; and Public Policy. Grants are made to organizations but not to individuals.

Financial Data

(Year ended 3/31/01)	
Assets:	$ 542,651,730
Total grants paid:	$ 29,986,439
Highest grant:	$ 300,000
Lowest grant:	$ 10,000
Median grant size:	$ 50,000

Application Procedures

Since 1995, the foundation has received applications for grants from its various funding partners through a single process. Applications are received throughout the year. The Grant Application Guidelines of The Minneapolis

Foundation are available on the website at www.MinneapolisFoundation.org or by calling (612) 672-3861. These guidelines describe the goals, approaches and application procedures.

Grant Limitations

In the competitive grants category, the foundation will not consider grants to the following types of organizations for the following purposes: religious organizations for direct religious activities; annual contributions to ongoing operating budgets; deficit financing; multi-year support; dollar-for-dollar replacement of reduced or eliminated government funding; membership in civic organizations or trade associations; individuals; political organizations or campaigns; fraternal organizations; societies or orders; courtesy advertising or benefit tickets; telephone solicitations; and national fundraising efforts. Competitive grants are awarded only in Minnesota.

Meeting Times

Funding partners meet throughout the year to approve grants.

Publications

The foundation publishes an annual report.

CHARLES STEWART MOTT FOUNDATION

503 S. Saginaw Street, Suite 1200
Flint, Michigan 48502-1851

PHONE: (810) 238-5651

FAX: (810) 766-1753

EMAIL: infocenter@mott.org

WEB: www.mott.org

Contact Persons*

An-Ma Chung, Education
Ray Murphy, International
Ronald White, Community Development and Community-Based
    Organizations
Jack Litzenberg, Economic Development
Lois DeBacker, Sandra Smithey, Environment
Karen Eason, Flint
Chris Sturgis, Families & School to Work

Purpose

The foundation, since its founding in 1926, has funded programs aimed at improving the quality of life for individuals and their communities. The foundation's approach to grantmaking is guided by certain underlying values to support efforts that promote a just, equitable, and sustainable society.

The foundation is primarily interested in:

• Fresh approaches to solving community problems in our defined program areas.

• Approaches that, if proven successful, can generate long-term support from other sources and/or that can be replicated in other communities when appropriate.

• Public policy development as well as research and development activities to further existing programs as well as to explore new fields of interest.

• Approaches and activities that lead to systemic change.

---

*General questions concerning the foundation's program, and funding guidelines and grantmaking procedures can be answered by obtaining a copy of "Philosophy, Programs and Procedures." This and other foundation publications are available by calling the Mott Foundation's "Publication Hotline" 1-800-645-1766. Grant proposals should be clearly marked on the outside of the envelope and addressed as follows: Office of Proposal Entry, Mott Foundation, Mott Foundation Building, 503 S. Saginaw Street, Suite 1200 Flint, Michigan 48502-1851.

**Areas of
Interest**

Civil Society

Through our grantees, Mott helps build cohesive communities around the world. We support nonprofit organizations working to develop a strong civil society in the United States, Central/Eastern Europe and Russia, South Africa and at the global level.

Our grantees work to:
- strengthen the nonprofit sector,
- promote citizen rights and responsibilities, and
- improve race and ethnic relations.

At home and abroad, grantees try to achieve these goals while consciously including people who have been historically excluded from society's decision-making process, such as women, people from racial and ethnic groups, those with low-income, and others.

Environment

Through two funding priorities, the foundation aims to create institutions, policies and development models that secure environmental quality in the United States and around the world:

- **Reform of International Finance and Trade** works to reform the environmental policies and practices of international financial and trade institutions.

- **Conservation of Freshwater Ecosystems** in North America advances the conservation and restoration of freshwater ecosystems, with an emphasis on the Great Lakes region and select ecoregions in the Southeastern United States.

Flint Area

C.S. Mott created the foundation as a way to share responsibility for the well-being of the Flint community. He believed strongly that people within connected institutions—schools, health care and human service agencies, law enforcement agencies, churches, social organizations, and families—contribute to a community's health.

The C.S. Mott Foundation funds projects that show promise of long-term positive impact for the greater Flint community. The grantmaking is guided by four principles:

- All people should live in a caring, safe and nurturing community that offers economic opportunity.
- Diversity is a basis for community wholeness.

- Progress can be achieved only by encouraging citizens and leaders to partner together to address shared challenges.
- Flint's future is deeply connected to the future of its surrounding communities.

The Flint Area Program employs a set of three "Strategic Lenses" for its grantmaking: Issues, Public Capital and Areas. Proposals submitted to the program must address all three of these lenses simultaneously.

Pathways Out of Poverty

When Charles Stewart Mott established the foundation that bears his name, it was with the belief that:

- an individual's well-being is inextricably linked to the well-being of the community;
- individuals are essentially in an informal partnership with their community; and
- by working together, individuals can make a difference in our society and our world.

Those beliefs are perhaps no more readily apparent than in our grantmaking to address poverty in the United States. We have consistently supported efforts to help ordinary citizens come together to strengthen their communities, grow through their participation in educational opportunities and attain economic self-sufficiency by engaging more fully in our economy.

Increasingly, we have come to see community organizing, education and economic opportunity as critical to moving low-income Americans toward greater prosperity. In fact, those three areas have become the pillars for the foundation's grantmaking plan for addressing poverty in the United States.

Ultimately, this grantmaking plan is based on the foundation's desire not only to relieve the distress of living in poverty, but also to empower people to escape poverty entirely. It is also our belief that by concentrating our efforts on select aspects of education, work and community, we can touch on the essential areas in which children, adults and families must have access and opportunities in order to escape poverty.

The work also reflects our belief that racism contributes to and shapes poverty in the United States.

CHARLES STEWART MOTT FOUNDATION

**Financial
Data**

(Year ended 12/31/00)	
Assets:	$ 2,880,296,978
Total grants paid:	$ 152,970,798
Number of grants paid:	606
Highest grant:	$ 8,500,000
Lowest grant:	$ 1,500
Median grant size:	$ 200,000

**Application
Procedures**

Grant applications may be handled in one of two ways. The prospective grantee may either submit a brief letter outlining the details of the project or may send a full proposal. Both are processed as if they are requests for support. Projects are generally funded for a single year, but multi-year budgets may be submitted. In any event, the following basic information is needed: a description of the project and what will be accomplished; a statement of why the project is needed; a statement concerning the population to be served; a brief line-term budget, including distribution of funds if a multi-year grant; information on the organization seeking the funds and its accomplishments to date; and the starting and ending dates and plans for post-grant funding and project evaluation. Applicants should allow about four months to process proposals.

**Meeting
Times**

The board of trustees meets quarterly.

Publications

The foundation publishes an annual report that details each program interest and lists each grantee. Other foundation publications include "Programs, Policies and Procedures," a booklet setting forth the foundation's program philosophies, and "Facts on Grants," which contains a thorough summary of grant awards.

MS. FOUNDATION FOR WOMEN

120 WALL STREET, 33RD FLOOR

NEW YORK, NEW YORK 10005

PHONE: (212) 742-2300

FAX: (212) 742-1653

EMAIL: info@ms.foundation.org

WEB: www.ms.foundation.org

Contact Persons

Marie Wilson, President

Sara Gould, Executive Director

Purpose

The Ms. Foundation for Women is a national, multi-issue women's fund supporting the efforts of women and girls to govern their lives and influence the world around them. It funds and assists women's self-help organizing efforts and pursues changes in public consciousness, law, philanthropy, and social justice policy. The foundation directs resources to break down barriers faced by women of color, low-income women, older women, lesbians, and women with disabilities.

Since its inception in 1972, the foundation has supported the efforts of grassroots women to fight discrimination and violence, protect children and develop healthy families, achieve economic and social empowerment, launch non-sexist, multiracial curriculum programs, and safeguard reproductive rights.

Areas of Interest

The foundation makes grants available in three major categories:

• Economic Justice. Workplace organizing and labor rights for women workers, rural and urban poverty, welfare organizing, non-traditional employment, and economic development.

• Safety. Prevention of all types of violence against women and girls, such as domestic violence, sexual assault, incest, lesbian battering, and hate crimes against women.

• Girls. Activities that challenge gender role stereotyping of girls, address the increase of violence in girls' lives, and sustain the self-confidence and vitality of adolescent girls, ages 9 to 15.

Special consideration is given to groups that support newly-emerging feminist issues as women organizing define them; have limited access to funding sources; encourage cooperation across race and class lines; are of special benefit to women of color and women isolated by geography or class; may be replicated by other groups or in other parts of the country; are run by women affected by the problem being addressed; and will empower women and girls to make their own decisions in the future.

**Financial
Data**

> (Year ended 6/30/00)
> Total revenue: $ 15,014,308

**Application
Procedures**

Requests for funding may be made for a specific project, for general support, or for start-up costs. Applications for funding must include a proposal summary sheet which can be obtained by writing or calling the foundation for its grant guidelines. The foundation asks that applicants, in five to ten pages, describe the organization, purpose, history, constituency or membership (including race and class composition), decision-making structure, programs and accomplishments, and relationships to other organizations; if applying for a specific project, outline the need, purpose, goals and methods, staff capabilities and responsibilities, time frame, and evaluation plans; and describe the community in which the organization works and the need for the organization.

Applicants are also asked to attach to their submission the project budget, and if the project is only one part of the applicant's general work, an organizational budget; a list of past and current funding sources and amounts and a list of potential funding sources and requests that are outstanding; the names of other individuals or organizations (with telephone numbers) who are not part of the organization, but are familiar with its work; resumes of key staff; and proof of tax-exempt status.

Most grants range in size from $5,000 to $25,000. Renewal funding may be awarded upon annual re-application.

**Grant
Limitations**

The foundation funds local and national women's organizations that are grassroots and activist. The foundation does not fund cultural or media projects, publications, individuals, scholarships, research, school sponsored programs, university projects, international projects, state agencies, or religious organizations. Projects must be tax-exempt under Section 501(c)(3) of the Internal Revenue Code.

**Meeting
Times**

The board of directors meets three times a year in the winter, spring, and fall.

Publications

The foundation distributes an annual report, a list of grant awards, and guidelines for prospective applicants.

A.J. MUSTE MEMORIAL INSTITUTE

PHONE: (212) 533-4335

FAX: (212) 228-6193

EMAIL: info@ajmuste.org

WEB: www.ajmuste.org

339 LAFAYETTE STREET

NEW YORK, NEW YORK 10012

Contact Persons

Murray Rosenblith, Executive Director

Jane Guskin, Program Associate

Purpose

The A.J. Muste Memorial Institute funds innovative and experimental projects that promote the principles and practice of nonviolent social change within its areas of interest. Grants are made to local, national, and international projects.

Areas of Interest

The institute seeks to fund projects concerned with the issues to which A.J. Muste dedicated his life: peace and disarmament, social and economic justice, racial and sexual equality, and the labor movement.

Financial Data

(Year ended 6/30/00)	
Assets:	$ 429,661
Total grants paid:	$ 336,297
Number of grants paid:	39
Highest grant:	$ 2,000
Lowest grant:	$ 500
Median grant size:	$ 1,500

Application Procedures

Proposals must be no longer than five pages and must include a description of the project, including its relevance, targeted community, and evidence of the group's ability to carry it out, a contact name, with day and evening telephone numbers, detailed project budget and annual organizational budget with a list of other funding sources, brief relevant biography of project coordinator(s), list of advisors to the project or organization, amount requested, preferably a line item from the project budget, or, if applying for a sponsorship request, the ceiling amount for transfer between the time sponsorship is granted and the end of the calendar year.

Supporting material such as printed matter or press clippings may be attached. Applicants must submit two copies of the complete proposal and attachments and five copies of a one-page summary of the project. Each proposal that passes an initial review is assigned to a board member who may contact the organization for additional information. That board member will also receive a copy of the complete proposal and supporting materials. The board will consider a maximum of ten proposals in each funding cycle. Be sure to include the organization's name and address on the first page of the proposal and in the summary; include the amount requested in both the summary and the proposal.

Because deadlines vary from year to year, applicants should contact the institute directly before submitting a proposal.

Grant Limitations

The institute does not fund organizations or projects that can secure funding from traditional sources and generally does not support projects that have budgets exceeding, or organizations whose annual budget exceeds, $500,000. Grants are not made to academic projects or individuals. The institute will not accept a new request from a previously funded group for two years after a grant.

Meeting Times

The board of directors meets approximately six times a year and grant requests are considered at four of these meetings.

Publications

The institute publishes a quarterly newsletter and grant application guidelines.

THE NEEDMOR FUND

42 SOUTH SAINT CLAIR STREET

TOLEDO, OHIO 43602

PHONE: (419) 255-5560

EMAIL: needmorfund@sbcglobal.net

WEB: www.fdncenter.org/
grantmaker/needmor

**Contact
Persons**

Dave Beckwith, Executive Director

Frank Sanchez, Senior Program Officer

Purpose

The mission of the Needmor Fund is to work with others to bring about social justice. We support people who work together to change the social, economic, or political conditions which bar their access to participation in a democratic society.

We envision a nation committed to democracy. We believe that citizens should be free and equal to determine the actions of government and the terms of public policy and thus assure their right to:

- justice
- political liberty
- the basic necessities of life: food, shelter, access to health care, and safety
- an education which enables them to be contributing members of society
- the opportunity to secure productive work with just wages and benefits and decent working conditions

We believe that all citizens should be free to exercise these rights regardless of race, ethnic origin, gender, sexual orientation or religious persuasion.

Our grantmaking philosophy fosters a spirit of individual and collective responsibility. We strive to remove systemic barriers to the practice of democracy by encouraging the efforts of people who have come together to work for justice and the common good. We seek always to engage those whose participation in the affairs of their community has been systematically denied, because we believe our nation will operate most equitably when all of its citizens can be actively involved in crafting the vision, values, and specific policies that guide its operation.

Areas of Interest

The focus of our grantmaking is community organizing. The Needmor Fund has identified community organizing as the most effective process by which low and moderate income people can build power, can address the systemic barriers to the practice of democracy, can hold public and corporate officials accountable for their actions, and can begin to participate in shaping public policy.

We look for multi-issue, membership-based community organizations in low and moderate income communities which show promise for creating significant social change (impacting significant public or private institutions which influence low and moderate income communities.) Potential grantees need to exhibit the following qualities:

- structures which reflect ownership and democratic control by the membership
- a membership which is fully involved in both development and implementation of strategies to affect institutional change and to alter the relationships of power
- strong internal leadership development
- an understanding of power relationships within their community along with the capacity to determine and implement solutions suggested by this understanding
- a process to help members understand the root causes of problems being addressed and an action plan to address these problems
- effective plans to attract new members and to build the organization
- commitment to, and strategies for, developing diverse non-grant income

Financial Data

(Year ended 12/31/00)	
Total grants paid:	$ 2,516,000
Highest grant:	$ 75,000
Lowest grant:	$ 5,000

Application Procedures

The Needmor Fund has two grantmaking cycles per year. You may submit your application at any time during the following months, but no later than the specific deadlines:

For applicants located in AL, AZ, southern CA, LA, MS, NM, and southern TX (including San Antonia), the Application Form is accepted during the months of November through the January deadline.

For applicants located elsewhere in the United States, the Application Form is accepted during the months of April through the June deadline.

Needmore utilizes the National Network of Grantmakers common grant application. Include the cover sheet, five-page proposal, and all attachments. Please note that these attachments will not be "checked below by the funder" if you accessed the application on the internet.

We do not accept video or audio tapes. We cannot accept handwritten applications or faxed applications. Submit the original and one additional copy to our office. Please use paper/binder clips to hold your proposals together, not staples.

Grant Limitations

Some of the things for which Needmor will not consider proposals for funding are:

- community development corporations;
- scholarships/fellowships;
- personal businesses;
- direct services or training programs (e.g., counseling programs, medical services, job training, referral services, childcare programs, emergency shelters);
- cultural enrichment programs; films, TV or radio production;
- books, publications, or research;
- conferences;
- capital improvement;
- litigation;
- projects outside the United States;
- and government sponsored or controlled projects.

Meeting Times

The fund has two grantmaking cycles each year. Funding decisions are usually made by the advisory committee in May and November.

Publications

The fund distributes a program description, application guidelines and a list of grantees upon request.

NEVADA WOMEN'S FUND

770 SMITHRIDGE DRIVE, SUITE 300

RENO, NEVADA 89502

PHONE: (775) 786-2335

FAX: (775) 786-8152

EMAIL: info@nevadawomensfund.org

WEB: www.nevadawomensfund.org

Contact Person

Fritsi H. Ericson, President & CEO

Purpose

The Nevada Women's Fund is a community foundation created in 1982 to respond to inadequate funding of many women's and children's programs and projects in Nevada. Through public support the fund helps women by making grants in recognition of and in response to the special needs of women.

Areas of Interest

The fund supports educational and charitable projects relevant to women and children in Nevada including: training and counseling to become self-sufficient and self-supporting; scholarships, internships, and projects that promote career development for women and girls in nontraditional fields such as science, the arts, the professions, athletics, and business; counseling and training programs for displaced homemakers, single, minority, rural, disabled and elderly women; children's services; organizations helping women and families in emergency or crisis.

All grantees must be Nevada residents or organizations that are working on a project that will benefit women and children in Nevada. Grants are awarded for specific projects to be accomplished within specified time frames, and preference is given to applicants who are not likely to receive funding from more traditional sources. All grantees are required to participate in an evaluation process during the grant period and to submit a final report on their work.

**Financial
Data**

```
(Year ended 12/31/00)
Assets:                            $ 1,507,825
Total grants paid:                 $ 106,904
Number of grants paid:                     17
Highest grant:                     $ 15,000
Lowest grant:                      $ 800
Median grant size:                 $ 7,636
Total scholarships paid:           $ 134,500
Number of scholarships paid:               83
Highest scholarship:               $ 5,000
Lowest scholarship:                $ 500
Median scholarship size:           $ 1,622
```

**Application
Procedures**

Interested applicants should write or telephone the fund and request a copy of the grantmaking criteria and application guidelines. Deadlines for submitting applications vary, so applicants should be certain to ask about the timing of a request.

Among the items that must be included in a grant application to the fund are descriptions of the documented need for the program; measurable objectives; clear and concise program procedures; an evaluation scheme related to the identified objectives; the personnel involved in the program and their qualifications; a detailed budget including other sources of funding and the specific proposed use of grant funds; a time schedule for meeting objectives; and a timetable for reporting to the fund on progress toward meeting the program objectives.

There are separate application procedures and guidelines for scholarships that can be used by Nevada residents for education outside the state. Among the factors the fund takes into consideration in making scholarship awards are need, goals, previous and current community involvement, plans after completing course of study, and the nontraditional field a candidate desires to enter.

**Grant
Limitations**

Applications may be downloaded from our website. Only hard copies mailed or hand delivered to the office will be accepted. Preference for grant funding is given to 501(c)(3) agencies and institutions in northern Nevada. Scholarships are awarded annually for academic study and vocational training. Preference is given to northern Nevada residents and those attending schools in the northern Nevada university and community college system.

**Meeting
Times**

The board of directors meets monthly. In the fall the board considers grant applications; in the spring the board considers scholarship applications.

Publications

The fund publishes newsletters and Nevada Women's Fund informational packets and reports.

THE NEW HAMPSHIRE CHARITABLE FOUNDATION

PHONE: (603) 225-6641

FAX: (603) 225-1700

EMAIL: info@nhcf.org

WEB: www.nhcf.org

37 PLEASANT STREET

CONCORD, NEW HAMPSHIRE 03301-4005

Contact Person

Lewis M. Feldstein, President

Purpose

The New Hampshire Charitable Foundation is New Hampshire's statewide community foundation. Established in 1962, the fund makes grants, loans, and scholarship awards to respond to community problems and needs across the state.

Areas of Interest

The foundation's grantmaking focuses principally on the arts and humanities, education, the environment, health, social and community services, and the voluntary sector. In awarding project grants and support from unrestricted funds, decisions are guided by the following interests: structural innovation and reform, direct services and support, funding transitions and planning for adversity, nonprofit management and governance, demonstrations and advocacy, startup funding or service expansion and diversity, participation, and self-help.

Application Procedures

Application deadlines are April 1 and September 1. Application letters should explain carefully the purpose of the project and describe how it will be accomplished. Each submission must include an itemized income and expense budget for the project, the organization's operating budget, and last available financial statement, along with a copy of the IRS tax-exemption letter.

Proposal guidelines and a coversheet are available on request.

**Financial
Data**

```
(Year ended 12/31/00)
Assets:                          $ 237,664,323
Total grants paid:                $ 12,670,538
Total loans:                         $ 451,968


2000 Grants by
New Hampshire Charitable Foundation
                                  $ 12,670,538
2000 Number of grants paid:      1,685 grants
            and 1,451 scholarships and loans
Highest grant:
Lowest grant:
Median grant size:
```

**Grant
Limitations**

Grant and loan eligibility is limited to tax-exempt organizations and public agencies in the state of New Hampshire. General operating support is usually not provided from discretionary funds for ongoing programs, and grants will not be made for endowments or to eliminate deficits. Generally, grants are not made for capital projects such as acquisition of land, buildings, major equipment, or the construction or renovation of facilities.

**Meeting
Times**

The boards of the New Hampshire Charitable Fund and affiliated trusts make grantmaking decisions twice a year.

Publications

The foundation publishes an annual report and grant application guidelines.

NEW YORK COMMUNITY TRUST

2 PARK AVENUE, 24TH FLOOR

NEW YORK, NEW YORK 10016

PHONE: (212) 686-0010

FAX: (212) 532-8528

EMAIL: info@nycommunitytrust.org

WEB: www.nycommunitytrust.org

Contact Person

Judith Lopez, Executive Assistant

Purpose

The New York Community Trust is a community fund whose mission is to award grants to help make New York City a better place to live. Grants are awarded to strengthen families, develop youth, build community, promote multicultural understanding and meet basic human needs in New York City. The trust also mobilizes people and resources to tackle important problems in the city by convening groups from the private, nonprofit, and government sectors to focus community attention on important issues and special initiatives.

Areas of Interest

The trust makes grants in four major areas of interests: children, youth, and families; community development and the environment; education, arts, and the humanities; and health and people with special needs.

• Children, Youth, and Families. Projects in the areas of girls and young women, hunger and homelessness, social services and welfare, substance abuse, and youth development (including employment, recreation and services, and juvenile justice).

• Community Development and the Environment. Programs in civic affairs, conservation and the environment, economic development, housing, neighborhood revitalization, and technical assistance.

• Education, Arts, and the Humanities. Programs in arts and culture, education, and human justice.

• Health and People With Special Needs. Research in biomedical research, health services, health systems and policy, and people with special needs (such as AIDS, elderly, mental health and retardation, visual disabilities, and children and youth with disabilities).

The trust also has a loan guarantee program that assists nonprofit organizations in obtaining short-term commercial financing.

Financial Data

(Year ended 12/31/00)	
Assets:	$ 1,930,370,263
Total grants paid:	$ 143,950,743

Application Procedures

Applicants are specifically requested not to telephone for appointments or to discuss a proposed project until a letter describing the project or a proposal has been submitted. Applicants should phone and ask the receptionist for the trust's general data sheet entitled "Guidelines for Grant Applicants" and for any additional grantmaking guidelines in your specific program area.

Applications should include a cover letter on the applicant's letterhead signed by the director and a complete New York Community Trust Proposal Cover Sheet. The proposal, no longer than ten pages, should include: agency background, project description (problem addressed, goals and objectives, target population, project activities, staff resumes), evaluation plan, and project budget.

Supporting materials should include: identification of the organization's board members, the organization's most recent audited financial statement and annual report, a copy of the organization's current operating budget, and evidence of tax-exempt status.

All proposals are acknowledged with a postcard, and the trust notes that sometimes applicants may not hear again from the staff for six to ten weeks following acknowledgment. The trust may request a meeting to obtain additional information if it appears that a meeting would be productive.

Grant Limitations

Grants usually range from $5,000 to $100,000 for one year. Some grants are made at higher levels or for longer periods, but they are extremely competitive.

The distribution committee concentrates its selection primarily on organizations in the New York City area. Support is not made to individuals, for endowments, building campaigns, general operating support, or for religious purposes.

**Meeting
Times**

The distribution committee meets in February, April, June, July, October, and December.

Publications

An annual report and specific application guidelines are available upon request.

NEW YORK FOUNDATION

PHONE: (212) 594-8009

350 FIFTH AVENUE, ROOM 2901

NEW YORK, NEW YORK 10118

WEB: www.nyf.org

Contact Person

Maria Mottola, Executive Director

Areas of Interest

The New York Foundation makes grants in the metropolitan New York area to groups that are working on problems of pressing concern to disadvantaged, handicapped, or minority populations. In general, the foundation supports projects that have strong community roots and that seek to enable members of New York's neediest groups to make some difference in their own lives. Nearly one-half of the foundation's grants are made to projects serving youth or the elderly. The foundation also considers support for public education and advocacy programs whose effect is to increase the participation of its target populations in public debate on issues of pressing concern. It is particularly interested in reviewing proposals to coordinate and improve communication among programs working on similar issues.

Projects stand the best chance of receiving a grant if they: involve New York City or a particular neighborhood of the city; address a critical need of a disadvantaged population and involve those affected in seeking to meet that need; are strongly identified with a particular community; require an amount of funding to which a New York Foundation grant would make a substantial contribution; and clearly identify a role for the foundation's funds.

Although the foundation supports a diversity of issues, all its grants fall into one of the following categories: start-up grants to new, untested programs, frequently involving a high element of risk; grants for new community projects of established institutions that offer a high probability of ongoing support in the future, or that anticipate only a limited life; general support to organizations meeting the foundation's guidelines, usually relatively new programs; and grants offering technical assistance, either by support of organizations providing technical assistance or by direct provision of services to grantees.

NEW YORK FOUNDATION

Financial Data

(Year ended 12/31/00)	
Assets:	$ 82,355,000
Total grants paid:	$ 4,862,000
Number of grants paid:	115
Highest grant:	$ 80,000
Lowest grant:	$ 25,000
Median grant size:	$ 40,000

Application Procedures

The foundation's deadlines for proposals are November 1, March 1, and July 1. The foundation was the initiator of the project that developed a Common Application Form for use by area nonprofits. It strongly encourages applicants to submit proposals in this form. A simple first step, however, is to send a letter outlining the project and the budget. The foundation can often make a quick determination without a full proposal.

Applicants will usually receive a response to this initial letter within ten days. If the foundation decides that a project fits within its guidelines, the applicant will receive proposal information and required financial forms. The foundation staff meets personally with applicants to evaluate proposed projects and will visit the program site before making recommendations to the board.

Grant Limitations

The foundation does not make grants to individuals and rarely supports capital campaigns. It is unlikely to fund research studies, films, conferences, or publications, unless initiated by the foundation itself. The foundation makes no grants outside the United States.

Meeting Times

The board of directors meets three times a year, in February, June, and October.

Publications

The foundation publishes an annual report.

THE NEW YORK TIMES COMPANY FOUNDATION

PHONE: (212) 556-1091

FAX: (212) 556-4450

229 WEST 43RD STREET

NEW YORK, NEW YORK 10036-3959

WEB: www.nytco.com/foundation

Contact Person

Jack Rosenthal, President

Purpose

The New York Times Company Foundation provides funding to projects that are innovative and capable of showing concrete and relatively quick results for improving social, educational, cultural, or environmental conditions. They also focus on organizations that have become negatively affected by government cutbacks. Some national and international activities receive contributions, but the majority of grants are concentrated in the New York area and in localities served by The New York Times affiliated companies.

Areas of Interest

Grants are divided into five major categories: cultural affairs, education, community services, journalism, and environmental concerns. In the arts, grants are made to museums and libraries and major cultural institutions, as well as to smaller performing arts groups. A continuing concern of the foundation, in education and journalism areas, is improving opportunities for minorities. A large part of the educational fund is directed to inner-city schools, mainly for literacy programs, mentoring and tutorial assistance, dropout prevention, special approaches to troubled or learning-disabled children and scholarship programs for the gifted. Community service and environmental grants contribute to improvements on an urban, national, and international level.

**Financial
Data**

> (Year ended   / /   )
> Assets: NA
> Total grants paid:
> Total number of grants:
> Highest grant:
> Lowest grant:
> Median grant size:

**Application
Procedures**

Grants should be requested in a letter describing the purpose for which funds are sought and providing information concerning the costs of the specific venture and details of other potential sources of support. A financial report of the organization as well as proof of tax-exempt status from the Internal Revenue Code must accompany the letter.

Meetings with applicants are arranged at the discretion of the foundation only when such a meeting is essential to the determination of a response.

**Grant
Limitations**

The foundation does not make grants to individuals, to sectarian religious institutions and causes, or for health related purposes. In the urban affairs area, grants are generally not made on the neighborhood level. Some national and international activities receive contributions, but the majority of grants are concentrated in the greater New York area and in localities served by affiliates of The New York Times Company.

**Meeting
Times**

The board of directors meets at least twice annually, in the first and third quarter of each calendar year, to review the president's recommendations and approve grants.

Publications

The foundation publishes an annual report.

NORMAN FOUNDATION

147 East 48th Street

New York, New York 10017

PHONE: (212) 230-9830

FAX: (212) 230-9849

EMAIL: info@normanfdn.org

WEB: www.normanfdn.org

Contact Person

June Makela, Program Director

Purpose

Since the late 1950's the Norman Foundation has supported efforts to promote fairness and opportunity, primarily by empowering the unempowered to challenge the conditions and institutions that control major aspects of their lives. For some time the foundation has been focusing particularly on economic justice and environmental justice issues, while maintaining its broad and historic commitment to civil rights.

Areas of Interest

Economic justice grants are awarded to organizations that seek to create wider and fairer access to decent employment, education, housing, and other basic needs. Environmental justice grants support projects addressing government and corporate abuses of power that threaten human health and safety, especially where the harm falls disproportionately on those already suffering economic and social deprivation. Civil rights grants aim at fighting systemic discrimination and violence and towards greater equity.

The foundation provides general support and also funds issue-specific projects that hold some promise of effecting change on a national level. Proposals most likely to be successful will combine a fundamental substantive approach with a component of persuading larger groups to follow an example. Collaboration between local grassroots groups and national organizations are encouraged. In addition, the foundation favors proposals that aim to secure and build upon recent specific accomplishments, such as a group's precedent-setting campaign or achievement.

The foundation encourages proposals from new organizations and grassroots groups that may lack previous fundraising experience.

The foundation also welcomes innovative proposals designed to increase the influence or financial stability of social change organizations working in the foundation's areas of interest. Generally, such proposals should seek to tap underutilized resources, broaden the group's base of support or disseminate models of proven effectiveness. In this area of grantmaking, strong preference will be given to organizations that have already earned the foundation's confidence through successful completion of a previous substantive grant project.

Financial Data

(Year ended 12/31/00)	
Assets:	$ 25,207,736
Total grants paid (1999)*:	$ 1,719,500
Number of grants paid:	77
Highest grant:	$ 30,000
Lowest grant:	$ 6,600
Median grant size:	$ 18.000

*No grants made in 2000 due to transition.

Application Procedures

The foundation has instituted deadlines which are posted on its website. There is no formal application form. However, prospective grantees may use the National Network of Grantmakers or New York Area Common Application Form. Prospective grantees are encouraged to initiate the application process by sending a short letter of inquiry to the program director. This letter should explain the scope and significance of the problem to be addressed; the organization's proposed response and (if appropriate) how this strategy builds upon the organization's past work; the specific, demonstrable effects the project would have if successful; and how the project promotes change on a national level and otherwise relates to the foundation's guidelines.

All inquiries will be acknowledged. If a proposal is deemed promising, the organization will be encouraged to submit a full proposal which should include a more detailed description of the proposed project as outlined in the initial letter; detailed organization and project budgets, including a breakdown of current and prospective income from foundation and other sources; background on project staff and their ethnic and racial composition; a descriptive list of board members and their ethnic and racial composition; letters of support as appropriate (e.g. from organizations proposed as collaborators or as potential networks for project dissemination); and documentation of tax-exempt status.

Each proposal will be assessed by its ability to fulfill the following criteria: talented personnel, including innovative, creative, and sound managerial and personnel skills among the program's leadership; clearly articulated objectives and goals; active, ongoing equal-opportunity leadership development; and a substantial plan to acquire adequate support to complete the proposed project or to achieve self-sufficiency.

The foundation acknowledges receipt of proposals. The program director is generally unable to arrange appointments with prospective grantees prior to receipt and review of written proposals.

Grant Limitations

The foundation does not make grants to individuals or to support conferences, scholarships, research, films, media and arts projects, direct social service delivery programs, capital funding projects, fundraising drives or other grant-making organizations. Programs seeking funding must be tax-exempt and focused primarily on domestic issues.

Meeting Times

The board of trustees meets three times a year.

Publications

The foundation's grant reports, guidelines and deadlines for grant applications are available on the foundation's website, www.normanfdn.org.

NORTH STAR FUND

305 Seventh Avenue, 5th Floor
(between 27th and 28th Streets)
New York, New York 10001-6008

PHONE: (212) 620-9110

FAX: (212) 620-8178

EMAIL: info@northstarfund.org

WEB: www.northstarfund.org

Contact Persons

> Hugh Hogan, Executive Director
> Miriam Hernandez, Administrative Manager
> Sheila Stowell, Program Associate

Purpose

> The North Star Fund makes grants to projects that bring New York City activists together to work for social, economic, and political change. North Star considers applications from groups in New York City that: organize low-income and are working toward institutional, political, social, and/or economic change; are democratically structured, and are both responsive and accountable to their communities; and make links between different, but related, forms of oppression.

Areas of Interest

> The fund supports groups that educate the community on social and economic conditions and organize people to confront fundamental problems affecting their lives. Funding areas include: community organizing, women's rights, anti-racism organizing, lesbian and gay rights, housing advocacy, immigrants' rights, health care, youth empowerment, peace, and international solidarity. North Star also supports film, video, and cultural projects specifically related to New York City community organizing efforts.
>
> Grants awarded are between $500 and $6000, depending on the organization's budget, other sources of income, and its funding history with North Star. Emergency grants of up to a maximum of $500 are available to groups that need to respond to urgent political events or crises. North Star will also make interim grants of $500 to $2000 to organizations responding to unexpected needs, situations and opportunities that cannot wait until the next deadline.
>
> North Star maintains a $5,000 revolving loan fund to assist groups with start-up funds for particular activities or to help cover expenses while awaiting

payment of an approved grant. Organizations that have received North Star grants are eligible to apply for these loans.

Financial Data

```
(Year ended   /   /   )
Support and revenue:          NA
Total grants paid:
Number of grants paid:
Highest grant:
Lowest grant:
Median grant size:
```

Application Procedures

Application deadlines are in October and March. Potential grantees should telephone or write the fund and request an application form. The form contains summary sheets and outlines the information necessary to complete the proposal. All funding decisions are made by the community funding board made up of community activists representing a broad range of progressive perspectives. An applicant may be asked to attend an interview.

Grant Limitations

The North Star Fund does not fund projects that: are directed at constituencies outside New York City; solely provide direct services; have large budgets and access to traditional funding sources; are individual efforts; request travel expenses for individual speakers or conference participants; promote specific candidates for public office.

Meeting Times

Funding decisions are made twice a year in January and June. The funding board meets three times during a funding cycle and on other occasions for interviews and committee meetings. The board of directors meets every two months.

Publications

North Star publishes an annual report and a brochure. Grant guidelines and a recent grantee list are contained in the application forms.

THE NORTHERN TRUST COMPANY CHARITABLE TRUST

50 South LaSalle Street, MB-5

Chicago, Illinois 60675

PHONE: (312) 630-6000

FAX: (312) 444-3108

WEB: www.northerntrust.com/aboutus/
community/charitable

Contact Person

Kelly Mannard, Senior Vice President

Purpose

The Northern Trust Company Charitable Trust is funded through gifts from The Northern Trust Company. The trust provides grants in Chicago to projects that are responsive to the needs of low income residents, especially those designed to address systemic problems, promote self-help, and foster the independence of those served. Additionally, grants are made to cultural, educational, and health care institutions and organizations. Grantmaking is limited to the Chicago metropolitan area, with priority given to Cook County.

Areas of Interest

The fund has four areas of interest:

• Community Development. Projects that increase and improve affordable housing and promote creation of jobs in low- and moderate-income neighborhoods.

• Education. Projects that address the problems of early childhood education, focus on school failure prevention, and work to improve the Chicago public school system.

• Health and Human Services. Projects that strive to make primary health care services more accessible and affordable to low-income Cook county residents. Priority projects will address the problems of teen pregnancy and deal with prevention or treatment of substance abuse.

• Culture and the Arts. Projects aimed at sustaining well-established institutions as well as assisting a limited number of smaller and newer groups. Priority is given to programs which promote cultural diversity.

The trust has a matching gift program and a volunteer grants program which support the activities of Northern Trust Company. Additionally, the bank also makes a limited number of direct contributions to a variety of community activities.

Financial Data

> (Year ended 12/31/99)
> Total grants paid: $ 2,499,832
> Total number of grants:
> Highest grant:
> Lowest grant:
> Median grant size:

Application Procedures

Organizations should request an application form by calling the foundation at 312-444-4059. Along with the application form, an organization will receive instructions on the proposal requirements and supporting documentation.

Proposals from major educational, health care, and cultural institutions will be considered as received. For all other projects, proposals are reviewed in the month following the deadlines listed below:

August 1/November 1	Community Development
February 1/August 1	Health and Human Services
May 1	Education
May 1	Culture and the Arts

Grant Limitations

Grants are not made to support individuals, fraternal groups, individual churches or sectarian organizations, political activity, tickets or advertising for fundraising benefits, or general operations of United Way agencies. Grantmaking is limited to the Chicago metropolitan area. Organizations must provide a current IRS letter confirming 501(c)(3) tax-exempt status.

Meeting Times

The board of trustees meets bimonthly to consider grant requests.

Publications

The fund publishes an annual report and grant guidelines.

JESSIE SMITH NOYES FOUNDATION

6 East 39th Street, 12th Floor

New York, New York 10016

PHONE: (212) 684-6577

FAX: (212) 689-6549

EMAIL: noyes@noyes.org

WEB: www.noyes.org

Contact Persons

>Victor De Luca, President
>Millie Buchanan, Program Officer
>Wilma Montañez, Program Officer
>Kolu Zighi, Program Officer

Purpose

>The Jessie Smith Noyes Foundation is committed to protecting and restoring Earth's natural systems and promoting a sustainable society by strengthening individuals, institutions and communities pledged to pursuing those goals.
>
>The foundation makes grants in the areas of environment and reproductive rights. The components of our program are:
>- Toxics
>- Sustainable agriculture
>- Reproductive rights
>- Sustainable communities
>- Metro New York environment
>
>We favor activities that address the connections between these concerns and their broader implications, especially those activities that have a potential for widespread impact or applicability, as well as the ones that address the connections between environmental issues and issues of social justice.

Areas of Interest

>As of February 1, 2001, the guidelines for the Noyes Foundation's Toxic and Sustainable Agriculture Programs have been revised to reflect a deepening concern about the growing power and global reach of corporations and their impact on the environment, communities and society in general. The guidelines for the Reproductive Rights, New York Metropolitan Environment and Sustainable Communities Programs have not been changed. Requests for funding in these program areas that address corporate power and globalization issues should be made under the existing guidelines.

TOXICS

OBJECTIVE:

To reduce threats posed by toxics to the environment and human health.

PRIORITIES:

• To strengthen the organizing, advocacy, and technical capabilities of groups that fight toxic pollution, especially at the state and regional levels.

• To support efforts to change governmental and corporate policies and practices in order to reduce toxic threats to the environment and public health.

• To strengthen the movement for environmental justice by developing leadership and participation by low-income people and people of color.

GEOGRAPHIC FOCUS:

United States, with emphasis on the Southeast, Southwest and the Rocky Mountain West

SUSTAINABLE AGRICULTURE

OBJECTIVE:

To help build a system of food and fiber production that sustains the environment and benefits people.

PRIORITIES:

• To strengthen the capacity of organizations promoting sustainable agriculture.

• To advance sustainable agriculture policies and practices that promote continuity and responsibility in the ownership of farmland, maintenance and restoration of soil quality and crop diversity, and efforts to counter the actions of public and private sector institutions that support the concentration of ownership in, and the industrialization of, agriculture.

• To demonstrate the agricultural and economic feasibility of sustainable agriculture; its social benefits; and its ability to strengthen rural communities and reduce the distance between producers and consumers.

GEOGRAPHIC FOCUS:

United States, with emphasis on the Northeast, Southern U.S. and Rocky Mountain West

REPRODUCTIVE RIGHTS

OBJECTIVE:

To ensure quality reproductive health care as a human right.

PRIORITIES:

• To broaden the base and the agenda of the reproductive rights movement through the involvement of new constituencies

• To support legal and policy initiatives at the state and national level to safeguard reproductive freedom

• To ensure that reproductive health is included in health care policies and reform initiatives

GEOGRAPHIC FOCUS:

United States

SUSTAINABLE COMMUNITIES

OBJECTIVE:

To promote communities that are environmentally sound, economically vital and socially just.

PRIORITIES:

• To support individuals and organizations in implementing local initiatives, technologies or systems that respect the inter-connectedness of human and natural communities.

• To strengthen local economics built upon inclusive and demographic decision making.

GEOGRAPHIC FOCUS:

United States

METRO NEW YORK ENVIRONMENT

OBJECTIVE:

To promote an environmentally sound New York metropolitan area through an active, informed and empowered local citizenry.

PRIORITIES:

• To strengthen the advocacy, outreach, analytical, technical and organizational capacity of organizations working on environmental issues, particularly community-based and grassroots groups

• To improve public policies and the responsiveness of public agencies charged with protecting the area's environment

• To develop effective coalitions and networks among different organizations,both within the environmental movement and between environmental activists and others, to enhance the quality of life in the New York metropolitan area

GEOGRAPHIC FOCUS:

New York: New York City, Long Island and Westchester and Rockland Counties

New Jersey: Bergen, Essex, Hudson and Union Counties

Financial Data

(Year ended 12/31/00)	
Assets:	$ 85,347,395
Total grants paid:	$ 4,223,900
Number of grants paid:	150
Highest grant:	$ 40,000
Lowest grant:	$ 3,000
Median grant size:	$ 25,000

Application Procedures

The first step should be a letter of inquiry of no more than three pages. Letters can be submitted at any time during the year and they are reviewed on a continuous basis. We welcome the opportunity to meet with prospective grantees, but prefer to wait until after we receive a letter to determine if the meeting will be useful.

The letter of inquiry should include the following:

• a statement of the issues to be addressed, the history and goals of the organization and your organization's involvement with these issues

• a summary of the activities for which you are requesting funding, including the objectives and anticipated outcomes

• the starting date and duration of the proposed activities

• the total amoung of funding needed and information about possible sources of support

We try to acknowledge the receipt of all letters of inquiry. Letters that do not fall within the foundation's program guidelines are immediately declined. If you do not hear from us within one month, please call the program officer.

Letters that are within the guidelines receive additional review and a full proposal may be requested. Proposals should be submitted to the foundation only upon request. The foundation accepts the common grant application form of the National Network of Grantmakers, which will be provided. Since the foundation receives more proposals than it can fund, you should not interpret a request for a proposal as an indication of likely support.

Program officers may request additional information from applicants. We also might consult with persons knowledgeable about the organization and/or the proposed activities. Finally, we will meet with the applicant preferably at your location or in New York City or at another appropriate site.

Grant Limitations

The foundation only makes grants to tax-exempt organizations with a 501 (c)(3) classification from the IRS.

The foundation will not consider requests for endowments, capital construction, general fundraising, deficit financing, or loans and grants to individuals. The foundation no longer provides scholarship or fellowship support to individuals. In view of the national scope of its program, it does not ordinarily consider projects that are primarily of local interest. The foundation does not make grants for research projects or give support to conferences, seminars, media events, or workshops unless they are an integral part of a broader program. The foundation also does not provide support for the production and development of television and radio programming.

Meeting Times

The board of directors meets three times a year in spring, summer, and fall.

Publications

The foundation publishes an annual report and a brochure outlining its program guidelines and procedures.

OTTINGER FOUNDATION

80 BROAD STREET, 17TH FLOOR
NEW YORK, NEW YORK 10004

PHONE: (212) 764-1508

FAX: (212) 764-4298

EMAIL: info@ottingerfoundation.org

WEB: www.ottingerfoundation.org

Contact Person

Michele Lord, Executive Director

Areas of Interest

The Ottinger Foundation is a private family foundation that funds non profit organizations that promote innovative policies and citizen activism to build a movement for change. We support organizations that address structural or root causes of social problems and focus on systemic social change rather than direct services. Organizations and projects funded by the Ottinger Foundation include a sound strategic vision, a concrete action plan, and strong components of advocacy and grassroots organizing. Projects must have national significance. We also favor organizations that are involved in coalition building as well as building leadership and organizational infrastructure.

Financial Data

(Year ended   /   /   )
Assets: NA
Total grants paid:
Number of grants paid:
Highest grant:
Lowest grant:
Median grant size:

Application Procedures

A brief letter of intent (no more than three pages) is required to determine whether the foundation's present interests and funds permit consideration of the request. Letters of intent will be accepted from organizations working on economic security and development throughout the United States.

The letter should include:

- The purpose of the project for which funds are being requested and how it furthers the objectives of the Economic Security and Development Program.
- Background information about the prospective grantee.
- A list of other organizations involved in similar programs and how the proposed project is different or collaborative.

Along with the letter, please send the following attachments:

- Estimated overall budget for the project and/or organization.
- Qualifications of those who will be engaged in the project, including staff and board profiles.

After receiving the letter, foundation staff members may ask the grantseeker to submit a formal proposal. If requested, a complete proposal should be written concisely and its narrative sections should not exceed ten pages. All proposals must include the following information:

- A clear statement of the need for support, the project's goals, and an action plan for achieving those goals. Preference is given to proposals that include detailed and pragmatic notes on strategy and project implementation rather than those that focus on the need for support.
- Methods for evaluating the project's success must be included.
- A determination letter of 501(c)(3) tax-exempt status issued by the I.R.S.
- A list of other sources of financial support already committed.
- Project and organizational line-item budgets as well as audited financial statements.

The foundation's staff will contact applicants if further information is needed.

Grant Limitations

The foundation only makes grants to tax-exempt organizations in the United States. It does not make grants to organizations which traditionally enjoy popular support such as universities, museums, or hospitals. It does not support academic research, film or video projects, construction or restoration projects, profit-making businesses, or local programs without national significance.

Meeting Times

The board of directors meets twice a year to review grant proposals.

Publications

None.

PEACE DEVELOPMENT FUND

P. O. Box 1280

Amherst, Massachusetts 01004-1280

PHONE: (413) 256-8306

FAX: (413) 256-8871

EMAIL: pdf@peacefund.org

WEB: www.peacedevelopmentfund.org

Contact Person

Aleah Vaughn, Director of Grants and Training, Ext. 105

Purpose

Peace Development Fund works to strengthen a broad-based social justice movement that embodies, embraces, and honors many cultures to create the new systems and institutions essential to building a peaceful, just, and equitable world. We are a public foundation providing grants, training, and other resources in partnership with communities, organizations, trainers, and donors with whom we share a common vision for change.

Areas of Interest

PDF's current grant program priorities are in the following areas:

• Unifying movement sectors to develop a common vision, a shared analysis for change and action.
• Empowering people in traditionally marginalized communities by connecting political education with action to address social change issues.
• Eliminating forms of systemic oppression and the violence that arises from them using an analysis that links the oppressions.
• Building networks with a common vision and shared analysis for change amongst individuals and/or organizations capable of collectively addressing progressive issues nationally and internationally.

The Peace Development Fund gives priority to the following types of organizations and projects:

• Projects that focus on local communities, but make the connection between local, national and international issues or struggles.
• Groups and projects with a social change agenda, committed to using political education within the context of organizing previously under-organized constituencies.

• Efforts that foster and use movement building and networking as key strategies to build unity amongst existing groups.

• Groups with a diverse leadership that reflects the communities in which they are organizing.

• Groups and organizations of proven effectiveness, or new projects or groups that have that potential.

• Efforts that have difficulty securing funds from other sources.

• Projects that emphasize transnational organizing amongst workers in Canada, Mexico, and the United States.

• Efforts from indigenous communities in Canada, Mexico, and the United States that are working to address local, regional, national, or international challenges.

Financial Data

(Year ended 6/30/00)	
Assets:	$ 3,025,213
Grants awarded:	$ 693,322
Highest grant:	$ 10,000
Median grant size:	$ 7,000

Application Procedures

Guidelines are available in English and Spanish.

The first step in applying to the Peace Development Fund is sending three (3) copies of a letter of intent no longer than three (3) pages. The letter should provide:

• Basic information about your organization, including a brief statement of its activities and history.

• A brief summary of the kind of change you are trying to bring about, including your objectives, strategies and tactics.

• A clear explanation of the root causes of the injustice or inequity that your organization is working to transform.

• A brief and concise statement of how your group uses political education in your community to achieve organization goals. Provide examples of topics, ideas or approach.

• A brief and concise outline of the Budget information, including: the total budgets of the organization, the total budget for the project, the total amount requested from the foundation and other sources of support, both assured and requested.

1. Letters of intent deadlines are September 1 and February 1. Letters must be in the Amherst office by these dates in order to be considered. We do not accept letters by fax or e-mail. The Peace Development Fund requires three (3) copies of the letter of intent. Decisions on letters of intent are generally made within three weeks following the deadline.

    The Board will not approve funding for a project that has already been completed or is nearly over by the time a proposal is considered. Applicants should keep this in mind when describing their programs.

2. Proposals are accepted by invitation only. If your organization is invited to send a full proposal we require six (6) copies of the proposal and accompanying materials, unless otherwise specified. Decisions on grant awards are generally made within two months following the proposal deadline.

3. PDF is using the National Network of Grantmaker's Common Grant Application Form for funding proposals. Please follow the instructions carefully, and fill out all items on the enclosed application cover sheet, in the spaces provided. Use 8-1/2 by 11 sheets only. If you are using a computer or work processor, please repeat the questions and items from the cover sheet, and use only the same amount of space provided on the application.

4. Please be sure that all the components of each copy of your proposal are properly collated, with the application cover sheet on top. Please do not bind your proposal.

Grant Limitations

The Peace Development Fund does provide general support funding. Grant size is determined by using the following criteria:

*   Financial need and access to other sources of funding
*   Effectiveness of program or organization
*   Current PDF funding priorities

Groups may only receive funding from the Peace Development Fund once a year. Proposals will be considered for projects, organizations, and national/international networks based in the United States and its territories, Canada, and Mexico.

The Peace Development Fund does not fund:

*   Individuals
*   Research projects
*   Conferences and other single events

- Production of audio-visual materials
- Direct services that are not part of an organizing strategy
- Scholarships
- Academic institutions

Meeting Times

Decisons on letters of intent are generally made within three weeks following the deadline. Full proposals are accepted by invitation only after a letter of intent is screened into consideration. Decisions on grant awards are generally made within two months following the proposal deadline.

Publications

The fund publishes an annual report and newsletters. These are available on our website or by contacting the office.

PENINSULA COMMUNITY FOUNDATION

1700 SOUTH EL CAMINO REAL, NO. 300

SAN MATEO, CALIFORNIA 94402-3049

PHONE: (650) 358-9369

FAX: (650) 358-9817

EMAIL: see website

WEB: www.pcf.org

Contact Person

Ellen Clear, Director of Programs

Purpose

The Peninsula Community Foundation promotes philanthropic giving and innovative grant making in San Mateo County and Northern Santa Clara County (Palo Alto, Mountain View, Los Altos Hills). Grants are made to organizations providing services in this region for education, human services, health, and cultural affairs.

Areas of Interest

The foundation dedicates sixty percent of its grantmaking to services for children, youth and families, twenty percent to adult services of various kinds, fifteen percent to housing and homelessness issues, and five percent to public benefit, including annual support of a resource center for nonprofits.

Financial Data

(Year ended 12/31/00)	
Assets:	$ 450,000,000
Total grants paid:	$ 65,000,000
Number of grants paid:	1,250

Application Procedures

Written guidelines, available on request, recommend that applicants attend a monthly orientation in the foundation's library. (Telephone (650) 358-9392 for the date of the next briefing.)

A letter of inquiry, of less than two pages, may be submitted at any time. If the program fits within the foundation's funding priorities, the organization will be invited to submit a formal proposal. The process may take two to six months depending upon the number of pending applications received earlier.

**Grant
Limitations**

Organizations seeking funding must be located in San Mateo County or Northern Santa Clara County or must operate a program that serves residents of that geographic area. No grants to individuals or for commercial activities.

**Meeting
Times**

The distribution committee meets six times a year.

Publications

The foundation publishes an annual report and a quarterly newsletter.

THE WILLIAM PENN FOUNDATION

Two Logan Square, 11th Floor

100 North 18th Street

Philadelphia, Pennsylvania 19103-2757

PNONE: (215) 988-1830

FAX: (215) 988-1823

EMAIL: moreinfo@wpennfdn.org

WEB: www.wpennfdn.org

Contact Persons

Kathy Engebretson, President

Purpose

The William Penn Foundation is a private regional foundation seeking to improve the quality of life in the Delaware Valley including Bucks, Chester, Delaware, Montgomery, and Philadelphia Counties in Pennsylvania and Camden County, New Jersey. The foundation supports expanding affordable rehearsal and performance space in the South Broad Street cultural corridor; increasing the stock of new and rehabilitated low-income housing in North Philadelphia; protecting the Delaware River watershed; and improving opportunities for minority young people to undertake careers in science, mathematics, engineering, and teaching.

Areas of Interest

The foundation's priorities are:

• Human Development. Programs that address the educational, human services, and health care needs of individuals and families.

• Culture. Programs that promote high quality in performances and exhibits, to increase access to the arts, and to promote conservation of cultural artifacts.

• Environment. Projects that improve urban development patterns by preserving and creating urban open space, assisting land banking efforts, supporting community gardening, enhancing public parks, and supporting urban planning projects.

• Community Fabric. Projects that concentrate on relations between the people and the institutions upon which they rely to make society function. Of particular interest are projects which improve human relations among cultural, racial, ethnic, age, and other groups; increase and renovate low income housing and provide permanent housing for the homeless; train law and justice system officials; improve the effectiveness of community institutions; increase access to community-based health care; and improve adult education and literacy.

THE WILLIAM PENN FOUNDATION

Financial Data

```
(Year ended    /   /   )
Assets:                              NA
Total grants paid:
Number of grants paid:
Highest grant:
Lowest grant:
Median grant size:
```

Application Procedures

The foundation accepts and reviews written requests for support throughout the year. There are no formal deadlines. A single copy of a proposal is sufficient, and the foundation has no standard application form. The foundation states that there is no reason for proposals to be lengthy, elaborate, or expensively packaged. There are, however, a few rules to follow. Because the foundation reviews only written requests, potential applicants should not telephone for an appointment with the staff. If additional information is required, applicants will be contacted.

A complete application should have the following elements: a one-page summary outline, information about the organization making the request, a complete description of the proposed project, and background financial data. Included with every request should also be proof of tax-exempt status from the IRS, a list of the officers and directors of the organization, the organization's most recent annual program report, and the most recent financial statement, preferably audited. Each of these elements is more completely described in the foundation's guidelines.

Grant Limitations

Foundation grants are limited to organizations in the five southeastern Pennsylvania counties and Camden County, New Jersey, which are defined as tax-exempt public charities under Section 501(c)(3) of the Internal Revenue Code. In the case of the environment program area, geographic eligibility encompasses a larger area—approximately a 100-mile radius of Philadelphia. The organization does not fund grants to individuals or for scholarships, fellowships, or travel. Nor does it support religious activities, political lobbying or legislative activities, organizations wishing to distribute grants at their own discretion, tax-exempt organizations which pass funds on to non-exempt groups, profit-making enterprises, loans, programs concerned with a particular disease, addiction treatment programs, recreational programs, or films.

Meeting Times

The board of directors meets five times a year, in January, April, July, September, and December, to consider grant requests.

Publications

The foundation publishes an annual report that includes application guidelines. It also distributes a brochure entitled *Foundation Priorities and Grant Application Procedures*.

THE PEOPLE'S FUND

810 NORTH VINEYARD BOULEVARD

HONOLULU, HAWAII 96817

PHONE: (808) 845-4800

FAX: (808) 845-4800

EMAIL: peoples@lava.net

Contact Person

Nancy Aleck, Executive Director

Purpose

The People's Fund provides financial support and technical assistance to progressive and radical grassroots social change organizations working for a more equitable distribution of wealth, resources, and power in Hawaii and the Pacific.

Areas of Interest

The fund makes grants available to organizations who are working against discrimination, struggling for the rights of workers, promoting self-determination in low-income and other oppressed communities, creating alternative arts and media; promoting peace and responsible U.S. foreign policy, or addressing issues of Hawaiian sovereignty.

Financial Data

Assets:	NA
Total grants paid:	
Total number of grants:	
Highest grant:	
Lowest grant:	
Median grant size:	

Application Procedures

The fund has its own application form which can be obtained by calling the fund. Proposal writing assistance is available. Deadlines are March 1 and September 1.

Proposals are evaluated by staff and a grantmaking committee made up of board members and community activists. Finalists are invited to give a presentation to the committee. The board usually approves the grantmaking committee's recommendations.

Grant
Limitations

The maximum grant amount is $2,000. Emergency grants are available throughout the year with a maximum amount of $300.

Meeting
Times

The fund's board meets twice a year in April and October.

Publications

The foundation publishes an annual report and a spring and fall newsletter.

THE PHILADELPHIA FOUNDATION

PHONE: (215) 563-6417

FAX: (215) 563-6882

EMAIL: parkow@philafound.org

WEB: www.philafound.org

1234 MARKET STREET, SUITE 1800

PHILADELPHIA, PENNSYLVANIA 19107-3794

Contact Person

R. Andrew Swinney, President

Purpose

Created in 1918, The Philadelphia Foundation is a nonprofit community foundation and a professional clearinghouse for enlightened philanthropy. We serve the community needs in Bucks, Chester, Delaware, Montgomery and Philadelphia counties.

The foundation links resources with needs by building a growing pool of more than 400 permanent, charitable funds from people who want to "give something back" to their community. We administer these funds, invest them wisely, and use their revenue, which is generated to provide grants and scholarships to organizations that are solving problems in this remarkable region we call home.

Areas of Interest

The Foundations areas of interest are:
- Arts and Cultures
- Education
- Health
- Environmental
- Public & Community Development
- Human Services

Financial Data

(Year ended 2000)	
Assets:	$ 222,000,000
Total grants paid:	$ 14,000,000
Number of grants paid:	786
Highest grant:	$ 153,250
Lowest grant:	$ 3,500
Median grant size:	$ 20,000

Application Procedures

All applications are due at The Philadelphia Foundation on the DEADLINE DATE. Applications submitted after the deadline date will not be considered.

Grant Limitations

Organizations that are located in one of the following counties: Bucks, Chester, Delaware, Montgomery and Philadelphia, are classified by the Internal Revenue Service under Section 501 (c) (3), and are not private foundations, will be given funding consideration. The foundation rarely makes grants to the following types of organizations or projects:

- Affiliates of national or international organizations
- Government agencies
- Organizations outside the five counties
- Private schools
- Umbrella funding organizations
- Endowments
- Capital campaigns
- Deficit financing
- Publications, research projects, tours and trips
- Individuals

Meeting Times

The board of managers meets twice a year to vote on grant applications, usually in November and April.

Publications

The foundation publishes an annual report. The following are just a few of the brochures published by the Foundation:

- *Donate today . . . Impact Tomorrow*
- *The Planned Giving Design Center*
- *Thinking About Creating Your Own Foundation*

THE PHOEBUS FUND

1500 WALNUT STREET

SUITE 1305

PHILADELPHIA, PENNSYLVANIA 19102

PHONE: (215) 731-1107

FAX: (215) 731-0453

EMAIL: info@breadrosesfund.org

WEB: www.breadrosesfund.org

Contact Person

John Hopkins, Trustee

Purpose

The Phoebus Fund is a private family foundation that supports strategies in the economic, political, and social systems promoting justice, encouraging progressive change, and leading to greater empowerment of the disadvantaged. The fund is particularly interested in projects which typically do not have access to more traditional funding resources.

Areas of Interest

Funding is concentrated in three areas:

• Central America. Projects, especially grassroots ones, which focus on community development, public policy, and education projects.

• Domestic Violence. Projects that address the causes and impact of this problem, aimed at policy changes, advocacy, prevention and protection of victims or potential victims, and those that influence the response of legal and medical authorities.

• Reproductive Rights. Projects aimed at developing and disseminating medical, legal, and political information regarding services, practices, and policies. Also considered are policy development, media, or direct service projects.

**Financial
Data**

```
(Year ended   /  /   )
Assets:                              NA
Total grants paid:
Number of grants paid:
Highest grant:
Lowest grant:
Median grant size:
```

**Application
Procedures**

Proposals should not exceed five typed pages and should include information on the organization including its goals, programs, and other sources of support. For local projects in the greater Philadelphia area, applicants should use the common grant application form available through Philadelphia Foundation or the Bread and Roses Community Fund.

**Grant
Limitations**

Grantmaking is limited to projects in the three areas of interest.

**Meeting
Times**

The board meets twice a year.

Publications

The foundation publishes application information and a list of grantees.

PLAYBOY FOUNDATION

680 N. LAKESHORE DRIVE

CHICAGO, ILLINOIS 60611

PHONE: (312) 751-8000

FAX: (312) 266-8506

WEB: www.playboy.com

Contact Person

Cleo Wilson, Executive Director

Areas of Interest

The Playboy Foundation seeks to foster social change supporting projects of national interest and scope involved in fostering open communication about, and research into, human sexuality, reproductive health and rights, and protecting and fostering civil rights and civil liberties, including women, people affected by HIV/AIDS, gays and lesbians, racial minorities, the poor and the disadvantaged, and eliminating censorship and protecting freedom of expression.

Financial Data

(Year ended 12/31/00)	
Total grants paid:	$ 665,000
Total number of grants:	50
Highest grant:	$ 30,000
Lowest grant:	$ 250
Median grant size:	$ 5,000

Application Procedures

The foundation accepts grant proposals throughout the year. The board of directors generally meets in the fall to consider proposals. Grants range from $5,000 to $30,000. Requests for funds should include a description of the organization, including a summary of its background, purpose, objectives and experience in the area for which funds are sought; itemized project budget and proposed funding sources, amount of funds requested, their proposed use and over what time period; names and qualifications of people involved with the project; organizational expenses and income for previous, current, and coming fiscal year; list of board members, their titles, outside affiliations and phone numbers; Internal Revenue Service verification that the organization is not a private foundation and is exempt from taxation under Internal Revenue Service sections 509(a) and 501(c)(3). A copy of the IRS tax-exempt letter must accompany the proposal along with an audited financial statement or Form 990 for the most recently completed fiscal year.

The foundation does not award grants for direct service projects. It is especially interested in projects where a small grant can make a difference. As a small corporate giving program, the foundation's budget is small and competition for support is very high. Proposals should be addressed to the executive director.

Grant Limitations

No grants are made for scholarships, capital campaigns, endowments, or for religious purposes. The foundation does not make grants for the reduction of an operating deficit or to liquidate a debt.

Meeting Times

The board of directors meets several times a year to consider grant proposals.

Publications

The foundation publishes a brief brochure describing its priorities and grant-application procedures. The foundation does not publish an annual report.

PLOUGHSHARES FUND

Fort Mason Center, B-330

San Francisco, California 94123

PHONE: (415) 775-2244

FAX: (415) 775-4529

EMAIL: ploughshares@ploughshares.org

WEB: www.ploughshares.org

Contact Persons

Sally Lilienthal, President

Naila Bolus, Executive Director

Purpose

The Ploughshares Fund is a public grantmaking foundation established in 1981 to stop the spread of weapons of war, from nuclear arms to landmines.

Areas of Interest

In order to meet its goals, the fund makes grants concentrated on the following areas: halting the proliferation of nuclear weapons, controlling the international arms trade, promoting new approaches to international security, and confronting the legacy of the arms race. As a public foundation, Ploughshares also supports individuals directly and spends a portion of its resources on grassroots and national political lobbying. In addition, Ploughshares launches initiatives in response to needs that are not being met by existing programs.

Financial Data

(Year ended 6/30/00)	
Assets:	$ 15,192,382
Total grants paid:	$ 3,428,511
Number of grants paid:	139
Highest grant:	$ 80,000 (2 year)
Lowest grant:	$ 1,000
Median grant size:	$ 25,000

Application Procedures

The initial request should be a letter briefly describing the project and indicating the financial needs. It should give the qualifications of the personnel involved and a concise description of the methods by which the project goals will be carried out. It should also identify other sources of existing support as well as those pending or contemplated. Proof of tax-exempt status and a list of the board of directors for sponsoring organizations should be enclosed. If it is determined that the project falls within the priorities and interests of the fund, a full proposal will be requested for further consideration. There are no application deadlines.

Grant
Limitations

The fund does not support the production of films, videotapes, or books. It also does not fund the research and writing of academic dissertations.

Meeting
Times

The board of directors meets four times a year (generally in January, April, June, and October), with additional meetings of a small grants committee to consider grants of up to $10,000. Proposals must be received two months prior to be eligible for consideration at a board meeting. Ploughshares may also consider emergency funding for grants of up to $5,000 on an immediate basis.

Publications

The fund publishes an annual report that includes a complete list of grants and a statement of the fund's policies, programs, and guidelines.

PROSPECT HILL FOUNDATION

99 PARK AVENUE, SUITE 2220

NEW YORK, NEW YORK 10016-1601

PHONE: (212) 370-1165

FAX: (212) 599-6282

EMAIL: ashipley@prospect-hill.org

WEB: www.fdncenter.org/
grantmaker/prospecthill

**Contact
Person**

Laura Callanan, Executive Director

Purpose

The Prospect Hill Foundation provides grants to organizations working on issues of environmental conservation, nuclear weapons control, family planning in Latin America, social services, and arts, culture and education.

**Areas of
Interest**

The foundation has five areas of interest.

Environmental Conservation

The foundation's environmental grantmaking concentrates on habitat and water protection in the northeastern region of the United States. In addition, a few grants are awarded each year to advance habitat and ecosystem preservation in Latin America. We encourage proposals from organizations exhibiting leadership that:

• Offer strategies and policies for the conservation of significant private and public lands

• Strengthen policies and initiate means of improving water quality and protecting coastal areas

Nuclear Weapons Control

The foundation seeks through its grants relating to nuclear weapons control to limit reliance on the availability of nuclear weapons, and to enhance the sensitivity of national leaders to their collective responsibility to assure a habitable world. We seek proposals that:

• Implement strategies for limiting the proliferation of nuclear weapons, nuclear weapons materials, and the capacity to manufacture nuclear weapons

• Lead to commitments among national leaders to eliminate or reduce nuclear weapons arsenals

Reproductive Health

Concern about unplanned population growth in relation to natural resource availability, food supply, and an opportunity for a satisfying and healthy life for all underlies our giving for family planning services in Latin America. In addition, upon invitation only, a few related grants are made each year for domestic programs. We encourage proposals targeting Latin American countries that:

• Provide a full range of family planning services
• Enable and/or expand the provision of family planning services

Arts, Cultural, and Educational Institutions

Major commitments have been made to institutions already identified by the directors and only a limited number of new grant requests from arts, cultural, and educational institutions receive favorable response. Applications for such grants should be made only upon invitation.

Social Services

The directors have allocated a portion of the foundation's resources for activities (primarily in the New York area) that improve the quality of life for people in our society. Applications for such grants should be made only upon invitation.

Financial Data

(Year ended 6/30/00)	
Assets:	$ 83,000,000
Total grants paid:	$ 3,970,625
Total number of grants:	101
Highest grant:	$215,000
Lowest grant:	$ 5,000
Median grant size:	$15,000

Application Procedures

Applicants may submit grant requests to the Executive Director at any time of year. The request should be in the form of a letter (three pages maximum) that summarizes the applicant organization's history and goals; the project for which funding is sought; and the contribution of the project to other work in the field and/or to the organization's own development. In addition, requests should include the organization's total (current and proposed) budget and staff size; the project budget; project dates; potential sources of project support;

and a list of the organization's board of directors. We favor project support over general support requests. Please submit this information in duplicate.

All material is reviewed by the Executive Director and one or more members of the Board of Directors. Response is generally provided within four weeks. If there is interest in the proposal, more detailed information is normally required including line-item organizational and project income and expense budgets; a list of committed and prospective sources of support for the project; a timetable for completion of the project; qualifications of key personnel involved with the project; a list of other organizations involved in similar projects with a description of how the proposed program is different from or complementary to those efforts; a list of the project's expected results and criteria the applicant wishes the foundation to apply when evaluating the completed project; the I.R.S. letter determining 501 (c)(3) tax status; the most recent audited statement; and the most recent I.R.S. 990 tax form.

Grant Limitations

The foundation does not consider grants to individuals, for scholarly research, sectarian religious activities or organizations that are not tax exempt.

Meeting Times

The board of trustees meets five times a year to consider grant requests.

Publications

The foundation publishes an information brochure including a grants list and application guidelines.

PUBLIC WELFARE FOUNDATION

1200 U Street, NW

Washington, DC 20009

PHONE: (202) 965-1800

FAX: (202) 265-8851

EMAIL: general@publicwelfare.org

WEB: www.publicwelfare.org

Contact Person

Larry Kressley, Executive Director
Proposals should be addressed to the Screening Committee.

Purpose

The Public Welfare Foundation is dedicated to supporting organizations that provide services to disadvantaged populations and work for lasting improvements in the delivery of services that meet basic human needs.

Areas of Interest

The foundation's funding has no geographic restrictions, but emphasizes seven initiative and two program areas: criminal justice, environment, disadvantaged elderly, health, disadvantaged youth, population, reproductive health, human rights and global security, and community economic development and participation.

Financial Data

(Year ended 10/31/00)	
Assets:	$ 444,900,000
Total grants paid:	$ 18,102,277
Number of grants paid:	517
Highest grant:	$ 450,000
Lowest grant:	$ 1,000
Median grant size:	$ 42,268

Application Procedures

Proposals may be submitted at any time during the year. They are reviewed daily by the screening committee. Within one month, the foundation will notify the organization in writing whether the request has been accepted for consideration. Within three to four months, the organization will be notified in writing whether the request has been approved for funding.

Preferred initial contact is via one copy of the proposal with cover letter. A "Guide to Grant Requests," giving full details of the proposal format and the application process, is available upon request, as is the foundation's annual report which provides a complete program description and grants list.

Grant Limitations

The foundation generally does not accept requests to fund conferences, seminars, workshops, scholarships, graduate work, individuals, publications, research projects, foreign study, or endowments.

Meeting Times

The board of directors or a committee of the board meets to consider funding requests eight times during the year.

Publications

The foundation publishes an annual report and funding guidelines which are both available at www.publicwelfare.org.

REEBOK HUMAN RIGHTS FOUNDATION

1895 J.W. FOSTER BOULEVARD

CANTON, MASSACHUSETTS 02021

PHONE: (781) 401-7707

FAX: (781) 401-4806

EMAIL: rhrfoundation@reebok.com

WEB: www.reebok.com/x/us/
humanRights

Contact Person

Associate Director

Areas of Interest

Its current prinicpal areas of interest are:
- Children-at-risk projects in the greater Boston area.
- Human Rights programs in the United States and abroad. The foundaiton makes grants to human rights workers who have made an outstanding contribution toward the struggle for human rights.
- National organizations such as the National Urban League and the NAACP Legal Defense and Education Fund, which are devoted to strenghtening American pluralism.

Financial Data

(Year ended / /)	
Assets:	NA
Total grants awarded:	
Number of grants awarded:	
Highest grant:	
Lowest grant:	
Median grant size:	

Application Procedures

The foundation has its own application form that must be completed before consideration. Prospective applicants should contact the office for a copy.

**Grant
Limitations**

The foundation normally does not make grants to individuals, for advertising, medical research or dinner table sponsorship. Support is limited to the greater Boston area.

**Meeting
Times**

The board of trustees meet quaterly.

Publications

None.

Contact Person

Lisa E. Goldberg, President

Purpose

The Charles H. Revson Foundation seeks to advance public welfare. Of specific interest to the foundation are the forces shaping the future of New York City, the changing role of women, the impact of modern communications on education and other areas of life, and the need in a democratic society to keep government accountable to citizens. In some cases, these themes help to define a program; in others, they cut across grantmaking program lines.

Areas of Interest

The foundation's grantmaking activities are concentrated in the following areas: urban affairs and public policy with special emphasis on New York City; education; biomedical research; and Jewish philanthropy and education.

In addressing the problems and future of New York City, the foundation funds primarily research and model programs with the potential for impact on public decision-making. The foundation does not support community-based or direct service delivery organizations.

Grants relating to the changing role of women emphasize the participation of women in politics and the political process. In addition to a series of foundation-sponsored fellowship programs designed to provide younger women with firsthand experience in policy-making at the city, state, and local levels, the foundation has supported research and training activities. Throughout its program the foundation desires to support organizations committed to increasing the participation of women and minority group members.

The foundation supports a wide variety of organizations that address the problem of a lack of access to information about government activities and strengthen the voices of citizens in policy debate including projects in the area of international human rights policy, and research that educates the public.

**Financial
Data**

```
(Year ended    /   /   )
Assets:                                    NA
Total grants paid:
Number of grants paid:
Highest grant:
Lowest grant:
Median grant size:
```

**Application
Procedures**

Applicants should submit a letter briefly outlining the proposed project to the foundation's president. The letter should include a description of the proposed project, expected results, plans for evaluation and future funding, other sources of support (if any), amount sought, the purpose and duration of the requested amount, and the background and purpose of the sponsoring organization. Attachments should consist of: the organization's latest audited financial statements, a copy of the IRS letter confirming tax-exempt status, a current and projected budget, and a list of the board of directors and their organizational affiliations.

**Grant
Limitations**

The foundation generally does not approve grants to individuals; community-based organizations; book projects; local arts groups; endowments; building, renovation, or construction; local or national health appeals; charity events; travel expenses; and general institutional support.

**Meeting
Times**

The board of directors meets quarterly.

Publications

The foundation publishes a report once every two years.

Z. SMITH REYNOLDS FOUNDATION

147 SOUTH CHERRY STREET, SUITE 200

WINSTON-SALEM, NORTH CAROLINA

27101

PHONE: (336) 725-7541

FAX: (336) 725-6069

EMAIL: info@zsr.org

WEB: www.zsr.org

Contact Person

Thomas W. Ross, Executive Director

Purpose

The Z. Smith Reynolds Foundation supports a wide variety of activities in North Carolina including projects dealing with women and minorities, and economic and environmental issues, among others.

Areas of Interest

The foundation's grants are generally grouped into the following categories:

• Women. Efforts to put economic independence for women at the top of the public policy agenda for the state.

• Minorities. Projects that empower Black people and open the doors of opportunity.

• Economic development. Community projects that will help promote economic independence for women, minorities, and other disadvantaged groups.

• Environment. Programs that protect North Carolina's environment and preserve ecologically sensitive areas.

• Education. Pre-school, elementary, and secondary education projects, with special emphasis on projects which improve the quality of teaching and which combat the problem of school dropouts.

In addition, the foundation has a catch-all miscellaneous grantmaking program. Grants in this category have been made to projects working in such areas as grassroots organizing, the arts, inter-generational programs, and various social service programs.

Financial Data

> (Year ended 12/31/00)
>
> | | |
> |---|---|
> | Assets: | $ 470,905,223* |
> | Total grants approved: | $ 12,428,218 |
> | Number of grants approved: | 265 |
> | Highest grant: | $ 1,200,000 |
> | Lowest grant: | $ 8,000 |
> | Median grant size: | $ 30,000 |
>
> *This represents the combined assets of the Zachary Smith Reynolds Trust and the W.N. Reynolds Trust.

Application Procedures

The foundation requires that every applicant fill out and submit a three-page form in addition to a proposal. One copy of the complete application package must be postmarked or delivered to the office no later than February 1 and August 1. The application form includes detailed instructions concerning deadlines, procedures, and proposal guidelines for submitting a complete application package. Applicants are also advised to review the guidelines contained in the foundation's annual report.

In brief, the application form asks for background information on both the organization and the project, including a breakdown of board and staff membership by sex and minority representation, fiscal information, and the need for the project. The form must be signed by an authorized official of the organization. The proposal, which is not to exceed three single-spaced pages, must state the amount requested in the first paragraph. Attachments must include a one-page, line-item budget including anticipated income and expenditures for the period for which funds are being requested and for the proposed project; a board of directors list with a description of how they are elected; and proof of tax-exempt status as a public charity from the IRS. Additional supporting materials for the proposal are optional.

Grant Limitations

The terms of the foundation's charter limit its grantmaking to charitable activities in the state of North Carolina. The policy is to make grants only to nonprofit, tax-exempt organizations falling under Section 501(c)(3) of the Internal Revenue Code or to governmental units. No grants are made to individuals for any purpose. Organizations that operate both within and outside the state may be eligible for consideration for programs operated exclusively in North Carolina. In general, the foundation gives very low priority to endowments and to brick-and-mortar projects.

Meeting Times

The board of trustees meets twice annually to consider grant applications: the third Friday in May and the third Friday in November.

Publications

The foundation publishes an annual report and an application form.

ROCKEFELLER BROTHERS FUND

437 MADISON AVENUE, 37TH FLOOR

NEW YORK, NEW YORK 10022-7001

PHONE: (212) 812-4200

FAX: (212) 812-4299

EMAIL: rock@rbf.org

WEB: www.rbf.org

**Contact
Person**

Benjamin R. Shute, Jr., Secretary

Purpose

The major objective of the Rockefeller Brothers Fund is to improve the well-being of all people through support of efforts in the United States and abroad that contribute ideas, develop leaders and encourage institutions in the transition to global interdependence. It seeks to counter world trends of resource depletion, militarization, protectionism, and isolation that threaten cooperation, trade and economic growth, arms control, and conservation.

Four "touchstones" relating to the fund's approach to its substantive concerns (as opposed to specific areas of interest in and of themselves) are key to the fund's consideration of grant proposals:

- education of key individuals, special target groups, and the general public;
- leadership, such as the identification and encouragement of a new generation of leaders around the fund's specific program interests;
- leverage, using combinations of trustees and staff as well as related organizations to work toward common goals; and
- synergy, developing related projects so as to have an impact beyond the sum of the parts.

**Areas of
Interest**

The fund makes grants in five general areas.

- "One World". This program is made up of two components: Sustainable Resource Use and World Security, as well as the connections between global resource management and global security. The first advocates a global perspective in support of projects in forestry, agriculture, fisheries and renewable energy. World Security seeks to strengthen arms control and international relations.

- New York City. In its New York City program, community-based organizations involved in the rehabilitation and construction of low-cost and affordable housing and in neighborhood preservation; encourage reforms and improvements in city public schools; and focus attention on effective action on public health, services public policy development, and related issues involved with the AIDS crisis in New York City.
- Nonprofit Sector. Programs promoting the health and vitality of the nonprofit sector, nationally and internationally, the fund supports basic research and public education with respect to nonprofits, efforts to develop new sources of income for and improved management of nonprofits, and greater international grantmaking.
- Special Concerns. Programs that strive to improve the accessibility of basic education in South Africa through literacy, reading and learning programs and efforts to improve teaching methodology.
- Education. Projects which increase the numbers and quality of teachers, especially minority teachers.

Financial Data

(Year ended 12/31/99)	
Assets:	$ 795,991,600
Total grants paid:	$ 18,897,203
Median grant size:	$ 25,000 - $ 300,000

Application Procedures

There are no application deadlines. Initially, the fund recommends that applicants send a two or three page letter of inquiry to the fund's Secretary, including a succinct description of the project or organization for which support is sought and its relationship to the fund's program, information about the principal staff involved, a synopsis of the budget, and an indication of the amount requested from the fund. All such inquiry letters are reviewed by one or more staff members who try to be prompt in notifying applicants when their projects do not fit program guidelines or exceed budgetary restraints. If a project is taken up for grant consideration, staff members will ask for additional information, including a detailed proposal and almost certainly a meeting with the project's principal organizers.

Grant Limitations

To qualify for a grant from the fund, applicants must be either a tax-exempt organization or an organization seeking support for a project that would qualify as tax-exempt. The fund does not make grants to individuals, nor as a general rule does it support research, graduate study, or the writing of books or dissertations by individuals.

Meeting Times

The board of trustees meets four times a year, in March, June, October and December.

Publications

The fund publishes an annual report and application guidelines, list of grants, and informational brochures.

ROCKEFELLER FAMILY FUND

437 Madison Avenue, 37th Floor

New York, New York 10022

PHONE: (212) 812-4252

FAX: (212) 812-4299

EMAIL: mmccarthy@rffund.org

WEB: www.rffund.org

**Contact
Persons**

> Mr. Lee Wasserman, Director
> Maureen McCarthy, Grants Administrator

Purpose

> The Rockefeller Family Fund supports advocacy programs that are likely to yield tangible public policy results. Of preference to the foundation are entrepreneurial organizations that seek to maintain or expand their programs by raising money in innovative ways to gain greater self-sufficiency.

**Areas of
Interest**

> In 1999, the Rockefeller Family Fund made grants in five program areas:

> ### Economic Justice for Women

> The Family Fund's program for women supports projects designed to promote economic justice. In particular, the program seeks to provide women with equitable employment opportunities and to improve their work lives.

> Examples of past grants which fit these criteria include national advocacy, research, and public education efforts aimed at achieving pay equity; support to state-level "economic agenda" coalitions to train women in leadership and public policy skills; advocacy efforts on behalf of contingent and part-time workers; a public education campaign designed to increase awareness of economic inequities women face in retirement; and advocacy designed to eliminate sex discrimination in the insurance industry.

> ### Environment

> The Family Fund's Environment program emphasizes conservation of natural resources, protection of health as affected by the environment, the cessation and cleanup of pollution caused by the Department of Energy and the Department of Defense, and domestic efforts to broaden the definition of national security to include environmental protection.

Examples of past grants which fit these guidelines include support for a coalition of grassroots groups to undertake advocacy campaigns in Alaska; funding for a national environmental group to encourage field organizing and media expertise; support for a new organization working on health and environment issues; and support for efforts to curb pollution at the nation's bomb production facilities and military installations.

Institutional Responsiveness

Institutional Responsiveness traditionally is the most open-ended of the Family Fund's program areas. Its purpose is to help provide organizations with the means to affect the policies and actions of public and private institutions.

Examples of past grants which fit these guidelines include support for: advocacy designed to reduce wasteful government spending; efforts to ensure that government records are open to the public and for parallel efforts to oppose government secrecy; efforts to protect citizen privacy in the development of policies governing the Internet and electronic record keeping; and to promote greater accountability of financial institutions to consumers and their communities.

Self-Sufficiency

The Self-Sufficiency program area emerged out of a recognition that advocacy groups need help in developing renewable sources of funding, rather than depending too heavily on support from private foundations. This program supports efforts to increase and diversify organizational support.

Examples of past grants which fit these guidelines include support for a coalition of environmental groups forming a workplace-giving federation; assistance to pay the salary of a development director; a grant to cover part of the cost of a direct mail campaign for a consumer organization; funding for groups to increase their technological capacity; and support for an organization that provides fundraising training for activist groups.

Citizen Participation & Government Accountability

This program encourages the organized participation of citizens in government, and seeks to make government more accountable and responsive. Grants in this program area support the efforts of nonpartisan organizations to help citizens exercise the right to vote, advocate for structural improvement to systems of government, and otherwise increase opportunities to participate in public policy formation. Particular emphasis is placed on the electoral process, but grants are not restricted to this arena.

Examples of past grants include support for public education and voter registration drives aimed at under-represented communities; efforts to expand access to government information; advocacy to promote electronic disclosure of campaign contributions; support for innovative electronic voter education systems; training of activists on voter mobilization methods; and a broad range of program initiatives aimed at holding various government agencies and public officials accountable for their actions.

The Family Fund provides support for advocacy efforts within these program areas that are action-oriented and likely to yield tangible public policy results. Funding is also given to organizations that seek to maintain or expand their financing in innovative ways or from non-foundation sources.

Financial Data

(Year ended 12/31/00)	
Assets:	$ 69,511,147
Total grants paid:	$ 8,528,789
Number of grants paid:	112
Highest grant:	$ 435,000*
Lowest grant:	$ 3,000
Median grant size:	$ 30,000
*Includes a two-year grant.	

Application Procedures

Applicants should submit a letter of inquiry of no more than two pages summarizing the goals of the project, the strategy or plan for achieving the goals and the amount of funding requested. Letters of inquiry may be sent at any time. The Family Fund responds to all inquiries, and applicants should allow two to four weeks for staff to review and answer a letter of inquiry. Those organizations that are invited to submit a full proposal will be provided with guidelines for material to include. All grants are made by the board of trustees or by the executive committee acting on its behalf. The director does not have a discretionary fund.

Letters of inquiry may be mailed to the Rockefeller Family Fund or to the following e-mail address: mmccarthy@rffund.org. For more information on our grant programs, and links to other Rockefeller philanthropies, you can visit our web site at www.rffund.org.

Grant Limitations

Within its program guidelines, the Family Fund supports tax-exempt organizations engaged in activities of national significance. Thus, the fund does not ordinarily consider projects which pertain to a single community, except in the rare instance where a project is unique, strategically placed to advance a national issue, or is likely to serve as a national model.

Because the fund has limited resources, it is unable to assist most applicants. Grants are rarely made to organizations which traditionally enjoy popular support, such as universities, museums, hospitals, or endowed institutions. The Family Fund does not make grants for academic or scholarly research, or for social or human service programs. Nor are grants made to support individuals, scholarships, international programs, domestic programs dealing with international issues, profit-making businesses, construction or restoration projects, or to reduce an organization's debt. In addition, grants are normally made to the same organization for no more than two years at a time, and except in extraordinary cases, are not given to the same organization for more than three or four consecutive years.

Meeting Times

The full board meets twice a year; the executive committee usually meets three additional times.

Publications

The fund publishes an annual report which is available to the public; the report usually comes out in July.

WINTHROP ROCKEFELLER FOUNDATION

308 EAST EIGHTH STREET

LITTLE ROCK, ARKANSAS 72202

PHONE: (501) 376-6854

FAX: (501) 374-4797

EMAIL: programmanager@
wrfoundation.org

WEB: www.wrfoundation.org

Contact Person

Program Manager

Purpose

The Winthrop Rockefeller Foundation's vision is Arkansas as a state where economic, racial, and social injustice is universally valued and practiced. Our mission: to improve the lives of Arkansans. Using its resources, the foundation continues to build and sustain strong communities for Arkansans by supporting and strengthening organizations that serve them.

Areas of Interest

The Winthrop Rockefeller Foundation provides grants to Arkansas-based nonprofit organizations that provide service in the following foundation program areas:

• Economic Development, to empower individuals and institutions to improve the standard of living and economic viability of low-income communities.

• Education, to enable all children and adults to develop fully their capacities to improve themselves and to contribute to the educational, cultural, economic, civic, and social vitality of their communities.

• Economic, Racial, and Social Justice, to engage institutions and individuals in the struggle for pervasive justice in the lives of All Arkansans and their communities.

Application Procedures

The Winthrop Rockefeller Foundation accepts concept papers of no more than three pages describing initiatives compatible with our current program areas: Economic Development; Education; and Economic, Racial, and Social Justice.

Your concept paper should address the following items:
- A summary of the goals and objectives of the proposed initiative
- A brief description of the targeted beneficiaries and how the initiative will impact them
- A description of how the initiative will make a difference and how the difference will be measured
- If appropriate, a description of collaborative partners and their roles

The following documents must accompany each concept paper:
- A budget and timeline for carrying out the initiative. The budget should address the entire project and not just the amount being requested from the foundation.
- A completed Request Information Form (RIF), available on our website. Other attachments are discouraged.

All concept papers will be formally acknowledged. Concept papers without a RIF or budget and timeline information will be acknowledged, along with a request for the missing documents. The foundation will wait four weeks to receive the missing documents. At the end of four weeks, incomplete packages will be automatically declined, and you will be required to resubmit a complete package to start the process again. Please see our website for current information.

Financial Data

(Year ended 12/31/00)	
Assets:	$ 161,327,026
Total grants paid:	$ 2,823,644
Number of grants paid:	32
Highest grant:	$ 500,000
Lowest grant:	$ 1,000

Grant Limitations

Foundation grants are limited to entities whose work will benefit Arkansans. We do not fund capital initiatives, fellowships or scholarships directly to individuals, and rarely consider endowments.

Meeting Times

The board meets quarterly.

Publications

The foundation publishes an annual report which is available upon request.

ROSENBERG FOUNDATION

47 KEARNY STREET, SUITE 804

SAN FRANCISCO, CALIFORNIA 94108-5528

PHONE: (415) 421-6105

FAX: (415) 421-0141

EMAIL: rosenfdn@rosenbergfdn.org

WEB: www.rosenbergfdn.org

Contact Person

Kirke Wilson, President

Purpose

The Rosenberg Foundation makes grants in the state of California for projects to benefit children and youth, with particular emphasis upon children who are minority, from low income families, and immigrants. Usually the foundation itself does not operate programs.

Areas of Interest

The foundation has two priority grantmaking categories. The first focuses on children in poverty and their families in rural and urban areas of California. In this area, the foundation is particularly interested in programs which reduce dependency, promote self-help, create access to the economic mainstream, or which address the causes of poverty among children and families. The second focus is the changing population of California. The emphasis of this program is on programs and activities which promote the full social, economic, and cultural integration of immigrants as well as minorities into a pluralistic society.

The foundation states that grants are made for projects that have the greatest feasibility and significance. Feasibility of a project includes the extent to which the leadership, setting, scale, and design are adequate to achieve its goals. Significance includes the importance of issues addressed and the potential of the project as a model, a source of permanent institutional reform, or a contribution to public social policy related to children and youth. The foundation also pays particular attention to projects sponsored by groups they are designed to serve.

**Financial
Data**

(Year ended 12/31/99)	
Assets:	$ 74,000,000
Total grants paid:	$ 4,000,000

**Application
Procedures**

The foundation does not use standardized application forms, but prefers brief letters of inquiry that describe the proposed project, the applicant organization, and the estimated budget. If the project appears to fall within the foundation's program priorities, a complete application will be requested. That application must include a full narrative proposal, an itemized budget, and materials describing the applicant organization. The foundation publishes a full listing of the required contents of this application, which is available on request.

After an application has been accepted, the foundation staff usually arranges a visit to the project site. Because the foundation reviews a large number of applications, there is normally a two- or three-month waiting period before applications are considered by the board.

**Grant
Limitations**

Except for a small number of grants in the field of philanthropy, the foundation does not make grants for programs outside California. Foundation policy also precludes grants to continue or expand projects started with funds from other sources or to match grants from other sources. Grants to purchase equipment, produce films, or publish materials are made only when such activities are a necessary part of a larger project supported by the foundation. No grants are made to individuals or for basic research, construction, scholarships, or operational expenses of ongoing programs.

**Meeting
Times**

The board of directors meets six times a year.

Publications

The foundation publishes an annual report.

SAMUEL RUBIN FOUNDATION

777 UNITED NATIONS PLAZA

NEW YORK, NEW YORK 10017

PHONE: (212) 697-8945

FAX: (212) 682-0886

EMAIL: info@samuelrubinfoundation.org

WEB: www.samuelrubinfoundation.org

Contact Person

Lauranne Jones, Grants Administrator

Purpose

The purpose of the Samuel Rubin Foundation is to carry on the work of its founder, who pursued peace and justice and searched for an equitable reallocation of the world's resources. The foundation believes that these objectives can be achieved only through the fullest implementation of social, economic, political, civil, and cultural rights for all the world's people.

Areas of Interest

The foundation's emphasis is on national and international organizations. Generally, the foundation provides funding in the areas of civil and constitutional rights, environment, peace and disarmament, education, public policy, and arts and culture.

Financial Data

(Year ended 6/30/00)	
Assets:	$ 15,300,070
Total grants paid:	$ 1,238,943
Total number of grants:	125
Highest grant paid:	$ 170,543
Lowest grant paid:	$ 1,000
Median grant size:	$ 5,000

Application Procedures

The foundation prefers that an applicant's initial contact be made with the submission of a full proposal (one copy) which includes a budget and an IRS tax determination letter. The foundation does not acknowledge receipt of applications. After the proposal has been submitted, however, the foundation may request an interview. Following the board meeting all applications are acknowledged.

Grant Limitations

The foundation makes no grants to individuals or for scholarship, for capital or building funds.

Meeting Times

The board of directors meets three times a year. Deadlines for applications are the first Friday in January, May, and September.

Publications

The foundation will distribute a program policy statement upon request, and information is available on its website www.samuelrubinfoundation.org.

THE SBC FOUNDATION

(formerly The Ameritech Foundation)

PHONE: (800) 591-9663

FAX: (210) 351-2599

130 EAST TRAVIS, SUITE 350

SAN ANTONIO, TEXAS 78205

WEB: www.sbc.com/foundation

Contact Person

Laura Sanford, President

Purpose

The SBC Foundation (formerly known as The Ameritech Foundation) supports multi-state and national programs in regional education, economic development, and public policy. It was established in 1984 to plan, develop, and implement the contributions program of Ameritech, the parent of the Bell companies serving Illinois, Indiana, Michigan, Ohio and Wisconsin and several other communications-related companies.

Areas of Interest

Areas of interest include health and human services, civic and community, elementary and secondary education, higher education, and arts and culture. Priority is given to grant requests that advance the applications of technology in ways that improve these program areas. Types of support include program development, annual campaigns, capital campaigns, matching funds, fellowships, and research grants. Communications-based programs must clearly demonstrate that they are unique and innovative model programs and have the potential for other nonprofits to emulate or consider using. The foundation also considers organizational support for projects and special programs that make communities where the corporation operates better places to live, learn, and work, principally in the Great Lakes region.

Financial Data

(Year ended / /)	
Assets:	NA
Total grants awarded:	
Number of grants awarded:	
Highest grant:	
Lowest grant:	
Median grant size:	

THE SBC FOUNDATION (formerly Ameritech Foundation)

Application
Procedures

Grant applications are accepted throughout the year. Preliminary inquiries by telephone or personal visits are discouraged. Rather, initial inquiry should be made by letter before a formal proposal is submitted. This letter should include: a description of the organization, its history and purpose; an overview of the proposed project; a summary of the program's budget and an indication of the level of support requested; a list of sources and amounts of other funding obtained, pledged, or requested for the project; the population and geographic area served by the organization or project; and proof of 501(c)(3) tax-exempt status.

If the initial review is favorable, a formal proposal will be requested. There is no deadline for submitting proposals. If the review is not favorable, the foundation will convey the reasons for declining to provide funding. Organizations are asked not to submit a preliminary proposal more than once in any twelve-month period.

Grant
Limitations

The foundation does not make grants to organizations which do not have a 501(c)(3) status from the IRS, individuals, individual community organizations, local chapters of national organizations, religious groups for religious purposes, political activities or organizations established to influence legislation, advertising, or national or international organizations with limited relationships to local Ameritech operations.

Meeting
Times

The board of directors meets four times a year, in March, June, September and December.

Publications

The SBC Foundation distributes an annual report which sets forth application guidelines and includes a list of grants awarded.

**Where to
Apply to
SBC State
Organizations:**

SBC Illinois
Director, Contributions
225 W. Randolph, Room 27B
Chicago, IL 60606

SBC Indiana
Manager, Contributions
240 N. Meridian Street, Room 1827
Indianapolis, IN 48204

SBC Michigan
Director, Contributions
444 Michigan Avenue, Room 1700
Detroit, MI 48226

SBC Ohio
Director, Contributions
45 Erieview Plaza, Room 1600
Cleveland, OH 44114

SBC Wisconsin
Director, Contributions
722 North Broadway, 18th Floor
Milwaukee, WI 53202

THE SAN FRANCISCO FOUNDATION

PHONE: (415) 733-8500

FAX: (415) 477-2783

EMAIL: rec@sff.org

WEB: www.sff.org

225 BUSH STREET, SUITE 500

SAN FRANCISCO, CALIFORNIA 94104

Contact Person

Derek Aspacher, Director of Grants Management

Purpose

The San Francisco Foundation seeks out and encourages projects that add to the quality of life in the Bay Area by contributing to the aesthetic, physical, and social well-being of the community. Usually such projects fall into one or more of the following areas: enhancing the enjoyment and appreciation of life through the arts, culture, and the humanities; developing public policy; testing new methods of addressing problems; changing institutional behavior; and coordinating the activities of two or more established agencies.

The foundation's grantmaking is limited to the following counties in northern California: Alameda, Contra Costa, San Francisco, San Mateo, and Marin.

Areas of Interest

The foundation's activities may be grouped into the following broad general categories:

• Arts and Humanities. Projects that enhance the capacity of both individuals and communities to think creatively and critically about the aesthetic, ethical, and humanitarian issues of our times. Projects that have a significant public benefit, projects that enhance and encourage individual creativity, and grants that support organizational advancement are given priority.

• Community Health. Projects that influence public policies to expand and improve access to health and social services, create coordinated systems of care, develop strong organizations, and those that empower clients to take control of their lives. Topic areas include mental health, women's health, AIDS, elder services, and health reform.

• Education. Projects that promote school success and the capacity of children and youth for civic participation and leadership in a culturally diverse society. Priority is given to efforts that include school improvement and reform, academic assistance and youth development activities in the community to prevent school failure, early childhood development and family support, and projects that promote higher education opportunities for underrepresented minorities and address the needs of non-literate adults.

• Environment. Programs that protect and restore the ecosystems of the Bay Area; promote a livable, sustainable and healthful urban environment for Bay Area residents; promote multicultural participation and leadership in setting the Bay Area environmental agenda; promote environmental literacy and expand career preparation and opportunities (especially for young people of color); and that protect parks, open spaces, and outdoor recreation opportunities for all Bay Area residents.

• Social Services and Urban Affairs. Projects strengthening the capacity of nonprofit housing sponsors to produce and preserve affordable housing for low- and moderate-income people; increasing the support of permanent housing units and supportive services; capacity building and leadership development within communities; improving employment, job training, and self-sufficiency opportunities for at-risk groups; and enhancing community justice through juvenile justice reform and expanding legal advocacy for the disadvantaged.

In addition to the grants described above, the foundation also provides short-term technical assistance grants to permit organizations to bring in expert assistance to strengthen management or otherwise improve the capacity to deliver services.

Financial Data

(Year ended 6/30/00)	
Assets:	$ 41,675,931
Grants paid:	$ 7,894,927

Application Procedures

Applicants should obtain a copy of the foundation's application guide, "How We Can Serve You," and telephone the foundation to arrange to attend one of the foundation's workshops, "How to Apply for a Grant."

The first step in applying is to submit a letter of intent of no more than three pages. The letter should be addressed to Applicant Services and should cover the following: a project outline including goals, methods, project budget, and how much is requested from the foundation, as well as from other potential sources of funding; definition of the problem or issue to be addressed, expected results of project, and how the project fits the foundation's goals; and a description of the organization's purpose, programs, size of annual budget, and sources of current support.

Letters of intent are reviewed by staff, and applicants are notified within four to six weeks whether a full proposal is encouraged. If so, the foundation will send an application package with complete instructions on the requirements for the proposal. All proposals are reviewed by a program executive, and recommendations are prepared for the foundation's board of trustees. The process of review and recommendation for proposals normally takes two to four months.

The most successful applications are those that include either problem-solving projects, capacity-building efforts, or short-term technical assistance.

Grant Limitations

In addition to the geographic limitations mentioned above, the foundation makes grants only to tax-exempt, nonprofit organizations with appropriate financial records and controls. Grants are not made for endowments, budget deficits, medical research, direct assistance to individuals, or for scholarships.

Meeting Times

The board of trustees meets monthly, with the exception of April, August, and November, to make grant decisions.

Publications

The foundation publishes an annual report and distributes information on guidelines, procedures, and deadlines for applications.

THE SCHUMANN FUND FOR NEW JERSEY

PHONE: (973) 509-9883

21 Van Vleck Street

Montclair, New Jersey 07042

WEB: www.fdncenter.org/
grantmaker/schumann

Contact Person

Barbara Reisman, Executive Director

Purpose

In 1998, Florence Schumann and her children created the Schumann Fund for New Jersey to continue the lifelong philanthropy of Mrs. Schumann and her husband John. The Schumann Fund for New Jersey traces its roots to the Florence and John Schumann Foundation. A separate board of New Jersey residents serves as trustees of the Schumann Fund for New Jersey. That board has designated early childhood development, environmental protection, and statewide public policy, with a special focus on school innovation, as grant-making priorities.

Areas of Interest

The Schumann Fund for New Jersey is a tax-exempt, private foundation, incorporated as a corporation not for pecuniary profit under the laws of the State of New Jersey. Schumann Fund program priorities fall into four broad categories:

• Early Childhood Development: We support efforts to heighten the chances of academic and social success for young children, especially the urban poor, by supporting programs and policies that provide good quality early child-hood education and care to children from birth to eight years old.

• Environmental Protection: We support the conservation of natural resources, the revitalization of New Jersey's urban centers, and the restoration and protection of New Jersey's environment. We believe that sustainable economic growth and sound and coordinated land use planning, at regional, state and local levels, are essential to this goal.

• Public Policy: We support efforts to enhance the informed discussion of important policy issues facing the State of New Jersey, particularly in the areas of school reform and educational innovation, environmental planning and protection, and effective delivery of educational and social services to families with young children.

• Essex County: We support local programs directed at meeting community needs, with particular focus on social and educational services for families with young children that will have a long-term impact on addressing community problems.

Financial Data

```
(Year ended 12/31/00)
Assets:                    $ 39,361,711
Total grants paid:         $ 2,272,222
Number of grants paid:
Highest grant:
Lowest grant:
Median grant size:
```

Application Procedures

There is no standard application form to be used in presenting a request to the Schumann Fund for New Jersey, but organizations may use the New York/New Jersey Common Application Form, if they choose. We ask that a written proposal be submitted which includes a clear description of the purpose of the grant, the need or problem that will be addressed, the work to be undertaken, the staffing plan for project implementation, and the means of evaluating progress. The proposal must be accompanied by:

• a copy of the organization's latest audited financial statement;

• current organizational and project budgets identifying all sources of revenue and categories and amounts of expenditures;

• brief resumes of key organization and project staff;

• the project's time frame and projected sources of future funding;

• a list of the organization's Board of Directors;

• Internal Revenue Service documents confirming the organization's status as a 501(c)(3) organization.

The Schumann Fund Board of Trustees meets quarterly, in March, June, September and December. Application deadlines are January 15, April 15, July 15 or October 15. Action on proposals may be deferred to a later quarter, but we will notify organizations promptly as to the status of all requests.

In reviewing grant proposals, the Schumann Fund for New Jersey gives special consideration to those that:

1. offer the hope of permanent and positive change in the way that our society addresses the need for quality education and social services, and environmental preservation with sustainable economic development;
2. demonstrate the capacity to make effective use of all available private and public resources for support;
3. indicate a high level of time and/or money contributed from the group to be served, and
4. describe a clear strategy for meeting program goals and an effective means of evaluating progress toward those goals.

Grant Limitations

In general, the Schumann Fund for New Jersey does not accept applications for capital campaigns, annual giving, endowment, direct support of individuals, or local programs in counties other than Essex. Projects in the arts, healthcare, and housing development normally fall outside Schumann Fund priority areas.

Meeting Times

The board of trustees meets quarterly in March, June, September, and December.

Publications

The fund publishes an annual report and application guidelines. See our website for more information.

GARDINER HOWLAND SHAW FOUNDATION

PHONE: (781) 455-8303

FAX: (781) 433-0980

EMAIL: ghsfound@aol.com

10 LINCOLN ROAD, 2ND FLOOR

FOXBORO, MASSACHUSETTS 02035

Contact Person

Thomas Coury, Executive Director

Purpose

The Shaw Foundation was established for the study, prevention, correction, and alleviation of crime and delinquency, and the rehabilitation of adult and juvenile offenders. The foundation limits its grants to programs in Massachusetts.

Areas of Interest

The foundation concentrates its support on projects that explore new ideas and approaches to criminal justice issues. Special consideration is given to projects which clearly demonstrate the ability to use Shaw Foundation support to attract new public and private resources to the field of criminal justice and those projects which serve women and minority offenders. The foundation has the following funding priorities:

- Programs that divert court-involved youth and juvenile offenders from escalating involvement in the criminal justice system.
- Programs that promote alternatives to incarceration and intermediate criminal sanctions.
- Innovative and effective approaches to rehabilitation for detained and incarcerated juvenile and adult offender.
- Methods that improve the administration of justice and quality of services for individuals appearing before the criminal court.
- Initiatives that effect current public policy in criminal justice through education, training and effective advocacy.

The foundation provides grants for start-up funds, general operating support and project support for successful programs with the potential for local and national replication.

Financial Data

```
(Year ended    /   /   )
Assets:                          NA
Total grants paid:
Number of grants paid:
Highest grant:
Lowest grant:
Median grant size:
```

Application Procedures

Potential applicants are encouraged to telephone the foundation to discuss their ideas prior to submitting a proposal. All new applicants should submit a concept paper describing their organization and the purposes for which funds are being sought, along with a budget and evidence of tax-exempt status before submitting a full proposal.

Deadlines for applications are January 2, May 1, and September 1 for consideration at the meeting the month after each deadline. Grant applicants are asked to submit brief proposals, three to five pages in length, explaining the problem to be addressed, clients to be served, program objectives and methods, evaluation plan, and the specific grant request. The following materials must be attached: IRS proof of tax-exempt and public charity status; brief profiles of staff and key volunteers; names of board members (with affiliations); budget for the proposed project and the organization; an independent audit, IRS Form 990, or a Massachusetts Form PC; and plans for future funding.

Grant Limitations

The trustees have made it a policy not to fund substance abuse or mental health counseling, the arts, endowments, capital requests, or proposals from individuals. The foundation does not consider requests for proportional support of programs that happen to serve offenders among a much larger, more diverse client group.

Meeting Times

The board of trustees meets to consider grant applications in February, June, and October.

Publications

The foundation publishes an annual list of grants.

THE SISTER FUND

116 EAST 16TH STREET 7TH FLOOR

NEW YORK, NEW YORK 10003

PHONE: (212) 260-4446

FAX: (212) 260-4633

EMAIL: info@sisterfund.org

WEB: www.sisterfund.org

Contact Persons

Kanyere Eaton, Executive Director

Sunita Mehta, Director of Grants and Programs

Purpose

The Sister Fund is a private women's fund which supports justice and fullness of life for women and girls in our society. We seek to identify and support programs that foster women's spiritual empowerment through the promotion of social, economic, political, and spiritual justice. The Sister Fund is committed to making explicit the relationship between spirituality and social justice. By valuing women's social justice work as spiritual, we work to strengthen all movements for universal equity in our society.

Areas of Interest

The Sister Fund supports the women's movement in that it seeks to liberate the human spirit. We believe that through spiritual empowerment, women will infuse social justice work with a new energy and determination. We seek to respond to the problems of racial and gender discrimination, AIDS, environmental neglect, violence, growing inequality and widespread poverty—issues that cannot be resolved without the leadership and participation of women. The Sister Fund gives primary consideration to those organizations that both serve and are led by women most affected by economic, social, mental, and physical oppression, especially women of color, lesbians and economically disadvantaged older or disabled women. In recognizing women's contribution to the web of human interconnection, we endeavor to uphold the sanctity and interdependence of life.

The Sister Fund gives priority to the following four program areas:

1. Community programs, including those that are faith-based, that empower women and girls with the ways and means to bring about necessary changes in their lives and communities;

2. Programs and organizations that seek to radically transform social, economic, political, and religious institutions and dogma that oppress women and girls;
3. Efforts to develop liberative women's theologies that encompass our diversity, including feminist, womanist, mujerista, Asian, and Native American theologies and that reflect on the religious understandings and practices of grassroots women; and
4. Activities that encourage dialogue and collaboration between women's movements and expressions of women's spiritualities that seek justice.

In addition, The Sister Fund continues to support the women's funding movement as well as transformative social justice efforts. We seek programs and projects that enable women to organize and mobilize effectively to bring about structural change, especially those that work with other community groups and help to build coalitions. Ultimately, we give preference to organizations that establish policies that embody just and empowering ways of knowing, doing, and relating.

Application Procedures

Initial contact with the fund should be a brief proposal of five to ten pages (double spaced) which outlines the project and includes a one-sentence statement of purpose, the amount of the grant request, a needs statement, goals and objectives of the organization and the project, the history and mission of the organization and the project, project design and implementation description, fundraising plan and long-range plans and plan for evaluation and follow-up. Supporting documentation should include proof of Section 501(c)(3) tax-exempt status, current budget and most recent financial statement, list of members of the board of directors, list of current funding sources and a statement of policy and practice regarding representation of population of concern in board and staff leadership.

Deadlines are January 2 for the April meeting, April 1 for the July meeting and August 1 for the November meeting, but these dates are subject to change. Proposals received after the deadline for one cycle will be held over for consideration until the next grant cycle.

**Financial
Data**

(Year ended 11/30/00)	
Support and revenue:	
Total grants paid:	
Number of grants paid:	
Highest grant:	$ 90,000
Lowest grant:	$ 5,000
Median grant size:	$ 20,000

**Grant
Limitations**

Grants usually are in the range of $5,000 to $30,000. The fund only supports public charities recognized by the IRS and preference is given to projects located in metropolitan New York. National or international advocacy and public education programs as well as occasional board solicited and sponsored local programs are also funded. The fund does not support state, county or municipal agencies, capital or building acquisition or improvements, research, scholarship funds or student aid, or deficit financing.

**Meeting
Times**

The board of directors meets three times a year in April, July, and November.

Publications

The fund publishes a newsletter three times a year, as well as guidelines.

STEELCASE FOUNDATION

PHONE: (616) 246-4695

FAX: (616) 475-2200

LOCATION CH.4E

P.O. BOX 1967

GRAND RAPIDS, MICHIGAN 49501-1967

Contact Person

Susan Broman, Executive Director

Purpose

The Steelcase Foundation funds projects that improve the quality of life where our manufacturing plants are located. The foundation only awards grants in which the company has operations: Kent & Ottawa Counties in Michigan; Orange County, California; Athens, Alabama; Asheville, North Carolina, and Markham, Ontario.

Areas of Interest

The foundation awards grants in the following areas of interest: human services, health, education, community and economic development, arts, and the environment. Special consideration is given to projects helping people who are disadvantaged, disabled, young, or elderly.

Financial Data

(Year ended 11/30/00)	
Assets:	$ 124,477,408
Total grants paid:	$ 7,833,409
Total number of grants:	110
Highest grant:	$ 1,000,000
Lowest grant:	$ 2,000
Median grant size:	$ 25,000

Application Procedures

Before submitting a full proposal, applicants are required to submit a letter of inquiry. Applicants should obtain an application form, which should be submitted at the same time as the letter of inquiry. The letter should be on organization letterhead and should describe the organization, the proposed project and its intended results, and amount of funding required. This letter should be accompanied by a copy of the applicant's proof of tax-exempt status under the Internal Revenue Code. Foundation staff will review the letter of inquiry and notify the organization whether or not to submit a full proposal.

Deadlines are approximately every three months and applicants will be informed of the next deadlines when the application form is requested.

Grant Limitations

The foundation does not make grants outside the geographical limits identified above. Grants are not awarded to individuals, to support conferences, seminars, or similar events, or for religious purposes. The foundation makes only one grant per year per organization and does not wish to be the sole on-going support of a program. Only tax-exempt nonprofit organizations under section 501(c)(3) are eligible for funds.

Meeting Times

The board of trustees meets quarterly to consider grant requests.

Publications

The foundation publishes an annual report and application guidelines.

THE STERN FAMILY FUND

PHONE: (703) 527-6692

FAX: (703) 527-5775

EMAIL: sternfund@starpower.net

WEB: www.sternfund.org

P.O. Box 1590

ARLINGTON, VIRGINIA 22210-0890

Contact Person

Elizabeth Collaton, Executive Director

Purpose

The Stern Family Fund supports government and corporate accountability projects that encourage citizens to vigilantly monitor and guarantee the responsiveness of public and private institutions that wield substantial power over their lives. Specifically the fund seeks to support systemic reform efforts that attack the root causes of problems rather than providing direct services; projects that strive for a more equitable distribution of political and economic power; and action-oriented projects with the potential for significant regional and national influence.

Areas of Interest

The fund seeks to achieve these goals through two grant programs, the Public Interests Pioneer Program and the Strategic Support Grant fund.

• Public Interest Pioneer Program. Individuals who can create a cutting-edge project designed to stop or prevent government and corporate abuses. The fund supports one or two individuals who "possess the skills, experience and passion to succeed; propose strategies that are likely to yield dramatic and long-lasting results; and display the potential to create enduring institutions or develop programs that can be replicated." These grants range from $60,000 to $100,000 with a potential for renewal.

• The Strategic Support Grants. Projects or organizations which have specific short-term financial needs at critical junctures in their development. These are situations where grants of $5,000 to $20,000 can have a significant impact on the success of the project.

THE STERN FAMILY FUND

Financial Data

> (Year ended 6/30/00)*
> Highest grant: $ 50,000
> Lowest grant: $ 5,000
>
> *The foundation does not distribute financial information or
> a list of grants.

Application Procedures

Each program has its own application procedures and deadlines.

Prospective Public Interest Pioneers should submit three copies of a concept paper of no more than three pages long. All concept papers are kept confidential. The board reviews the concept papers and selects a limited number for development into full proposals. Deadline for concept papers is January 4 and grant decisions are announced in June.

Applicants for Strategic Support Grants should submit a formal proposal or a summary proposal to ascertain the fund's interest in their request. A proposal sent to another foundation would be welcome. Every proposal should include a statement of the need for support, the project's goals, and an action plan for achieving these goals (proposals that include detailed plans on strategy and project implementation, rather than focus on the need for support are given preference); a timetable for the project and evaluation methods; the projected budget of the organization for the fiscal year for which funds are being sought, and a detailed budget for the specific project proposed; a list of current sources of support and sources from whom additional funds are being solicited; staff resumes or profiles; and a statement as to whether other organizations are involved in similar programs and, if so, their identities.

The deadline for submissions is February 1 for decisions in May and August 25 for decisions in November. Applicants are discouraged from making inquiries by phone.

Grant Limitations

The fund does not support organizations that traditionally enjoy popular support such as universities, museums, or hospitals. Grants are not made to international programs, domestic programs dealing with international issues, capital campaigns, academic research, scholarships, endowments, benefits, films, or social service programs offering ongoing or direct delivery of service.

THE STERN FAMILY FUND

**Meeting
Times**

The board of directors meets three times per year.

Publications

None.

THE STREISAND FOUNDATION

2800 28TH STREET, SUITE 105

SANTA MONICA, CA 90405

PHONE: (310) 535-3767

FAX: (310) 314-8396

WEB: www.barbrastreisand.com/

bio_streisand_foundation.html

**Contact
Persons**

Margery Tabankin, Executive Director

Suzy de Blois, Program Assistant

Purpose

Since its inception in 1986, The Streisand Foundation has made grants totaling over 12 million dollars. In the early years, we provided assistance to national organizations working on the issues of nuclear disarmament, preservation of the environment, voter education, and the protection of civil liberties and civil rights.

In 1993, the foundation added additional priorities. We began focusing on women's, children's and youth-related issues. Under these new priorities, we provided assistance to an array of national organizations, including those working to promote and protect women's rights and to provide aid and enrichment programs to economically at-risk children in Los Angeles.

**Areas of
Interest**

National advocacy organizations promoting or supporting:

- environmental issues
- women's issues including choice and health-related concerns
- civil liberties and democratic values
- civil rights and race relations
- children's and youth-related issues with a focus on the economically disadvantaged (Los Angeles-based only)
- AIDS research, advocacy, service and litigation

Financial Data

> (Year ended 12/31/00)
>
> | | |
> |---|---|
> | Assets: | $ 4,000,000 |
> | Total grants paid in 2000: | $ 587,510 |
> | Number of grants paid in 2000: | 40 |
> | Highest grant: | $ 25,000 |
> | Lowest grant: | $ 1,000 |
> | Median grant size: | $ 10,000 - $20,000 |

Application Procedures

The foundation does not require an application form. Organizations should submit all of the following items together: a one- to three-page summary of project proposal (separate and detached from the full proposal); a full proposal stating the problem, project goals and strategies for achieving these goals, proposed solutions, and the value or impact on society; organizational budget; project specific budget; a statement of current and projected income; a list of members of the organization's governing board; and an up-to date copy of the organization's IRS tax determination letter indicating 501(c)(3) and public charity status. Should an organization have a sponsor for this purpose, it must include a current copy of the sponsor's tax exemption determination letter. Letters of inquiry are accepted from September 1st to December 1st only, with grants announced the following summer.

Grant Limitations

The foundation funds both general and project specific support. Awards range from $1,000 to $25,000; the average award amount is between $10,000 and $20,000. At this time, The Streisand Foundation only considers requests from United States based non-profit organizations that are working on a national level.

As a rule, the foundation does not fund local organizations. However, we do make exception for projects in Los Angeles providing educational and extra-curricular programs for disadvantaged children and youth. We do not provide support to individuals, start-up organizations, or endowment or capital campaign grants. In addition, we generally do not fund documentaries or other types of audio-visual programming nor do we fund the publication of books or magazines.

THE STREISAND FOUNDATION

**Meeting
Times**

The board of directors does not have fixed meeting dates. Grants are made at least once per year.

Publications

Guidelines may be requested by calling 310-535-3767.

SUNFLOWER FOUNDATION

PHONE: (212) 682-0889

305 MADISON AVENUE, SUITE 1166

NEW YORK, NEW YORK 10165

Contact Person

Richard Parker, President

Purpose

The Sunflower Foundation provides support for progressive groups involved in educating and organizing for change by addressing the root causes of problems in society, rather than those treating the surface symptoms of the problems.

Areas of Interest

The broad interests of the foundation include community organizing, Third World or women's organizing, legal and health care organizing, and related social and political activities. Occasionally the fund provides support for international groups interested in these activities.

In the past, the foundation has funded projects working on the immediate shelter needs of the homeless, alternative farming and energy techniques designed to meet the environmental and economic needs of the future, legal assistance for Haitian immigrants, the mobilization of workers toward improvement of working conditions, conservation of threatened forest and mountain regions, and educational projects working to promote public awareness of the various cultures and species in society.

Financial Data

Total grants paid:	NA
Number of grants paid:	
Highest grant:	
Lowest grant:	
Median grant size:	

Application Procedures

Applicants should send a stamped, self-addressed envelope for guidelines before submitting a proposal. Organizations seeking funds should include in their proposal a description of the project (or that portion of a larger project) for which funding is sought and the amount requested; plans to achieve financial self-sufficiency; and the applicant's members, key staff, board members (if any), and goals. In addition, applicants should provide proof of tax-exempt status (or that of a sponsor) and the names of other foundations or donors from whom support is received, to whom proposals have been sent, and to whom it is contemplated proposals will be sent.

The foundation does not have a formal schedule. It suggests that proposals be submitted before October 15th for the annual meeting in December. Timely submission does not guarantee when a proposal will be considered. On occasion the foundation makes decisions at a preliminary meeting. Other times proposals are held over to subsequent meetings.

Grant Limitations

The foundation does not support direct services provisions, individuals, films, or books.

Meeting Times

The board of directors meets once a year in December.

Publications

The foundation does not publish an annual report. It will make guidelines available upon request.

SURDNA FOUNDATION, INC.

330 MADISON AVENUE 30TH FLOOR

NEW YORK, NEW YORK 10017-5001

PHONE: (212) 557-0010

FAX: (212) 557-0003

EMAIL: request@surdna.org

WEB: www.surdna.org

Contact Person

Edward Skloot, Executive Director

Purpose

The Surdna Foundation supports projects that foster catalytic, entrepreneurial programs offering solutions to difficult, systemic problems in the areas of environment and community revitalization in the United States.

Areas of Interest

The foundation's two areas of interest are:

• Environment. Projects that have main themes of biological and cultural diversity; energy and transportation; and restoring the environment in urban and suburban areas. The goals of all three themes are to prevent irreversible damage to the environment; support government, private and voluntary actions that will produce a sustainable environment and enhance livability; and to foster a citizenry which is environmentally informed and activist.

• Community Revitalization. Projects that seek to integrate comprehensive, multi-service local programs of community revitalization; support public/ private/voluntary partnerships; develop community self-help programs; revise service delivery funding; offer training programs for community leaders; disseminate information about effective community revitalization strategies; and support efforts to change public policy and funding toward community revitalization.

**Financial
Data**

```
(Year ended  /  /  )
Assets:                                    NA
Total grants authorized:
Total number of grants:
Highest grant:
Lowest grant:
Median grant size:
```

**Application
Procedures**

Before submitting a full proposal applicants are encouraged to submit a two or three page letter of inquiry. The letter should describe the organization's purpose and activities. It should briefly and concisely state the proposed project as well as its objectives, significance and intended results, the project timetable, and the funding strategy for the project including the total budget for the project and the organization. This letter should be accompanied by a copy of the applicant's proof of tax-exempt status under the Internal Revenue Code, the most recent audited financial statement, and names and qualifications of key personnel. Foundation staff will review the letter of inquiry and notify the organization whether or not to submit a full proposal.

Inquiries and proposals are accepted throughout the year. Grants are awarded three times a year in February, May, and September.

**Grant
Limitations**

The foundation normally does not make grants for endowments, capital or building programs, or to individuals. Projects which focus on the United States are preferred. Only tax-exempt nonprofit organizations under section 501(c)(3) status from the IRS are eligible for funds.

**Meeting
Times**

The board of trustees meets three times a year to consider grant requests.

Publications

The foundation publishes an annual report and grant guidelines.

TACONIC FOUNDATION

c/o **J.P. Morgan Private Bank**

Global Foundations Group

345 Park Avenue, 4th Floor

New York, NY 10154

PHONE: (212) 464-2443

FAX: (212) 464-2305

WEB: www.fdncenter.org/
grantmaker/taconic

Contact Person

Hildy J. Simmons, Managing Director

Purpose

The Taconic Foundation directs most of its grants to programs in the New York City area that are aimed at furthering equality of opportunity in various aspects of life, including those related to economic well-being.

Areas of Interest

The foundation places special emphasis on youth development and housing and community development. Some support is also available for projects related to broader civil rights issues. Grants usually range from $5,000 to $25,000.

Financial Data

(Year ended 12/31/99)	
Assets:	$26,203,988
Total grants awarded:	$747,500
Number of grants awarded:	44
Highest grant:	$30,000
Lowest grant:	$5,000
Median grant size:	$15,000 - $20,000

Application Procedures

The foundation does not require a special application form and reviews proposals throughout the year. The foundation specifically requests proposals that have well-defined goals, specific plans for achieving and financing the project, and that take into consideration other related work.

Grant
Limitations

The foundation does not make grants to local community programs outside New York City except in special instances directly related to the foundation's program priorities. Regional projects are occasionally supported, and national programs only rarely. Nor does the foundation make grants for the following purposes: buildings or endowments, higher education, scholarships and fellowships, the elderly, arts and cultural programs, mass media, crime and justice, health, medicine, mental health, the environment, and international programs. Only public charities with IRS section 501(c)(3) certification are eligible for funding.

Meeting
Times

The board of directors meets four to six times a year.

Publications

The foundation publishes a biennial report and distributes, on request, a yearly listing of grants.

S. MARK TAPER FOUNDATION

PHONE: (310) 476-5413

FAX: (310) 471-4993

EMAIL: guidelines@smtfoundation.org

12011 SAN VICENTE BOULEVARD

SUITE 400

LOS ANGELES, CALIFORNIA 90049

Contact Person

Executive Director

Purpose and Areas of Interest

The S. Mark Taper Foundation seeks to quicken the pace of finding solutions to the most intransigent problems of social justice, homelessness, poverty, civil rights, environment, and domestic violence, among others, facing communities in California. The foundation awards grants for general purposes, special projects, and seed money.

Financial Data

(Year ended / /)	
Assets:	NA
Total grants paid:	
Total number of grants:	
Highest grant:	
Lowest grant:	
Median grant size:	

Application Procedures

The foundation discourages telephone inquiries. Organizations seeking support should first send a brief one or two page letter to the executive director outlining the project and projected cost. The executive director will contact applicants after reviewing the initial inquiry.

Grant Limitations

Grantmaking is limited to California and no grants are awarded to individuals.

**Meeting
Times**

The board of trustees meets as needed.

Publications

The foundation provides grant guidelines in response to written requests.

TARGET CORPORATION

(formerly Dayton Hudson Foundation)

1000 NICOLLET MALL, TPS-3080

MINNEAPOLIS, MINNESOTA 55403

PHONE: (612) 696-6098

FAX: (612) 696-5088

EMAIL: guidelines@target.com

WEB: www.targetfoundation.org

Contact Person

Bridget McGinnis, Associate Specialist

Purpose

The Target Foundation is the major vehicle through which the Target Corporation contributes to nonprofit, tax-exempt organizations. The foundation policy is primarily to fund projects in those communities in which the corporation has operating company headquarters, mostly around the Minneapolis-St.Paul area. The foundation gives a limited number of national grants for programs that compliment the local involvement of the operating companies, promote philanthropy or that research and analyze public policy issues in the foundation's priority areas.

Areas of Interest

The foundation allocates eighty percent of its giving to two areas where it believes it can have significant effect—social action and the arts.

• Social Action. Programs and projects that result in the economic and social progress of individuals or the development of community and neighborhood strategies that respond effectively to critical community social and economic concerns. Priority is given to efforts that help low-income adults prepare for work in order to leave or avoid welfare and efforts that strengthen indigenous community leadership and leaders.

• Arts. Programs and projects that result in artistic excellence and stronger artistic leadership in communities or increased access to, and use of, the arts as a means or community expression. The remaining twenty percent is provided to special community needs and opportunities. Funds in this category are limited and are generally allocated to projects of special and current interest to Target Foundation and other local community leadership.

TARGET CORPORATION (formerly Dayton Hudson Foundation)

Financial Data

```
(Year ended  /  / )
Total grants awarded:              NA
Number of grants awarded:
Highest grant:
Lowest grant:
Median grant size:
```

Application Procedures

The first step in applying for a grant is to identify the Target Company operating in your community. (Contact Target for the facility nearest you.) Areas of special interest, priorities and applications procedures may differ. If you apply to more than one Target facility, you should indicate so in your formal request.

Generally, the foundation prefers a one-page preliminary application letter that states the following: applicant's name, address, telephone number, and IRS tax-exempt status; the specific amount requested; and how the funds would be used. No additional information is needed at this stage. The foundation specifically requests that preliminary inquiries not be made by telephone or personal visits. Preliminary applications have no deadlines. The foundation or company usually responds to these inquiries within one month either by declining support or by asking for a formal application.

The foundation does not use an application form. If a formal application is requested, it should be made in a letter of not more than two typewritten pages (four hand written pages) that includes, but is not limited to the following: a description of the proposed program or project, the need, the people to be served, and the time period to be covered by the grant; an explanation of the results to be accomplished by the proposed program or project, and how the results will be evaluated; a request for a specific amount of money, with an explanation of how the funds will be used; and a description of your organization, including its purposes and objectives and the name(s) and qualifications of the person(s) who will administer the grant. If the request is to support a capital drive or specific project, the letter should include information about the need to be addressed, the geographical area and population to be served, and a timetable for the project.

Attached to each letter should be the following: a copy of the organization's most recent tax-exempt ruling; a list of the organization's officers and directors; a financial report for the most recently completed year of operation; an organizational budget for the current operating year showing anticipated expenses and income by sources; and a donor's list, either complete or representative, showing private, corporate, and foundation, contributors to organization during the past twelve months. Applications without the basic information and attachments listed above will not be considered until all such material is provided.

Grant Limitations

The Target Corporation makes grants for general program, project, and capital support. It limits capital grants to programs supported by the foundation and to unusual community opportunities. Its support of endowments is even more limited.

It does not usually support health, education, recreation, therapeutic and residential programs, housing and living subsidies, care of disabled persons or emergency care. Nor does it make grants to individuals, religious groups for religious purposes, fund-raising dinners, testimonials and other similar events.

Meeting Times

The board of directors meets three times a year, in December, March, and June.

Publications

The foundation publishes an annual report and will make available upon request an information sheet, "Information for Applicants," and a list of Target facilities.

Operating Companies

Requests from Minnesota organizations should be addressed to the foundation. All other requests should be sent to the appropriate Target company. Please contact Target for the facility nearest you.

THE TIDES FOUNDATION

P.O. Box 29903

San Francisco, California 94129-0903

PHONE: (415) 561-6400

FAX: (415) 561-6401

EMAIL: info@tides.org

WEB: www.tidesfoundation.org

Contact Person

Tanya Diaz, Outreach and Communications Associate

Purpose

Tides Foundation actively promotes change toward a healthy society, one which is founded on principles of social justice, broadly shared economic opportunity, a robust democratic process, and sustainable environmental practices.

Tides Foundation is a public charity, founded in 1976, that offers philanthropists a vehicle for their charitable giving through Tides Donor Advised Funds. Tides Foundation manages over 300 of these funds, each of which has a Fund Advisor who has the privilege of making grant recommendations from her/his fund. Most Fund Advisors direct their own grantmaking, but some Fund Advisors look to Tides staff to recommend organizations working in their interest areas. Tides staff relies on the Letter of Inquiry (LOI) process to gather information about a wide range of organizations working for social change.

Areas of Interest

Tides Foundation provides grants in the following issue areas:
- Arts, Culture and Alternative Media
- Civic Participation
- Economic Development
- Economic and Racial Justice
- Environment
- Environmental Justice
- Gay, Lesbian, Bisexual and Transgender Issues
- HIV/AIDS
- Native Communities
- Women's Empowerment and Reproductive Health

- Violence Prevention
- Youth Development and Organizing

For detailed descriptions of each issue area, please visit our web site at www.tidesfoundation.org. If your organization's work does not fall into these issue areas you may not be considered.

Financial Data

(Year ended 12/31/00)	
Assets:	$ 159,354,730
Total grants paid:	$ 56 million
Number of grants paid:	2,400
Highest grant:	$ 50,000
Lowest grant:	$ 1,000
Median grant size:	NA

Application Procedures

In order to be considered for Tides Foundation funding, an organization must complete an online Letter of Inquiry (LOI) submission form. The submission form, along with LOI information, criteria, guidelines and deadlines are posted on Tides' web site (www.tidesfoundation.org).

While we discourage non-electronic LOI submission, in limited circumstances (if you have no way to access the web, or have significant technical problems that we are unable to assist you with) we will accept LOI submissions through the mail. To do this, you may request that materials be mailed to you by sending your request and mailing address to info@tides.org, or by calling 415-561-6400.

LOIs may be submitted throughout the year and are reviewed by Tides program staff twice yearly. Following each review, applicants are informed if Tides will be able to hold their inquiry on file for one year. During this one-year period, program staff seek to match held applications with the interests of current donor-advised fund interests. If a potential match is found, program staff may request a full proposal from the applicant. Please note that in 2000, Tides donor-advised funds were able to provide grants to less than 5% of organizations that submitted LOIs.

Grant Limitations

Tides grants to 501(c)(3) non-profit organizations and provides limited funding to 501(c)(4) organizations.

Tides does not accept LOIs from universities, schools, individuals or corporations; nor for capital campaigns, endowments, or film production.

Tides only considers organizations with budgets under $2 million. In limited cases Tides will consider projects of organizations with budgets over $2 million if the project budget falls below this ceiling and the project operates relatively autonomously from the parent organization.

Please refer to www.tidesfoundation.org for a complete list of grant limitations.

Meeting Times

The board of directors meets three times a year.

Publications

The foundation publishes an annual report and grant guidelines.

TIGER FOUNDATION

101 PARK AVENUE 48TH FLOOR

NEW YORK, NY 10178

PHONE: (212) 984-2565

FAX: (212) 949-9778

EMAIL: see website

WEB: www.tigerfoundation.org

Contact Persons

Phoebe Boyer, Executive Director
Amy Schoenberg, Program Officer
Julia Hernandez, Grants Administrator

Purpose

The Tiger Foundation's goal is to help break the cycle of poverty in New York City and to give disadvantaged children and families the chance to build successful lives. It seeks preventive programs designed to address the root causes of poverty and not merely its symptoms.

Areas of Interest

Primary funding consideration is given to those organizations that address the educational, developmental, vocational, and health needs of young people and their families. In particular, the foundation supports early childhood programs, teen pregnancy prevention, and educational reform projects.

Financial Data

(Year ended 6/30/00)	
Assets:	$ 7,961,573
Total grants paid:	$ 3,599,389
Total number of grants:	46
Highest grant:	$ 190,000
Lowest grant:	$ 25,000
Median grant size:	$ 75,000

Application Procedures

The foundation accepts the New York Area Common Application Form. Applicants should submit a three-page letter request which includes a brief history of the organization, population served, and services offered. Applications should also include the organization's operating budget, amount of funding requested, and a list of supporters.

Grant
Limitations

Grantmaking is primarily in the New York City area. The foundation does not fund individuals, annual or capital campaigns, endowments, benefits/special events, public policy and lobbying groups, legal aid, existing obligations or debt liability.

Meeting
Times

The board of trustees meets quarterly.

Publications

The foundation publishes grant guidelines.

THE TIMES MIRROR FOUNDATION

PHONE: (213) 237-3945

FAX: (213) 237-2116

202 WEST FIRST STREET

WEB: www.timesmirrorfoundation.org

LOS ANGELES, CALIFORNIA 90012

Contact Person

Michelle Williams, Executive Director

Purpose

The Times Mirror Foundation provides grants for operating support, capital campaign, and special projects in the broad areas of culture and arts, civic and community, education, and health and human services. The company itself also provides grants, primarily to civic organizations in Southern California region, and Times Mirror operating units make cash and in-kind contributions to nonprofit organizations serving communities in areas where Times Mirror owns a business.

Areas of Interest

Both the foundation's and Times Mirror Company's area of interests are culture and arts, civic and community, education, and health and human services. Operating unit charitable contributions are made in the areas of publishing and television.

Application Procedures

Please read our mission statement and eligibility statements carefully and complete the online grant summary form. In addition, please submit a clearly written and concise proposal that addresses the following points:

• Statement of the Problem or Issue that your program addresses: How does this problem relate to the foundation's mission and priorities?

• Qualifications: What are the strengths and skills of your organization and personnel?

• Program Goals: What are you going to accomplish? Who will benefit? What is the time frame?

• Methodology: How are you going to accomplish your goals?

• Evaluation: How will you measure your program's accomplishments and effectiveness?

• Budget: Include both administrative and project costs.

If you do not submit all of the above application requirements, we regret that we will be unable to consider your proposal.

Proposals are accepted year-round but must be received by April 15 or October 15 for possible consideration at the board of directors meetings in June and December, respectively.

Grant
Limitations

Contributions are not considered for production costs, films, videos or television programs, religious or fraternal purposes, publication, conferences, or to individuals.

Financial
Data

(Year ended 12/31/00)	
Assets:	
Total grants made:	$ 4,165,811

Meeting
Times

The board normally meets twice a year, in June and December to consider grant requests.

Publications

The foundation publishes a contributions annual report.

TOWN CREEK FOUNDATION

121 NORTH WEST STREET

EASTON, MARYLAND 21601

PHONE: (410) 763-8171

FAX: (410) 763-8172

EMAIL: info@towncreekfdn.org

WEB: www.towncreekfdn.org

**Contact
Person**

Christine B. Shelton, Executive Director*

Purpose

The Town Creek Foundation is an unstaffed funding resource that was created in 1981 with the goal of playing a role in the achievement of a livable and sustainable environment, and the search for a just society and a peaceful world.

**Areas of
Interest**

Grants are made in the following program areas: preservation and enhancement of the environment in the United States, and monitoring federal, state, and local officials and bodies that are responsible for enforcement of legislation enacted to protect the environment; dissemination, via public radio and television throughout the United States, of news and commentary significant to people concerned about the world around them and the future in order to provide them with a basis to examine what is happening and to act to improve many aspects of society and government; the search for ways to secure a peaceful and democratic society, supporting projects that challenge and redirect the military economy, reduce the risk of war and promote a government responsive and accountable to its citizens; and improvement of the quality of life and opportunities for advancement for the people of Talbot County, Maryland and its communities, where such opportunities have been adversely affected by economic and social conditions.

---

*The staff consists of one part-time executive director who is generally in the office on Mondays and Wednesdays.

Financial Data

```
(Year ended 12/31/00)
Assets:                          $ 60,457,482
Total grants paid:               $ 2,901,600
Number of grants paid:                    88
Highest grant:                   $ 250,000
Lowest grant:                    $ 2,250
Median grant size:               $ 25,000 - $ 75,000
```

Application Procedures

A letter of inquiry (up to two pages) may be submitted before a full proposal is prepared. The letter of inquiry may be submitted by fax or email and we will respond as soon as possible as to whether a full proposal will be considered. Grant decisions are made by the Board of Trustees three times a year, during March, July and November. Grant application deadlines are January 15th, May 15th and September 15th, and full proposals must be received by those dates. If the deadline date falls on a holiday or weekend, it is postponed to the next business day.

The proposal must be submitted unbound, printed on both sides of recycled paper. Fax or email applications will not be accepted. None of the materials will be returned unless a stamped self-addressed envelope is provided. Brevity in the proposal is suggested. However, fundamental components of the application package are:

A cover letter on the organization's letterhead briefly introducing the proposal and specifying the dollar amount sought;

The body of the application, not to exceed eight pages, type-written and numbered. The foundation gives preference to proposals which describe strategy and implementation plans rather than those which focus primarily on the need for support. The body of the proposal must contain:

- a paragraph describing the organization and its goals and objectives
- a statement of the organization's assets and total revenues and expenses for its most recent fiscal year
- a clear statement of the need for support, either for a specific project or for general support
- if the request is for a specific project, the project's goals
- description of the geographic scope of the organization and the project (national, regional, etc.)

- description of the strategies to be used (grassroots organizing, advocacy, collaboration, etc.)
- the action plan and timeline
- outcomes expected and methods for evaluation.

Fiscal and administrative information, as a supplement:
- the current year operating budget for the organization
- the total budget for the project, if the request is for project support
- a copy of the organization's 501(c)(3) tax exemption letter from the Internal Revenue Service. If the request is for a project under the fiscal management of another organization, a letter from the fiscal agent and a copy of its IRS approval letter and financial statements is required.
- organizational capacity for carrying out the work, including a brief paragraph describing the qualifications of key staff and a list of the board of directors and their affiliations
- the most recent financial statements or annual report
- a list of other sources and amounts of support, requested and received, within the last 12 months

Other possible inclusions:
- sample brochure and most recent newsletter
- one or two newspaper or magazine articles
- an executive summary for any books or reports produced. Do not send the full report or publication.

Grant Limitations

The foundation does not fund programs outside of North America nor does it make grants to individuals, primary and secondary schools, hospitals, religious organizations, or for endowment, capital and building fund campaigns, or the purchase of land or buildings. It does not make grants to colleges or universities, except when some aspect of their work is an integral part of a program supported by the foundation. It does not fund research, scholarship programs, conferences, the publication of books and periodicals, or visual or performing arts projects.

Meeting Times

The board of directors meets to review grant requests three times a year.

Publications

The foundation publishes a brochure describing its program interests and application procedures.

THE TRAVELERS FOUNDATION

PHONE: (310) 828-1288 or (860) 954-2775

2101 WILSHIRE BOULEVARD, SUITE 225

SANTA MONICA, CALIFORNIA 90403

EMAIL: see website

WEB: www.travelers.com/foundation

Contact Person

John Motley, President

Purpose

The Travelers Foundation is a company-sponsored foundation whose funds are donated by The Travelers, Inc. Its principal focus is public education. The foundation looks for projects which improve the readiness of children to enter and succeed in school and those which provide students with skills and knowledge for employment. Grants are also awarded to nonprofit organizations which address societal needs in the area of human services, childcare, homelessness, civic development, and culture.

Areas of Interest

The foundation gives primarily in areas of company operations with a special emphasis on New York. It provides support for operating budgets and special projects in the following areas of interest:

• Child Development. Projects that improve the readiness of children to enter and succeed in school are a priority. Included are projects that improve early childhood education, parenting programs that provide comprehensive services to disadvantaged children and their families, and programs that improve the quality of childcare.

• Education and Job Readiness. Support is provided to school-based programs that provide students with skills and knowledge for employment.

THE TRAVELERS FOUNDATION

Financial Data

```
(Year ended   /  /  )
Assets:                        NA
Total grants paid:
Number of grants paid:
Highest grant:
Lowest grant:
Median grant size:
```

Application Procedures

The foundation will consider either brief descriptions of one or two pages, including a clear statement of goals and objectives of the program for which support is sought, or full proposals. Applications are accepted throughout the year. After reviewing initial submissions, additional information may be requested by the staff of the foundation.

Applicants submitting complete proposals should be certain to include: a description of the nature and purpose of the organization; a clear description of the project for which funding is sought, including a line-item budget, identification of the population served by the project, a list of recent contributors, and a description of the methodology to be used in evaluating the project's effectiveness; financial information, including the organization's most recent annual report and budget; a copy of the organization's 501(c)(3) determination letter from the IRS; and proof that the organization does not discriminate in its practices or services on the basis of race, sex, age, creed, or national origin.

There are no application deadlines and applicants are notified within three to four months of application date.

Grant Limitations

Grants are only made to organizations which possess a letter from the IRS identifying them as tax-exempt pursuant to Section 501(c)(3). Support is not provided for endowment funds, annual campaigns, publications, individuals, deficit financing, special events, or loans. Support is limited to areas where The Travelers, Inc. has corporate locations in New York, New York; San Francisco, California; Wilmington, Delaware; Duluth, Georgia; Baltimore, Maryland; Fort Worth, Houston, and Irving, Texas.

Meeting Times

The board of directors meets as required and has its annual meeting in February.

Publications

The foundation publishes an annual report and application guidelines.

TRIO FOUNDATION

1563 SOLANO AVENUE #174

BERKELEY, CALIFORNIA 94707

PHONE: (510) 527-4605

WEB: www.foundationcenter.org/
grantmaker/trio

Contact Person

Lyda Beardsley, Ph.D., Executive Director

Purpose

The primary purpose of the Trio Foundation is to "provide opportunities for young children of all cultures, who are growing up in poverty to achieve their fullest and brightest potential." The foundation is especially interested in organizations that are community based and serve the residents of Alameda and Contra Costa counties of California. Trio's secondary focus is to fund projects sponsored by Jewish organizations serving Jewish children in need or serving a multi-cultural clientele.

Areas of Interest

The foundation will consider projects that affect children from birth to eight years of age and projects offering family support in the pre-natal period and beyond. Specifically the foundation looks for projects which do one or more of the following: develop new ways of providing care or support for young children in poverty; strengthen low-income families; advocate for changes in child care and family services policy; cultivate leadership that is rooted in the community; establish models that may be used by other communities.

Grants range in size between $5,000 and $20,000.

Financial Data

(Year ended / /)	
Assets:	NA
Total grants paid:	
Total number of grants:	
Highest grant:	
Lowest grant:	
Median grant size:	

Application Procedures

The foundation does not have an application form and applicant's initial contact should be a letter, no longer than one page, outlining the purpose for which the funding is being sought. The letter should include a one sentence summary of the proposed project and answer the following questions:

- What is the significance of the issue you seek to address?
- What are the changes you seek to bring about?
- What project are you proposing to Trio, and approximately how much funding are you requesting for it?
- How will this project bring about the changes you seek?
- If the proposed project matches its funding priorities, the grant seeker will be asked to submit a longer proposal.

Deadlines for grant applications are February 1 for a June decision and August 1 for a December decision.

Grant Limitations

Only organizations serving the residents of Alameda or Contra Costa counties are eligible. The foundation does not ordinarily award grants for general operating support, loans, scholarships, support to individuals, or large capital expenditures. Only organizations classified as tax-exempt under Section 501(c)(3) of the Internal Revenue Code or those that are affiliated with such an organization are eligible.

Meeting Times

The board of trustees meets in June and December.

Publications

The foundation publishes an informational brochure and a grants list.

UNITARIAN UNIVERSALIST VEATCH PROGRAM AT SHELTER ROCK

PHONE: (516) 627-6576

FAX: (516) 627-6596

EMAIL: jan@veatch.org

WEB: www.uucsr.org/veatch

48 SHELTER ROCK ROAD

MANHASSET, NEW YORK 11030

Contact Person

Marjorie Fine, Executive Director

Purpose

The Veatch Program supports Unitarian Universalism and nondenominational organizations whose goals reflect a belief in the inherent worth and dignity of every person; justice; the rights of conscience and the use of the democratic progress and other principles of Unitarian Universalism. Veatch is not a foundation; it is the grantmaking program of the church.

Areas of Interest

In its nondenominational grantmaking, Veatch supports organizations engaged in community organizing, environmental justice, workplace organizing, workers' rights, global democracy, and civil and constitutional rights.

Financial Data

(Year ended 6/30/00)	
Assets:	Not endowed
Total grants paid:	$ 10,150,000
Number of grants:	210
Highest grant:	$ 1,100,000
Lowest grant:	$ 15,000

Application Procedures

The program has no application forms and no deadlines. Applications are considered throughout the year in the order in which they are received.

The initial contact may be a short letter or full proposal. The program prefers that requests for support be made by written proposal, rather than by phone inquiry or request for personal meeting. Proposals prepared for other foundations are accepted. Applications should be concise and brief (narrative of five to fifteen pages) and contain a one-page cover sheet including the name, address, and telephone number of the applicant; the amount being requested; the time period for which funding is being solicited; and a one-paragraph description of the proposed project.

A complete application should also include an organizational profile, including its history, purpose and objectives, accomplishments, decision-making structure, sources of financial support, and staff composition; background of the problem that the project seeks to address and an explanation of why the applicant is particularly well-qualified to undertake the proposed activities; an outline of the specific activities to be undertaken during the course of the project with particular attention paid to what will be done; the methodology to be employed; the proposed timetable; and the anticipated results.

Finally, the program requires an itemized budget detailing all proposed project costs in addition to a copy of the general operating budget of the organization for the two preceeding years; a list of other sources and corresponding amounts of project support, committed and solicited; audited financial statements (if available); annual report; and recent copy of IRS determination letter indicating tax-exempt status under Sections 501(c)(3) and 509(a) of the Internal Revenue Code.

Receipt of application is acknowledged by postcard. Once an application is deemed complete, every effort is made to provide a definitive response regarding support within ninety days.

Grant Limitations

The Veatch Program's nondenominational grantmaking is limited to U.S.-based organizations with activities in the United States. Support is generally provided only to nonprofit, tax-exempt organizations as defined under section 501(c)(3) of the Internal Revenue Code. The program does not make grants to individuals or government institutions, nor in the following categories: capital projects, endowments, historic preservation, direct services, academic research, film or video production, publications or cultural activities.

Meeting Times

The board of governors meets regularly throughout the year (approximately 5-6 meetings per year).

Publications

The Veatch Program publishes an annual report and a spring newsletter.

LAWSON VALENTINE FOUNDATION

PHONE: (860) 570- 0728*

FAX: (860) 570-0728*

EMAIL: vdoyle@compuserve.com

1000 FARMINGTON AVENUE, SUITE 105A

WEST HARTFORD, CONNECTICUT 06107-2184

Contact Person

Valentine Doyle, Program Officer

Purpose

The Lawson Valentine Foundation is a small family foundation that supports grassroot efforts in the areas of natural and human environment. New applicants must be working in the areas of environmental or economic justice or food systems.

Areas of Interest

The foundation funds projects in the areas of environment, improved race relations, and human rights. Most grants are within the $5,000 to $30,000 range.

Preference is given to organizations that use local individuals, are based in the community in which they serve, that address a specific unmet need, and use volunteers. New organizations and organizations that have trouble finding funds are encouraged to apply.

Financial Data

(Year ended 12/31/00)	
Assets:	$ 18,000,000
Total grants paid:	$ 1,040,300
Highest grant:	$ 35,000
Lowest grant:	$ 500
Median grant size:	$ 20,000

*Letters are preferred as there is usually no one available to answer phones. Call before a fax is sent.

Application Procedures

For grants up to $5,000, organizations should submit the "foundation's request for grant consideration" which can be obtained by writing to the foundation. For grants larger than $5,000, organizations should submit a letter of inquiry describing their work and the size of the organization, and attach the following information: a statement of need, program objectives and how they will be achieved, expected benefits, population served, proposed method of program evaluation, and a defined budget including other sources of financial support committed and pending. Supporting documentation should include a copy of the organization's most recent audited financial statement, a copy of its tax-exempt status under IRS Code 501(c)(3), and a list of the board of directors and their organizational affiliations.

The Board makes grants in spring and fall.

Grant Limitations

Grants are awarded only to organizations that have received tax-exempt status under the IRS Code 501(c)(3). Additionally, organizations are expected to meet acceptable standards for effective management, fiscal accountability and efficient delivery of services. The foundation does not make grants to schools, medical research, land trusts, religious institutions, or organizations working with animals.

Meeting Times

The board's meeting times vary each year, but generally occur in the spring and fall.

Publications

None.

VAN AMERINGEN FOUNDATION

PHONE: (212) 758-6221

509 MADISON AVENUE SUITE 2010

NEW YORK, NEW YORK 10022-5501

WEB: www.vanamfound.org

Contact Person

Eleanor Sypher, Executive Director

Purpose

The van Ameringen Foundation is primarily devoted to furthering the field of mental health and related social issues. The foundation seeks to stimulate prevention, education, and direct care programs in the mental health field, and emphasizes projects which have a direct effect on disadvantaged and deprived populations. Grants are made almost exclusively in the New York metropolitan area and the urban Northeast corridor. Rarely does the foundation make grants on a regional or national basis.

Areas of Interest

The foundation's concern is with access to and delivery of appropriate and effective therapeutic care. The foundation is particularly interested in preventive and early-intervention strategies, especially those programs that work in tandem with education programs; that demonstrate the relative merits of various therapies; that feature the creative mixing of public and private efforts on behalf of mental health clients; that increase the accessibility of mental health services to the poor and needy; and that incorporate self-help models. Several grants have been made for AIDS-related services, including the problems of turn-over, stress, and burnout among health care professionals and volunteers working with AIDS victims.

Financial Data

(Year ended 12/31/00)	
Assets:	$ 58,337,416

Application Procedures

All inquiries and grant requests should be in writing and addressed to the President, Mr. Henry van Ameringen. Interviews are initiated by the foundation. A full proposal should incorporate the following elements:

1. Cover Letter—This summarizes in no more than two pages what is being requested, the objectives and significance of the proposed program and the major activities planned.

2. Proposal—The proposal itself should not exceed five pages and may be shorter.

   It should include:

   a) a detailed description of the program design and what is to be accomplished during the proposed grant period;

   b) a statement of the qualifications or capabilities of the organization to carry out the proposed project;

   c) a description of how the project will be evaluated;

   d) a budget noting all planned expenditures, anticipated income, sources of income, and plans for future fundraising for the project if applicable.

3. Additional Documentation—Each proposal must be accompanied by a copy of the Internal Revenue Service letter indicating tax-exempt status; the most recent financial statement (preferably audited); a current organizational operating budget; a list of directors and officers of the organization; and the latest annual report. Applicants may also include relevant publications or news articles. Foundation grants are made only to nonprofit, charitable organizations that are tax-exempt under Section 501(c)(3) of the Internal Revenue Code.

Grant Limitations

Applications outside the geographic focus of the foundation are not encouraged, and regional or national grants are made only occasionally. Foundation policy excludes consideration of applications for endowment purposes, capital projects, annual fundraising drives, and support of international activities and institutions in foreign countries. Grants are made to tax-exempt organizations; under no circumstances are grants made in direct support of individuals.

**Meeting
Times**

The board of directors considers grant proposals three times annually, generally in March, June, and November.

Publications

The foundation has two publications, an annual report and a booklet, "The Foundation and Its Program," which includes application procedures.

VANGUARD PUBLIC FOUNDATION

PHONE: (415) 487-2111

FAX: (415) 487-2124

EMAIL: vpf@vanguardsf.org

WEB: www.vanguardsf.org

383 RHODE ISLAND STREET, SUITE 301

SAN FRANCISCO, CALIFORNIA 94103

Contact Person

Randall Miller, Grants Director

Purpose

The Vanguard Public Foundation is a partnership of donors and community activists dedicated to the promotion of peace and social justice. The major purpose of Vanguard's grantmaking is the empowerment of historically disenfranchised sectors of society through community organizing and advocacy. Through its general fund and donor-advised programs it promotes the development of a grassroots, progressive, and democratic movement for social change, and seeks to enhance the power of both community activists and donors. Although the foundation concentrates its direct funding on projects located in Northern California (all counties north of Monterey), the foundation supports progressive social change nationally and internationally.

Areas of Interest

The foundation funds new and existing organizations involved in direct organizing or advocacy that are based in Northern California (all counties north of Monterey). The foundation's interests are in civil rights, economic justice, workers' rights, women's rights, education, disability, health, housing, environment, cultural activism, indigenous peoples' rights, and international solidarity, and projects that involve and empower those communities most affected by the unequal distribution of economic resources and political power. Preference is given to those projects which have the greatest potential to have significant and long term influence on the empowerment of communities that have been left out of the democratic process. Priority is given to projects without traditional sources of funding, those that are controversial or of low priority. Vanguard seeks coalitions that emphasize joint strategies and projects.

Specifically, the foundation provides funds to organizations that seek to alter the underlying causes of injustice, poverty, and disenfranchisement; involve low-income and working class people in achieving self-determination; work toward a society free from racism, sexism, homophobia and economic exploitation, and support the rights of all people; and incorporate affirmative action guidelines and practices.

Financial Data

> (Year ended 6/30/00)
> Grantmaking activity of both the general fund and the donor-advised fund is combined below.
>
> | | |
> |---|---|
> | Support and revenue: | $ 4,485,075 |
> | Total grants paid: | $ 3,336,162 |
> | Highest grant: | $ 10,000 |
> | Lowest grant: | $ 250 |
> | Median grant size: | $ 4,500 |

Application Procedures

A statement of Vanguard's funding guidelines and an application form and instructions may be obtained by telephoning the foundation. Applicants must complete the application form and include a cover sheet, a narrative (no more than four pages), and the required attachments. A checklist of required items is included in the foundation-supplied material. Proposal deadlines are July 1, October 1, January 1, and April 1.

The funding process requires an initial review and an in-person interview prior to any decision. All applicants are informed at the end of the first review stage whether or not they have been selected for an interview. Applicants should expect the whole process to last approximately five months. Grants range from $1,000 to $10,000 with the average being $4,500. Past grantees may apply for additional funding on a schedule described in the foundation's application package.

Meeting Times

The community and donor board meets quarterly.

Publications

The Vanguard Foundation publishes an annual report and distributes program guidelines and application forms upon request.

VICTORIA FOUNDATION

946 BLOOMFIELD AVENUE

GLEN RIDGE, NEW JERSEY 07028

PHONE: (973) 748-5300

FAX: (973) 748-0016

EMAIL: info@victoriafoundation.org

WEB: www.victoriafoundation.org

Contact Person

Catherine M. McFarland, Executive Officer

Purpose

The Victoria Foundation primarily supports projects focusing on education, environment, ethnic and geographic communities, and youth and families in New Jersey.

Areas of Interest

The foundation's current areas of interest are:

• Education. Core and enrichment programs in the public and private schools that promote greater readiness for and access to college education for disadvantaged students, and other educational programs such as career guidance and adult literacy.

• Environment. Organizations that are addressing urgent environmental problems within New Jersey, including toxics, preservation of pinelands, wildlife, and shoreline and resource recovery.

• Ethnic and geographic communities. Self-help programs within minority and disadvantaged communities dealing with issues including housing, job training, health services, and education.

• Youth and family. Programs dealing with such issues as adolescent pregnancy and parenting, mental health and counseling, wellness promotion, tutoring and training, and families in crisis.

In addition to these areas, the foundation makes grants for a number of other issues including drug and alcohol abuse, support services for small businesses, and services to prisoners.

VICTORIA FOUNDATION

**Financial
Data**

(Year ended / /)	
Assets:	NA
Total grants paid:	
Number of grants paid:	
Highest grant:	
Lowest grant:	
Median grant size:	

**Application
Procedures**

Prospective grantees may submit either a brief letter outlining the details of the project or a full proposal. A two-page written summary is preferred. Deadlines for receiving proposals are February 1 for spring consideration and August 1 for fall. Grant application guidelines are available from the foundation.

**Grant
Limitations**

Organizations outside the state of New Jersey are requested not to apply for grants. Rarely are out-of-state grant awards made, and only at the initiation of the foundation and not in response to applications. The foundation makes no grants to individuals, or for programs dealing with specific diseases, afflictions, geriatric needs, or day care.

**Meeting
Times**

The board of trustees meets semi-annually, usually in May and December.

Publications

The foundation publishes an annual report and guidelines for grant applications.

VIRGINIA ENVIRONMENTAL ENDOWMENT

1051 East Cary Street

Suite 1400

Richmond, Virginia 23219

PHONE: (804) 644-5000

FAX: (804) 644-0603

EMAIL: info@vee.org

WEB: www.vee.org

Contact Person

Gerald P. McCarthy, Executive Director

Purpose

The purpose of the Virginia Environmental Endowment is to improve the quality of the environment in Virginia. It also funds projects related to water quality and the effects of water pollution on human health and the environment in the Ohio River and Kanawha River valleys. The endowment prefers constructive, result-oriented projects carried out by existing organizations. Activities that bring business, government, and environmental groups together to address environmental opportunities are encouraged.

Areas of Interest

The foundation makes grants in two major areas: the Virginia Program and the Kanawha and Ohio Water Quality Program.

Virginia Program priorities are as follows:

• Water quality research and monitoring of water quality conditions throughout Virginia;

• Land and open space conservation;

• Chesapeake Bay fisheries conservation, research and education;

• Environmental education.

The Kanawha and Ohio River Water Quality Program emphasizes water quality and the effects of water pollution on public health in the Kanawha & Ohio River Valley region.

Financial Data

(Year ended 3/31/01)	
Assets:	$ 17,372,200
Total grants authorized:	$ 1,689,318
Number of grants authorized:	38
Highest grant:	$ 639,092 over 3 years
Lowest grant:	$ 300
Median grant size:	$ 25,000

Application Procedures

Proposals for the Virginia Program are welcome at any time. Those received by 5:00 p.m. Eastern Time on April 15, August 15, and December 15 will be considered at the June, November, and March board meetings respectively. Proposals for the Kanawha and Ohio River Valley Program are considered once each year and are due by April 15.

The endowment does not use application forms, nor does it review preliminary proposals. Applicants should submit two copies of their full proposal signed by the chief executive officer or board chairman.

Proposals should include a project description (about five pages) stating the need for the project, its objectives and how they will be achieved, how project results will be measured, and relevance to other work being done in the field; information about the organization, qualifications of key personnel, a list of the board members, and proof of tax-exempt status; a line-item budget showing all sources and amounts of matching funds, all anticipated income and expenses and plans for future support; a project schedule; plans for continuing project activities and raising financial support beyond the grant period; and a detailed plan for evaluation stating method and criteria.

Grants are normally made for one year. Matching funds in equal amounts from other sources are required, and challenge grants may be offered to provide leverage in fundraising efforts. Approved grants are paid in installments on a reimbursement basis. Grantees are required to submit periodic reports of progress and expenditures as well as a final evaluation report at the end of the grant period.

Grant Limitations

Ordinarily funds are not provided for overhead, indirect costs, building funds, endowments, or lawsuits.

**Meeting
Times**

The board of directors usually meets in March, June, and November.

Publications

The endowment publishes an annual report.

WISCONSIN COMMUNITY FUND

1202 WILLIAMSON STREET, SUITE D

MADISON, WISCONSIN 53703

PHONE: (608) 251-6834

FAX: (608) 251-6846

EMAIL: info@wisconsincommunity
fund.org

WEB: www.wisconsincommunityfund.org

**Contact
Person**

Steven Starkey, Executive Director

Purpose

The Wisconsin Community Fund is a progressive foundation that supports organizing for social change and progressive nonprofit organizations throughout the state of Wisconsin with cash grants, comupter equipment, and technical assistance programs.

**Areas of
Interest**

The fund supports organizations based in Wisconsin that are involved in issues of Native American rights; environment and safe energy; Central American solidarity; gay and lesbian rights; peace and disarmament; mental health consumer advocacy; workers' rights; literacy; senior rights; multi-cultural education; sustainable agriculture and family farm preservation; anti-racist organizing and training; and sexual assault and domestic abuse prevention.

**Financial
Data**

(Year ended 6/30/01)	
Assets:	$ 210,000
Total grants paid:	$ 1,250,000
Number of grants paid:	525
Highest grant:	$ 100,000
Lowest grant:	$ 100
Median grant size:	$ 2,500

**Application
Procedures**

Applications are only accepted during the funding cycle which begins in August. A funding cycle is approximately four months long and the Wisconsin Community Fund currently has one funding cycle per year. The staff and Grant Allocation Committee determine whether the applications meet the funding guidelines. If the program described in the grant proposal is consistent with the fund's objectives and areas of interest, it is considered for funding. A grant application form includes an organizational section, narrative section, a budget section and requires proof of nonprofit status with the IRS.

Grant Limitations

WCF supports only social change groups working in Wisconsin that have federal tax-exempt status or a tax-exempt fiscal sponsor. The fund does not support projects that are individual, national, academic or religious in nature; social or community service, research, education or cultural projects, unless there is an organizing or direct action component; annual fund drives, endowments or capital campaigns.

Meeting Times

Meeting times vary each year for the Board of Directors and the Grant Allocation Committee.

Publications

The fund publishes a newsletter twice a year, an annual report, and brochures. WCF also has a program book/ad book for our annual banquet.

THE WOMEN'S FOUNDATION*

340 PINE STREET, SUITE 302
SAN FRANCISCO, CALIFORNIA 94104

or 3550 WILSHIRE BLVD., SUITE 610
LOS ANGELES, CALIFORNIA 90010

PHONE: (415) 837-1113
    or (213) 388-0485
FAX: (415) 837-1144
    or (213) 388-0405

EMAIL: info@womensfoundca.org

WEB: www.womensfoundca.org

Contact Person

Patti Chang, President and CEO
Patricia L. Murar, Vice President

Purpose

TWF suuports organizations that serve low-income women and girls throug-out California, primarily the fifty counties in northern and central California, and more recently, southern California and the Mexico side of the US/Mexico border. We fund programs for preventing violence against women and girls, girls' leadership, health, and economic justice. TWF targets programs that promote and protect the human rights of women and girls in the civil, politi-cal, economic, and social arenas. In addition to grantmaking, The Women's Foundation develops collaborations between individuals, organizations and institutions, who can combine their efforts towards creating the changes neccesary to achieving gender equality and social justice.

Areas of Interest

The Women's Foundation is commited to the following goals for all programs:

• Policy Change/Systems Change
  The Women's Foundation believes that many of the policies and systems in our communities, institutions and state are not designed to support the needs and interests of women and girls. Our goal is to transform systems and policies so that environments are created where women and girls may thrive. Proposals should focus on: promoting leadership among women and girls to increase their capacity to access resources and strengthen their communities; providing tools for organizations to build their constituency base by conducting meaningful outreach, developing new and effective organizing tools, mobilizing public opinion, and forging alliances with other organizations around a common agenda; or

*The Los Angeles Women's Foundation has now merged with The Women's Foundation of California.

advocating for a specific policy that would improve the lives of women and girls.

- Organizational Effectiveness

  The Women's Foundation supports the intentional work of organizations to strengthen and improve their internal capabilities to be more effective in achieving their mission and sustaining themselves over the long term.

  Our goal is to assist in creating strong, effective, sustainable, and stable organizations. Projects focused on organizational effectiveness may include, but are not limited to: board recruitment and training, strategic planning, development of financial systems, diversification of funding, and technological capacity building.

- Protecting and Promoting Human Rights

  It is The Women's Foundation's goal to support the protection and promotion of the human rights of women and girls in both access and equity in the civil, political, economic, social, and cultural spheres. Our partnership in the passage of San Francisco's historic Convention on the Elimination of All Forms of Discrimination Against Women (CEDAW) Ordinance, modeled after the United Nations CEDAW, made the city the first in the U.S. to support the implementation of the Convention's underlying principles on a local level. Projects focused on protecting and promoting women's rights may include, but are not limited to the issues of: domestic violence, reproductive health access, immigrant rights, economic security, health, lesbian rights, racial justice, and environmental justice.

**Financial
Data**

> (Year ended   / /)
> Assets: NA
> Total grants paid:
> Number of grants paid:
> Highest grant:
> Lowest grant:
> Median grant size:

**Application
Procedures**

Applicants should write or telephone the foundation and request guidelines and application forms. Deadlines vary from year to year so applicants should check with the foundation regarding forthcoming deadlines. The Women's Foundation awards grants ranging in amounts from $5,000 to $30,000. For work of a longer duration, an additional one to two years of funding, for a total three-year period, will be considered for a select number of established projects and organizations previously funded by the Foundation. We make general operating and project-specific grants. We give serious consideration to requests for start-up grants, especially for emerging issues and new organizations. Funding for publications and one-time events such as retreats and conferences will only be considered if they are integrated within a larger strategy for social change.

To be considered for a grant, an organization must:
- Benefit low-income women and girls in California
- Have tax-exempt status or a fiscal sponsor
- Have submitted final reports/financial accounting from any past Women's Foundation grant

Grant Limitations

The foundation does not fund direct services. Grants are not usually made to organizations with budgets over $500,000. We do NOT fund capital improvements, endowments, loans, individuals, debt reduction, expenses that occur prior to the date of the grant award, or fundraising events. Size and amount of grants vary by specific fund.

Meeting Times

The allocations committee meets twice a year, in the spring and fall.

Publications

The foundation publishes an annual report and a quarterly newsletter, and provides funding guidelines and application forms upon request.

WOMEN'S FOUNDATION OF MINNESOTA

155 FIFTH AVENUE SOUTH, SUITE 900

MINNEAPOLIS, MINNESOTA 55401-2549

PHONE: (612) 337-5010

(888) 337-5010 (in Minnesota)

FAX: (612) 337-0404

EMAIL: contactus@wfmn.org

WEB: www.wfmn.org

Contact Person

Nancy Smith, Senior Program Officer

Purpose

Women's Foundation of Minnesota adds power to women and girls organizing for economic, political, and social equality, by providing resources and a vital voice for their cause.

Areas of Interest

The Women's Foundation of Minnesota supports programs, projets, groups, and organizations within the state of Minnesota that are directed toward changing the underlying causes of gender discrimination. Grants are made in the following area:

1) Social Change/Systems Change

Projects by and for women and/or girls designed to have a significant impact on societal attributes and behaviors, or results in needed systemic change benefitting women and girls are of primary focus. In other words, projects which extend substantially beyond the women and girls immediately involved in the projects. Grants in this area may be made to grassroots groups or more established organizations.

2) Grassroots Empowerment

Grants are available to help people bring together previously unorganized, traditionally underserved groups of women and/or girls as an initial organizing step in the process of social/systems change. Grants in this area are generally limited to grassroots groups and organizations.

3) Women, Money and Social Change

Grants are intended to fund new and innovative efforts that will stimulate giving and increase support for organizations, projects and efforts benefitting women and/or girls. Projects and programs should be innovative educational or advocacy efforts to increase the support of policy makers, funders and the general public for organizations and efforts by and for women and girls.

Funds are provided for start-up costs, program and project support, general operating support and technical support.

Financial Data

(Year ended 3/31/01)	
Assets:	$ 10,580,426
Total grants paid:	$ 411,100
Number of grants paid:	53
Highest grant:	$ 50,000
Lowest grant:	$ 500
Median grant size:	$ 7,757

Application Procedures

The deadline for receipt of the grant application is March 1. Please note that proposals must be received in the Women's Foundation of Minnesota office by the due date. Grant decisions are made in approximately five months. Staff can be reached at 612-337-5010, or toll free in Minnesota at 888-337-5010, if you have any questions about the guidelines, application, or review process.

Meeting Times

The board meets bi-monthly.

Publications

The foundation publishes an annual report, newsletter, and grant guidelines and application.

WOODS FUND OF CHICAGO

PHONE: (312) 782-2698

FAX: (312) 782-4155

EMAIL: application@woodsfund.org

WEB: www.woodsfund.org

316 N. Michigan Avenue

Suite 1600

Chicago, Illinois 60601-3809

Contact Person

Ricardo A. Millett, President

Purpose

The Woods Fund of Chicago seeks to strengthen the community by improving opportunities for people in Chicago. The fund supports a wide range of nonprofit activities that include issue analysis, public policy development, advocacy, and citizen participation in efforts to improve the functioning of the city and its neighborhoods.

Areas of Interest

The foundation's two funding priorities are community organizing and public policies that affect families. Two other areas of interest are the Chicago school reform and government accountability. The fund's grantmaking is not limited to these specific issues. A listing of grants (available in the annual report) reveals a wide range of support and the funding patterns of the foundation. Nonethless the major grantmaking priorities are:

• Community organizing. Community organizing that develops independent, community-controlled organizations that elect their own leaders and determine their own issues and approaches—as opposed to community outreach efforts to recruit participants into a planned initiative. The fund welcomes proposals from new and emerging as well as well-established community organizations.

• Public policies affecting families. Projects focusing on public policies affecting the employment possibilities for Illinois' poorest residents. Specifically the foundation has been most interested in welfare-to-work policies. The fund encourages policy-oriented proposals from community-based as well as larger organizations, from recipient groups, local job creation and economic development practitioners, and from people recommending both policy improvements and strategies for getting them implemented.

• School reform. Organizations working to make public school reform in Chicago a reality.

• Government accountability. Civic and community groups building more responsive and accountable relationships between citizens and public institutions intended to serve them.

In addition the fund has awarded grants for projects in public policy and planning, housing, jobs and economic development; justice, governance and equal opportunity; pre-collegiate education; the performing arts; and the arts and humanities.

Financial Data

(Year ended   /   /   )
Assets: NA
Total grants paid:
Number of grants paid:
Highest grant:
Lowest grant:
Median grant size:

Application Procedures

Applicants should request a copy of the fund's guidelines, procedures, and timetable. Applicants should either submit a two-page summary request and budget or telephone the foundation to determine the viability of proceeding with a full proposal.

If a proposal is requested, the outline provided in the fund's annual report should be used by the applicant as a guide and checklist.

The timetable for submitting proposals is as follows:

Submission Dates	Board Meeting
March 1 - April 15	June (includes all arts proposals)
June 1 - July 15	September
September 1 - October 15	December

Proposals that arrive well before the deadline have a better chance for careful review. Proposals neither clearly within the fund's priority areas, nor clearly ineligible, are screened by the fund's local board members. If at least one board member seeks board meeting discussion of the proposal it can be considered for funding.

Grant Limitations

Grants are limited to organizations in metropolitan Chicago. Occasionally the fund reviews proposals from outside the city if the proposed activities have statewide impact or are designed for wide application. The fund will not consider: fundraising benefits or program advertising; individual needs; endowments; scholarships or fellowships; residential care, treatment programs, clinics, or recreation programs; social services, except special projects with a clear public policy strategy or projects expressly planned for wide duplication; health care institutions; medical or scientific research; national health, welfare, educational, or cultural organizations or their state or local affiliates; or religious programs.

Meeting Times

The board of trustees meets four times a year, in March, June, September, and December.

Publications

The fund publishes an annual report and application guidelines.

AN OVERVIEW OF THE NONPROFIT SECTOR
THE RANGE OF THE NONPROFIT WORLD

BY DANIEL L. KURTZ*

There exists no wholly reliable census of the number of nonprofit organizations nationally. The Internal Revenue Service, the most comprehensive collector of data in this field, treats as nonprofit more than two dozen distinct varieties, a total of almost 800,000. And this figure excludes most churches and many other religious organizations, the addition of which would increase these numbers by almost 50 percent.

Even within the 300,000 or so charitable nonprofits, there is an almost bewildering variety of types and sizes. On the one hand, there are the major exemplars of America's high civilization: the grant-making foundations with vast endowments, our preeminent educational institutions, the largest, most complex, and sophisticated centers for medical care and research, the leading institutions of both established culture and experimentation in the arts. On the other hand, there are the myriad community-based organizations, grass-roots providers of social services, day care, housing for the poor, job training.

Charity is practiced in the religious activities of millions of Americans on a daily basis; it channels enormous sums of money into research on, and the treatment of, every conceivable psychological and somatic ailment. And there is that uniquely American phenomenon—what we now call advocacy organizations—first identified by de Tocqueville in his observation on our propensity to associate for the promotion of a cause. Whether it has been temperance, nuclear disarmament, opposition to slavery, or the right to work, advocacy organizations have been and continue to be at the forefront of virtually every public issue.

From an economic perspective, nonprofits produce a dazzling array of goods and services. Although still largely unmeasured, their contribution is substantial; total nonprofit revenues may well approach $200 billion nation-

---

*Daniel L. Kurtz has specialized in nonprofit corporate law for the last thirty years. Before going into private practice he was Assistant Attorney General-in-charge of the Charities Bureau in New York. Reprinted with permission from *Board Liability: Guide for Nonprofit Directors,* Moyer Bell, 549 Old North Road, Kingston, RI 02881.

ally, and total nonprofit assets are substantially higher. Nonprofits dominate certain occupational and geographic markets. In particular fields, nonprofit organizations are major employers—for example, almost 15 percent of professional and technical employees work for nonprofits and in particular industries—educational services for example—nonprofits account for as much as 90 percent of all jobs.

In recent years, a number of theories have been proffered by legal scholars, philosophers, economists, sociologists, and others to account for and to explain nonprofits. Some see them as filling interstices in the free market economy, while others see nonprofits as functioning essentially outside the free enterprise system. Fortunately, for our purposes, it is not necessary to resolve this increasingly complex debate. As stated by Lord McNaghten in the nineteenth century:

> "Charity" in its legal sense comprises four principal divisions: trusts for the relief of poverty; trusts for the advancement of education; trusts for the advancement of religion; and trusts for other purposes beneficial to the community not falling under any of the preceding heads.

The fourth of these common law categories—of public benefit—is universally recognized as the key to defining charitable activity and "may be applied to almost anything that tends to promote the well-doing and well-being of social man."

The Essential Characteristics of Nonprofits

Almost all charitable organizations are created under the separate legal systems of the fifty states and the District of Columbia. While there are differences from state to state, most state laws provide for: (1) the limitation of activities to the pursuit of specified objectives benefiting the public (the "mission"), and (2) the prohibition on the distribution by nonprofits of any earnings or profits for private purposes (the "nondistribution constraint").

Some states permit the incorporation of charitable organizations with a charter proclaiming only a simple general statement of purpose; others require greater specificity. However, even those organizations formed with only a "general purpose" clause will have to submit a detailed description of proposed activities when seeking tax exemption from the Internal Revenue Service. Virtually all state laws and the Internal Revenue Code impose some variation of the nondistribution constraint on nonprofit activities.

The "mission" and the "nondistribution constraint" largely define the character of nonprofit organizations. The importance of the relationship between organizational objectives and board conduct can be seen most clearly by a comparative examination of the nonprofit organization with the business corporation.

Profit-Making and Nonprofit Corporations

As described in a landmark study of corporate governance, the "business corporation is an instrument through which capital is assembled for the activities of producing and distributing goods and services and making investments . . . with a view to enhancing corporate profit and shareholder gain." This prescription marks them off from nonprofit corporations, where there are a multiplicity of specific missions. Shareholders, by and large, do not care whether the objectives of a business enterprise are met by making widgets or wickets, cars or cucumbers.

The current trend in corporate nomenclature emphatically underscores this point. Today, for example, American Tobacco is American Brands, International Harvester is Navistar, and U.S. Steel is USX. The kind of business actually pursued is almost irrelevant. The corporation simply becomes a means to attain superior financial results, not an industry specific end. For nonprofits, while there is legitimate and increasing concern with financial performance, the pursuit of particular objectives—the "mission"—remains paramount, even when it is not legally binding.

The ability to ascertain progress toward attaining objectives also is a critical difference between business and nonprofit organizations. Business activities are uniformly translated into a "bottom line." For nonprofits, there are no adequate measurements of the key nonfinancial objectives. No one measurement of performance or even series of measurements can tell a university how well it is doing its job, or an environmental organization what its influence is on the quality of the environment much less on public discourse. Consequently, whether directors are doing their jobs capably is not always easy to judge.

The pursuit of profit-maximizing behavior by business organizations is an obligation due only to the corporation's shareholders. Shareholders may subordinate this pursuit to allow for social objectives (like corporate philanthropy). However, unlike business organizations, which are owned by their shareholders collectively, *no* individual has a proprietary interest in nonprofits. The general public is the ultimate beneficiary of the activities of charitable organizations. It is the public—that broad yet undefined class—that benefits from the goods and services that nonprofits provide. When fundamental nonprofit objectives are altered, the participation and assent of some representative of the general public—for example, a state attorney general—and the agreement of a court may be required.

The use of the corporate form by charities has many advantages. Apart from tax-based considerations, incorporation solves many of the same problems that it does for private entrepreneurs: limited liability, organizational continuity, administrative convenience, familiarity, etc. However, there are fundamental differences in the two distinct types of endeavors. The business corporation remains our dominant form of economic organization and the preferred instrument for capital formation; nonprofit corporations, while also needing capital to sustain their activities, pursue a multitude of goals.

PLANNING FOR FUNDRAISING

BY TRICIA RUBACKY*

Successful fundraising begins with a clear organizational mission and people committed to achieving it. These ingredients are critical; without them, your attempts to raise money will surely suffer. Assuming your organization satisfies these basic conditions, my advice is to follow these three commandments of fundraising:

I. Thou shalt always plan, plan, and plan some more;
II. Thou shalt always strive for a diversified fundraising plan;
III. Thou shalt tie thy program and budget planning to thy fundraising planning.

The information on funding sources in this book can prove lucrative for your organization. However, without careful planning, your investment in grantseeking can have disappointing—even disastrous—results.

A frequent complaint from grantseekers is: "I sent in all these proposals and I haven't heard anything from the foundations. We're headed for a financial crisis if we don't hear something soon!" This is the classic "blame the funder" approach, which you should decide right now to abandon. It assumes it is up to the foundations to prevent your funding problems.

A plan alone cannot solve a financial crisis. However, it can help prevent one, because it incorporates the steps you must take over a prescribed period of time, the strategies you can employ to make your program attractive to a variety of funding sources, and the internal back-up systems for times when your strategies and plans fall short.

A fundraising plan is much more than a list of funders and amounts requested. A real plan reflects an income goal that is tied to your organization's program goals and incorporates the following components:

---

*Tricia Rubacky, a consultant and trainer in fundraising and development, is Senior Development Advisor for the Center on Budget and Policy Priorities, Washington, DC.

(1) A list of all sources from whom you are seeking funds (both grant and nongrant fundraising) organized by likelihood of support and priority of effort;

(2) A calendar including all deadlines and a follow-up schedule;

(3) An income projection based on likely funding; and

(4) A cash flow projection.

The most successful fundraising plans also demonstrate a commitment to diversified fundraising. Diversity in fundraising prevents organizational over-dependence on one source of funding (e.g., foundation grants or direct mail), and provides a greater margin of safety for those inevitable times when circumstances prevent one source from continuing its support. In addition, dependence on a single type of fundraising limits your group's exposure in other arenas—exposure which is necessary to achieving familiarity needed for attracting new support. It is true that considerable organization resources must be used to achieve funding diversity; however, it is also true that your organization's future could be in serious jeopardy without the stability provided by diverse income streams.

A good fundraising plan also produces important management benefits. It can forestall the need for crisis-mode fundraising and keep you informed of where you stand at all times. A plan helps you identify progress and anticipate problems, and it forms the basis for informed decisions and budget adjustments as new developments occur or new information is received. A plan also helps you set and balance priorities and avoid the pitfalls of competing goals and timetables. Finally, a plan helps build the organization's confidence in its fundraising capacity.

Step One: Goals and Timelines

Before making a plan, considerable preparation work is needed. First, you must have a ballpark idea of how much money you need to raise and when it is needed. This ballpark figure will help you build the plan, but it is important that the program and budget goals are informed by the fundraising plan and vice versa.

The most logical place to start is with the amount you raised during the previous year. Later, armed with a realistic estimate of what can be raised and from what sources, you may decide that no increases for new programs are feasible. Or you may determine that adding to your program and budget is feasible in light of your fundraising potential and the time and resources you have available for raising the funds. Before committing to a budget and a fundraising plan all the people involved in your program, including financial managers, fundraisers and members of your governing board, should review the plan and reach agreement that the goals are realistic and achievable.

Step Two: Identify Potential Funding Sources

The next step is to create a list of all the potential sources of income for your organization. Here are some possibilities to consider:

Grant Fundraising. Sources of grants include corporations, foundations, government programs, religious organizations, and individuals who make grants through philanthropic institutions, labor unions, or professional associations.

Nongrant Fundraising. This fundraising can be grouped in two categories, as follows: (1) Individual solicitation, including personal requests, phonathons, telemarketing, mail appeals via the media (radio or telethons), workplace and payroll deduction, special events, canvassing, and membership drives; and (2) Earned income, including sales of products, fees for services, and interest income.

While you may already be raising funds through a variety of means, as part of the planning process you must determine whether to try to raise more from current sources or to explore new avenues. Some combination of tested and untested sources is a positive goal for any organization if the resources are available to undertake new ventures. Before deciding, you need to do some research and learn as much as you can about both grant and nongrant fundraising. Armed with this information, you are in a position to determine what the potential is for your group.*

Step Three: Record Keeping

Once you have decided which avenues of support you will pursue, you need a system for managing the information you compile about these sources. Essential facts (such as contact person, address, phone number, deadlines, and board meeting dates) and strategy should be organized for every source you

---

*There are many excellent reference works available to help you formulate and diversify your fundraising program. Among the best are the books by Klein, Flanagan, and Seltzer, which are listed in the bibliography.

Figure 1. Fundraising Strategy Sheet

Name of funding source:

Address:

Telephone:
Fax number:

Contact person:

Other known staff/board members:

History of contact/funding:

Who can help us here?

Known interest areas:

Total annual grants: Average grant size:

Step 1:
    Results:

Step 2:
    Results:

Step 3:
    Results:

Notes from meetings, telephone calls, etc.:

are planning to approach. This information should be kept within easy reach at all times, either in a notebook or on a computer. (See Figure 1 for a sample strategy-sheet format.)

Basic information on individual contributors, whether major donors or members, should also be well organized in a profile book, a card file, or a computer data base. There are several good donor data-bases already developed and on the market, or you may want one customized for your organization's purposes. (See Figure 2 for a sample of a basic donor profile record.)

Figure 2. Basic Individual Donor Profile Record

Name:

Home address: Telephone:

Business address: Telephone:

Title/Occupation:

Preferred place for being contacted:

Personal/financial background information:

General philanthropic interests:

Any foundation connections?:

Who knows/can help us?

Donor history:

Date   Amount   Restricted/Unrestricted

The information system you devise should be easy to update regularly, since grantseeking requires you to handle many important details at once and you cannot afford to allow any to fall through the cracks. Indeed, the system itself is critical to developing and refining your strategy in approaching funders and should be considered among the most priceless tools of your plan. In addition, you need to establish a filing system on funders to provide new staff and board members with a sense of the organization's history with its funders, and with those from whom it has tried unsuccessfully to raise funds. This information is critical to the future relationship of organizations to their grantmakers, and holds many clues to understanding problems a group may be having raising funds from particular sources.

Step Four: The Calendar

The next component in organizing your fundraising is a calendar, preferably a fifteen-month calendar to plan fundraising for the year—since much of fundraising requires advance planning that you normally need to begin at least three months before your fiscal year even starts.

As you lay out your plan, keep the calendar nearby and fill in as many deadlines or dates for your fundraising activities as possible. You will add to the calendar and change it frequently throughout the year. The calendar will also help you decide whether new program activities can be added or must be deferred because they compete with each other or with other organizational activities. You may want to set aside a copy of your original calendar and go back to it at the end of the year to see how realistic it was as a planning tool.

Deadlines mean nothing unless they are accompanied by a work plan. Your next step, therefore, is to take the deadlines calendar and create another calendar for all the activities listed. Every aspect of your fundraising, including preparation of proposals, letters, printing newsletters, travel, board and committee meetings, individual meetings, events, and all follow-up should be built into the work plan calendar. If the work plan is mapped out using the same fifteen-month format, then, when you are ready, the fundraising and work plan calendars can be integrated and converted to whatever calendar system works best for you—six-month, three-month, one-month, or weekly.

Keep in mind, in order to be effective planning tools, the calendars must be developed in conjunction with your overall program and fundraising plans, incorporating enough of your organization's activity to know what will affect or drive your fundraising.

Step Five: Income Projections

A significant part of the fundraising plan is an income projection. Because budget and program decisions will be based upon the fundraising plan, extra caution must be taken not to overestimate the potential for funding from any source, whether a traditional one or an entirely new one. All income projections should be made according to likelihood rating based on your most informed judgment. For example, all things being equal, your potential for raising $45,000 from an annual event that always yields in that range should be very likely. However, before counting on that income, you must ask yourself if all factors that produced that level of response last year are unchanged. Maybe you have a different person or committee running the event, or maybe there is competition from another organization holding an event the same date. There could be increased opportunities that could enable you to raise more money. Use this kind of information to estimate your proceeds, and when in doubt, err on the conservative side.

In terms of foundation grants, try using a percentage likelihood method to gauge your income projection. Group the grant applications together in order of likelihood. Even if last year Foundation A made a $30,000 grant last year, and the year before also made a $30,000 grant, is it safe to assume Foundation A will renew again? Your answer must be based on your most recent information about the funder. Have you stayed in touch with them to know their impressions of your work? Does the foundation still fund groups working on the same issues? Has there been staff turnover at the foundation? Has anything happened that would affect their level of grants, or the timing of their grant cycles?

The point is that in order to anticipate income realistically you must have current information upon which to base your probability estimates.

The following hypothetical annual fundraising plan gives an idea how to approach this task. This hypothetical organization had a fundraising goal of $300,000 and the fundraising plan is laid out to illustrate how the groups will meet that goal.

Figure 3. Sample Fundraising Plan 1995

| Organization: | Women's Health Clinic | |
| Goal | $300,000 | Adopted 12/15/94 |

Sources	Income Projected	Notes
I. Grants	117,250	modest increase over 1994
Very Likely: (est. at 85%)		
Fnd. A $30,000		decision in April 1995
Fnd. B. 10,000		decision in May 1995
Fnd. C. 45,000		decision in June 1995
Sub-total	$85,000	
	x.75 = $72,250	

Sample Fundraising Plan continued on next page

Sample Fundraising Plan 1995 *(continued)*

Possible (est. @ 50%)			
Fnd. D. $50,000			decision in June 1995
Fnd. E. 25,000			decision in April 1995
Fnd. F. 15,000			decision in September 1995
	Sub-total	$90,000	
		x.50 = $45,000	
II.	Fees for Services	100,000	Assumes same service provision as 1994 Assumes no increase in fees
III.	Spring Event	45,000	4th yr of event; goal is $60,000
IV.	Annual Fund	30,000	Assumes increase of 10% over 1994
V.	Payroll Deduction Gifts	10,000	Assumes same as 1994; could go up if we improve publicity
VI.	Holiday Card Sales	13,000	Demand far exceeded supply in 1994; this assumes a 20% incease over 1994
Total Income Projection		**$315,500**	

This kind of plan enables an organization to evaluate its progress continuously, to monitor its fundraising successes and evaluate its program accordingly, and to correct for disappointments in a timely manner. As the fundraising plan is being drafted, the calendar should be developed alongside to make sure adequate time is allotted to achieve the fundraising plan.

A few rules in the preparation of income projections should be followed to increase their reliability.

1. Base percentages on an informed sense of what is likely, even if the sources in a category are only twenty-five to fifty percent likely.

2. Do not include "prospects" in the income projection. (A prospect is a source that is untried as well as one for which you have no reliable experience or information upon which to evaluate the probability of support.) Groups often become so caught up with efforts to raise funds from other categories of support that they never get around to the prospects list. Therefore, it is better to treat income from these sources as the funds to expand your program if they are raised. If prospects do not yield success, your existing program will not suffer if they were not included in your original income projection.

3. Once the plan is approved, do not change the placement of sources or the likelihood rating you assigned to each category. If you change the plan midyear, you will not be able to evaluate your original projections, nor will you be able to make informed judgments about expenditures during interim budget review periods.

4. Remember that you are developing a plan, and like any plan, it needs constant monitoring to determine progress. It is not a foolproof calculation and should not be considered immune to failure. Your projections may be wrong, but if they are, you will know what the impact will be relative to your other fundraising activity.

Step Six: The Income Cash Flow Projection

The last piece of the fundraising plan is the income cash flow projection. This is a necessary complement to the expense cash flow projection which your organization needs in order to meet monthly bills. To prepare your income cash flow projection, begin with an accounting sheet with twelve columns. List all the sources of income on your fundraising plan down the left side, and label the top of each column with the names of the months. (See Figure 4.)

Then, go over your potential sources and make a realistic and conservative projection of when grants might be expected, when income from individual contributions is likely to be received, when the proceeds from sales and events are possible. Put the conservative projected amount in the column under the month the income is anticipated.

It will soon be obvious which months will be your high income months and which will be low. This will help you plan your expenses, especially those which can be deferred or spread over time.

As you can see from the sample, none of the prospect income is included in the cash flow plan. Because you have not made an income projection for the sources in that category, you should not include those sources in the cash flow plan. You should also exercise caution with some of sources you have categorized as "possible." It may be advisable to project less income or to put the projection later in the year when it is not as vital. While this conservative approach means that your cash flow projection will not equal your income projection, this is a precautionary measure to prevent over-extending your organization's cash flow.

Figure 4. Sample Income Cash Flow Projection 1995

	Jan.	Feb.	Mar.	April	May	June	July	Aug.	Sept.	Oct.	Nov.	Dec.
Foundations												
Fnd A					15,000							15,000
Fnd B						10,000						
Fnd C							30,000					
Fnd D							25,000					
Fnd E						12,500						
Fnd F										7,500		
Fees for services	8,000	8,000	8,000	8,000	8,000	8,000	8,000	8,000	8,000	8,000	10,000	10,000
Individuals/Events												
Spring Event			5,000	20,000	20,000							
Payroll Deduction Campaign			1,000	1,000	1,000	1,000	1,000	1,000	1,000	1,000	1,000	1,000
Annual Fund									6,000	5,000	12,000	7.000
Product Sales												
Holiday Cards										3,000	5,000	5,000
Total	8,000	8,000	14,000	29,000	44,000	31,500	64,000	9,000	15,000	24,500	28,000	38,000
	Jan.	Feb.	Mar.	April	May	June	July	Aug.	Sept.	Oct.	Nov.	Dec.

You should regularly adjust the cash flow plan based on new information about your funding sources and the projected outcomes of fundraising events. Constant oversight of income and expenses is one way of preventing a cash flow crisis, provided that the other facets of the fundraising plan are being followed carefully throughout the year.

Planning an organization's fundraising does not require sophisticated systems. All the suggestions offered here are, rather, means to help keep fundraising efforts organized. They are simple to use, and can be modified to meet an individual organization's particular needs. While planning alone cannot guarantee fundraising success, it can do the next best thing: It can enhance the organization's capacity and bring order to what is too often an overwhelming process.

FUNDRAISING FROM INDIVIDUALS

BY KIM KLEIN*

There are two broad sources of funds for America's nonprofit organizations: the public sector, which is all types of government funding, and the private sector, which is made up of foundations, corporations, and individuals. Surprisingly, ninety percent of the money donated by the private sector is given by individuals.

Every year, the American Association of Fund Raising Counsel (AAFRC) compiles and analyzes philanthropic giving by the private sector from the previous year. For the past thirty-five years that AAFRC has compiled these figures, the percentages have varied by only one or two points, and have consistently shown that ninety percent of the money given away by the private sector took the form of donations and bequests from individuals. Figure 1 illustrates private sector giving for 1992, the latest year for which figures are available.

Who Are These Individuals?

Many studies have profiled the people who tend to be donors. Some surprising facts have merged. One of the most recent studies, conducted for the Rock-

Figure 1.

Contributions (in billions)		Contributions as Percent of total	
Individuals	$101.83	Individuals	81.9%
Bequests	8.15	Bequests	6.6
Foundations	8.33	Foundations	6.7
Corporations	6.00	Corporations	4.8
TOTAL	**$124.31**		

SOURCE: American Association of Fund Raising Counsel, *Giving USA*, 1993

---

*Kim Klein is a fundraising consultant specializing in individual donor programs for small nonprofits. She is the author of *Fundraising for Social Change* and the publisher of the *Grassroots Fundraising Journal*. She lives in Berkeley, California.

efeller Brothers Fund by Yankelovich, Skelly and White, showed that households with incomes of $50,000 and over (13 percent of all households) gave 37 percent of the total given, while 63 percent came from households with incomes of $50,000 and under.[1] A 1985 United Way study showed that 85 percent of all money contributed by individuals came from households with incomes of $50,000 and under.[2] Organizers and service providers who work with low income people bear out the fact that generosity increases with lack of resources. Measured as a percentage of income, poorer people give away much more income than wealthy people do. Although the precise figures vary from study to study, the conclusion is the same: It is the middle class and below that give away the most money in America.

Studies consistently show that even among the very wealthy, tax advantages for giving are the least important factor in deciding whether or not to be a donor. In her book, *America's Wealthy and the Future of Foundations*, Teresa Odendahl describes a study done by Eugene Steuerle. Steuerle showed that wealthy people tended to retain their assets during their lifetimes, making their largest contributions as bequests. Odendahl remarks: "This pattern of wealth retention is remarkable in light of the fact that lifetime giving offers more tax advantages than do bequests. In effect, the rich hold on to wealth that they will most likely never consume, and they pay a greater price for it. . . . The wealthy tend to show a preference for wealth-holding itself, regardless of the tax consequences."

Other studies show that people who attend religious services tend to give more to all charities than people who do not. In 1984, according to Yankelovich, Skelly and White, 86 percent of people attending religious services made 94 percent of the total contributions to all charities.[3]

A great deal has been written about the $9 trillion transfer of wealth that will take place over the next two decades as baby boomers come into inheritances. Many nonprofits hope to be the beneficiaries of some percentage of this money and probably many will. However, it would be foolish to count on that money in any way. Many other sectors have their eye on it, such as the government, insurance companies, the health care industry and the like. Much of that money will be used to finance the chronic and acute health care needs of an aging population. It is also unclear what percentage of that money will come to people for whom giving away money is a value.

---

[1] Yankelovich, Skelly and White, Inc. In *Giving USA*. (New York: American Association of Fund Raising Counsel, 1987).
[2] *Grassroots Fundraising Journal*. (Knoxville, August, 1987).
[3] Yankelovich, Skelly and White, Inc.

However because the prime giving ages are 35–64, and more and more people are entering that age bracket, we can expect giving by individuals to increase through the next decade.

Where Did This Money Go?

AAFRC divides nonprofits into eight broad categories and analyzes amount and percent of giving to each. These categories and the 1992 figures for each appear in Figure 2.

The vast majority of private sector funding goes to religion. Religious institutions—primarily churches—raise money through a combination of three basic techniques:

1. Churches ask for money constantly.
2. Churches encourage everyone to give. If you have $1.00 to give, they encourage you to give it. If you have $1 million, you are equally encouraged. No gift is too small or too ostentatious.
3. Churches provide a variety of places to give. You are expected to give not only to the general collection but also to overseas missions, the building fund, flowers for the sanctuary in memory of someone, the soup kitchen or homeless shelter run out of the church basement, and the local shelter for battered women as a domestic mission of the Women's Group.

None of the above techniques are restricted to religious institutions. Any organization can request funds, encourage donors to give as much as they possibly can, and ask for additional gifts for special programs all year long.

Figure 2.

Distribution (in billions)		Distribution as Percent of total	
Religion	$56.71	Religion	45.6%
Education	14.02	Education	11.3
Undesignated	12.56	Undesignated	10.1
Human Services	11.57	Human Services	9.3
Health	10.24	Health	8.2
Arts, Culture	9.32	Arts, Culture	7.5
Public/Society Benefit	5.04	Public/Society Benefit	4.1
Environment	3.12	Environment	2.5
International	1.71	International	1.4

SOURCE: American Association of Fund Raising Counsel, *Giving USA*, 1992.

Basic Principles

Four basic principles govern all fundraising, and can be extrapolated from organizations with successful fundraising records. These principles are as follows:

1. People give out of self-interest.

Your organization is a business. Perhaps it is incorporated and has tax-exempt status from the federal government as a Section 501(c)(3) or Section 501(c)(4) organization. Certainly, someone must keep track of money coming in and going out, and provide budgets, financial reports, and so on. From a fundraising standpoint, the fact that your organization is a business means that your donors are customers who "buy" your "products," which are your services, your organizing, your advocacy, or whatever it is you do.

People will give their money to your organization when it serves their self-interest to do so. Some rewards of giving to support social change are that a donor helps to move the world a little closer to his or her vision of what it should be. Maybe a local situation is changed and the "little guys" win. Or maybe the donor is recognized by friends as a generous or caring individual. Sometimes self-interest is more direct: the donor's water is cleaned up, the donor's candidate wins, the donor is no longer discriminated against because of sex, race, or sexual orientation.

The first task in effective fundraising is to figure out the different rewards donors will have if they give to your group. Each donor will have multiple motives, and donors will have different motives from each other. However, if you do not touch on one of their motives, you will not get your gift.

2. Fundraising is a long-term process.

It is not enough to get a donor to give; we must always be thinking about how to get that person to give again, to give more, to encourage friends to give, and to become involved. The first gift is just that. As you develop strategies to raise money, you need to balance your fundraising plans by including some strategies whose main purpose is to bring in new donors (i.e. direct mail, special events, canvassing) as well as strategies to encourage donors to give bigger gifts (i.e. personal solicitation, pledge programs) and strategies to encourage donors to give several times a year (i.e. special mail appeals, phonathons, house parties).

3. Personal contact is most effective.

In general, the most effective strategies for raising money involve personal contact with the donor. The most effective specific strategy is for one person to ask someone he or she knows in the context of a personal visit. As a rule, the closer you get to the donor, the more likely you are to get the gift.

4. Diversify funding sources.

To implement principles 1, 2, and 3, you need two things: diversified sources of funding and an active volunteer force involved in fundraising. (An active volunteer force means five or more people committing eight to ten unpaid hours a month to your organization. For service organizations, this group of people would be in addition to hotline volunteers, crisis counselors, and so forth.) This volunteer force should be generally led by the main decision-making body of the organization. An organization cannot maintain successful diversity without also having a large number of people working on fundraising. Further, an organization that relies on one or two people, whether paid or volunteer, to do all the fundraising is no more secure than an organization with only one or two funding sources. The same things happen to people that happen to funding sources: they die, they move, they move on, they get mad, they run out of energy, or they change their priorities.

Summary of Basic Principles

Successful fundraising is built on marketing and sales principles, facts of life that sometimes make progressive people and organizations queasy.

It is important to understand that like money itself, marketing and sales are neutral. Positive values and behavior can be marketed, such as wearing seat belts, or practicing safe sex. Important "products" can be "sold" such as a bilateral, verifiable nuclear arms freeze, or pay equity. "Abolish Apartheid" is as much a sales slogan as "Coke Is It."

There are now 1.2 million registered 501(c)(3) and (c)(4) nonprofit tax-exempt corporations in America,[4] and up to eight million organizations that may not have any kind of tax exemption.[5] With all these groups raising money, there is a great deal of competition for the billions of dollars available. As more and more organizations are forced to raise private sector dollars to replace previous federal funding, the competition increases every day. The organizations that will survive and grow in the next few years will be those who apply the adage "Work smarter, not harder" to their fundraising by implementing effective fundraising techniques.

Fundraising Strategies

The rest of this chapter will describe briefly the most common fundraising strategies. All these strategies involve, to varying degrees, identifying pros-

---

[4]*Non-Profit Times*. Vol. 1. Princeton: 1987.
[5]Carl Bakal, *Charity USA*.

pects and asking for money. There is really no such thing as fundraising if it does not involve these two points. Therefore, we begin the strategy discussion with them.

Identifying Prospects

A prospect is someone who is likely to give. A prospect is different from a stranger, and is not just a name. For someone to be a prospect, three things must be true of the person:

1. He or she must have the *ability* to make a gift. Part of prospect identification is to determine what size gift is possible and what strategy should be used in getting the gift.
2. He or she must believe in your cause or in something similar to your cause.
3. He or she must be known to the group in some way. The organization must have a way to contact the person.

When you have positive verifiable evidence of these three factors, you have a prospect. Depending on your strategy, your prospect may be an individual (for a major gift solicitation) or may be a part of a group that exhibits the above characteristics (all the donors to one group may be approached by mail for another group).

Asking for Money

Asking for money seems to be the great stumbling block to raising money, which is unfortunate since there is really no other way to raise money effectively. The reason why people find it difficult to ask for money is simple: we find it difficult to talk about money. If we can't talk about it, clearly we can't ask for it.

Most people in the United States are raised to think that it is rude to ask someone what her salary is or what he paid for his house. At the same time, most people are curious about other people's salaries or purchases, and will use alternative methods to find out.

Our attitudes are full of contradictions on the subject. On the one hand, we believe, "If you are a good person and work hard, you will get what you deserve." At the same time, we assert that you cannot measure a person's character by how much money he or she has. We fiercely maintain that money can't buy happiness while thinking that we would be happier if only we had more money. We claim: "Time is money," yet ask each other for time much more easily than for money, and do not value large gifts of time from our volunteers nearly as much as large gifts of money.

The inability to get money we need for social justice work comes, in great part, from the inability to ask for money. This is learned behavior. Children have no trouble asking for money, or anything else. We learn it, and we can retrain our thinking in order to raise the money we need for our work.

There are two things to remember in asking for money:

1. Success is *asking*. Whether you get the money or you don't is up to the prospect, not up to you. The only thing you can do is *ask*—ask straightforwardly and clearly, but *ask*. Failure in fundraising is a failure to ask.

2. Most people will say no. If you ask through a direct mail appeal, up to ninety-nine percent of the people will not respond; in a phonathon, up to eighty-five percent of the people will turn you down; and even in the most successful strategy, the personal visit, up to fifty percent of the people will say no.

Fundraising is a numbers game. If you ask enough people, you will get your money. Once you know that your task is simply to ask and that you will get turned down some of the time, there is no longer anything to fear—and no longer any reason not to do it.

The Strategies

Personal Solicitation

First, identify your prospect. The prospect usually should have a giving ability of $50 or more because of the time involved in getting each gift, and should also be personally known to someone in the organization. He or she does not have to be known to the solicitor, but the solicitor will need to use someone's name to gain access to the prospect, i.e. "Fred Murphy gave me your name. . . ."

In the most formal approach, the solicitor writes the prospect a letter which says, in effect: "I am raising money for Good Organization. I would like to talk with you about being a major donor. I'll call you in a few days to see when we can meet." The letter is then followed by a phone call to set up the meeting, and the meeting to get the answer to the request. In each step, keep in mind the purpose of the step.

Step One: The letter is to tantalize the prospect. Don't say much about your organization. Simply tell the person you want to talk to him or her about making a gift, but ask the prospect, in effect, not to decide until you have had a chance to visit personally.

Step Two: The phone call is to set up the meeting. Sometimes the prospect will wish to make a decision on the phone, and you should accept graciously. However, you should offer to meet with all your prospects even if some of them give the money with just a phone call.

Step Three: The meeting's purpose is to ask for the money. The meeting, however, has been preceded by at least one, and perhaps two, indications that you are going to talk about money (the letter and the phone call). In the meeting, then, you don't focus on the prospect's money but on your organization, and why it is important. Remembering the basic marketing principle of the first part of this chapter, you should prepare for the meeting by thinking through why it is in this prospect's self-interest to support your group. What does he or she support now? Believe in? Whom does he or she want to look good in front of? What kind of self-image does he or she have? By thinking through these things, you can focus the conversation on the prospect's interests and concerns.

The most important aspect of each step is what is called "the close"— where you name what it is you want. In the case of the letter, it is simple. The close is "I'll call you to set up a meeting." Don't say "Call me if you want to meet" or "I'm hoping we can run into each other sometime."

The "close" of the phone call is "When can we meet?" Or "Tuesday is better than Wednesday for me. How is it for you?" Not "Shall we meet?" or "I was hoping that sometime we could see each other."

Clearly, the most difficult and critical close takes place in the meeting. At this close, the prospect will either become a donor or will reject your offer. You must decide if the prospect is ready to tell you a decision, and then you should look straight at him or her say clearly and distinctly, "Will you help us with $" and name an amount. After you say exactly what you want, you have nothing else to say, so be quiet.

The close must be specific and clear. Sometimes solicitors will claim that they asked someone for money but that they don't know what the person's response was. This is impossible unless the solicitor has amnesia or the prospect lapsed into a foreign language at the end. If you ask clearly and unambiguously, the prospect can only say "yes" or "no" or "I'll think about it." In the case of the latter, respect the person's need to think. Many people cannot make decisions in a hurry. However, set a time by which the thinking will be done. Say, "May I call you Wednesday?" Or "I'll call you next week if that will be enough time?"

The final point to clarify in individual solicitation is how the money will be paid. Let's assume you have asked for $1,000. The prospect says she would be delighted to give. After thanking her, you say, "How would you like to pay that?" The donor says, "I'll give you a check" or "I'll send stock or a check" or whatever.

The end of the whole interaction is a thank-you note.

Direct Mail

The purpose of direct mail, which means simply two hundred or more identical letters sent by bulk mail rates, is to acquire donors. Here the prospects are all of one group, and the group meets the three criteria, although each individual within the group may not. Also, the level of personal contact is greatly reduced. Your contact with these people is an address list.

Mass direct mail (sending ten thousand to one million letters) is generally not a strategy small social change organizations can or even should undertake. However, even the smallest group can compile a list of all the people they know, send that group a mail appeal, and ask the respondents for names of people they know.

There are three parts to a mail appeal: the "carrier envelope" (the outside envelope), the letter, and the enclosures (which are the return envelope and the reply device). Direct mail must be easy to understand and should carry an emotional message rather than relying on an intellectual grasp of the subject.

For organizations seriously considering direct mail, there are many good books available.

Special Events

Special events are the most common grassroots fundraising strategy and probably the most misunderstood. Special events such as dances, auctions, luncheons, walkathons, and so forth, should be used first to promote the organization, second to increase the overall visibility of the organization, and only third to raise money. For the amount of time they take, special events are an inefficient way to raise money, but they are the most efficient way (short of a media campaign) to get attention.

The variety of special events is almost limitless. Organizations contemplating or planning a special event should consult some of the many excellent books and articles on the subject.

Fundraising by Telephone

Telephone solicitation is rapidly becoming as common as direct mail appeals, but unfortunately is much more disliked by the public. Many people feel that phone solicitation is an invasion of privacy, and many people distrust phone solicitors, and thus the organization doing the phoning. Still, it is an effective way both to raise money and to teach volunteers how to ask for money directly in a less charged setting than a major gift solicitation.

Names of prospects are critical. To get names, send an appeal to your current donors and ask them for names, addresses, and phone numbers of people they think would be interested in your organization. Ask volunteers to bring the names of five people who they think would be interested but whom they are uncomfortable about asking for a large gift face-to-face. Those volunteers will trade names. Call all the people who gave you money last year but have failed to respond to renewal letters this year. Or call to follow up on a mail appeal.

Set aside a three-hour block of time, ideally six to nine on any evening from Monday to Thursday. Ask volunteers to come thirty minutes before the phoning for orientation and to stay thirty minutes afterward to finish up and clean up. Have in place: phones, lists of names, and instructions for handling gifts. Each volunteer should be able to call twenty people per hour, so you can figure out how many volunteers you will need for your prospects.

Provide volunteers with a script which they are free to adapt, a list of common and hard questions about your organization, and make them practice with each other. Let them know that most people will say no, and some will say it rudely. Success in a phonathon is a donation from about fifteen percent of the people reached.

Workplace Fundraising

Once the sole domain of the United Way, federated fundraising, or raising money through payroll deduction, is now being used by many alternative funds around the United States. The most well known of these are the Black United Funds, Womens Way in Philadelphia, and Community Shares in Knoxville, Tennessee.

The first step in workplace fundraising is to see if the United Way will accept your organization as an agency. if you are in social change or social justice work, the answer is almost certain to be no. However, if you are a service provider, you may have a chance. United Ways vary from community to community and are worth looking into. If the United Way says no, check to see if there are alternative funds in your community that you could join. If there are none, or you do not qualify, you can create your own federation.

Canvassing

Canvassing involves a team of people going door to door to request contributions for your work. Canvassing is used extensively by local groups and by local chapters of state or national organizations.

While part-time or temporary canvasses can be run with volunteers, most canvassing is a full-time operation involving salaried or commissioned employees who work forty hours a week and solicit in neighborhoods on a regular and revolving basis. Well-run canvasses can bring in $50,000 to

$500,000 or more in gross income. Because they are labor intensive, however, the high cost of most canvasses absorbs at least sixty percent of their gross earnings.

Canvassing works best when the organization has an issue that effects the people being canvassed, when that issue is easy to explain, and when the canvass is run in a metropolitan area. Although there have been rural canvasses, they have not lasted because of the distance between homes or towns, and the labor required to reach a small population.

Summary

There are dozens of other fundraising strategies, and within each of the strategies described here there are hundreds of variations and applications. Many people wonder how to choose a fundraising strategy. The first part of picking strategies is fairly simple: every organization, regardless of size, location, or age, should raise some money from personal solicitation, some from mail appeals, and some from special events. Every organization should use a variety of strategies, so it is not a question of picking one strategy, but picking several. In choosing which variation or application of a strategy, groups need to look at considerations such as volunteers available, amount of money needed and when, front money available, and other goals of the strategy (such as recruiting new donors or getting publicity).

The basics of individual donor fundraising are the same throughout all the strategies, and are simple and straightforward. To summarize, to raise money from individuals, you must:

1. Ask for it by name, clearly and boldly.
2. Know what the money will be used for, and make it clear that the donor is important to the success of the organization.
3. Ask for additional gifts during the year.
4. Use a broad base of volunteers led by the board of directors to do fundraising. It should not be a staff-dominated activity.
5. Use a wide variety of strategies to maximize visibility, the number of donors, and sources of income.
6. Remember that people give money when it serves their self-interest, and that fundraising is built on principles of marketing and sales.
7. Remember that success in fundraising is asking for the money; failure is a failure to ask.
8. Remember this old fund-raisers' saying, if you are having trouble talking about money: "If you are afraid to ask for money, kick yourself out of the way and let the cause talk."

REFERENCES

Achieving Excellence in Fundraising, Henry Rosso, 1991, Jossey Bass

America's Wealthy and the Future of Foundations, 1987, Teresa Odendahl, The Foundation Center

Chronicle of Philanthropy, bi-weekly publication, Chronicle Publishers, Washington, DC

Giving USA Annual Report, American Association of Fundraising Counsel

Grassroots Fundraising Journal, bi-monthly periodical, Chardon Press, Berkeley California

Fundraising for Social Change, Third Edition, 1994, Kim Klein, Chardon Press, Berkeley, CA

Grassroots Fundraising Book, update and revised 1992, Joan Flanagan, Contemporary Books

RESPONSIVE PHILANTHROPY

BY NATIONAL COMMITTEE ON RESPONSIVE PHILANTHROPY*

TRENDS IN PHILANTHROPY
MORE GROUPS, FEWER DOLLARS

You knew this, intuitively, as you struggled to make ends meet, but now we'll give you the facts behind your intuition. Giving fell behind inflation in 1993 [the most recent reportable year].

Despite a sluggish recovery economy, however, Americans did maintain a strong commitment to supporting nonprofit organizations in 1993, according to *Giving USA*, the annual report prepared by the American Association of Fund-Raising Counsel (AAFRC) Trust for Philanthropy. In total, individuals, foundations, and corporations granted $126 billion to nonprofits in 1993, an increase of 3.6% over 1992 giving.

Nevertheless, this increase lagged behind inflation, which jumped 3.9% in 1993, as measured by the Gross Domestic Product.

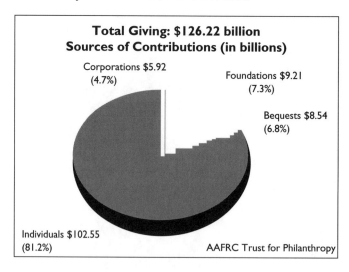

Total Giving: $126.22 billion
Sources of Contributions (in billions)

Corporations $5.92 (4.7%)

Foundations $9.21 (7.3%)

Bequests $8.54 (6.8%)

Individuals $102.55 (81.2%)

AAFRC Trust for Philanthropy

---

*Reprinted from *Responsive Philanthropy* (quarterly, $25/year), with permission from the National Committee for Responsive Philanthropy, 2001 S St. N.W., Suite 620, Washington, D.C. 20009.

Don't despair! There are some good economic signs for the future. Personal income grew 4.7% in 1993 and unemployment dropped to 6.4%, after a high of 7.7% in December 1992.

The $126 billion total charitable giving is about 2% of Gross Domestic Product, the total measure of the U.S. domestic economy. "This is a slightly higher percentage than the 1974–1985 period, and a slightly lower percentage than we saw in the 1960s and early 1970s, but giving has hovered at around two percent of GDP for decades," states Martin Grenzebach, Chairperson of AAFRC.

As usual, the largest share of philanthropic giving in 1993 came from individuals (living and by bequest), whose contributions accounted for $0.88 of every charitable dollar, or $103 billion. The remaining $0.12 of the charitable dollar came from foundations (7.3%) and corporations (4.7%).

576,000 501(c)(3) Organizations

Have you wondered why it seems harder every year to raise money even though private donations continue to rise every year? According to *Giving USA*, "We have been in the midst of a virtual explosion in the formation of new voluntary associations all over the globe."

In the U.S. *alone*, there were 576,000 501(c)(3) charities in 1993, an increase of about 80% since 1981. Additionally, there are nearly 600,000 other tax exempt entities registered with the IRS.

Also, have you ever wondered about so many nonprofits being small and a few huge? Actually, the 68% of nonprofits with assets under $500,000 receive only 5% of all nonprofit revenue. These numbers probably underestimate the situation, since they come from IRS 990 reports, which are not required of organizations with annual revenue under $25,000.

As for the big corporations, those with assets above $10 million (!) constitute only 5% of nonprofits but collect 79% of all revenue. (The middle 27% of nonprofits receives 16% of the revenue.) (See graph, p. 549)

Foundation Grants Up

At 7.3% of total U.S. private giving, foundation giving was at its highest percentage in a long while. One has to go back to the 1965–1974 period to find foundations with a stronger influence on the nonprofit sector. During that ten-year span, foundation giving ranged from 7.7% to 9.0% of all private giving.

Also noteworthy, foundation giving grew faster in 1993 then individual or corporate giving, increasing by 6.6% to $9.2 billion. Some of this increase may be attributed to the growth in foundation assets. According to a report by the Foundation Center, *Foundation Giving 1994*, foundation assets (excluding corporate foundations) grew eight percent in 1992, reaching $170 billion.

Community foundations, although accounting for only 1% of all U.S. foundations in 1991, made 6.2% of all foundation grants, received 12.4% of all gifts to foundations, and held 4.9% of all assets in 1992, according to the Foundation Center report. "These trends emphasize the significance of community foundations in philanthropy and the active role living donors are playing in community foundation growth," states *Giving USA*.

Fast expansion of foundation giving shouldn't set you racing to your computer to submit more and bigger proposals, however. Keep some perspective! Remember that a 50% increase in foundation giving over the past five years amounts to $3.0 billion, while a more modest 28% growth in individual giving over the same five years has put $22.5 billion more into nonprofit circulation.

Corporate Giving, No Change

Corporate giving at nearly $6 billion in 1993 remained at the 1992 level (and the 1991 level, and the 1990 level). But what a change eight years makes! In 1985, corporate giving amounted to 6.6% of all private donations, but by 1993 this percentage had dropped to 4.7%. That's almost a 30% drop in influence in the nonprofit sector.

The decline of corporate giving is even more striking when looking at corporate giving versus pre-tax income. Again, using 1985 as a base year, we see corporate income at $225 billion. By 1993 income had grown to $450 billion. That's exactly double in eight years. But growth of corporate gifts hasn't kept pace. From $4.8 billion in 1985, corporate donations went to only $5.9 billion last year. That's only a 23% growth in contributions compared to a 100% increase in pretax income. The Council for Aid to Education and the U.S. Department of Commerce supplied our numbers here, courtesy of *Giving USA*.

The amount company foundations donated to charities exceeded the amount they received from their parent companies, a pattern that has occurred in every year since 1986. According to *Corporate Contributions 1992* , a report published by The Conference Board, corporate philanthropy began declining in 1987 after steady growth in the mid-1980s. "Corporate restructuring, reorganization, divestiture, and downsizing, coupled with turmoil in the world and in the U.S. economy, have slowed annual contributions growth rates from double- to single-digits," states the report. "Contributions executives forecast virtually no growth in . . . 1994."

Meanwhile, corporate giving overseas has increased 500% in ten years, according to The Conference Board. The 1992 median overseas contributions budget was $589,000. But Hitachi Foundation estimates that Japanese corporate giving in the U.S., at $400 million, is about equal to U.S. corporate giving overseas.

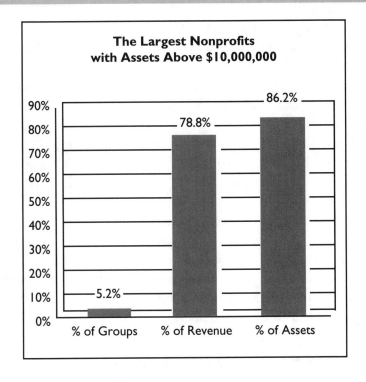

**The Largest Nonprofits
with Assets Above $10,000,000**

- % of Groups: 5.2%
- % of Revenue: 78.8%
- % of Assets: 86.2%

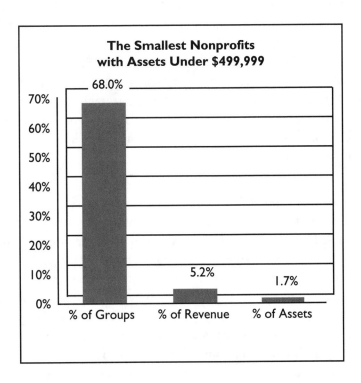

**The Smallest Nonprofits
with Assets Under $499,999**

- % of Groups: 68.0%
- % of Revenue: 5.2%
- % of Assets: 1.7%

Religious Giving Remains Tops

Contributions to religious causes consumed the greatest chunk of charitable giving in 1993. Giving to religious organizations reached $57 billion, which accounts for 45% of total giving. Giving to religious causes increased by 4.1% (only 0.2% after inflation). Religious contributions come primarily from individuals.

One explanation for the strong support religious organizations receive is their wide community involvement. Martin Grezebach, Chair of the AAFRC, explains, "Religious congregations are the hub of social change, community building, and health and human service provision. They are also active in the arts, in international affairs, in education, and in conservation activities."

In 1993, 92% of religious organizations surveyed for Independent Sector's report *From Belief to Commitment*, said they provided welfare and human services. Ninety percent said they provided health services. In addition, 62% reported providing services for public/society benefit, 53% for educational activities, and 40% for environmental programs.

Education, 40% Real Growth, 10 Years

Education was the last largest recipient after religion. Education giving over ten years has shown steady growth every year. In 1983, education got $6.7 billion of total private giving; in 1993 it received $15 billion, a 40% growth in real inflation adjusted dollars.

The report notes a marked interest in public school reform in 1993 educational giving. One such interest was demonstrated by Walter Annenberg, who in 1993 announced $500 million in education grants to organizations involved in reforming public elementary and secondary schools. The Annenberg Institute for School Reform, at Brown University, will administer the awards over a five-year period.

International Giving Up

The strongest percentage growth in contributions went to international affairs, which demonstrated an 8.5% increase (4.4% after inflation), bringing it to $1.9 billion. $380 million of that amount was pledged by George Soros towards education reform in the former Soviet Bloc countries.

"The increase [in giving to international affairs] comes amid a worldwide increase in the numbers of nonprofit or non-governmental organizations. The international nonprofit sector is growing in importance and numbers, a sign that organizations of this kind, when allowed to form, are natural components of civil society," according to the *Giving USA* press release.

Public Benefit, Human Services Both Up

Public/Society Benefit and Human Services both received a strong upsurge in contributions as well. Human Services, which garnered $12.5 billion, and Public/Society Benefit which totalled $5.4 billion, each had increases of 7.8% (3.7% after inflation).

The report states that the rise in Human Service funding might partly be attributed to the unusual number of natural disasters afflicting the nation in 1993. The long term picture of giving to Human Services, however, is grim. Such giving was only 10.8% of all giving in 1993. While this is a little better than the two previous years, it is far, far from the 16.8% figure posted in 1963, or even the 15% figures of 1969–1972.

The Public/Society Benefit category includes a wide range of organizations involved in public policy, community improvement, civil rights, and scientific research. Trends in this category are difficult to analyze because donors interested in social/community improvement may sometimes give to the health, education, or religion categories instead. In addition, the inclusion of scientific research in the category obscures research that may not necessarily be for the public good. The contribution of $65 million to the Houston Advanced Research Center (HARC) by the family of Houston oilman George P. Mitchell (Mitchell Energy and Development Corporation) raises such a question. HARC focusses on "research and technology development in energy, medicine, the environment, and related fields."

Community-Based Development Strong

A report by the Council for Community Based Development does, however, indicate improvement in the funding of community-based development programs. The study found that between 1989 and 1991 the number of funders rose 66%, reaching 512. Total grant support increased by 72% in that period, rising from $104 million to $179 million.

The long-term picture of Public/Society Benefit giving is quite opposite to that of Human Services. Public/Society Benefit giving is now 4.7% of all private giving, the highest percentage in 31 years (except in 1990, at 4.9%). The percentage had been only 2.5% in 1970 and 3.2% in 1963 (as far back as the data go).

Environmental and Arts Giving Down

Areas showing drops in 1993 funding after consideration of inflation were arts, culture and humanities, which fell by 1.2%, and environment, suffering a 1.7% drop. In 1992, environmental organizations had reported the largest rates of increase in contributions among surveyed organizations.

Both environmental and arts organizations were expected to benefit from the 1993 tax act, which restored the full deductibility of gifts of appreciated property, including both land and works of art. Since the value of land and art have not recently appreciated significantly, however, and because such gifts take a long time to arrange, it may be a while before the fruits of the tax law are evident.

Nevertheless, since separate records have been kept by *Giving USA* on both environmental and international giving, they have both gone up steadily as a percentage of total private giving. Environmental giving rose from 1.9% in 1989 to 2.8% in 1993, and international giving moved from 1.1% in 1987 to 1.6% in 1993.

Environmental Donor Surveys

Surveys conducted by Craver, Mathews, Smith & Company to determine what effect Bill Clinton's election would have on contributions to environmental causes found that giving had increased in the first quarter of 1993. Moreover, by April, more environmental donors (41% as opposed to 31% right after the election) said there would be a greater need to support conservation groups over the next four years. Only nine percent said the need would be less; all other respondents said it would remain the same.

The commitment donors are expressing may be explained by another survey finding. Immediately after the election, 71% of environment donors said they expected substantial gains in environmental protection in the next four years. By April that percentage had dropped to 49%.

Health Giving Unaffected

Health. In the news. Spotlight on health care by President Clinton, the First Lady, and Congress. But according to Grenzebach, Chairperson of the AAFRC Trust, "The 1993 numbers do not indicate that the debate about health care has affected giving."

A look at the long-term picture from 1983 to 1993 shows that giving to health has kept pace with inflation, but that's all. Health giving peaked in 1987–1988, when it was about 12–13% higher in inflation adjusted dollars.

One highlight of giving to health was AAFRC's cautious estimate that 1992 voluntary contributions to AIDS service organizations had reached between $575 and $850 million. That sum went to more than 18,000 programs.

References

Giving USA's 1994, the yearbook on philanthropy, for $45, prepaid, from the AAFRC Trust for Philanthropy, 25 West 43rd Street, Suite 820, New York, NY 10036.

CAPITAL AREA UNITED WAY OPENS ITS DOOR

New Opportunity or Uninformed Choice?

In 1994, the United Way of the National Capital Area in Washington, D.C. launched an unprecedented change in its workplace fund raising campaign. For the first time, United Way opened wide its doors to outside nonprofit organizations that wanted to be included in United Way's workplace fund raising drive.

In effect, United Way canceled the privileged membership status of its former recipient agencies and required all new and old members to compete on an equal basis for donor dollars. "We are market driven," explains Ken Unzinger, United Way's Director of Corporate Affairs. "We are giving donors what they asked for—a wide array of choices—and they will determine how the system works."

Traditionally, United Way in the District of Columbia, like all United Ways in the U.S., raised money for a limited number of organizations whose focus was health and human services. Undesignated donations were divided among member agencies by a United Way Citizens' Review Board.

Overall contributions have been dropping for United Ways since the 1992 scandal surrounding William Aramony, chief executive officer of United Way of America. It was revealed then that Aramony was receiving over $400,000 a year in salary and benefits, and that substantial funds had been transferred to spin-off organizations in which Aramony, his family, and top UWA officials had financial stakes.

The scandal created a crisis of confidence in United Ways, leading many potential donors to question whether United Way was really the best way to donate their workplace dollars. In 1992 United Ways' total contributions fell by 4.1%, the first decrease since World War II. Non-United Way charities, however, experienced a 5.3% increase in workplace contributions in 1992.

Undesignated donations, which United Way may distribute according to its own allocation process, have been steadily dropping as well. In the last 20 years, Capital Area United Way's undesignated funds fell from 85% to 30% of contributed money.

The Expanded Umbrella

In response to the growing trend of employees looking outside United Way to donate their dollars, United Way brought the outside in: 699 agencies participated in the fall 1994 campaign, in contrast to 270 the year before. The same eligibility requirements imposed by the U.S. Government's Combined Federal Campaign (CFC) were employed by United Way. "Employees have indicated that they are concerned about where their money goes," Unzinger says, "and we're selling them choice—the opportunity to make an intelligent decision about where to give their money."

Dropping the emphasis on health and human services opens the United Way of the National Capital Area campaign to many causes that were previously excluded, such as environmental conservation and protection, international relief and development, arts and culture, gay and lesbian rights and services, occupational health and safety, social justice advocacy, and national health issues.

Among the 699 charities that participated in the fall 1994 campaign, eight federations, both local and national, have signed up with the United Way campaign, including: Earth Share, Combined Health Appeal, United Arts Organization, International Service Agencies, United Black Fund, Independent Charities of America, Local Independent Charities, and National United Service Agencies.

A Question of Access

The issue, in the perspective of many newly joined federations, is one of access. Jeanne Oats Angulo, Executive Director of the Combined Health Appeal of the National Capital Area (CHA), explains, "Through the Combined Federal Campaign, we had access to 150,000 employees in the D.C. area. United Way gives us access to 600,000 more."

"The United Way campaign is an enormous opportunity for us," says Aldus Chapin, President of the United Arts Organization, "It takes us beyond the public sector into the private."

Employees in the private sector, often better-paid than government employees, present a particular draw. Arnold Swope, Deputy Executive Director of National United Service Agency (NUSA), explains, "There are roughly 55% of private employees, with good pay and job security, who do not give to anyone at work. By broadening the base of choice, we are hoping to offer more of these potential donors access to NUSA and its member charities."

Still Imperfect

The access that participation in the expanded United Way will provide is not considered perfect, however. United Way is printing 900,000 pledge cards that will contain an alphabetical list of all participating agencies, along with their phone numbers, and their CFC number.

But a twenty-five word description of each agency will not appear on the pledge card, as it does in the CFC brochures, meaning that donors without predetermined choices may be hard pressed to figure out what many of the listed agencies actually do.

Also, the alphabetical listing may frustrate donors looking for specific types of charities. For example, all health charities will be spread across the entire list rather than being grouped under their federation banner, the Combined Health Appeal, or if they are independent, simply being listed under a "health" category. "People will get an undifferentiated mass of agencies with no way for a donor to distinguish among them," says Kevin Ronnie, Director of Field Operations at the National Committee for Responsive Philanthropy. "The majority of donors won't have enough information to make an informed decision, and will be playing Pin the Tail on the Donkey."

Ken Unzinger replies that the alphabetical listing is donor driven. "It's designed for the case of the contributor," he says. "Contributors know what they want, and an alphabetical listing is the simplest way for them to find it."

A survey conducted by Independent Charities of America about CFC workplace contributing reveals, however, that 90% of donor/respondents do not know who they will give to before they open the CFC brochure.

United Way is printing a smaller number of directories similar to the CFC brochures, with twenty-five word blurbs describing the activities of participating organizations, an overhead percentage, telephone number, and CFC number. United Way has not disclosed how many of these directories will be printed. The ICA survey found that 93% of respondents felt the twenty-five word statements found in the CFC brochures were either "very important" or "important and helpful to donors."

"The cost of printing 900,000 directories is prohibitive," said a United Way official, "but we are doing everything we can to assist companies in getting information to employees."

The pledge card will give donors two options. They may write in the CFC number of any agency they choose from the attached list or they may check off one of nine local geographic districts in which they want their money spent. Specific agencies written in will directly receive the donors' contributions. They do not have to submit budget reports to United Way, nor open themselves up to site visits.

If a donor checks off a geographic district, his or her money will be channeled into a United Way Community Service Fund. UW volunteers will then determine where in the chosen community the money will be spent, after evaluating applications submitted from nonprofits serving that community. "In this way, United Way will continue to have its influence even in a campaign that will become a designated campaign," says Swope.

The Free Market Approach

The big challenge that federations will face is how to make themselves stand out amidst the nearly 700 competitors in the Capital Area United Way. Instead of promoting themselves as a concrete bloc made up of 15 or 30 units, federations will have to promote 15 or 30 fragmented units in a sea of hundreds of similar sounding units.

Some smaller local federations have decided that the costs of participating with United Way outweigh the benefits. The Environmental Federation of Maryland (EFM), a local federation serving twenty-one member groups, declined joining. "Participating would not be advantageous for us," says Jim Eacker, Executive Director of EFM. "If we list our members alphabetically, we'll lose them. A donor wanting to give to the environment will have to scan through hundreds of organizations. If the listing was by federation, it would be much easier because the total number of federations is small."

In addition, Eacker explains, EFM did not want to give up its listing as an independent federation in the CFC campaign. The Capital Area United Way will require local federations that join with United Way to list under United Way in the CFC. "It is clear that United Way is seeking to dismantle its competition," says Kevin Ronnie.

National federations in the CFC, however, are approved for participation directly by the U.S. Office of Personnel Management, not by United Way, and cannot thus be compelled to list under United Way.

Another concern of local federations is how to compete with national federations for D.C. dollars. Given that many national federations have their headquarters in Washington, D.C., and redistribute contributions nationwide, local groups fear that the District's needs may be overlooked. The United Way pledge card does not distinguish between national and local agencies.

Whatever the arrangement, "Any federation that thinks it can just sit back and wait for the money to come in is fooling itself," says Swope. "It is the responsibility of federations to make sure their member agencies are being promoted equitably in the campaign." NUSA is planning widespread advertising campaigns in metro stations, cafes, newspapers, and on the radio.

Foundations in the D.C. area are concerned about the haste with which United Way's new policy has been implemented. They fear being deluged with requests for grants from United Way's former member agencies. In a letter to Sheldon Fantle, President of United Way, The Meyer Foundation's President, Julie Rogers, and Chairman of the Board of Directors, Theodore Lutz, wrote, ". . . we are concerned that the affected agencies have not had enough notice to adjust to drastic changes in their budgets. . . . The Meyer Foundation has already received numerous proposals from agencies that anticipate being cut out of the United Way system under the proposed changes." Another foundation leader suggested that United Way should have had a phase-in period over the next few years, providing member agencies with decreasing funding and training before they were cut off entirely.

"As in every competitive market, there will be winners and losers. A flashy or well-recognized name is going to be the most important factor in this campaign," says Ronnie. The Northwest Settlement House, for example, lacking both a glitzy name and recognition, is the kind of charity that is likely to drown in the sea of agencies. The Settlement House, a former United Way member, relied on United Way contributions for 50% of its revenues. An all-inclusive social service agency providing cradle-to-grave services for the indigent community it served, the Settlement House lacks the money to launch a publicity campaign to promote itself. Ronald Wilmore, Director of the Settlement House, worries about its extinction. "How does a community lose an agency like this and still be safe?" he asked.

United Way has not provided any funds or services to help its former members through the transition, but claims that members have been warned for nearly ten years about the impending changes. Unzinger says that the Settlement House is an exception because two-thirds of United Way's former members got less than ten percent of their budget from United Way. "I think it's fair to assume that if this is really a deserving agency and if it serves a real need, then it should feel confident that it will be supported through the Community Fund," said Unzinger. Wilmore, however, worries about competition for community funds from other campaign participants, since so many more agencies are now eligible to apply.

CAUSE RELATED MARKETING: DOING WELL BY DOING GOOD?

American Express' Charge Against Hunger Campaign may be a model for cause related marketing, which has been greeted with skepticism and cynicism by some fundraisers since its inception. By putting aside two cents from every purchase made with an American Express card from October 5 to December 31 of last year [1993], American Express raised $5 million to go to groups fighting hunger in America.

Kmart, Century 21, Galleries Lafayette, and Liz Claiborne raised additional funds in a tie-in campaign with the Charge Against Hunger. Stevie Wonder made a personal contribution of $50,000 and Campbell's Soup Company donated 30,000 cans of food. According to American Express, many members expressed strong support for the entire initiative.

Cause Related Marketing, Risks and Benefits

Though this is the largest single amount raised to combat hunger in America, American Express is certainly not acting in a vacuum. According to the Cone/Roper Benchmark Survey on Cause-Related Marketing, 78% of respondents said they are more likely to buy a product that is associated with a cause they care about and 54% percent said they would pay more for it. In fact, one third of respondents said that after price and quality, a company's responsible business practices are the most important factor in deciding whether to buy its products.

In a highly competitive market, where products, like credit cards, are difficult to distinguish from one another, a progressive image can provide a powerful marketing edge. Ed Keller, Executive Vice President of Roper Starch Worldwide, which partnered with Cone Communications in the survey said, "To succeed in the 1990s, brands will aspire to people—products will have to meet not only the price and quality demands of consumers, but their personal values as well. Given that environment, cause related marketing is a dramatic way to build brand equity."

Cause related marketing (CRM) is also a chance for companies to compensate for their decline in traditional corporate philanthropy. According to a recent Conference Board report, corporate contributions have been dropping since 1985 (after inflation is taken into account), after their heyday in the early 1980s.

Yet nonprofits should pause before casting their lot with corporate America and the consumers of its products. Since CRM is a marketing strategy, corporations will make selections based on perceived attractiveness to customers rather than the needs of charities. Hunger, which, according to the

Congressional Hunger Center, is identified by over 90% of Americans as a problem, is likely to draw far more corporate interest than the more political issues related to empowerment of the poor, gays and lesbians, women, and minorities. The danger, as an Independent Sector survey of CRM indicated, is that "controversial, unappealing, or smaller causes lose out in attracting corporate sponsorships."

The Cone/Roper survey findings confirm this projection. Respondents indicated that corporations should be doing more to address the problems of crime, the quality of environment, and homelessness, and that enough has been done in seeking equal rights for minorities and women.

In addition, CRM may end up being just that: marketing. There is the danger that partnerships between companies and nonprofits may be disproportional, where the former uses the image of the latter for its promotions but gives little of substance in return. Bill Shore, founder and Executive Director of Share Our Strength, the hunger relief organization that administered the proceeds raised by American Express, says, "Cause related marketing has the potential to be a very positive thing, if it's doing something significant rather than giving away a very small amount."

Christine Vladimiroff, President and CEO of Second Harvest, a Chicago-based hunger relief agency, offers three criteria in judging a company's performance in a CRM campaign. First, she suggests, the company should be evaluated for truthfulness in its representation of the cause. Is the issue it is presenting exaggerated? Is the presentation distorted?

Second, the authenticity of statements made and figures used in the press should be verified. Is the company distorting a cause for marketing effect?

Third, the integrity of the process of grantmaking and reporting to the public should be confirmed. Is the company truly donating all or most of the money it raised for a cause to that cause? How closely does the allocation of funds correspond to what was advertised in the campaign? How open is the company to consumers and to the wider public in disclosing the results of grantmaking? Is the company showing any long term commitment to the cause it is sponsoring?

Charge Against Hunger

Applying these questions, this article began as an investigative piece to mercilessly uproot any irresponsibility, breach of ethics, or deceit in American Express' Charge Against Hunger campaign, yet could unearth no such evidence. In many ways, the Charge Against Hunger could be a model for other corporations interested in leading a responsible CRM campaign.

The campaign is exemplary in the extent to which it involved employees, the publicity it provided for the problem of hunger in America, the amount of money it raised, the number of agencies it affected, the creative approach it utilized, the degree to which it plans to keep members informed of the results, and the commitment it has shown to sustaining its support.

The campaign was formed in partnership with Share Our Strength (SOS), a hunger relief organization founded by Bill Shore, former campaign adviser to Gary Hart and former chief of staff to Senator Bob Kerrey. American Express' relationship with SOS goes back several years to its annual sponsorship of SOS's Taste of the Nation. A week long benefit involving wine tastings and dinners prepared by notable chefs at more than 100 cities across America, Taste of the Nation raises $3 million annually that is distributed to local and national hunger relief programs. American Express employees were instrumental in identifying hunger as an issue the company should address, both through company opinion surveys, and American Express-sponsored volunteer initiatives for its employees.

Speaking to campaign administrators at American Express about the program, one may forget that these are marketing executives. The talk is all of good citizenship and social awareness. Yet choosing hunger may not have been an entirely selfless motive. SOS's strong connection to restaurateurs may offer an opportunity for American Express to sweeten the bitterness caused when American Express charged a higher service fee to restaurants that accepted the Card back in 1991.

Publicity

Nevertheless, American Express is widely praised for the widespread attention it has brought to the issue of hunger in America. "The Charge Against Hunger campaign helped put hunger on the political map," says Max Finberg, of the Congressional Hunger Center. "It got people to sit up and notice. No single hunger organization has the access to tap into the mass media the way American Express did." American Express used its normal advertising budget to promote Charge Against Hunger. Ads ran on primetime TV, as well as during the popular morning show hours. Bill Shore appeared in an interview on Good Morning America, and Stevie Wonder was featured at a Thanksgiving Day Parade and during the Superbowl singing a song he wrote for the campaign.

Truth in Advertising

Other kudos went to American Express for doing what it said it would. One press conference was held at the start of the campaign to announce the company's intention to raise and donate $5 million for hunger relief, and another held on January 13 to declare that the goal had been met. True to its promise, the $5 million was distributed widely, to a total of 257 recipients in all 50 states. In addition, American Express donated $200,000 to SOS in administrative grants so that all of the $5 million raised could go directly to hunger relief.

A creative and thoughtful approach characterized the campaign, one which sought to make hunger relief organizations and those who depend on them sufficient. Five allocations categories were established, including expansion of federal school breakfast programs, perishable food rescue projects, food assistance programs in undeserved areas, Super Pantry programs to teach nutrition and food preparation to people who regularly use food banks, and child malnutrition clinics. The programs targeted "America's fastest growing segment of hungry people, children and their families," according to an SOS brochure.

Integrity

The integrity of the allocation process was another area where the campaign can be commended. In any large scale CRM campaign, there is the chance that only a few favored cronies may receive the proceeds, or that the availability of funds is not widely communicated to interested groups. In this campaign, Request for Proposal forms were distributed through all the major hunger relief networks. SOS estimates that 80% of recipients had never received money from SOS before. The average grant size was $20,000, although some grants for school equipment was as low as $1000 and one grant for the national Campaign to End Childhood Hunger was $305,000.

The impact that grants will make varies. The Kentucky Food Bank, for example, with an annual budget of $370,000 received a $2,000 grant that will allow it to extend credit to four needy agencies that depend on the Food Bank for supplies. The Farm Project of the Capital Area Community Food Bank in Washington, D.C., however, with a budget of $53,000 last year, received a grant of $20,000. The Farm Project, which grows produce for low-income people, will be able to increase its crop from 11,000 pounds of produce last year to 25,000 pounds this year, and 30,000 pounds next year.

Approval criteria included the following: clearly defined and realistic goals; meeting local needs and capacities; having the potential to make a significant impact; demonstrated stable and effective operations; and a demonstrated financial need.

"SOS has an extensive nationwide network and has done a good job in getting the money out," commented Christine Vladimiroff of Second Harvest.

Finberg, of the Congressional Hunger Center, remarks that, "SOS was very interested in having as many people know about the possibilities of getting grants. They are professional and thorough. I feel very comfortable that they were not just picking favorites."

Recipients are expected to spend the money in the way outlined in their proposals, and are asked to submit a six-month and one-year assessment of what impact the money had. In its expectations of grant recipients, "SOS strikes the right balance between accountability and flexibility," says Finberg.

Commitment

The Charge Against Hunger grows out of the commitment to hunger issues that American Express displayed in its support of Taste of the Nation. It plans to extend this commitment by running the campaign again next year, with the hope of raising another $5 million. "There's an equity in doing it a second time," said Gregory Tarmin, Public Affairs Manager for the campaign at American Express. "People know more about the issue and have an added chance to get involved."

Accountability

A key concern about CRM is how to insure philanthropic accountability in the context of corporate marketing needs. No law requires a corporate sponsor to disclose whether and how it spends funds raised in a CRM campaign. The absence of regulation opens the field to abuse of the public trust.

In this respect too, officials at American Express appear concerned about maintaining accountability to their members. SOS has recently completed a list of grant recipients, which includes names, grant amounts, and intended purposes. Natalia Cherney, who managed publicity for the Charge Against Hunger Campaign at American Express, says that ". . . a key focus of the next few months is communicating to cardmembers and service establishments through newsletters, brochures, press releases, and advertisements where their money went and how it was spent."

Although finding a corporate sponsor may not be easy (SOS has not been approached by other corporate sponsors), the Cone/Roper survey suggests that cause related marketing will be a growing trend. Any nonprofits who do partner with a company in such a campaign must be prepared to ask the right questions. Otherwise, they may just end up buying a lemon.

COMMUNITY ORGANIZING
Moves Past the 'Hood

Beyond the Politics of Place, a recent report by Gary Delgado, Director of the Applied Research Center in Oakland, California, takes community organizing beyond the neighborhood backyard into the shifting boundaries of community identity. And, in a concluding section, Delgado identifies opportunities for funders interested in basic community development.

"The ground-breaking work, the innovation, the experimentation, and the motivating livid anger of the truly oppressed is at the heart of the work in immigrants' rights organizations, gay and lesbian groups, disabled people's organizations and organizations of people of color," Delgado explains. "It is these formations, compelled always to struggle with the politics of difference, that will force the practitioners of traditional community organizing to move beyond 'the politics of place' to address the cultural dimensions of power in their own organizations, as well as in society at large."

The traditional method of community development was to convene representatives of the community elite—business leaders, government officials, heads of nonprofits—and then to expand outward. Neighborhood organizing turned the equation on its head. As a bottoms up approach, it brought the needs, desires, and insights of the disenfranchised, dispossessed, and disadvantaged into the process of building and shaping a community.

But community organizing has taken new turns in recent years. The rise of identity politics has challenged or transformed notions of "place" as the terrain for collective action.

"Community organizing seeks to develop and articulate a community of interest by devising more equitable policies, building political pressure to fight for local resources, and developing indigenous leadership," explains Delgado. Whatever the specific issue, the most essential goal of community organizing is community building. As Andres Sarabia, first president of the Communities Organized for Public Services in San Antonio, put it, "We came to see that the issues we work on are like dessert. The main meal is the rebuilding of communities. . . ."

Movement Accomplishments

Currently 6,000 community organizations operate in the United States, with most having formed in the last ten years. Their accomplishments are significant.

Community organizing has helped residents in particular communities understand local issues in a larger political context. "Thus, the demand for a corner stop-light is related to plans to reindustrialize some low-income neighborhood, the unavailability of loans to small businesses in a neighborhood is explored in relationship to bank and insurance redlining and future plans for a different 'brand' of neighborhood, . . . and toxic exposure is related to the reduction of toxic pollution," writes Delgado.

The training of leaders is another accomplishment of community organizing. Besides emphasizing traditional qualities of leadership such as creativity, innovation, and the ability to articulate the aspirations of a constituency, community organizing also teaches the concept of "functional leadership": different people using different skills at different times to forward the interests of the organization. Community organizations are an excellent training ground for young people as well, offering them the opportunity to engage in meaningful activity on behalf of their communities.

Community organizing also gives voice to people un/under-represented in the political system. The movement has had a great effect on the distribution of Community Development Block Grant funds and the disposition of private mortgage funds using the Community Reinvestment Act.

Combining youth training with local political action, for example, the Association for Community Organizing and Reform Now (ACORN) completed a "Summer of Service" program that trained 50 youth to inform New York residents and officials of the dangers of lead paint. This effort resulted in a 35% increase in building inspections, and over 2,000 emergency repairs.

The community organizing credo of "no permanent allies and no permanent enemies" allows community organizations to hold local politicians accountable by alternating working with or opposing local politicians on a variety of issues. "This pragmatic flexibility has allowed local community organizations to be consistently active in the political arena without compromising the interests of their constituents," writes Delgado.

In Boston, community organizations have influenced job allocation and have had a strong voice in development through the eminent domain process. Oakland and San Francisco community organizations have changed the "color, complexion, and operational style of public health care," according to Delgado. Baltimore and San Antonio schools are more responsive to the needs of low-income communities after the intervention of community organizations. In New York, Chicago, Detroit, Atlanta, Denver, and other cities, financial institutions are now watching their "Ps and Qs."

Shifting Organizing Contexts

The changing role of government in the '80s hindered the progress of community organizing, however. Federal and state budget cuts subjected the movement to a war of attrition, in which groups fought to keep one social service from collapsing while losing several others simultaneously. As Dave Bockmann, former organizer for Washington Fair Share, notes in the report, "We'd keep a neighborhood health center open and across town, the public hospital would cut free services to low-income patients."

Globalization of the economy necessarily affects community organizations as well. Decisions affecting particular neighborhoods are now being made hundreds, even thousands of miles away. One organizer quoted by Delgado says, "We have as much at stake in an equitable trade agreement as we have in getting block grant money for rehab in poor communities."

Trends in Community Organizing

Amid these changing conditions, two trends have emerged: the explosion of independent organizations in communities of color and the growth of organizing training intermediaries. These trends, Delgado asserts, will have the most dramatic effect on the future of community organizing.

Organizations in communities of color evolved not out of a preplanned goal of winning power for the community, but rather because there was no other choice. As one activist Delgado quotes put it, "We never went to Alinsky's school, but we still had to learn how the system works." Racial inequalities in housing, job opportunities, social entitlements, and treatment in the criminal justice system were an integral factor in the formation of these groups. "With no roadmap or model," Delgado writes, "these organizations build bold, interesting, and effective organizations that combine an understanding of their own cultural base with an assessment of how the world can be changed to benefit their constituents."

Organizations in communities of color have borrowed from and transformed what Delgado identifies as the three traditional approaches to community organizing: building a membership base, working in coalition, and organizing through religious institutions. Community organizations of color have evolved into a wide variety of forms, but can be categorized under seven different types: single issue mobilizations, multi-racial community organizations, monoracial community organizations, immigrant rights groups, community-based workplace initiatives, economic development efforts, and professional advocacy groups.

Most common are single issue mobilizations, which function more as ad-hoc committees than as organizations. They mobilize around specific crisis situations (e.g. an incident with the police, toxic poisoning) and may expand to include other issues. Examples of such groups include the Committee Against Police Violence in Los Angeles and the Bilingual Parents Advocacy Group in Oakland, California.

Mono-and multiracial organizations usually address, through the prism of race, a wider set of issues not confined to the local community. They form strategic alliances with each other, and with groups in the white community. The Southwest Organizing Project in Albuquerque, New Mexico, for example, has successfully worked on issues of school reform, police violence, water quality, toxic pollution, and immigrant rights with a base in the Chicano community.

Immigrant rights groups, perhaps the newest and most tenuous segment of the community organizing movement, work to obtain access to jobs and services for immigrants, to ensure fair treatment by INS officials, to organize against racial violence, to build communities, and to address the problems of capital flight. Organizers, who have traditionally worked on a citizenship model of neighborhood mobilization, must find new and creative means to mobilize members and address their needs. Asian Immigrant Women Advocates in Oakland for example, has used English as a Second Language classes to build a base among women in the Korean, Vietnamese, and Chinese communities.

The Rise of Training Intermediaries

The expansion of organizing in communities of color has occurred side by side with the growth of training intermediaries. They have initiated projects, trained leaders, and developed organizers. The number of these intermediaries more than doubled between 1979 and 1991. Some provide technical assistance to particular geographical areas (e.g. Community Resource Center in Denver), while others build formidable organizing networks (Industrial Areas Foundation). Still others work either with specific types of constituencies (Center for Community Change) or on specific issues (Citizen's Clearinghouse for Hazardous Waste and National Training and Information Center). These kinds of groups are now the most stable component of the community organizing movement, Delgado asserts, with the widest scope of work and the most professional staff. "They are the most likely instruments for improving, refining, and consolidating community organizing activities."

Opportunities for Funding

Existing resources have been insufficient to support network expansion or development. In fact, Delgado reports, "External support for most community organizations is spotty, small, and inconsistent."

Ample opportunities exist, however, for strategic funding initiatives by the philanthropic community. According to Delgado, "Support for community organizing may be viewed as an empowerment strategy, an effective approach to leadership development, a component of community development, an efficient mechanism to influence public policy, or as one approach to increase public participation and to ensure civil rights," Delgado writes.

The Campaign for Human Development of the Roman Catholic Church (CHD), the Woods Charitable Fund, and the Wieboldt Foundation in Chicago are among the few foundations that have significantly supported community organizing. CHD, for example, invests nearly $5 million annually in community organizing groups that empower the poor. The Woods Charitable Fund offers its support because, as noted in its brochure, "community organizing does nothing less than provide people with the means to exercise their democratic rights and responsibilities on a continuing basis."

Delgado identifies several areas where funding could make a significant difference in the field of community development. Among them are the following:

• Emerging Communities of Interest. Delgado suggests that funders could provide much needed startup capital to networks and intermediaries that provide training, organizational development assistance, and help with leadership development to such emerging community groups. The most underserved constituencies in this area include communities of color, immigrant rights groups, and networks to support the development of effective organizations in the gay and lesbian, women's, and disabled communities.

• Multiple year core support for key national networks and major community organizing training intermediaries. National People's Action's work on housing, ACORN's banking and campaign reforms, and Citizen Action's utility reform campaign demonstrate that "the most successful reform efforts growing out of the movement have come from the ability of national networks to initiate campaigns that combine local action with the ability to apply pressure at the national level," writes Delgado.

• Leadership development for poor, indigenous people. Many major funding initiatives have targeted professional community leaders. Delgado suggests that funders consider emphasizing the development of indigenous leaders who have a following and are accountable to an organization.

• Small grants to local organizations. Delgado recommends that funders wishing to support local organizations consider a regranting partnership with a training intermediary, who could assist funders in understanding and evaluating local organizing efforts.

References

Beyond the Politics of Place is available for $16 plus $3 for shipping and handling, prepaid, from the Applied Research Center, 25 Embarcadero Cove, Oakland, CA 94606.

FAYE WATTLETON ON CONTROVERSY AND FUND RAISING

A growing trend in the politicization of philanthropic giving threatens many social change nonprofits. Organizations seeking to guarantee equal rights to gays and lesbians, to protect women's reproductive rights, and many others have been finding themselves in the limelight of rightwing attacks on their sources of funding. Faye Wattleton, president of Planned Parenthood of America from 1978 to 1992, has front line experience in how to turn controversy around to an organization's advantage.

In the late 1980s, Planned Parenthood was the target of abortion opponents trying to deprive the organization of its institutional support. Threatening nationwide boycotts, the right demanded that General Mills, AT&T, American Express, Pillsbury, Dayton Hudson, J.C. Penney, Union Pacific, Eastman Kodak, and many other corporations, as well as United Way, defund Planned Parenthood. As a result, United Ways in King County and Kennewick, Washington; Boise, Idaho; Hilo, Hawaii; and El Paso, Texas dissolved their partnerships with Planned Parenthood. A number of corporations, such as J.C. Penney, Union Pacific, and AT&T, succumbed to the pressure as well. Dayton Hudson dissolved its relationship with Planned Parenthood, but later reinstated it.

Using the negative publicity to its advantage, Planned Parenthood was able to enlist a new corps of supporters as well as to raise contributions often in excess of what it lost. In Hawaii, within two years of being dropped from United Way, Planned Parenthood increased its membership from 300 to 2,000. In Boise, contributions rose 10% to 12% per year after the local United Way dropped Planned Parenthood.

Here, talking with NCRP editor Svetlana Tsalik, Faye Wattleton reflects on how other organizations threatened by controversy can use it to their advantage.

ST: Is adversity something that's good for an organization or something to be avoided at all costs?

FW: I don't think any organization seeks controversy or desires to be engaged in adversity. But I think that when controversy occurs, to not fully take advantage of the opportunities that arise from it is really a miscalculation of the value that such diversion can be for an organization.

ST: How can a group facing this kind of crisis use it to its advantage?

FW: One has to be very clear about one's mission and forthright in defending it. One has to be ready to stand up for the mission and not try to rearrange it or adjust it around the edges with the hope that adversity and controversy will go away. It's very easy to run for cover and to try to alter one's values to accommodate the conflict. I think in the long run, organizations lose when they do so.

I've always been of the opinion that donors come to you because they believe in the guiding principles of your organization and that long term donors will stay with you if you stay true to those principles. If long term principles are altered and embroidered, I find that you create a reactionary phenomenon. Donors who are supportive of you because of your firmness and the work you are doing will feel alienated because you would appear to be capable of changing in an opportunistic way, as opposed to staying true to the mission and simply trying to reassure the donor that his or her support is in fact credible, as it was in the first instance.

ST: How can a threatened organization use the added media attention to its advantage?

FW: I think there's always the opportunity to use media, but I think this should be done only in a carefully planned and executed strategy. Episodic attempts to try to gain attention through the media can be disastrous and often not productive to getting one's story told. Any group's great temptation is to react and to assume a bunker mentality. But I think often adversity is the time to stop and say, "Let's just take the long view of this. Let's look at what our short term and our long term strategies are." And realize that you may not see immediate results, but if you keep at it, in the end, people will support you for the same reasons they came to you in the first place. It is not necessarily because they like you but because they believe you are doing important work. It's important for organizations to realize that they're not going to be loved by everyone all of the time. There are always going to be people who are unhappy with some aspect of what you do and that is why it is so important to remain true to one's guiding principles.

ST: In a crisis situation, should the goal be to win back corporate support or to raise individual awareness and contributions?

FW: It depends on the situation. Get reliable professionals who can develop a good strategy both to reinforce the organization among those people who are supportive and to appeal to larger groups who are potential supporters.

ST: What can a group do to prepare for or try to prevent a loss in funding due to its controversial position?

FW: Controversy doesn't come about because a group happens to do something. Often it is due to the opposition of outside forces to the group's work. I think keeping donors well informed about controversial developments is essential. For larger organizations, that may be very difficult. But donor information is really very important, even outside the course of a controversy. Fully understanding the nature of the opposition to one's work and where that opposition is coming from is also very important.

ST: So is it a good idea to keep track of your opposition's work, even before a problem occurs?

FW: Well I don't think it's very necessary. I never spent any time tracking the opposition to Planned Parenthood's work. What I did was to keep in mind the way the opposition tried to position Planned Parenthood's work, not as a defensive strategy, but to make sure we offensively told our story in as many ways and through as many channels as possible. Certainly the explosion of modern technology gave us the capacity to communicate in ways we never could have dreamed of ten years ago. It gives tremendous potential to organizations.

ST: Is there greater potential for funders to withdraw support for controversial causes with the growth in strength of the religious right in recent years?

FW: I think it's always a possibility that the so-called religious right will have an impact. I think there is also a real possibility that there will be a backlash to their extreme tactics as well. And it is really important for donors to come to appreciate that giving in to a narrow opposition does not solve controversy. It only emboldens those who want to create controversy. It is very empowering to the opposition to have an effect and get the results it seeks. That's often a hard lesson for donors to learn who are feeling the heat for their support. But the best way to defang controversy is simply to continue supporting the same groups one had been funding all along.

ST: Do you see any trend in funders trying to avoid controversial organizations in the first place?

FW: Generally people don't like controversy and most often do not see it as an opportunity but rather as a threat. I happen not to see the glass in that fashion. I always tried to use controversy as an opportunity to advance the work of the organization that I headed.

ST: What convinces a funder to fund or to reinstate a controversial cause? For example, do you think economic boycotts are effective in preventing corporate grants?

FW: Well, I have never seen an economic boycott that was effective against an organization. But that doesn't matter. The perception is that these boycotts can be damaging and dangerous. It is certainly a very sensitive subject with corporate donors. Even though the evidence does not bear any semblance to the perception, they still run with the first mention of boycott and other economic sanctions. When you have a donor that is not willing to stand up to the courage of its original conviction to support an organization, even when that organization has been faithful to its guiding principles and has kept the donor well informed about the issue, then you have to realize that some donors are going to leave you. Donors leave you all the time. It's important for an organization to seek many ways of positioning its message and its work and not simply to assume, if it's doing good work, that it will be funded. The philanthropic world is too competitive for any such complacency. While it may seem like a very difficult experience, it can often be, if managed well, an experience in which an organization can rebound more strongly.

ST: Are there any risks in protesting against a funder's decision to deny funding? Are there times that can work against you?

FW: I think if a funder defunds you, that's the end of that. If you have a funder that's so sensitive that it chooses to defund you because of controversy, it's not likely to reinstate that funding. The potential downside is that others who may have been considering funding you may choose simply to avoid the controversy. But it goes back to what I just said. If you give in and go quietly away, it only emboldens those people who want to force their will on any number of organizations. That is empowerment that just simply should not be tolerated, whatever the risk.

INDEX OF GRANTMAKERS BY FIELD OF INTEREST

This index represents the editors' judgment of the subject-matter interests of the funders. Here are 156 categories that describe a wide aray of interests. These catagories are subjective and represent most of the interest for nonprofits. Many grantmakers describe their priorities in language that defies easy "key word" categorization. For example, one funder may use the word "education" to mean only educational programs in classrooms, another may use the word in the broader sense of "public information," and a third may mean both. While every attempt has been made to list funders according to the categories they use to describe their own programs, tempered with the reality of their grants lists, each category is subject to some variation.

Some funders have defined interests evidenced by their guidelines and grants lists that make them easily susceptible to categorization. Others deliberately take a more open-ended approach to their grantmaking, making it next to impossible for any two people to use the same categories to describe their priorities.

The effort here has been for inclusion rather than exclusion. The material that follows merely represents the interpretations of the editors. Its greatest utility is as a place to start research. The ultimate authority on the interests of any grantmaker is always that funder's annual reports, grants lists, and other printed materials.

A

abortion, see reproductive rights

ageism, 25, 130, 191, 193, 230

aging, 226, 369

agriculture, 357, 470

AIDS (and HIV), 14, 59, 102, 120, 138, 144, 189, 220, 246, 249, 278, 307, 310, 313, 342, 379, 396, 411, 419, 427, 441, 460

animal welfare, 71, 155, 322

animals and wildlife, 12

anti-Semitism, 25

arms control, 69, 136, 262, 332, 381, 383, 395, 406, 470

arts and culture, 27, 32, 42, 44, 49, 67, 69, 71, 75, 82, 91, 95, 107, 109, 113, 116, 120, 130, 136, 141, 144, 148, 154, 159, 163, 165, 169, 172, 175, 180, 191, 196, 202, 212, 214, 218, 226, 230, 238, 246, 263, 273, 276, 289, 301, 313, 315, 318, 340, 342, 347, 354, 367, 369, 372, 374, 384, 392,

199, 219, 243, 251, 266, 278, 281, 289, 301, 329, 342, 352, 386, 392, 395, 402, 422, 438, 441, 448, 478

economic exploitation, 25, 59, 230, 464

economic globalization, 133

economic issues, 36, 69, 133, 136, 191, 206, 473

economic justice, 1, 4, 55, 59, 65, 193, 235, 243, 283, 307, 329, 332, 49, 398, 402, 419, 424, 441, 463

economic rights, 179

education, 16, 27, 32, 42, 44, 49, 57, 62, 71, 75, 80, 84, 93, 95, 102, 105, 109, 116, 121, 125, 128, 136, 138, 141, 144, 146, 148, 154, 157, 159, 167, 172, 175, 179, 185, 187, 196, 199, 206, 210, 212, 214, 219, 227, 230, 235, 238, 246, 251, 260, 266, 273, 276, 287, 289, 292, 296, 301, 309, 315, 318, 321, 326, 334, 340, 342, 345, 347, 354, 363, 367, 374, 384, 388, 390, 392, 395, 402, 406, 408, 411, 414, 422, 444, 446, 451, 463, 465, 478

education (business), 226

elderly, 42, 91, 95, 136, 208, 222, 227, 249, 253, 256, 309, 323, 329, 337, 342, 345, 386, 411, 419, 422, 470

employment, 57, 95, 151, 258, 260, 273, 278, 310, 329, 354, 412, 477

energy, 46, 395, 430, 432, 470

environment, 10, 12, 38, 40, 44, 46, 59, 65, 67, 69, 82, 107, 109, 121, 128, 134, 136, 144, 155, 159, 165, 191, 199, 202, 208, 219, 224, 227, 230, 238, 249, 260, 262, 269, 276, 281, 283, 289, 301, 307, 313, 326, 340, 342, 347, 357, 369, 374, 383, 386, 392, 398, 412, 414, 419, 422, 427, 430, 436, 441, 448, 458, 463, 465, 470

environmental justice, 1, 4, 18, 69, 191, 349, 357, 441, 456, 473

epilepsy, 321

equipment, 89

ethnicity, 25, 62, 141, 146, 230, 273, 326, 369, 465

F

families, 34, 40, 42, 51, 53, 57, 84, 120, 161, 177, 185, 187, 196, 222, 238, 241, 273, 296, 310, 323, 326, 329, 337, 342, 367, 404, 412, 415, 444, 451, 454, 465, 477

family planning, 107, 123, 136, 138, 161, 167, 354, 384, 465

farm policy, 136, 357, 430, 470

food distribution, 91, 266, 357

food security, 134, 266, 384

foreign policy, 21, 69, 130, 165, 191, 372

G

gay rights, 26, 59, 130, 191, 193, 307, 312, 334, 352, 379, 441, 470

general, 118, 157, 216, 235, 293, 318, 361

girls, 25, 55, 95, 206, 228, 329, 337, 342, 472, 475

government management, 189

government responsibility, 424, 448, 478

H

Hawaiian sovereignty, 372

health, 16, 32, 36, 38, 42, 44, 47, 57, 59, 62, 73, 84, 93, 95, 109, 116, 121, 128, 134, 167, 172, 196, 206, 220, 227, 253, 255, 260, 266, 287, 292, 301, 303, 315, 318, 340, 374, 386, 396, 411, 444, 460, 463, 473

health (biomedical), 253, 342

INDEX OF GRANTMAKERS ARRANGED BY GEOGRAPHIC PREFERENCES

This index groups grantmakers with specific geographic interests and limitations by state, which can be misleading to one who does not read carefully. Many funders specify a city, county, or region within a state—for example, the five-county region know as the Bay Area of northern California. Others define their geographic limitations as a major metropolitan area which may encompass more than one state; greater Philadelphia, for example, may include Camden County, New Jersey, or the District of Columbia may include northern Virginia and parts of Maryland. There are also grantmakers who specify interests in terms of a region of the country whose boundaries may be open to interpretation; the *Southwest*, the *Pacific basin*, the *Southeast*, and *Appalachia* are all examples. Where the specific list of states for a funder is ambiguous, this list errs on the Iinclusive rather than the exclusive side.

Every effort has been made to identify the specific geographic interests of corporations that favor communities where they have facilities and other major business interests, but in the case of major companies with multiple subsidiaries, the reference may be incomplete.

INDEX OF CONTACT PERSONS

INDEX OF CONTACT PERSONS

FOUNDATION CENTER

The Foundation Center is an independent agency that researches, stores, and disseminates information on philanthropic programs. The Center operates five reference libraries which offer a wide variety of materials, including books and periodicals, foundation annual reports, newsletters, press clippings, and center publications. The New York City and Washington, D.C., libraries also keep on file IRS tax returns for all currently operating private foundations in the U.S. The Cleveland and San Francisico collections house the tax returns for foundations in the midwestern and western states respectively. The Center libraries are open to the public. Please telephone them for information and their specific hours of operation.

HEADQUARTERS:
NEW YORK
79 Fifth Avenue/16th Street
New York, NY 10003-3076
Tel: 212-620-4230
www.fdncenter.org
Library: www.fdncenter.org/newyork

FIELD OFFICES:
ATLANTA
50 Hurt Plaza, Suite 150
Atlanta, GA 30303-2914
404-880-0094

CLEVELAND
1422 Euclid Avenue, Suite 1600

Cleveland, OH 44115-2001
216-861-1934
Library: www.fdncenter.org/cleveland

SAN FRANCISCO
312 Sutter Street, Suite 606
San Francisco, CA 94108-4314
415-397-0902
www.fdncenter.org/atlanta

WASHINGTON
1627 K Street, NW, Third Floor
Washington, DC 20006-1708
202-331-1400
Washington, D.C., Library home page: www.fdncenter.org/washington

COOPERATING COLLECTIONS

In addition, the Foundation Center has cooperating collections in most major cities in the U.S. Generally these collections are located within public institutions such as libraries; however, in some instances the cooperating collection may be housed and maintained by foundations or area associations of foundations. These Collections are free funding information centers in libraries, community foundations, and other nonprofit resource centers that provide a core collection of Foundation Center publications and a variety of supplementary materials and services in areas useful to grantseekers.

To find the Cooperating Collections nearest you, check online at http://fdncenter.org/collections/index.html or call toll-free 1-800-424-9836.

FUNDING EXCHANGE

The Funding Exchange is described best by their executive director, Ellen Gurzinsky, "Bringing about a more just society means amplifying voices rarely heard and ensuring the visibility of progressive perspectives at home and abroad. As the only nationwide network of community-based foundations with solid grassroots connections and proven experience engaging front-line activists in grantmaking, the Funding Exchange network is an exceptional resource for both donors and grantees."

National Office:
Funding Exchange
666 Broadway, Suite 500
New York, NY 10012

phone: (212) 529-5300
fax: (212) 982-9272
WEB: www.fex.org/
EMAIL: info@fex.org

Network Member Funds:

Appalachian Community Fund
107 West Main St.
Knoxville, TN 37902
(865) 523-5783
(865) 523-1896 (Fax)

Chinook Fund
2418 West 32nd Ave.
Denver, CO 80204
(303) 455-6905
(303) 477-1617 (Fax)

Bread and Roses Community Fund
1500 Walnut St.
Suite 1305
Philadelphia, PA 19102
(215) 731-1107
(215) 731-0453 (Fax)

Crossroads Fund
3411 W. Diversey #20
Chicago, IL 60647
(773) 227-7676
(773) 227-7790 (Fax)

Network Member Funds (continued):

Fund for Santa Barbara
924 Anacapa St.
Santa Barbara, CA 93101
(805) 962-9164
(805) 965-0217 (Fax)

Fund for Southern Communities
315 W. Ponce de Leon Ave.
Decatur, GA 30030
(404) 371-8404
(404) 371-8496 (Fax)

Hawai'i People's Fund
810 North Vineyard Blvd.
Honolulu, HI 96817
(808) 845-4800

Haymarket Peoples Fund
42 Seavers Ave.
Boston, MA 02130
(617) 522-7676
(617) 522-9580 (Fax)

Headwaters Foundation for Justice
2801 21st Ave S. Ste 132-B
Minneapolis, MN 55407
(612) 879-0602
(612) 879-0613 (Fax)

Liberty Hill Foundation
2121 Cloverfield Blvd.
Suite 113
Santa Monica, CA 90404
(310) 453-3611
(301) 453-7806 (Fax)

McKenzie River Gathering Foundation
2705 E. Burnside
Suite 210
Portland, OR 97214
(800) 489-6743

North Star Fund
305 Seventh Ave., 5th Floor
(Between 27th and 28th Streets)
New York, NY 10001
(212) 620-9110
(212) 620-8178 (Fax)

San Diego Foundation for Change
3458 30th St.
San Diego, CA 92104
(619) 692-0527

Three Rivers Community Foundation
100 N. Braddock Ave.
Pittsburgh, PA 15208
(412) 243-9250
(412) 243-0504 (Fax)

Vanguard Public Foundation
383 Rhode Island St.
Suite 301
San Francisco, CA 94103
(415) 487-2111
(415) 487-2124 (Fax)

Wisconsin Community Fund
1202 Williamson St.
Suite D
Madison, WI 53703
(608) 251-6834
(608) 251-6846 (Fax)

SELECTED BIBLIOGRAPHY

Listed here are some of the many periodicals and books related to fundraising, management, and organizing. The list is by no means exhaustive. Rather, it is made up of selected publications recommended by various grantseekers and grantmakers alike over the years as particularly useful for community-based social- and economic justice initiatives. Most of these materials are available at the Foundation Center libraries cooperating collections, or your local public library (even if currently out of print). For convenience, however, the most recently available information on the publisher's address and the price of the publication are included.

REPRINTS AND BROCHURES

The Foundation Center has vastly expanded its publications since the last edition of the *Grant Seekers Guide*. They have a 37-page catalog, and they have new computer databases, services available on the Internet, etc. (world wide web site: http://fdncenter.org). The last edition cited their book on AIDS funding, but now they have directories of funders for over 30 other topics including Health, Aging, Education, the Environment, Social Services, the Arts. Call 1-800-424-9836 for the catalog.

Grantmanship Center, The. 1125 West 6 Street, 5th floor, Los Angeles, California 90017. The Grantsmanship Center publishes a number of reprints of articles that have appeared in the *Grantsmanship Center News*. Prices vary according to the length of the article, from $3 to $4 each, and quantity discounts are available. Among the articles that have stood the test of time are: "Program Planning and Proposal Writing" (expanded version), and "Exploring Corporate Giving."

PERIODICALS

Council on Foundations. *Foundation News. To* subscribe, write, Foundation News, 1828 L Street, N.W, Washington, D.C. 20036. Published bimonthly, $35.50/yr, (202) 466-6512.

Foundation Center, The. *Foundation Grants Index Quarterly.* This publication updates the *Foundation Grants Index Annual* (see below). To subscribe, write the publisher, 79 Fifth Avenue, New York, New York 10003. Published six times a year. $28/yr.

Grantsmanship Center, The. *Whole Nonprofit Catalog.* Quarterley. Available from the publisher, 1031 South Grand Avenue, Los Angeles, California 90015. Free.

Grassroots Fundraising Journal. Bi monthly. Each issue features a practical article on a specific fundraising method or issue, and includes ideas submitted by readers.

Independent Sector. *Update.* Monthly. Contains information about volunteers and fundraising for nonprofits. Available to members of Independent Sector, 1828 L Street, N.W, Washington, D.C. 20036.

Lutheran Resources Commission-Washington (An adjunct agency of the Lutheran Council in the U.S.A.) *Newsbriefs.* To subscribe, write the publishers at 733 15th Street, N.W, Suite 900, Washington, D.C. 20005. Published monthly. $60/yr.

National Committee for Responsive Philanthropy. *Responsive Philanthropy.* To subscribe, write the committee at 2001 S Street, N.W, Suite 620, Washington, D.C. 20009. Published quarterly. Subscription price is $35/yr. for individuals and $35-$300 for organizations (depending on the level of annual income).

Northern Rockies Action Group. *NRAG Papers.* To subscribe, write the publisher, 9 Place Street, Helena, Montana 59601. Published quarterly. $12/yr.

The Taft Group. *The Planned Gifts Counselor.* This 8-page, monthly news-letter covers the latest news on changes in tax laws, regulation and pending legislation that affects your planned giving program. $150. Available by calling 1-800-877-TAFT.

BOOKS

A

AIDS Funding: A Guide to Giving by Foundations and Charitable Organizations. New York: The Foundation Center, 1993. This book lists 450 grantmakers, and includes basic contact information about the funders, lists of AIDS-related grants, and data on recipients and grant awards. Available from the publisher at the address above. $75.

American Association of Fund Raising Counsel, Inc. *Giving USA 1995: Annual Report on Philanthropy for the year 1994.* Available from the American Association of Fund Raising Counsel, Inc., 25 W. 43rd St., Suite 820, New York, New York 10036. $40; and quarterly newsletter: *Giving USA Update,* both for $75.

Anderson, Albert. *Ethics for Fundraisers (Philanthropic Studies).* 1996. $10.36 pb.

Antos, John & James A. Brimson. *Activity-Based Management for Service Industries, Government Entities, and Nonprofit Organizations.* 1994. $74.95 cl.

Associates Smith, et al. *The Complete Guide to Nonprofit Management (Nonprofit Law, Finance, and Management).* 1994. $17.56 pb.

B

Bauer, David G. *The 'How To' Grants Manual : Successful Grantseeking Techniques for Obtaining Public and Private Grants.* Oryx Press, 1995. $35.50 cl.

Bauer, David G. & Mary L. Otto. *Administering Grants, Contracts, and Funds : Evaluating and Improving Your Grants System.* Oryx Press, 1996. $43.75 cl.

Bergman, Jed I., et al. *Managing Change in the Nonprofit Sector : Lessons from the Evolution of Five Independent Research Libraries.* Jossey-Bass, 1995. $30.95 cl.

Berry, Ellen. *Gifts That Make a Difference : How to Buy Hundreds of Great Gifts Sold Through Nonprofits.* 1992. $6.36 pb.

Berry, Ellen. *Gifts That Save the Animals : 1001 Great Gifts Sold by Nonprofits That Protect Animals.* 1995. $7.95 pb.

Blazek, Jody. *Financial Planning for Nonprofit Organizations (Nonprofit Law, Finance, and Management Series).* 1996. $54.95 cl.

Bowen, William G. (Editor), et al. *The Charitable Nonprofits : An Analysis of Institutional Dynamics and Characteristics.* Jossey-Bass, 1994. $41.45 cl.

Brinckerhoff, Peter C. *Financial Empowerment : More Money for More Mission (Mission-Based Management Series).* 1996. $34.95 cl.

Bryson, John M. & Farnum K. Alston. *Creating and Implementing Your Strategic Plan : A Workbook for Public and Nonprofit Organizations.* Jossey-Bass, 1995. $24.95 pb.

Burlingame, Dwight F. (Editor). *Critical Issues in Fund Raising (Nsfre/Wiley Fund).* 1997. $31.50 cl.

C

Carver, John. *Boards That Make a Difference : A New Design for Leadership in Nonprofit and Public Organizations.* Jossey-Bass, 1990. $27.95 cl.

Carver, John. *Boards That Make a Difference : A New Design for Leadership in Nonprofit and Public Organizations.* Jossey-Bass, 1997. $27.95 cl.

Center for Third World Organizing. *Directory of Church Funding Sources.* Oakland, California: Center for Third World Organizing, 1986. Approximately 45 pp. This contains a list of religious funding sources, including both local and national levels, with contacts, deadlines, restrictions, and other useful information. Available from the Center for Third World Organizing, 1218 E. 21 Street, Oakland, CA 94606. $15.

Collins, Sarah and Charlotte Dion, eds. *The Foundation Center's User Friendly Guide.* 3d ed. New York: The Foundation Center, 1994. This book is a comprehensive guide to the reference tools available at The Foundation Center that includes insights into how foundations operate and how best to approach them. Topics covered include what are foundations, how foundations fit into the total funding picture, who gets foundation grants and how to present your ideas to a foundation. Available from the publisher, 79 Fifth Avenue, New York, NY 10003. $14.95.

Conference Board, The. *Annual Survey of Corporate Contributions 1991 Edition.* 1991. This survey presents data on contributions ratios based on financial data and number of employees, and it tracks the distribution of contributions among different types of grantees. All data are derived from the Conference Board's own surveys and IRS documents. Available from the Conference Board, 845 Third Avenue, New York, NY 10022. $100 for 1991 edition.

D

De Pree, Max. *Leading Without Power : Finding Hope in Serving Community.* 1997. $14 cl.

Dove, Kent E. *Conducting a Successful Capital Campaign : A Comprehensive Fundraising Guide for Nonprofit Organizations (Management Series/Higher Education Series).* 1988. $36.45 cl.

Drucker, Peter F. *Managing the Non-Profit Organization : Practices and Principles.* 1992. $10.80 pb.

Drucker, Peter F. *Managing the Non-Profit Organization : Principles and Practices.* 1992. $15.30 Audio Cassette.

Drucker, Peter F. *The Five Most Important Questions You Will Ever Ask About Your Nonprofit Organization: Participant's Workbook (The Drucker Fundation Self-Assessment).* 1994. $11.95 pb.

E

Eadie, Douglas C. *Changing by Design : A Practical Approach to Leading Innovation in Nonprofit Organizations.* Jossey-Bass, 1997. $27.95 cl.

Edles, Peter L. *Fundraising : Hands-On Tactics for Nonprofit Groups.* 1995. $13.56 pb.

Edwards, Michael & David Hulme (Editors). *Beyond the Magic Bullet : No Performance and Accountability in the Post-Cold War World.* West Hartford, CT: Kumarian Press, 1996. $18.95 pb.

F

Flanagan, Joan. *The Grass Roots Fundraising Book.* 2d rev. ed. 1982. This book provides a compilation of fundraising how-to information, including a detailed analysis on how to choose an event that will be the most profitable for your organization, a description of what steps should be taken to arrange the event, and who should do what. Available from the publisher, 180 North Stetson Avenue, Suite 1200, Chicago, Illinois 60601-6790. $14.95.

Fojtik, Kathleen *M. The Bucks Start Here: How to Fund Social Service Projects.* Ann Arbor: Domestic Violence Project, Inc., 1978. This is a practical guide to the rules and requirements of grantmaking agencies. It includes a number of handy appendixes and references. Out of print.

Ford Foundation, The. *Meeting the Challenge: Foundation Response to* AIDS. New York: The Ford Foundation, 1987. This report, prepared on the basis of interviews with foundation trustees and staff in mid-1987, assesses the role of foundations in responding to the AIDS crisis. It is available from the Foundation Center, 79 Fifth Avenue, New York, New York 10003. $6.50.

Foundation Center, The. *The Comsearch Printouts.* These printouts arrange foundation information derived from the National Grants Index into subject categories and geographic areas. In the 1987 series, there were 66 subject printouts, 20 geographic printouts, 26 broad topic printouts, and three special-topic printouts. The materials are updated periodically. For a current list of *Comsearch Printouts,* contact The Foundation Center, 79 Fifth Avenue, New York, NY 10003. $18 each for the subject printouts on paper. $7 each for printouts on microfiche.

The Foundation Directory. 1995 Edition. New York: The Foundation Center. This reference contains information on all American foundations whose assets exceed 2,000,000 or whose annual grants total $200,000 or more, over 7,000 foundations in all. The entries contain brief information on the foundation purpose, financial data, key officers, and grant application procedures. The directory also is indexed by foundation name, subject, geographic focus, names of donors, types of support, and by names of donors, trustees, and officers. Available from The Foundation Center at the address above, or from the publisher at, 136 South Hudson, Irvington-on-Hudson, NY 10533. $85.

The Foundation Grants Index. 16th ed. New York: The Foundation Center, 1995. This volume describes 68,000 actual grants awarded by major foundations. It is indexed by subject areas, recipients, key words, and geographic focus. Available from the publisher at 79 Fifth Avenue, New York, NY 10003. $150.

The Foundation 1000. 4th ed. 1995-1996. October 1995. Features multi-page detailed profiles on the country's 1,000 largest foundations. Contact the publisher at 79 Fifth Avenue, New York, NY 10003, toll free 1-800-424-9836. 2,826 pp. $285.

Funding for Justice Project. *Religious Funds for Social Justice* 1987-88. 1987. 94 pp. Lists local, regional, and national church and church organizations that fund social change. Available from Greater Minneapolis Council of Churches 122 West Franklin Avenue, Room 218, Minneapolis, Minnesota 55404. $7 plus postage.

Furnari, Ellen; Carol Mollner; Teresa Odendahl; and Aileen Shaw. *Exemplary Grantmaking Practices Manual.* Minneapolis: National Network of Grantmakers. The Manual is purposely designed to stretch one's thinking while showing by example successful practices employed by other foundations. Funders are cited who have instituted these practices into their work. Available from National Network of Grantmakers, 2801 21st Ave S, #132, Minneapolis, MN 55407. 80 pages. $33.95 including shipping and handling.

G

Gidron, Benjamin, et al. *Government and the Third Sector : Emerging Relationships in Welfare States.* Jossey-Bass, 1992. $39.95 cl.

Gilpatrick, Eleanor. *Grants for Nonprofit Organizations : A Guide to Funding and Grant Writing.* 1989. $55.00 cl.

Grace, Kay Sprinkel. *Beyond Fund Raising : New Strategies for Nonprofit Innovation and Investment (Nsfre/Wiley Fund).* 1997. $20.97 cl.

Graham, Christine. *Keep the Money Coming : A Step-By-Step Strategic Guide to Annual Fundraising.* 1993. $15.16 pb.

The Grass Roots Organization: Getting Started and Getting Results in Nonprofit, Charitable, Grass Roots, and Community Groups. Chicago: Contemporary Books, 1981. This book presents an excellent picture of how to make an organization function effectively. It includes chapters on such subjects as a strategy for self-sufficiency, how to make meetings fair and effective, boards of directors (their members and committees), and the publicity committees. Out of print.

Greenfield, James M. *Fund-Raising : Evaluating and Managing the Fund Development Process (Nonprofit Law, Finance and Management Series).* 1991. $67.95 cl.

Greenfield, James M. *Fund-Raising Fundamentals : A Guide to Annual Giving for Professionals and Volunteers (Nonprofit Law, Finance, and Management).* 1994. $21.56 pb.

Gross, Malvern J., Jr. *Financial and Accounting Guide for Not-for-Profit Organizations.* 5th ed. New York: John Wiley & Sons, 1995. This is basically a readable reference book that concentrates on different types of accounting systems and options for financial statements. It includes a useful section on setting up and keeping books for a small organization. Available from the publisher's warehouse, One Wiley Drive, Somerset, New Jersey 08875, Attn: Order Department. $120.

H

Hawks, John K. *For a Good Cause? : How Charitable Institutions Become Powerful Economic Bullies.* 1997. $15.75 cl.

Herman, Robert D. (Editor) *The Jossey-Bass Handbook of Nonprofit Leadership and Management.* Jossey-Bass, 1994. $59.95 cl.

Herman, Robert D. & Richard D. Heimovics. *Executive Leadership in Nonprofit Organizations : New Strategies for Shaping Executive-Board Dynamics.* Jossey-Bass, 1991. $26.95 cl.

Herron, Douglas B. *Marketing Nonprofit Programs and Services : Proven and Practical Strategies to Get More Customers, Members, and Doners.* Jossey-Bass. 1996. $48 cl.

Herzlinger, Regina E. & Denise Nitterhouse. *Financial Accounting and Managerial Control for Nonprofit Organizations.* 1994. $83.95 cl.

Holland, Thomas P., et al. *Improving Board Effectiveness : Practical Lessons for Nonprofit Health Care Organizations.* 1997. $35 pb.

Hopkins, Bruce R. *Charity, Advocacy and the Law (Nonprofit Law, Finance and Management Series).* 1992. $145 cl.

Hopkins, Bruce R. *The Law of Tax-Exempt Organizations (Nonprofit Law, Finance, and Management Series).* 1992. $145 cl.

Hopkins, Bruce R. *The Legal Answer Book for Nonprofit Organizations (Nonprofit Law, Finance and Management Series).* 1996. $79.95 pb.

Hopkins, Bruce R. *A Legal Guide to Starting and Managing a Nonprofit Organization (Nonprofit Law, Finance, and Management).* 1993. $15.95 pb., $69.95 cl.

Horgen, Gregory C. *Playing the Funding Game: Where It Is, How to Get It, Keep It, Increase It and Manage It for Your Special Project or Organization.* Sacramento: Human Services Development Center, 1981. This book clearly states some of the common sense principles of grantseeking, starting with the initial steps of incorporation through post-grant evaluation. It identifies various types of prospective donors (from the usual corporate-giving programs to the less common unions and the unthinkable elements of philanthropy, adult-bookstore operators, the Mafia, and so on). Out of print.

Howe, Fisher. *The Board Member's Guide to Fundraising.* San Francisco, CA. Jossey Bass, 1991. Available from the National Center for Nonprofit Boards, 2000 L Street N.W. Suite 510 P, Washington, D.C. 30026. $32.

Howe, Fisher. *The Board Member's Guide to Strategic Planning : A Practical Approach to Strengthening Nonprofit Organizations.* Jossey-Bass, 1997. $19.95 cl.

I

Ingram, Robert W. *Accounting and Financial Reporting for Governmental and Nonprofit Organizations.* 1991. $28.75 pb.

SELECTED BIBLIOGRAPHY

K

Kahn, Si. *Organizing: A Guide for Grassroots Leaders.* New York: McGraw-Hill, 1982. This book is filled with the kind of sensible and astute advice only an experienced organizer can provide. It includes chapters on constituencies, leadership, strategy, tactics, and culture, all well illustrated by examples. Out of print.

Kearns, Kevin P. *Managing for Accountability : Preserving the Public Trust in Public and Nonprofit Organizations.* Jossey-Bass, 1996. $27.95 cl.

Keegan, P. Burke. *Fundraising for Non-Profits.* 1994. $12.80 pb.

King, George V. *Deferred Gifts: How to Get Them.* Ambler, Pennsylvania: Fundraising Institute, 1981. This book emphasizes the marketing and management aspects of deferred giving, a fundraising program aimed at securing gifts that can be used by the recipient only after the donor's death, e.g., bequests, life insurance gifts, and trusts. It includes advice on identifying and approaching donors. Out of print.

Klein, Kim. *Fundraising for Social Change.* Inverness, CA: Chardon Press, 1994 3rd ed. Describes techniques for low-budget organizations to develop and maintain a fundraising program in their community, with particular emphasis on individual donors. Available from the publisher, PO Box 11607 Berkeley, CA 94712.

Kuniholm, Roland. *The Complete Book of Model Fund-Raising Letters.* 1995. $24.47 cl.

Kurtz, Daniel L. *Board Liability: Guide for Nonprofit Directors.* Wakefield, RI: Moyer Bell, 1988. 196 pp. This book remains the only authoritative guide to avoiding liability, geared for boards of directors of nonprofit institutions and their lawyers. Readable and clear for the layperson. Available from the publisher, 549 Old North Road, Kingston, RI 02881. $22.50 cloth, plus $4.50 postage.

L

Lakey, Berit, et al. *Grassroots and Nonprofit Leadership : A Guide for Organizations in Changing Times.* 1995. $13.56 pb.

Lee, Lawrence. *The Grants Game: How to Get Free Money.* San Francisco: Harbor Publishing, Inc., 1981. This book is a practical guide to the rules of the game and the pitfalls to avoid from the planning stages to the follow-through. Out of print.

Lyndenberg, Steven. *Rating America's Corporate Conscience.* Reading, Massachusetts: Addison-Wesley, 1986. 499 pp. The major objective of this book, prepared for the Council on Economic Priorities, is to influence consumer-buying patterns. It matches consumer products to their Fortune 500 manufacturers, profiles each company, and rates each for factors such as representation of women and minorities on the board of directors and in top management, involvement in South Africa, conventional and nuclear weapons contracting, and corporate giving. It provides excellent insight into underlying factors that influence corporate grantmaking. Out of print.

M

MacKie, Sam A. *How to Form a Nonprofit Corporation in Florida : With Forms (Take the Law into Your Own Hands).* 1995. $15.95 pb.

Mancuso, Anthony. *How to Form a Nonprofit Corporation (3rd Ed).* 1996. $31.95 pb.

Mancuso, Anthony & Barbara Kate Repa (Editor). *The California Nonprofit Corporation Handbook (7th Ed)*. 1996. $23.95 pb.

Mancuso, Anthony & Barbara Kate Repa. *How to Form a California Nonprofit Corporation : With Disk.* 1995. $39.95 cl.

Marshall, Sue, and Neil Mayer. *Neighborhood Organizations and Community Development.* Washington, D.C.: Urban Institute, 1985. 230 pp. Contains descriptions of projects by groups in HUD's Neighborhood Self-Help Development Program, and provides a wealth of ideas for community groups and funders. Out of print.

Mason, David E. *Leading and Managing the Expressive Dimension : Harnessing the Hidden Power Source of the Nonprofit Secto.* Jossey-Bass, 1995. $27.95 cl.

Merrill Lynch. *How to Read a Financial Report.* 5th ed. 1994. This booklet is a good introduction on how to read corporate annual reports. It contains useful information pertinent to foundation annual reports as well. Available free of charge from your local Merrill Lynch office.

Moskowitz, Milton, Michael Katz, and Robert Levering, eds. *Everybody's Business, an Almanac: The Irreverent Guide to Corporate America.* New York: Harper & Row, 1980. While somewhat dated, the value of this book lies in the way it tells the corporate story, not in its statistical analysis. Through a combination of profiles, short essays, and background facts, the editors reveal the corporate personalities of about 317 large corporations. The entries, grouped by industry, include information on the corporation's founding and history, its reputation, and public image. Out of print.

N

National Committee for Responsive Philanthropy. *GRANTS : Corporate Grantmaking for Racial and Ethnic Communities.* Kingston, RI: Moyer Bell, 2000. 732 pp. A comprehensive collection of grants, broken down by industry. Graphs and charts accompany each entry as well as analysis and commentary. Available from the publisher, 549 Old North Road, Kingston, RI 02881. $89.95 paper, plus postage.

National Directory of Corporate Public Affairs. Washington, D.C.: Columbia Books, Inc., 1995. Contains listings on approximately 1,500 corporations, including their political and grantmaking activities and officers responsible for corporate contributions activity. Available from the publisher, 1212 New York Avenue, N.W, Suite 330, Washington, DC 20005. $90.

National Guide to Funding for the Economically Disadvantaged. 1st ed. 1993. Features names and addresses, funding priorities and sample grants for over 1,400 grantmakers. Available from publisher at 79 Fifth Avenue, New York, NY 10003. 506 pp. $85.

National Network of Grantmakers. *Payout for Change.* Minneapolis: NNG. Profiles a diverse funders and their successful balance of investments returns and increased grantmaking. Profiles of grantees who benefited from grants due to an increased payout. Analysis of the payout practices of NNG's member foundations. Available from National Network of Grantmakers, 2801 21st Ave S, #132, Minneapolis, MN 55407. 60 pages. $20.00 including shipping and handling.

Nicholas, Ted. *Complete Non-Profit Corporation Handbook.* 1996. $79.95 pb.

Nicholas, Ted. *The Complete Guide to Nonprofit Corporations/Step-By-Step Guidelines, Procedures and Forms to Maintain a Nonprofit Corporation.* 1993. $15.95 pb.

Nichols, Judith E. (Editor) *Lessons from Abroad : Fresh Ideas from Fund-Raising Experts in the United Kingdom.* 1997. $28 cl.

Nielsen, Waldemar A. *The Golden Donors.* New York: E.P. Dutton, 1985. 468 pp. This book puts forth Nielsen's view of the role that the really big (assets over $250 million) foundations play in setting and meeting public policy demands at both the national and regional levels. Out of print.

O

O'Connell, Brian. *Board Overboard : Laughs and Lessons for All but the Perfect Nonprofit.* Jossey-Bass, 1995. $23 cl.

P

Pifer, Alan. *Philanthropy in an Age of Transition.* New York: The Foundation Center, 1984. This book contains a series of essays by the former president of the Carnegie Corporation of New York that articulates his views on some of the major social issues of the last 20 years. It provides good insight into the way a well-respected member of the grantmaking community thinks and analyzes problems and issues. Available from the publisher, 79 Fifth Avenue, New York, NY 10003. $12.50.

Poderis, Tony. *It's a Great Day to Fund-Raise!* 1997. $18.36 pb.

Powell, Walter W. *The Nonprofit Sector: A Research Handbook.* New Haven: Yale University Press, 1987. 464 pp. A compilation of scholarly articles on the sociological, political, economic, and legal aspects of nonprofit organizations. Available from the publisher, 92A Yale Station, New Haven, CT 06520. $45.

Price, A. Rae, ed. *Increasing the Impact.* Battle Creek, Michigan: W. K. Kellogg Foundation, 1985. 234 pp. This collection of essays by experienced communications and public affairs officers at foundations and nonprofits explores communications in the high technology era, everything from television coverage for a town meeting to communicating by computer. It's filled with both practical tips and how-tos as well as a wealth of ideas adaptable to many organizations. Out of print.

Pynes, Joan E. *Human Resources Management for Public and Nonprofit Organizations.* Jossey-Bass, 1997. $32.95 cl.

R

Rados, David L. *Marketing for Nonprofit Organizations.* 1996. $59.95 cl.

Ross, Dorothy M. *Fundraising for Youth : Hundreds of Wonderful Ways of Raising Funds for Youth Organizations.* 1990. $7.95 pb.

Russell, John M. *Giving and Taking: Across the Foundation Desk.* New York: Teachers College, 1977. This book is a small philosophical treatise on foundation management written by the former president of the John and Mary R. Markle Foundation. It is not a how-to book, but it does contain valuable insights into the attitudes of foundation executives toward would-be grantees. Out of print.

S

Salamon, Lester M. & Helmut K. Anheier. *Defining the Nonprofit Sector : A Cross-National Analysis (Johns Hopkins Non-Profit Sector Series ; 3) Vol 1.* 1997. $29.95 pb.

Salamon, Lester M. & Helmut K. Anheier. *Defining the Nonprofit Sector : A Cross-National Analysis (Johns Hopkins Non-Profit Sector Series, 4).* 1997. $69.95 cl.

Salamon, Lester M. & Helmut K. Anheier. *The Emerging Nonprofit Sector : An Overview (Johns Hopkins Non-Profit Sector Series ; 1).* 1996. $27.95 pb.

Salamon, Lester M. & Helmut K. Anheier. *The Emerging Nonprofit Sector : An Overview (Johns Hopkins Nonprofit Sector Series, 1).* 1996. $49.95 cl.

Seltzer, Michael S. *Securing Your Organization's Future: A Complete Guide to Fundraising Strategies.* New York: The Foundation Center, 1987. This book is designed as a complete guide to fundraising, including an overview of funding sources for nonprofits and how to secure funding from individuals, foundations, businesses, corporations, and the government. It also discusses new, emerging funding opportunities and provides a blueprint for designing and implementing your own funding strategies. Available from the publisher, 79 Fifth Avenue, New York, NY 10003. $24.95.

Shim, Jae K., et al. *Handbook of Budgeting for Nonprofit Organizations.* 1996. $48.95 cl.

Siegel, Joel G. PhD & Jae K. Shim PhD. *Financial Management for Nonprofits : The Complete Guide to Maximizing Resources and Managing Assets.* 1997. $24.50 cl.

Slepian, Anne and Christopher Mogil. *Welcome to Philanthropy.* Minneapolis: National Network of Grantmakers. This book offers a guide for both the seasoned professional and those newly involved in giving. It gives a concise overview of social change philanthropy. It also introduces resources that can provide guidance to individuals and families who want their giving to be more effective and satisfying. National Network of Grantmakers, 2801 21st Ave S, #132, Minneapolis, MN 55407. 50 pages. $19 including shipping and handling.

Spomer, Cynthia R. *Federal Support for Nonprofits 1996.* 1995. $198 cl.

Standard & Poor's Corporation. *Standard & Poor's Register of Corporations, Directors and Executives.* New York: McGraw-Hill, 1996. (Published every January.) This three-volume set is one of the best references on corporations, who runs them, what they do, and how much money they have. For ordering information, contact Standard & Poor's Corporation, 25 Broadway, Post Office Box 992, New York, NY 10275. $650.

Steckel, Richard, et al. *Filthy Rich and Other Nonprofit Fantasies : Changing the Way Nonprofits Do Business in the 90's.* 1989. $11.95 pb.

Steckel, Richard PhD. & Jennifer Lehman. *In Search of America's Best Nonprofits.* 1997. $17.50 cl.

Stoesz, Edgar & Chester Raber. *Doing Good Better! : How to Be an Effective Board Member of a Nonprofit Organization.* 1997. $7.95 pb.

Sturtevant, William T. *The Artful Journey : Cultivating and Soliciting the Major Gift.* 1997. $28 cl.

T

Taft Corporation. *Taft Corporate Giving Directory, 1996 Edition.* Rockville, MD: Taft Corporation, 1995. This directory profiles the thousand largest corporate giving programs and foundations. Each entry includes contact person, funding priorities, plant locations, recent grants, and more. Available from the publisher, 12300 Twinbrook Parkway, Suite 520, Rockville, MD 20852. $395.

U

U.S. Internal Revenue Service. *Tax-Exempt Status for Your Organization.* IRS Publication 557. 44 pp. This pamphlet explains the requirements and rules necessary for an organization that seeks recognition by the Internal Revenue Service as a tax-exempt organization under Section 501(c) and classification as "not a private foundation" under Section 509(a). Available from your local IRS district office. Free.

W

Ware, Alan. *Between Profit and State: Intermediate Organizations in Britain and the United States.* 1990. $34.65 cl.

Warwick, Mal. *How to Write Successful Fundraising Letters.* 1996. $15.95 pb.

White, Virginia P. *Grants: How to Find OutAbout Them and What to Do Next.* New York: Plenum Press, 1979. This book provides a good overview of identifying potential funding sources and developing a fundraising strategy. Out of print.

Who's no in America, 52nd Edition 1995-1996. Chicago: Marquis Who's Who, Inc., 1995.

Wolf, Thomas & Barbara Carter (Illustrator). *Managing a Nonprofit Organization.* 1990. $10.40 pb.

Women's Action Alliance. *Struggling Through Tight Times.* New York: Women's Action Alliance, 1985. This resource handbook designed primarily for women's organizations can help organizations learn to diversify their funding base, improve their management, assess their potential for income-generating projects, and acquire new analytical skills. Out of print.

Wuthnow, Robert (Editor). *Between States and Markets : The Voluntary Sector in Comparative Perspective,* 1991, $15.95 pb.

Y

Young, Joyce, et al. *Fundraising for Non-Profit Groups : How to Get Money from Corporations, Foundations, and Government (Self-Counsel Business Series).* 1995. $10.36 pb.

Z

Zander, Alvin. *Making Boards Effective : The Dynamics of Nonprofit Governing Boards.* Jossey-Bass, 1993. $29.95 cl.

Zander, Alvin. *Making Groups Effective.* Jossey-Bass, 1994. $27.95 cl.

COLOPHON

The text was set in Times New Roman, a typeface designed by Stanley Morison (1889-1967). This face designed for *The Times* of London was the result of a criticism Morison made to the management of *The Times* complaining of the paper's typography. They asked him to improve it. Working for the Monotype Corporation, Morison designed a face based on Granjon, and delivered it for use beginning in 1932. It has since become one of the most widely used faces and often copied because of its readability. The display face is Eric Gills Sans in various iterations.

The *Grantseekers Guide* was composed by Rhode Island Book Composition and printed by McNaughton & Gunn, Saline, Michigan on acid-free paper.